Ishmael Instructs Isaac

A "Connections" Book

Ishmael Instructs Isaac

An Introduction to the Qur'an for Bible Readers

John Kaltner

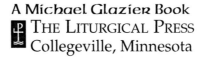

A Michael Glazier Book
THE LITURGICAL PRESS
Collegeville, Minnesota

Cover design by Ann Blattner. Watercolor by Ethel Boyle.

A Michael Glazier Book published by The Liturgical Press.

Library of Congress Cataloging-in-Publication Data

Kaltner, John, 1954–
     Ishmael instructs Isaac : an introduction to the Qur'an for Bible
readers / John Kaltner.
          p.   cm.
     "A 'Connections' book."
     Includes bibliographical references (p.   ) and index.
     ISBN 0-8146-5882-2
     1. Koran—Relation to the Bible.   2. Islam—Relations—
Christianity.   3. Christianity and other religions—Islam.
I. Title.
BP134.B4K35   1999
297.1'226—dc21   98-32326
                                                                                      CIP

To my parents,
John and Gladys,
who taught me to love our own family's story
and to respect and value those of others.

Acknowledgments

I wish to express a special word of thanks to those who assisted me in writing *Ishmael Instructs Isaac*: to my colleagues in the Department of Religious Studies at Rhodes College for their support and friendship; to the Faculty Development Committee of Rhodes for a grant during the summer of 1997; to the students in my course "Biblical Figures in the Qur'an" for their encouragement, feedback, and insights; and to Debra Bartelli for her love, companionship, and advice throughout the project.

Shukrān!

Contents

Introduction

*H*ow do non-Muslims learn about Islam? What sources do they draw upon in formulating their attitudes toward Muslims? How reliable a picture of the religion and its followers do these sources paint for them? Various answers are possible for these and similar questions. Those with relatives or close acquaintances who are Muslim or who have themselves spent time engaged in serious reading and study of Islam have probably been able to develop a fairly accurate impression of the religion. But others, perhaps the majority of people, often rely on other sources which can sometimes present a skewed image of Islam and those who practice it.

In the United States and other countries where Muslims are in a minority, exposure to Islam is primarily gotten through the media. Newspapers, magazines, television, radio and movies all convey information about many different topics, Islam included. More often than not, when this information reaches the public it has been filtered and edited in any number of ways. National interests, corporate agendas, political concerns, and personal biases can all leave their mark on the shape of the message which is communicated to us. In the entertainment industry, which is often more concerned with selling tickets or advertising time than it is with anything else, unfair stereotypes are frequently exploited and perpetuated in order to guarantee a laugh or boost the ratings.

It would be a serious mistake to overgeneralize and issue a blanket condemnation against the media on this matter. To be sure, there have been and continue to be many fine attempts to treat Islam in a fair and balanced way in all branches of the media. Such efforts should be applauded and others should be encouraged. But distortions and caricatures continue to be prevalent, and these can be equally influential in shaping the public's perception. Sometimes, the dissemination of misinformation is undertaken in a deliberate attempt to undermine the image of Islam and the reputations of Muslims. At other times, the intention is simply to amuse or to inform people about some unusual aspect of a religion that is foreign to many of them.

A few examples will help to illustrate this point. Recently, there have appeared in print a number of stories related to Islam which have alternately raised concerned eyebrows and induced cynical chuckles. The following is a sampling from them. The Libyan leader Muammar al-Qaddafi blasted Christians and Jews as racists because they do not name their sons Muhammad. After complaints from angry Muslims, a well-known athletic shoe company was forced to recall thousands of pairs of a new model because its logo resembled the word "Allah" in the Arabic script. The Taliban, a conservative Muslim faction which has taken over most of Afghanistan, banned the use of paper bags because recycled paper might contain pages from Islam's sacred text, the Qurʾan. When a young Muslim girl in Britain sliced a tomato in half she was shocked to discover the Islamic profession of faith spelled out in Arabic in its veins. To the outrage of the Muslim community, the new line of a European fashion designer included dresses upon which verses from the Qurʾan were stitched as decoration. Muslim organizations in the United States unsuccessfully argued for the removal of a statue of Muhammad in the Supreme Court building that is part of a group depicting some of the great lawgivers of history. A major publishing house had to recall all four thousand copies of a children's book on famous religious figures which presented Muhammad, the prophet of Islam, as a bloodthirsty villain with a penchant for women and food who hated Jews, Christians, poets, painters, and anyone who criticized him.

The image of Islam that emerges from such news items is not a flattering one. It comes across as a very defensive, almost paranoid, religion that goes to great lengths to correct what it perceives to be any injustice done to it. These stories can exert as much influence as any oped column or carefully researched article does on the perceptions non-Muslims form of Muslims and their faith. One might be tempted to object that this is being overly sensitive to the feelings of Muslims and is a selective reading of the newspaper. After all, countless similar articles appear in print on a regular basis that also place Jews and Christians in an equally vulnerable position as the potential objects of amusement or derision. One need only think of the coverage that accompanied the recent discovery in Florida of an image on the side of an office building that many claim bears a resemblance to the Virgin Mary. While many Christians scoff at the idea that this is some kind of heavenly sign, the media have recounted the words and impressions of others who have visited the site as pilgrims convinced of its authenticity. Surely, the argument might go, when it comes to reporting the news, Jews and Christians should be as concerned about the treatment they receive as Muslims are.

The point is well taken, but there is an important difference. In many places, Muslims are at a distinct disadvantage because their religion is unfamiliar to most people. As an example, consider the United States where the two dominant religions are Christianity and Judaism. It is commonly asserted, both explicitly and implicitly, by preachers, politicians, pundits and the public at large that the heritage and values of the United States are "Judeo-Christian" in nature. This statement is accurate because adherents of those two faiths have been, and continue to be, very influential in shaping American society. People in the United States are knowledgeable about the beliefs and customs of Christians and Jews. Churches and synagogues are commonplace features of the American landscape throughout much of the country, and interaction between Jews and Christians is often a routine part of everyday life. Furthermore, a level of intimacy exists between the two groups themselves due to their common roots in history and their shared textual tradition since the Jewish Hebrew Bible is virtually identical to the Christian Old Testament.

The net result of all this is a feeling of familiarity, at times even a sense of family, about Judaism and Christianity in the United States. Jews and Christians may not always agree, even among themselves, but what family does not occasionally experience this same problem? This context plays an important role for people in the United States when they pick up the newspaper and read something controversial or uncomplimentary about Christianity or Judaism. Their familiarity with these religions allows them to consider and evaluate the material they read and to see how it resonates with their experience and knowledge. They are usually able to distinguish between information that accurately portrays Judaism or Christianity and information that is either a distorted stereotype or not representative of the entire group.

Islam does not enjoy the same benefit. In places like the United States, despite the fact that millions of Muslims live there, it remains a mysterious and misunderstood religion. Consequently, when Americans read an article on Islam or watch a movie portraying a Muslim as a

Hollywood heavy, they often are unable to properly evaluate the information they take in or the image they see. The inability to do so is a problem that will become more acute with time. It is no longer possible to live an isolated existence in the world. Advances in technology and travel have brought all of us closer together, and, if we are to coexist peacefully, we need to learn about those who are different from ourselves. Islam is the fastest-growing religion in the world and will soon have more than one billion followers. To remain ignorant of the facts about something so influential and important for humanity would be irresponsible. The only solution to the problem of ignorance is education. Non-Muslims need to learn about Islam by whatever means available to them. For some, this can be done through direct contact by meeting Muslims and discovering their religion in conversations and visits to mosques. For others, reading and studying about Islam offers a viable alternative. There are many excellent books, articles, documentaries and films which present accurate, accessible information on Muslims and their faith.

This book attempts to introduce the reader to Islam through a study of the Qur'an, its sacred scripture. Muslims believe the Qur'an to be the definitive statement of God's will for humanity, and no other source has exerted more influence in shaping how they believe, think, and live their lives. It is therefore an excellent starting point for learning about Islam and those who practice it. The approach adopted here is a comparative one since the book is primarily written for someone who has some familiarity with the Bible and wants to explore the relationship between it and the Qur'an. It often comes as a shock to Bible readers that characters and stories that are part of their sacred text are also found in the pages of the Qur'an. At times, there is much in common in the way the two texts relate these shared traditions. At other times, there are significant differences in their descriptions of the same event or figure. A study of the similarities and divergences between the two texts on this common material allows for better appreciation of both what is distinctive about Islam and what it shares with Judaism and Christianity. This information can contribute much to one's personal understanding of what Islam is and can be a valuable aid in evaluating what others say it is.

WHAT IS THE QUR'AN?

Sometime around the year 610 C.E. an event occurred near the city of Mecca in modern day Saudi Arabia that changed the course of human history. A man named Muhammad, then about forty years old, was engaged in meditation when he heard a voice speak to him and order him, "Recite!" According to Islamic belief, that voice belonged to the angel Gabriel who had been sent from Allah to reveal a divine message to Muhammad that he was to deliver to his people. Over the course of the next twenty-two years, Muhammad continued to receive similar revelations until he died in the city of Medina in the year 632. For Muslims, the Qurʾan is the record of those revelations sent to him by Allah.

Prior to this turning point in his life, Muhammad was a typical citizen of Mecca. A city in the Ḥijāz, an area in the western part of the Arabian peninsula, Mecca was located along caravan routes running north/south and this location enabled many of the local people to involve themselves in trade and commerce. The early Islamic sources all agree that Muhammad made his living in this way and that he was quite good at what he did. Not much is known with certainty about his life prior to 610, but an event that is well established is his marriage at around age twenty-five to a woman named Khadijah, who was a wealthy merchant a bit older than he was. Mecca also enjoyed a reputation as a prominent religious center. It contained the Kaʿba, a shrine identified with a large number of gods and goddesses that was a popular site attracting many visitors from the surrounding area. Not surprisingly, Mecca's role as a pilgrimage destination had a positive effect on its economy.

The earliest revelations Muhammad received took the form of warnings directed toward his people. They are usually very brief, impassioned pleas that call for a rejection of polytheism and a return to the worship of Allah, the only God, or suffer the consequences of their false worship. Some of these texts threaten the community with divine retribution and punishment if they do not leave behind their idolatrous ways. This message was not well received by many of the people of Mecca since it demanded that they dismantle a religious system that enhanced their city's reputation and contributed a great deal to its coffers. Muhammad enjoyed some modest early success as small numbers of people were persuaded by his message and became his followers. But the primary response they received was rejection, at times accompanied by physical confrontation and social ostracism. During this early phase of Muhammad's career, referred to as the "Meccan period," the revelations he received were frequently addressed to various aspects of this context. For example, Muhammad is often encouraged and consoled in texts which urge him to be faithful and to persevere in the face of criticism from the people of Mecca.

The fortunes of the nascent Muslim community began to change when Muhammad was invited to move with his followers to the city of Yathrib, located about two hundred miles north of Mecca. As was the case in Mecca, the social system at Yathrib was tribal based, and a number of the tribes in this oasis area were Jewish. This was different from the situation in Mecca where Muhammad and his followers had very little contact with Jews or Christians. The people at Yathrib were interested in having Muhammad come live among them because they knew of his reputation as a leader and charismatic figure and were in need of such skills. They invited him to come and act as a judge who would help to settle disputes and other difficulties that arose among the various tribes and groups of the area. Muhammad agreed to this arrangement and, in 622, he and his followers, numbering no more than eighty to one hundred, made the journey to Yathrib. This migration or, as it is called in Arabic, the *hijra*, was the key moment in early Muslim history and is held to be the founding event of the community. To commemorate its significance, it was chosen as the starting point of the Islamic calendar which, as a lunar-based system, is organized by the phases of the moon.

Many of the people of Yathrib were receptive to Muhammad's message and converted to Islam. The city soon came to be referred to as "the city of the prophet," in Arabic *madīnat al-nabī*, and this was shortened to *madīna* ("city," spelled Medina in English), the name by which it has been known ever since. During his time in Medina, Muhammad continued to receive revelations but their tone and content changed in this new context. The brief, passionate warnings typical of the Meccan period that focused on the need to convert were replaced by lengthier, more detailed messages that addressed many of the issues that confronted Muhammad and his community as it began to grow and settle into life at Medina. Both internal matters, like worship and ethics, and external concerns, like relations with Jews and Christians, are frequently treated in these texts from what is referred to as the "Medinan period." Many of the passages that refer to biblical events and characters and will be discussed in this book come from this time of Muhammad's career.

Muhammad enjoyed much success at Medina as many people embraced Islam and accepted him as Allah's prophet. But there continued to be problems between the Medinans and Meccans that occasionally erupted in violence when one side would attack or raid members of the other. It was only toward the end of Muhammad's life that Mecca was brought into the Muslim fold and he was able to return to his hometown and institute monotheistic worship at the Kaʿba. By the time he died at Medina in 632, large portions of the Ḥijāz and its surrounding area within the Arabian peninsula had become Muslim. In the generation or two after his death, the religion had spread into Palestine, Egypt, and North Africa and Islam was poised to begin expanding into new areas, a process that continues to the present day. The message of the Qurʾan that was first heard among a small group of people almost fourteen hundred years ago is now proclaimed and practiced in every corner of the world.

After this brief sketch of the context out of which the Qurʾan emerged, we now turn to a consideration of the text itself. The Qurʾan, sometimes spelled Koran, is about the same length as the New Testament and is comprised of 114 chapters of varying length that contain approximately 6200 verses. Each chapter, or *sūra* in Arabic, has a title that is taken from some word or name that appears in that particular chapter. While it is typical for Muslims to refer to individual suras by their names, it is also common to designate them by their numbers and this latter alternative is the one used in this book. So, for example, the citation 19:30 should be interpreted in the same way it would be if it referred to a biblical text. The first number refers to the nineteenth sura (which goes by the name "Mary") and the second number indicates the thirtieth verse in that sura.

The term "Qurʾan" is a transliteration of an Arabic word that means "recitation, reading." According to Muslim tradition, the first revelation Muhammad received is found in sura 96 which begins with the command "Recite!" This word, *ʾiqra*ʾ in Arabic, is etymologically related to the word *quʾrān* ("recitation") and this meaning highlights the nature of the text for Muslims. It is an accurate recording of what Muhammad was told to recite in the revelations he received during the last twenty-two years of his life. Notice that what is believed to be the earliest message Muhammad received is found toward the end of the Qurʾan in sura 96. This points out an important feature of the text. Like the Bible, the Qurʾan is not presented in strict chronological order with the earliest passages first and the latest ones last. In fact, their exact historical sequence and the precise chronological relationship among the suras is a mystery since there are very few textual clues that allow for certain dating of chapters.

It was noted above that a distinction can be made between the Meccan and Medinan material of the Qurʾan based on data like their content and length. This division is a common way of categorizing the suras, although it is not without its problems. Most suras do not precisely state whether Muhammad was in Mecca or Medina when they were revealed, but the theme and tone of a chapter usually supply important evidence that points in the direction of one or the other city as the probable point of origin. Many translations of the Qurʾan do not designate whether suras are Meccan or Medinan, but copies in the original Arabic normally contain this information at the beginning of the sura immediately after its title. These geographic identifications are later additions to the text that are not found in earlier copies of the Qurʾan. Scholars have tried to refine this system by subdividing the categories further and arguing, for example, for early Meccan, middle Meccan, and late Meccan periods, but there is no complete agreement on this matter. The dating of individual suras and passages of the Qurʾan is a complicated matter that is very important for many areas of Islamic studies. It is less significant for the purposes of this book and will not be a major concern for us.

While an accurate chronological presentation of its contents is not found in the Qurʾan, it does make use of another organizing principle. The suras are arranged more or less by order of length with the longest ones coming first and the shortest ones at the end. The only notable exception to this structure is the first sura which is called the *Fātiḥa*, or "Opening," and is only 7 verses long. By contrast, sura 2 follows immediately after it and has 286 verses. At the other end of the spectrum is sura 108, the shortest chapter in the Qurʾan, which contains just 10 words in the original Arabic. Based on its length, the first sura should be found somewhere near sura 100, but its initial position derives from the role it plays as an introduction or prologue to the entire Qurʾan. To get a sense of the relative length of suras, note the following breakdown based on a popular English translation of the Qurʾan. The first 57 suras take up about 374 pages of text while the second 57 need only approximately 50 pages. The second sura alone comprises 31 pages and the final 31 pages of the text contain 45 complete suras.

This longest to shortest structure does have some connection to the issue of the chronology of the material in the Qurʾan. Because the Meccan suras tend to be briefer than the Medinan ones, most of them are found in the latter part of the text. For example, according to the traditional designations which are found after each sura's title, only 4 of the final 40 chapters are from the Medinan period. This means that reading the Qurʾan from back to front gives a much better sense of the general chronology of the material than reading it from front to back does.

Even though 90 suras are labeled Meccan and only 24 Medinan, the Qur'an contains more information from the latter period because these chapters are so much lengthier than the Meccan ones.

According to Islamic belief, Arabic is the only proper language for the Qur'an since this was the form in which it was revealed to Muhammad. Therefore, Muslims believe that any translation of the text is not truly the Qur'an but an interpretation of it. For this reason, all Muslims are expected to know some Arabic, even if they live in a part of the world where it is not spoken. In those places where very few Muslims know the language, the Arabic text will still be read by the community's leader during worship services and then translated into the vernacular for the congregation. When rendered into another language, the Qur'an loses much of what is undoubtedly its defining literary quality, its poetry. The Arabic form of the text makes masterful use of rhyme, meter, and imagery, and these elements help make the Qur'an a delight for the ear. As its name implies, this is a text that is meant to be spoken, not simply read. Recitation of the Qur'an is a high art form throughout the Muslim world, and the best practitioners have spent many years memorizing the entire text and honing their skills. To hear the Qur'an being recited by one of these experts is an aural delight even for the listener who does not understand a word of what is being chanted.

Reading the Qur'an can be a rich and rewarding experience for non-Muslims but it can also be a frustrating one, especially for the reader familiar with the Bible who expects the Muslim text to adhere to the conventions of his or her own scripture. The Qur'an and Bible are similar in many ways. They share many themes and characters and this can lend an air of familiarity to the text for the Bible reader that is not possible with the sacred books of religious traditions further removed from Judaism and Christianity. But the Qur'an is very different from the Bible in terms of the way its material is organized and presented. Much of the biblical literature, particularly that which is most frequently read in churches and synagogues, is in the form of a cohesive, organized narrative which is fairly easy to follow and presented in sequential chronological order. This is not the preferred mode of discourse of the Qur'an. It does contain narrative material and we will discuss much of it in the coming chapters. But the Qur'an typically uses such narrative to make a point rather than to tell a story. Therefore, it conveys only the information essential to make that point, is usually less detailed than the Bible in its presentation, and will often abruptly shift gears to discuss a seemingly unrelated point.

This approach can give the Bible reader the impression that the Qur'an is a very sparse text that tends to jump from one thing to another without staying focused on the same theme for long. This is a perfectly natural reaction for a person accustomed to the Bible whose first instinct might be to see how the Qur'an measures up to it, especially in those places where they are similar. But it is ultimately the wrong way to relate to the text. Rather, one needs to get used to the style and manner of the Qur'an by accepting it on its own terms and by trying to discover how it communicates its message rather than comparing its method to that of the Bible. Only then is it allowed to speak in its own unique voice.

One of the aspects of the Bible and Qur'an that can make this a challenging task is the presence of traditions which are found in both texts, and in this book we will be devoting a great deal of attention to much of this shared material. As we will see, this material is never found in an identical form in the two texts, but they do contain many intriguing similarities. Scholars from all three faiths have often attempted to explain the reasons for this phenomenon. One's own affiliation and theological perspective are very influential in determining how this question is answered. Muslims believe the Qur'an to be the final, definitive word of Allah which was sent to Muhammad to correct the errors in previous scriptures which were falsified by the followers of the prophets sent prior to Muhammad. Among these earlier scriptures are the Torah and Gospel which Allah revealed to Moses and Jesus but which, in their biblical form, have been distorted. Muslims therefore are predisposed to viewing the material common to the two texts as the Qur'an's attempt to counteract the errors in the Bible by setting the record straight and presenting the correct version of the events.

Jewish and Christian scholars, on the other hand, have tended to see the shared textual traditions as evidence of the influence of their religions on Islam which borrowed stories and ideas from Judaism and Christianity. In their view, both biblical and nonbiblical Jewish and Christian sources were drawn upon by early Muslims who adapted and reworked this older material to fit an Islamic context. Included among the types of nonbiblical sources available to them were the teachings and interpretations of the rabbis and the extracanonical gospels and other writings that were not included in the Bible. This touches on the important and complex question of the nature and degree of contact the early Muslim community had with Jews and Christians. As already noted, there was a Jewish presence in Medina during Muhammad's time and it is certain that Muslims interacted with Jews from the earliest days. Although there was less direct contact with Christians in the birthplace of Islam, Christianity was present in neighboring areas like Yemen, the southernmost part of the Arabian peninsula, and Abyssinia, an African kingdom across the Red Sea which was visited by Muslims during Muhammad's lifetime. As Islam spread, Jews and Christians were among those who converted and they brought with them knowledge and experience of their previous religions. Consequently, there is no reason to doubt that the early Muslim community had exposure to Judaism and Christianity, but questions still remain regarding the precise form it took and the influence it exerted on the Qur'an.

In this book, the possible historical reasons for the phenomenon of similar material in the Bible and the Qur'an will not be a focus of attention. As important and fascinating as this issue is, it falls outside the scope of our study which is an examination of the Qur'an that tries to answer the question "What does it mean?" rather than "Where did it come from?" The Qur'an, like the Bible, is the product of a complicated process of development that began with a period of oral transmission and culminated in its canonization when it was officially established as the definitive text of its community. Our primary interest is in the canonical text that continues to shape and inform the lives of Muslims today as it has done throughout history. As we study what the Qur'an and Bible have to say on particular themes and characters it will become apparent that the two texts use similar material in different ways which address the unique needs of their respective communities.

FROM SIBLING RIVALRY TO SIBLING REUNION

One of the aims of this book is to lay the foundation for a family reconciliation. Jews, Christians and Muslims all trace their roots back to Abraham, the father of Ishmael and Isaac, and therefore implicitly understand themselves to be somehow related to each other. It is often asserted that Ishmael is the ancestor of the Arabs, particularly Muslims, while Isaac is the forebear of Jews and Christians. Keeping in mind that this is an oversimplified reading of history, it is nonetheless a helpful and appealing image to use in discussing the relationships among members of these three faiths. Their common history, similar beliefs, and shared traditions suggest that Jews, Christians and Muslims are indeed relatives, even if distant ones. The sad fact is that for a long time the two sides of this large extended family have rarely been on speaking terms and, when they have communicated, they have usually not had nice things to say to each other. Their infrequent conversations have tended to repudiate, rather than celebrate, their common heritage.

Unfortunately, the sacred texts of this family, the Bible and Qur'an, have often been used as tools to further the estrangement among its members. Discussions of the relationships among them frequently begin and often end with one or more parties citing or implicitly relying upon the material found in these two bodies of sacred writing in a way that declares one "the winner." In other words, the Bible and Qur'an are often pitted against each other to bolster the claims of one side and negate the claims of the other. Such misuse of these writings prevents the recognition of the undeniable fact that the two texts have much in common.

That common ground is the ideal place to set up camp, sit down around the hearth, and begin to heal the centuries-old rift that has divided the family for far too long. Nothing brings families together like reminiscing and remembering days gone by. The wonderful thing about such gatherings is that no two family members recall the same event in exactly the same way, and as each person shares his or her own memories the complexity and richness of the family history are revealed to all. The Bible and Qur'an are, in a sense, the written record of one such family history told from different perspectives. Imagine a reconciliation between Ishmael and Isaac in which they sit around the fire swapping family stories and telling their own versions of what happened. How much they would learn about themselves and each other! Jews, Christians and Muslims have rarely stopped to listen to how the other side remembers the past or what the family's history means to the other. If they did, their appreciation of previously shunned relatives and their contributions to the family tree would grow immeasurably.

This book attempts to envision what such a reconciliation between the offspring of Ishmael and Isaac could be like. It is written from the perspective of Isaac's side of the family and tries to imagine the exciting things that can take place when we sit down with long-lost relatives and hear them retell familiar stories in new ways. Reading the Qur'an's accounts of biblical traditions can teach Jews and Christians much about Islam, but it can also teach them much about their own side of the family and how it has preserved their common history. In the same way, Muslims, as descendants of Ishmael, can benefit from such an encounter. This book is not written by one from among their ranks, but by a cousin who has a deep love and respect for their side of the family and who hopes they will feel welcome to join us around the fire.

It is important to remember that this book contains a selective reading of the Qurʾan. Because we are primarily considering only material that has biblical parallels, most of the Islamic text will not be discussed. Their familiar characters and similar stories help to make these among the most accessible passages for Bible readers, but it must be kept in mind that this is not indicative of the content and style of the entire Qurʾan. Nonetheless, the themes and subject matter of these texts are representative of the book as a whole and therefore they serve as a good starting point from which to begin to discover and study Islam's sacred scripture. But it is only a starting point. In order to get a proper sense of the entire text and how the passages studied here function within it, one should read the Qurʾan from beginning to end. At the very least, when reading this book it would be helpful to keep a copy of the Qurʾan near at hand and read the passages surrounding those we will be discussing so that their literary context can be understood and appreciated.

The English translations of the Qurʾan texts contained in the book are my own and a few brief comments about them might prove helpful. Throughout, I have tried to render the meaning of the Arabic in clear English while still giving the reader an experience of some of the literary and grammatical features of the original text. For example, the word order within sentences of the English attempts to mirror that of the Arabic, and this gives a sense of the Qurʾan's unique form and mode of expression. I have also used the same English word to translate every occurrence of a particular Arabic word within a given passage. This highlights the use of repetition and key words which are features commonly found in the Qurʾan that can be of assistance in interpreting texts.

In those places where personal pronouns are used to refer to Allah, I have opted for the masculine gender for the same reason. Arabic is a language that is much more gender-specific than English as is clearly seen in the difference between their verbal systems. In English, the form of the third person singular verb (for example, "speaks") remains the same whether the subject is masculine or feminine, and a personal name, noun, or pronoun ("he" or "she") must be supplied to specify the gender of the subject. This is not the case in Arabic where the verb itself has á different form depending on whether the subject is masculine or feminine. Throughout the Qurʾan the Arabic word "Allah" is grammatically masculine, and in order to accurately convey the sense of the original no attempt has been made to change that in the translation. It is common in the Qurʾan for Allah to speak in the plural by using pronouns like "we" and "our," and this has been preserved in the English translations in this book. This in no way violates the monotheistic belief of Islam, but is an example of the use of what is sometimes referred to as the "divine we" which elevates and exalts the deity. Such usage is not unique to Islam and is even sometimes found in the biblical literature. In Genesis 1:26, for example, God says, "Let us make humankind in our image, according to our likeness."

Much of the discussion in the following chapters entails comparative analysis of texts from the Qur'an and Bible in which the deity is frequently mentioned. To avoid confusion between the two texts and to more easily identify the deity in each, I have consistently referred to "God" when speaking of the Bible and "Allah" when speaking of the Qur'an. This approach is adopted only for the sake of convenience to assist the reader and does not have any theological significance. All biblical citations are taken from the New Revised Standard Version.

Each of the following six chapters discusses a particular biblical figure's role in the Qur'an. In order, those characters are Adam, Noah, Abraham, Moses, Mary, and Jesus. While these individuals are treated in the most detail, each chapter also explains the significance of other figures found in the Qur'an who are present in the Bible. For example, the chapter on Moses will also consider the roles of his brother Aaron, the Israelites, the Egyptian Pharaoh, and Moses' unnamed wife and father-in-law in the Islamic text. Not every passage in the Qur'an that mentions a figure is cited, but all of the most important ones are translated and discussed with particular emphasis placed on the events and themes of that individual's story which have been important and influential in Islam. Throughout each chapter, the similarities and differences between the Qur'an's and Bible's presentation of the material will be noted and explained. A glance at the table of contents shows that some chapters are quite a bit longer than others. This is primarily due to the relative amount of attention the Qur'an devotes to the individual characters. Some, like Moses and Abraham, are referred to frequently and treated in more detail than others, like Adam and Mary. Consequently, it takes more time to adequately explain their role in the Qur'an and Islam.

Each chapter concludes with a section that is titled "Cooperating Revelations." This is an attempt to explore how the Qur'an might be used to help the Bible reader discover new things about his or her own text. As noted above, the relationship between the two books is usually understood in a way that puts them in competition. If Jews, Christians and Muslims are truly part of the same family, their sacred texts should, at times, be able to cooperate rather than compete with one another. This is not to ignore or downplay the presence of the many profound differences between the Bible and Qurʾan that have significant theological and practical implications. Rather, it is to suggest that we need to look beyond the differences to discover the common ground and ask what the stories of the other side of the family have to contribute to those on our own side.

The "Cooperating Revelations" part of each chapter tries to do this by rereading a biblical passage in light of its counterpart in the Qurʾan. Revisiting a familiar Bible story with the theme and message of its Qurʾan parallel in mind can allow us to notice elements of it that have previously gone unrecognized. This is not an exercise in filling in the gaps that introduces material from the Qurʾan into the Bible to improve it in some way or to create a new story that is a hybrid of the two texts. It does not attempt to read anything into the biblical text that is not already there. It is, rather, a method that can shed light on things present within the Bible that are easily missed due to the subtle nature of their presence or the fact that the reader's attention is directed elsewhere in the story. When the texts cooperate in this way, the two sides of the family are brought closer together since the offspring of Isaac experience how much Ishmael's descendants can teach them about the family's history.

A more technical term that might be used to define this method is "intercanonical criticism," which describes the attempt to study texts from different canons or religious traditions in relationship to each other. Although this is undertaken in an explicit way at the end of each chapter, it is also, in a certain sense, the underlying aim of the entire book. One might question the legitimacy of such an approach and wonder what justification, if any, can be found for adopting this method of study. In fact, there is support for it among both those who read the Bible and those who read the Qurʾan.

The Islamic view of revelation, for example, acknowledges that Allah has spoken to a number of prophets throughout history and many of them, like Noah, Abraham, Moses and Jesus, are familiar to Bible readers. They were each given the same message, which is essentially that of Islam and the Qurʾan, but their followers distorted it making necessary the sending of Muhammad, the final prophet. But Islam maintains that many elements of the pre-Islamic scriptures are divine revelation and the only parts that must be rejected are those that conflict with the Qur'an. Jews and Christians are therefore commonly referred to in the Qur'an as "the people of the book," a term that acknowledges the legitimacy of their sacred writings. Some passages, like 5:68, express well the high status of the Bible in the Qur'an. "Oh people of the book, you have nothing until you observe the Torah and the Gospel and what has been revealed to you from your Lord."

In a similar way, the people of the book have, at times, recognized the value of Islam and its message. We see this in the Catholic tradition where some of the documents of the Second Vatican Council speak of Islam in commendable terms. For example, in paragraph 3 of the "Declaration on the Relation of the Church to Non-Christian Religions" we read, "The Church has also a high regard for the Muslims. They worship God, who is one, living and subsistent, merciful and almighty, the Creator of heaven and earth, who has also spoken to humanity." The final phrase, affirming Muslims' belief that the deity has spoken to humankind, can be understood as a legitimation of the Islamic view of revelation that suggests the Catholic Church sees this as a potential point of contact between Islam and itself. While these and other statements fall short of an explicit acceptance of the truth claims of the other regarding the locus and means of divine revelation, they at least signal a starting point from which to begin to work toward the goal of improving relations which is called for in the same Vatican II document. "Over the centuries many quarrels and dissensions have arisen between Christians and Muslims. The sacred council now pleads with all to forget the past, and urges that a sincere effort be made to achieve mutual understanding."

One of the ways such mutual understanding might be attained is through consideration of the relationship between the Qur'an and the Bible. In particular, when we study traditions that are shared by both texts we can learn a great deal about how the monotheistic religions converge and diverge on matters of faith. But a necessary precondition to such study is the adoption of a position of neutrality regarding the Qur'an and Bible that does not start with the premise that one got the story right and the other got it wrong. This does not mean that we trivialize the very real and important differences that exist between them, many of which are irreconcilable and the cause of profound theological and doctrinal conflicts. Rather, we must acknowledge the differences and try to understand how they contribute to the particular story's or tradition's function within the Qur'an or Bible.

Such an approach toward the texts can contribute a great deal to developing the mutual understanding among Jews, Christians, and

Muslims that is called for in statements like those of Vatican II. It allows us to recognize the fact that, their differences notwithstanding, there are significant and fascinating points of contact between our sacred scriptures and there can be, at times, a great benefit to reading and understanding one in light of the other. The Bible and the Qurʾan then cease to be competing revelations in which the legitimacy of each depends upon questioning the merits of the other, and they become co-operating revelations that work in tandem to inform and educate their readers.

1

Adam

*T*he Qur'an's view of Adam is strikingly similar to that of the
Bible. He was the first human created and is therefore the ancestor of all people. References to him in the Qur'an consistently reinforce this idea in their presentation of Adam. Either they
discuss his role in the context of the creation of humanity or they refer
to later individuals in a way that explicitly traces their lineage back to
Adam. In both cases, similarities with the biblical tradition are apparent
but it is clear that the Qur'an tends to present the material in a way that
makes it more Islamic and, consequently, relevant to its audience. The
following discussion will study examples of both these kinds of texts.

ADAM AND CREATION

Adam is found most frequently in texts that refer to the creation of
humanity and related events. But, different from the biblical tradition,
in none of these texts is human creation discussed in the context of the
creation of the world. The Qur'an does not begin with, or contain at all,
the same type of ordered and chronological account of creation we find
in Genesis 1 where humanity is the capstone and high point of the divine creative activity. Creation in the Qur'an is a given fact that is frequently alluded to and occasionally described in some detail, but it
lacks the narrative framework and drama that characterize the biblical
account. Nonetheless, the two texts share many common elements,
some of which will now be briefly discussed.

The Creation of the World

A concise description of Allah's creative role in the Qur'an is seen in 6:1 which states, "Praise be to Allah, Who created heaven and earth and made darkness and light." This verse, which neatly summarizes Allah's creative function, has a close connection with the biblical tradition where God first creates heaven and earth and then differentiates between light and darkness (Gen 1:1-5). In other places in the Qur'an we find references to divine creative activity that are also similar to certain biblical texts. Although it does not describe in much detail precisely how Allah brings things into being, in some places the Qur'an suggests that there is a verbal or oral element to the divine creative work. "Our word about something, if we will it, is that we say 'Be!', and it is" (16:40). This verse calls to mind the account in Genesis 1 where God adopts a similarly verbal approach ("And God said . . .") in bringing about the elements of creation.

We also sometimes find parallels in the Qur'an with the first chapter of Genesis regarding the amount of time it took Allah to create the world. "Truly, your Lord is Allah, who created heaven and earth in six days and then mounted the throne" (7:54). The Qur'an does not give us a day by day account of Allah's creative work, but elsewhere it identifies a clear division within the six-day period. "Say, 'Do you really disbelieve in the one who created the earth in two days? Do you set up equals (other gods) for Him?' That is the Lord of the worlds. He placed mountains above the earth. He then blessed it and in four days provided sustenance within it indiscriminately for those who seek" (41:9-10). This text has some interesting connections with Genesis 1 where God does not begin creating vegetation and other sources of sustenance until the third day.

Perhaps the most interesting aspect of the Qur'an's view of creation is the role of humanity within it. Although it does not convey the idea in as dramatic a fashion as the biblical tradition, the Qur'an also maintains that humans hold a privileged place in the world that makes them special and sets them apart. It sees the rest of creation as ultimately coming under the authority and domination of humanity. "It is Allah who created heaven and earth and sends down water from the sky by which He brings forth fruits for your sustenance. He subjects to you the ships that sail the sea by His command. He subjects to you the rivers. He also subjects to you the sun and the moon, persistent in their duties. And He subjects to you the night and the day" (14:32-33). This text underscores the dominant role humans have in creation in the Qur'an.

This same idea is found in Genesis, but a comparison between the two texts indicates that the Islamic tradition presents a loftier, more honorable view of humanity. In the biblical account, humans are given dominion only over the other living beings in creation (Gen 1:26-28). According to the Qurʾan, on the other hand, all of creation is subjected to humankind. This even extends to powerful forces of nature like rivers and seas and heavenly bodies like the sun and moon.[1] But the text is quick to point out that with this authority comes the obligation to always remember why humankind enjoys such a privileged place. It is the divine will that this be the way things are, and it is only at Allah's initiative that all of creation is subservient to humanity. The text begins by citing the supreme authority of Allah as creator and provider of human needs. It then describes in four sentences the subjection of creation to humanity. Each of these four sentences begins with the same Arabic words *wa sakkara lakum* ("and he subjects to you"), the verb of which carries the sense of "to constrain, compel, or make submissive." Rather than use the verb once and simply list the things that are subject to humanity, the text repeats the verb four times in a mantra-like attempt to remind the reader that it is ultimately by Allah's authority that humans have authority. The Qurʾan's order of things is thereby clearly established: the rest of creation is subject to humanity which is, in turn, subject to Allah.

The Creation of Humanity

When we consider the way the Qurʾan treats the creation of humanity the differences between it and the biblical tradition become most apparent. The Bible, in keeping with its aim to present a more or less chronological account of history, begins with an explanation of human origins and then traces the fortunes of the offspring of the first couple. It offers a sequential recounting of the human story in which Adam and Eve play important roles in the first four chapters of Genesis and are really not heard from again after that point. This is not at all the way the Qurʾan is structured. References to Adam and the creation of humanity are found throughout the text, and there is never any attempt to present a chronologically ordered record of human history that begins in the first sura and continues throughout the text.

This highlights one of the most important differences between the two texts that must be kept in mind when considering their relationship to each other. While a primary concern of the Bible is to present a logical, systematic history of the relationship between God and humanity, the Qur'an's focus is on something else entirely. Its main interest is in reminding its audience of its message that Allah is the one true God and Muhammad is Allah's prophet. It does this by adopting an approach that is more thematic than it is historical. When the Qur'an is considering an aspect of faith or Muslim life that can be illustrated in the lives of Adam, Abraham, Moses, Jesus or some other figure, it will refer to any or all of them in order to make its point. Frequently, the same story will be found in several places throughout the Qur'an. From a certain point of view, then, the Bible and the Qur'an are representatives of two entirely different types of writing.

But this does not mean they are written in completely separate genres that have nothing in common. The two works display both historical and thematic interests. While a chief concern for the Bible is in offering a cohesive, chronological narrative of human history, the text does so in order to validate its message that history is salvific and under the authority of the one God. In the same way, the Qur'an's emphasis on message does not mean a complete disregard for history. On the contrary, individuals and events from the past are frequently cited and discussed in order to authenticate or validate its message. The difference between the two texts in this regard is one of form: the Bible tries to achieve its purpose through chronological retelling of historical events while the Qur'an adopts a more thematic or message-centered approach toward the use of the traditions.

This aspect of the Qur'an is clearly seen in its treatment of the creation of humanity. Explicit references to this event are found in several places throughout the book (2:28-39; 7:10-25; 15:19-48; 20:115-122), and in each passage Adam plays a central role as the first human. All of these texts tell the same basic story, but each time it is presented a bit differently in order to deliver a particular message or illustrate some point. Each of the texts shares certain features with the biblical story of Adam and Eve in the garden where they are tricked by the serpent, but some are closer to the Genesis version than others. The form of the story in sura 7 is particularly interesting because it shows how the Qur'an can Islamize a tradition to have it speak directly to its intended audience.

[10] We have set you firmly on the earth and provided you with a livelihood, but you give little thanks. [11] We created you and then gave you shape. Then We said to the angels, "Prostrate yourselves before Adam," and they all prostrated themselves except Iblis, who was not among

those who prostrated. [12]"What prevented you from prostrating when I commanded you?" He asked. "I am better than he," he replied. "You created me of fire, but You created him of clay." [13]He said, "Go down from here! You are not to be proud here. Leave! You are now among the despised." [14]He replied, "Grant to me a delay until the day they are raised up." [15]"You are among those who are reprieved," said He. [16]"Because You have caused me to err," he declared, "I will surely lie in wait for them on Your straight path. [17]Then I will come upon them from the front and from behind, upon their right side and upon their left side. Then You will not find the majority of them thankful." [18]He said "Begone, banished and driven away! As for those that follow you, I will surely fill Hell with you all. [19] Oh Adam, you and your wife dwell in the garden, and eat from where you wish; but do not approach this tree or you shall be among those who do wrong." [20]But Satan whispered to them, so that he might reveal to them what was hidden from them of their shame. He said, "Your Lord has forbidden you to approach this tree only to prevent you from becoming angels or being among those who are immortal." [21]Then he swore to them "I am truly among those who give honest counsel to you." [22]Thus did he guide them by deceit. And when they had tasted of the tree, their shame became apparent to them, and they began to cover themselves with the leaves of the garden. Their Lord called out to them, saying, "Did I not forbid you to approach the tree, and did I not warn you that Satan is a clear enemy to you?" [23]They said, "Our Lord, we have harmed ourselves. If You do not forgive us and have mercy on us we shall surely be among the lost." [24]He said, "Go! Some of you will be enemies of each other. For a while, the earth will provide you a dwelling and life's necessities. [25]There you shall live and there you shall die, and from there you shall be brought out."

The latter part of this passage, beginning with verse 19, reads very much like the biblical account of Adam and Eve found in Genesis 2–3. But the first section, describing the creation of humanity and subsequent reluctance of Iblis to bow down to Adam, is without a biblical parallel.[2] The figure of Iblis is an intriguing one in the Qurʾan. Most scholars believe the word is not an Arabic one and many maintain it is a distortion of the Greek word *diabolos*, from which the English "devil" is derived. The only place Iblis is found in the Qurʾan is in the scene related here and elsewhere when, in his pride, he disobeys Allah and refuses to prostrate himself before the first human. The dialogue between Iblis and Allah highlights the former's proud and sinful nature. After Allah has granted him a temporary pardon from punishment (v. 15) Iblis immediately places the blame for his shortcoming on the deity

("Because You have caused me to err . . .") and boasts that he will ambush Allah's servants and bring about their destruction. At this point, Iblis is not referred to again. The agent responsible for the transgression of Adam and his wife is referred to as "Satan" (Arabic, *shayṭān*). We should understand this as another name or title of the same character since Satan goes on to deceive the first couple in the very way Iblis has threatened he will do. This identification of the two figures is in keeping with the history of Muslim interpretation which has consistently understood "Iblis" and "Satan" to refer to the same figure.

The scene describing the encounter between Satan and the couple shares much in common with the account in Genesis 2–3 but there are some important differences. Among the similarities are the following: the garden location, the admonition not to eat from a certain tree, a deceitful agent who presents himself as a confidante and then claims to reveal the deity's true motivations, the couple's recognition of their nakedness and covering of themselves with leaves, and a final conversation with the deity after which the couple leaves the garden. But the differences are equally prominent and important. Because the ways the two texts diverge can help to give us a clear sense of how the tradition functions in its Islamic context, five of the most interesting ones will be considered in some detail.

1. Human Creation

Several aspects of the Qurʾan's view of human creation as presented in this text deserve careful attention. In the first place, there is no detailed description of the moment of creation along the lines of what we find in the Bible at Genesis 2:7 where God forms the first human from the dust of the ground and then breathes the breath of life into his nostrils. This element may be absent here, but such anthropomorphic descriptions are not missing entirely from the Qurʾan. The parallel text in sura 15, for instance, presents the creation of humanity in a way that is remarkably similar to the biblical version. "Your Lord said to the angels, 'I am creating a human being from clay, formed mud. When I have fashioned him and breathed in him of My spirit prostrate yourselves to him'" (15:28-29). This is a good example of the Qurʾan's tendency, noted earlier, to present somewhat different versions of the same story.

This text from sura 7, and the Qurʾan in general, also lacks any detailed reference to the creation of the first female. Genesis 2:18-25 is clear about both the reason why Eve is created and how that work is accomplished, and its scene of a rib being taken from Adam in order to form a suitable mate is one of the most well known in all of biblical literature. But here, her creation is a given fact that is neither explained nor described. As will be seen below, this nondescript quality of Eve's character extends to other parts of this text and she, along with most women in the Qur'an, is a fairly anonymous figure in the text. In fact, Eve's name is never given in this or any other Qur'an passage and the only woman ever identified by name in the entire book is Mary, the mother of Jesus.

A part of the biblical account of human creation that has been the subject of much discussion is the statement in Genesis 1:26 that humanity was made in the image of God. What precisely this means and how it should inform our self-understanding are topics that have engendered much debate, but it is generally seen as a passage that somehow elevates humanity and gives us a special relationship with God that is lacking for other parts of the created order. The notion of humanity being created in the divine image is completely absent from the Qur'an and the reason for this is that the idea violates one of the central beliefs of Islam. As a faith that frowns upon any visual representation or depiction of the deity, Islam is a prime example of an aniconic religion. Allah, as a completely transcendent deity, is outside common human experience and therefore cannot be drawn, sculpted, painted, or imaged in any other way. To do so is one of the worst sins a Muslim can commit since it is an example of *shirk*, or associating something created with the eternal divine nature. This prohibition is taken extremely seriously and has had a profound effect on all aspects of the faith from Islamic theological discourse to Muslim art and architecture. It is therefore not surprising that an idea like humanity being created in Allah's image, which runs counter to a basic tenet of Muslim belief, is not found in Islam's sacred text.

2. Human Responsibility

When it is compared to the biblical version, the Qur'an's account of the transgression in the garden has some interesting things to say regarding human culpability. The Genesis text (3:1-7) identifies the woman as the one to whom the serpent first speaks. She decides to take his advice and then offers some of the forbidden fruit to the man who quickly eats it. This passage has often been interpreted in a way that presents a very negative depiction of Eve, and women generally, as the cause of the male's sin and downfall. Adam's words in 3:12 when confronted by God ("The woman whom you gave to be with me, she gave me fruit from the tree, and I ate") have often been used to reinforce this view, and the traditional understanding of the text has been that it assigns to Eve the bulk of the blame for their violation of the divine command not to eat of the tree. In recent times, biblical scholars have suggested alternative readings of the text which view Eve's role more positively, but for many Bible readers she remains the one who must bear the burden of responsibility.

The presentation of the scene in the Qurʾan does not allow for such a reading. In this and all other passages that describe the encounter with Satan, no distinction is made between the man and the woman since they are consistently depicted as a couple that acts and responds in tandem. Because Satan speaks to both of them (v. 20) and they both taste of the tree (v. 22) there is no way to determine if one or the other is more at fault. According to the Qurʾan, this is an act that each has shared in equally and a grammatical feature of the Arabic language helps to reinforce this fact. Unlike English and most other languages, Arabic can make use of dual forms and endings which are commonly employed when referring to two persons or objects. The shape and sound of these endings are quite unique and easily distinguished from the more common singular and plural endings. This passage is full of such forms since each time the couple is addressed by Satan or Allah and every time their actions are described the verbs and pronouns are grammatically dual. This has a profound effect on the reader's opinion of who is at fault. In the Arabic text, the section comprising verses 19 through 22 contains 28 dual forms. This is an incredibly high concentration of such usage in a very brief passage and it serves to reinforce the idea that there are two people involved in this transgression and they are equally culpable.

A further way the Qurʾan text conveys this idea is by the wording of the couple's appeal to Allah at the end of the passage. As noted already, in the biblical account Adam is quick to distance himself from the offense by shifting the blame to Eve. She attempts a similar maneuver by trying to implicate the serpent in 3:13 ("The serpent tricked me and I ate"). No such excuses are given in the Qurʾan as the couple acknowledges their mutual guilt and begs forgiveness of Allah. Their statement in verse 23 ("Oh Lord, we have harmed ourselves") is totally devoid of finger-pointing as they recognize their shared responsibility. This expression of solidarity is markedly different from the Genesis version and presents a more healthy and supportive picture of the relationship between the first man and woman.

3. The Agent of Deceit

While both the biblical and Qurʾanic traditions maintain the first couple was deceived by another being who convinced them to eat of the forbidden tree, they do not agree on the nature of that being. In Genesis it is the serpent, who is described as "more crafty than any other wild animal that the Lord God had made" (3:1). The Qurʾan, on the other hand, consistently portrays the deceiver as Satan who, as we have seen, has traditionally been identified with the figure of Iblis, the angel who refused to prostrate before Adam.

Part of the reason for this difference is theological and connected with the Islamic understanding of the nature of Allah. According to Genesis, one of the animals which God had created was partly responsible for the downfall of humanity. This raises important questions which have been asked frequently throughout the course of Judeo-Christian reflection on the text. Why would God create something that is capable of such evil? Does God have control over the created world? If so, why did God allow such a thing to happen? Did God, who is supposed to be omniscient, not know that the serpent would do this? What kind of a God is this?

The Qurʾan narrative softens this aspect of the story and reduces the need to ask such troubling questions. Here, it is one of the angels, rather than another member of the created order, who contributes to humanity's trouble. In the Islamic view, angels are supernatural beings that are not part of the earthly realm and, as such, have a different relationship with Allah. While not actually divine, they have powers and abilities that establish their authority over creation and humanity. By having an angel as the agent of deception, the Qurʾan has implicitly distanced Allah from the scene and focused the attention on one of these intermediary beings rather than the supreme deity. According to Muslim belief, God is only capable of good and does not create evil, which comes under the control of Satan and other supernatural beings. Ultimately, every individual makes a choice either to follow the way of Allah, which leads only to good, or to follow the way of Satan which leads to evil. "Whatever good comes to you comes from Allah, and whatever evil befalls you comes from yourself"(4:79). Given this worldview, it would be most inappropriate to present the garden scene in a way that might implicate Allah, however indirectly, in the transgression of the couple.

An interesting variant of this passage found in 18:50 points in this same direction. "When We said to the angels, 'Prostrate yourselves before

Adam,' they all prostrated except Iblis. He was one of the *jinn* and ne-glected the command of his Lord." The word *jinn* refers to another group of supernatural beings whose relationship to angels is not en-tirely clear. The singular of the word is *jinnī*, which is where the English "genie" comes from. No other text refers to Iblis as one of the *jinn*, but its mention here is intriguing, particularly in light of the meaning of the word during Muhammad's era. In pre-Islamic times, the *jinn* were the spirits found in the desert and other parts of the natural world which were hostile to humanity. A belief in their semidivine status car-ried over into Muhammad's day when many understood them to be vague, impersonal gods. The use of such a term to refer to Iblis might be a more explicit attempt to distance Allah from the garden scene by having a quasi-divine figure function as the antagonist.

4. The Outcome

The biblical account ends on a somewhat negative note as the ser-pent, Eve, and Adam are admonished in turn for their roles in the vio-lation of God's command (Gen 3:14-19). Each one is punished in a way that will have grave consequences for their post-garden existence: the serpent will now crawl on its belly, the woman will experience pain in childbirth and the man will have to toil and engage in hard work to sur-vive. A more serious result is the fact that now humans will experience death, which does not appear to have been a part of human existence prior to this moment. In an action that symbolizes the rupture of the divine/human relationship, humanity is then expelled from the garden, never to return. Traditionally, this episode has been understood as the "fall of humanity," which helped give rise to the notion of original sin, or the idea that all human beings are tainted at birth since they share in the sin of the first couple. This concept has been particularly influential in the Christian tradition.

Although the Qur'an considers the couple's transgression to be a serious mistake that has important consequences, it does not present such a bleak picture of its aftermath. In general, they are the same people at the end of the text that they were at the beginning. They do not undergo the transformation that Adam and Eve experience in Genesis, where they leave the garden cursed, rejected and mortal. The Qur'anic couple are expelled from the garden but not with the changed condition of their biblical counterparts. Allah does not curse them and it appears that mortality has always been a part of their human condi-tion since they are never explicitly threatened with it if they eat of the tree. In short, in the Qurʾan there is no "fall of humanity" or original sin. In the Islamic view, humans were created mortal with an innate capacity to do good, not evil. The first man and woman were tricked into violating the divine command, but this does not make them inherently bad or the first link in an unbroken chain of human sinfulness. If someone does sin, it is his or her own fault and not the inevitable consequence of some primordial transgression. The only result of the couple's mistake in the Qurʾan is their removal from the garden and the presence of Allah, but how are we to understand this outcome and how long will it last?

The answer to the latter question is found in the last verse of the passage. "There (on earth) you shall live and there you shall die, and from there you shall be brought out." The couple will be separated from Allah's presence as long as their lives last and then they will be "brought out." Brought out to where and what? This can be understood as a reference to a return to Allah after death, provided one has lived one's life in accordance with the message of Islam. The Qurʾan text ends on a positive note since it offers the possibility of a return to life in the garden after death. How different this is from the biblical version which holds out no hope for such a result. Adam and Eve are effectively shut out from the garden and cut off from God's presence with no hope of getting back. Ironically, God's words to Adam in 3:19 make use of the images of "bringing out" and "returning" but these are words of terror, not consolation, for humanity. "By the sweat of your face you shall eat bread until you return to the ground, for out of it you were taken; you are dust, and to dust you shall return."

5. The Image of the Deity

It should be clear at this point that an important difference between the Qurʾanic and biblical texts is that they present two different images of the deity which are hard to reconcile. The Genesis passage, as we have already seen, causes the reader to question God's power and control over the situation in the garden since, in several places, the deity does not appear to be omniscient and omnipotent. We have already seen how the serpent's manipulation of Adam and Eve raises puzzling problems about God's authority. Similarly, God does not seem to have full knowledge about what is going on, as the questions directed toward Adam in 3:9 ("Where are you?") and 3:11 ("Who told you that you were naked? Have you eaten from the tree of which I commanded you not to eat?") seem to suggest.[3] An even more troubling aspect of the divine nature is revealed at the end of the passage when God drives out humanity from the garden and then sets up the cherubim and flaming sword to prevent access to the tree of life. All contact with God is cut off and passage back into the garden is prohibited as the first couple are now left to fend for themselves in a strange, new environment. They have been abandoned by a God who seems to be quite different from the tender Artisan who carefully fashioned them and breathed life into them in the previous chapter.

This is not the image of Allah that emerges from the Qur'an text. As noted earlier, the fact that Satan, rather than the serpent, deceives the couple limits divine involvement. In the same way, Allah seems to be omniscient since the questions asked are of a rhetorical nature and not requests for information. "Did I not forbid you to approach the tree, and did I not warn you that Satan is a clear enemy to you?" (v. 22). Allah knows what they have done and reminds them that they should not have acted in this way since they were forbidden to do so.[4]

Allah's reaction to the couple's sin in the Qur'an is markedly different from that found in Genesis. This is not an angry, vengeful deity who rejects and abandons humankind. The couple's response to Allah is striking and points out the different relationship they have with their creator. The only recourse for the biblical Adam and Eve is to shift blame in order to avoid the anger and wrath of their God. Adam points his finger at Eve while she accuses the serpent of being the responsible party. It is as if they know their only hope to avoid certain punishment is to restore their reputations by denying any wrongdoing. Their Qur'anic counterparts adopt an entirely different strategy—they throw themselves on the mercy of Allah. After acknowledging their mutual responsibility they appeal to the compassion of their creator. "If You do not forgive us and have mercy on us we shall surely be among the lost" (v. 23). In Islam, the two most frequently cited qualities of Allah are mercy and compassion and this episode teaches that even in moments when one has violated the divine will one must remain confident and trust in divine mercy and forgiveness.[5] This has a significant effect on how we can interpret the outcome of the story. The couple asks for forgiveness and Allah responds not with a curse but with a command to leave the garden. We should understand humanity's removal to the earth as an expression of divine mercy rather than a punishment. Allah does not abandon them by expelling them from the garden and then sealing it off so they can never return. Rather, their separation from it is temporary. After living a good and faithful life, during which they are to learn how to submit themselves to the divine will, they will be "brought out" and back to the garden.

ISLAMIZATION OF THE TRADITION

The analysis of 7:10-25 up to this point has identified a number of ways and places in which the garden tradition has been made to reflect the interests and concerns of the Qurʾan. Certain themes have been highlighted and aspects of the scene have been presented in a way that enables the text to take on a distinctly Islamic flavor. Several other literary and thematic aspects of the passage have not yet been considered which also speak to its Muslim audience.

The use of direct address and point of view indicates that the purpose of the text is to instruct the modern reader or listener. By "modern" should be understood both people living during the time of Muhammad and any later individual or group who might read it. That this is the target audience is apparent in the first verse: "We have set you firmly on the earth and provided you with a livelihood, but you give little thanks." In the Arabic original of this verse the word "you" is found three times, always in the plural form. The addressee is therefore not only Muhammad or some other individual but a collectivity, probably humanity at large. This transforms the episode that follows from a simple recounting of a past event into an illustration of how it is that Allah provides but people are not thankful. We see here, then, an example of the different intentions of the biblical and Qurʾanic texts that were noted earlier. The presence of this initial verse shifts the attention of the reader to the message which the passage seeks to convey and how it might be applied in the contemporary context. The absence of a similar verse in the biblical account, while not completely dismissing its message, encourages the reader to view the text more as a recounting of a past event that may not speak as directly to his or her own situation.

The passage allows us to say more about the identity of its audience since it suggests that it is principally aimed at the Muslim community. Several of its features support this conclusion. In the first place, the nature of the transgressions of both Iblis and the couple fits well an Islamic context. They are all guilty of the same basic sin in that they refuse to submit themselves to the power and authority of Allah. Iblis does not obey the divine order to prostrate himself and the man and woman violate Allah's prohibition against eating from the tree. In this way, all of them have committed the same offense of rebelling against the divine will. While this type of sin is also frequently discussed in the Judeo/Christian tradition, it is even more central to the Islamic religious system since Islam (literally, "submission") insists that the only way one can be a true Muslim (literally, "one who submits") is to subject oneself to the will and authority of Allah.

Two other aspects of the text are even more explicit regarding its intended Muslim audience. The first concerns the manner in which Iblis threatens to waylay Allah's followers in verse 16: "I will surely lie in wait for them on Your straight path." As we will see in later chapters, the phrase "straight path" appears so frequently in the Qur'an and Islamic literature as a reference to the way Allah wishes Muslims to conduct themselves that it is virtually a synonym for the religion of Islam. Perhaps its most well known and frequently cited use is found in the *Fātiḥa*, the opening sura of the Qur'an, where verse 5 asks that Allah "Guide us on the straight path." Its presence in sura 7 Islamizes the passage as Iblis says he will tempt and turn away Muslims as they journey along the straight path of Allah. In yet another way, the form of Iblis' threat reinforces the idea that the text is meant for a modern audience. He says in verse 17 that the majority of those on the straight path will not be found thankful, and this recalls Allah's comment in verse 12 that people give little thanks. Texts like this play an important role in reminding Muslims that even Islam is not free from the presence of Satan. Believers must always be on guard against the deceiver and one's presence on the straight path is not a guarantee of salvation, as Allah's words in verse 18 warn: "As for those that follow you, I will surely fill Hell with you all."

A second feature of the passage that points to its Islamic audience is its immediate literary context. The verses immediately following the text are addressed directly to Muslims in a way that leaves no doubt that the tradition of the garden is here being recalled in order to teach them an important lesson. Four times in the section 7:26-38 the audience is addressed as "children of Adam" and then instructed regarding how to behave in order to avoid the mistake made by the first couple. This use of a vocative, explicitly linking them with Adam, and the attempt to apply the experience of the primordial couple to the situation of Muslims clearly highlight the way the garden scene is functioning in this section of the Qur'an.

"Oh children of Adam, we have sent down to you clothing to cover your shame as adornment. But the clothing of piety is better" (7:26).

"Oh children of Adam, do not let Satan seduce you as he sent out your parents from the garden. He stripped their clothing from them that he might show them their shame" (7:27).

"Oh children of Adam, take your adornments to every mosque. Eat and drink, but do not be unmindful for He does not love those who are unmindful" (7:31).

ADAM AS PRIMOGENITURE

These last citations serve as a good introduction to the other type of Qurʾanic material in which Adam figures prominently. Some texts that treat specific individuals or groups describe them in a way that directly connects them back to Adam as their prototype or the first in a series of generations. In this way, Adam's role as primogeniture is acknowledged. The passages just quoted do this by referring to the later Muslim community as "children of Adam," indicating the relationship they have with the first human.[6] Another text that does a similar thing is 19:58, which refers to some of those who have received favor from Allah as being from Adam's line. "These are the ones to whom Allah has been gracious: the prophets of the lineage of Adam and from among those We carried (in the ark) with Noah, and of the lineage of Abraham and Israel and from among those We guided and chose."

The Two Sons of Adam

Any consideration of the "children of Adam" by the Bible reader will immediately bring to mind two names: Cain and Abel. Most of the fourth chapter of Genesis is devoted to the story of these first two of Adam and Eve's offspring and it presents the well-known account of the Bible's first homicide in which Cain kills his brother and is then cursed by God. The Qurʾan also contains a version of this tradition but, in keeping with its presentation of other passages related to Adam and his family, the story here diverges somewhat from its biblical parallel. The passage in question is found at 5:27-32:

> [27]Relate to them in truth the story of Adam's two sons. When they presented an offering it was accepted from one of them but it was not accepted from the other. The one said, "Truly, I will kill you." The other said, "Allah accepts from the pious. [28]If you extend your hand against me to kill me, I will not extend my hand against you to kill you. I fear Allah,

the Lord of the universe. [29]I wish you would bear the sin committed against me and your other sins and be one of the people of the fire, for that is the reward of those who are wrongdoers." [30]And his mind aided him in the killing of his brother, so he killed him and became one of the lost ones. [31]Then Allah sent a raven which scratched on the earth in order to show him how to bury his brother's corpse. He cried, "Woe is me! Am I unable to be like this raven and bury my brother's corpse?" Then he became repentant. [32]Because of this, We laid it down for the children of Israel that whoever killed a person, except in the case of punishment for murder or causing corruption in the land, it would be as if he had killed all people. And whoever saved a person, it would be as if he had saved all people. Our messengers came to them with clear signs, but even after that many of them do evil in the land.

The first thing that strikes the reader when comparing this account with that of Genesis 4 is the relative lack of details regarding the brothers. The Qur'an does not provide us with certain information that the Bible gives us: their names (Cain and Abel), their occupations (tiller of the ground and keeper of sheep), what their offerings were (fruit of the ground and fat portions of the firstlings of the flock). Also missing is the encounter between God and Cain prior to the murderous act in which God reminds him of the need to master the sin that lurks at the door (Gen 4:6-7). These differences have a profound effect on how the reader understands the story. The only things we know about them in the Qur'an are the identity of their father and their relationship as brothers. But we are unable to differentiate between the two of them since we know nothing specific about either. This lack of biographical detail makes them less individualized and therefore more symbolic. Once again, this is a text that is concerned with presenting a message rather than recounting history, and so its characters are drawn in a way that allows that message to be apparent and more easily applied to the life of the reader.

The absence of the encounter between Cain and God in the Qur'an is equally interesting. In the biblical account, this makes God an important character in the story. The deity has warned Cain and reminded him of the need to avoid doing evil and yet he still kills his brother. This compounds Cain's guilt since he fails to follow God's explicit command. God is involved in the text even prior to this point, however, when we are told that after the brothers make their offerings, "the Lord had regard for Abel and his offering, but for Cain and his offering he had no regard" (Gen 4:4-5). The Bible makes it very clear that

God has preferred the offering of one brother over that of the other and this is the inciting moment that leads to the murderous climax. God is therefore a significant actor in this scene from its beginning.

Despite the lack of certain elements found in the biblical version, the Qur'an furnishes the reader with information not present in Genesis. Although there is no encounter between God and Cain prior to the murder, the Qur'an text does recount another encounter, only this time it is between the two brothers. This is a striking component of the text that gives an entirely new twist to it. According to Genesis 4:8, the only words ever spoken between the two brothers are decidedly one-sided: Cain says to his brother "Let us go out to the field." This invitation is particularly heinous since the motivation for it becomes obvious in the next sentence when Cain kills Abel in the very field to which he has lured him. Abel never utters a word in the Bible and the reader is left wondering how much, if at all, these two brothers spoke to each other.

The Qur'an does not leave this issue in doubt since it narrates a brief, but telling, conversation between the brothers. Once again, the killer speaks only one sentence, but this time it is not the overture to a sneak attack but a blunt statement of intent: "Truly, I will kill you." His brother responds in a most unusual way. Rather than ask for an explanation or somehow try to defend himself, he simultaneously expresses his faith in Allah and warns his brother of the fate that awaits him if he should carry out his threat. This response functions in the same way the conversation between God and Cain does in Genesis. The killer is being reminded of the result of his intended action and asked to make a choice between following the way of the deity and giving in to his own selfish desire. The difference here is that Allah is not doing the warning and, in fact, has been strangely absent from the entire scene up to this point. This becomes clear when we recognize that the offering scene has also been toned down to lessen divine involvement. Unlike the Genesis text, we are not told explicitly that Allah accepts the offering of one brother while rejecting the other's. The Qur'an text is more evasive by making use of the passive voice: "When they presented an offering it was accepted from one of them but it was not accepted from the other." One might properly conclude that Allah is the implied subject of the verb, but the resulting ambiguity, along with the absence of a direct divine role in this part of the story, put the deity in a very different light.

It appears, then, that Allah's role is being downplayed as the characters of the brothers are enhanced. This is the critical issue in understanding the main point of the text in the Qur'an. This is a passage that is concerned with addressing the matter of human faith and response to the deity. The two brothers, whose identities have been shorn of any individuality regarding name and occupation, symbolize two types of people. One, the victim, is a faithful believer who places all his trust in Allah, while the other, the killer, is a faithless unbeliever who takes matters into his own hands. The reason why the latter is rejected by Allah has nothing to do with his occupation or the type of offering he presents, a conclusion one might be tempted to reach when reading the biblical account. In fact, in the Qurʾan only one offering is presented jointly by the brothers. Its acceptance or rejection is based solely on the qualities of the individual, and the ensuing brief conversation between them indicates that the two brothers possess very different qualities. The victim is presented as the ideal Muslim believer and his words are typical of an adherent to Islam. In verse 28 he refers to Allah as "Lord of the Universe," which is a very common appellation for the deity in the Qurʾan as is seen, for example, in 1:1. "Praise be to Allah, Lord of the Universe." Similarly, the beliefs he articulates about the importance of piety and fear of Allah, as well as the reference to the punishment of Hell for wrongdoers, are views shared by all Muslims.

The killer, on the other hand, is presented as the stereotypical unbeliever. While his brother seeks guidance from Allah in determining how to live, his inspiration comes from another source. The motivation for his vile deed comes from within himself. "And his mind aided him in the killing of his brother, so he killed him and became one of the lost ones" (v. 30). The word "mind" is a translation of the Arabic *nafs*, which can have a number of meanings. The most common ones refer to intangible or immaterial aspects of the individual such as the "soul," "spirit," or "self." Sometimes, this is further refined and given the sense of the intellect or reason of a person. This is probably how we should understand its usage here, and "mind" captures well the point of the verse. This brother is depending upon himself and has no sense of relationship with or dependence upon Allah. He is therefore the antithesis of his believing brother, and the description of him as "one of the lost ones" is a fitting one since, according to Muslim belief, one who does not submit to Allah's will is damned. The reference to his being lost also establishes an interesting connection with his biblical counterpart who, after killing his brother, settles in the land of Nod (Gen 4:16), a name from a Hebrew root that means "to wander."

The Qurʾan text ends on a hopeful note as the murderer repents and acknowledges the error of his ways. The reason for his conversion and the way it is described fit well with the thematic focus of the passage that has just been discussed. The scene of the raven's appearance does not have a biblical parallel, but in the Qurʾan it is the critical moment that allows for the rehabilitation of the lost brother. When he sees the bird scratch on the ground he is overcome with guilt and realizes he has failed miserably in his fraternal relationship. But only the reader knows the real cause of his repentance: Allah has sent the raven which leads to his change of heart. The murderer does not know that the deity is behind the bird's appearance and this divine anonymity suits the purpose of the text very well in a couple of ways. In the first place, it remains consistent with the rest of the passage where, in comparison with the biblical account, the deity has been strangely absent. Allah is mentioned by name twice, but in the course of the entire scene never appears to either brother or utters a word. But this should not be mistaken for divine absence since Allah is implicitly present in the words of the victim and directly involved in the conversion of the killer by sending the raven. The narratorial mention of Allah's involvement, a step removed from the action itself, helps to maintain the sense of a deity who is busy working behind the scenes but is not the focus of attention.

A second way this divine anonymity works in the narrative is that it helps to support the analysis of the killer's character that was presented earlier. There, we saw that he is someone who acts according to his own "mind" and does not appeal to any outside source for help or guidance. This quality seems to be present in the scene with the raven as well, but with a strong ironic undertone. He sees the bird scratching on the ground and comes to the conclusion that this is a lesson for him. He realizes he has mistreated his brother. In his own mind, he has come to this insight of his own accord. Once again, just as in the matter of the murder of his brother, he is seemingly dependent upon only himself in making his decisions. But the reader knows better. His repentance would not have been possible if Allah had not sent the raven in the first place. The fascinating thing about this scene is that the killer repents without even being aware that Allah is involved in his rehabilitation. The text makes a profound point about Islam's understanding of the deity. Allah is present in all aspects of life and is the source of all that is good. Even when there appears to be no divine involvement and humans believe they are acting for their own reasons, Allah is involved. There is a degree of irony at work here in that the character, who has not professed an explicit belief in Allah and acts in ways that suggest a high degree of self-sufficiency and independence, is actually indebted to the anonymous deity for his salvation.

Even more irony can be uncovered when we read this text in light of its biblical counterpart. In Genesis 4:2-3 we learn of Cain's occupation and his skill at practicing it. "Now Abel was a keeper of sheep, and Cain was a tiller of the ground. In the course of time Cain brought to the Lord an offering of the fruit of the ground." The biblical murderer is someone who makes his living working the ground and the offering from him that God rejects is the result of his tilling the earth. After the murder, he is cursed by God in a way that indicates his relationship with the ground, just as that with his brother, has been damaged. Note the high frequency of terms connected with earth and ground in God's words. "What have you done? Listen; your brother's blood is crying out to me from the ground! And now you are cursed from the ground, which has opened its mouth to receive your brother's blood from your hand. When you till the ground, it will no longer yield to you its strength; you will be a fugitive and a wanderer on the earth" (Gen 4:10-12).

His occupation as a tiller is not mentioned in the Qur'an, but the scene with the raven does make use of the ground motif nonetheless. The killer in this text is hardly a tiller, since he must be shown by the raven how to scratch and dig in the earth. While Cain's livelihood is gotten from the earth, his Islamic counterpart does not know the first thing about working the land and must be shown how it is done by a bird! After the murder, Cain is cursed by God, loses his facility to work the land and is forced to wander the earth. But his Islamic counterpart is assisted by God, gains an understanding of how to dig in the earth and is no longer one of the lost. While in Genesis the ground is connected with Cain's punishment and rejection by God, in the Qur'an it is linked with his repentance and help from Allah. Once again, we see that the Qur'an's version of the tradition has resulted in a completely different outcome for a biblical figure. According to Genesis 4:16, Cain's story ends with his alienation from his God and other people ("Then Cain went away from the presence of the Lord, and settled in the land of Nod, east of Eden"), but the killer in the Qur'an, even if it is still unknown to him, has initiated a new relationship with Allah and humanity. His cry in verse 31, "Woe is me! Am I unable to be like this raven and bury my brother's corpse?," is another way of saying what Cain was forced to deny: "I *am* my brother's keeper."

A final aspect of the Qur'an's story of the two sons of Adam which suggests that its purpose is primarily didactic is found in its last verse, addressed to the reader. "Because of this, we laid it down for the children of Israel that whoever killed a person, except in the case of punishment for murder or causing corruption in the land, it will be as if he had killed all people. And whoever saves a person, it will be as if he had saved all people. Our messengers came to them with clear signs, but even after that many of them do evil in the land." The opening words of the verse, "because of this," indicate that the text of the two brothers is functioning as an etiology, a story that attempts to explain the cause or origin of something. The Qurʾan has recounted the brothers' tale in order to tell the reader how and why the Israelites were given the prohibition against murder. While not completely disinterested in the question of what happened to Adam's sons, the passage's main interest is in instructing the reader regarding what the text has meant for people in the past and what it might mean in his or her own faith life. In this way, the final sentence, with its reminder of the need not to ignore the messengers of Allah, ends on a distinctively Islamic note.

COOPERATING REVELATIONS

As noted earlier, there are several versions of the garden tradition in the Qurʾan, each with its own focus and main point. The one in sura 20 is the shortest of them and yet it contains many of the basic elements of the longer variants as seen, for example, in sura 7 which we have already examined in some detail. We now turn to this passage in order to see its contribution to the Qurʾan's vision of human origins and to consider how it might aid and advance our reading of the Genesis account.

> [115]Earlier, We made a covenant with Adam but he forgot. We did not find in him any resolve. [116]When We said to the angels, "Prostrate yourselves before Adam," they all prostrated except Iblis, who refused. [117]We said, "Oh Adam, this one is an enemy to you and to your wife. Do not let him drive the two of you out of the garden and make you miserable. [118]For in it you will not be hungry or naked, [119]you will not be thirsty or scorched by the sun." [120]Then Satan whispered to him saying, "Oh Adam, shall I show you the tree of immortality and a kingdom that does not pass away?" [121]And then they both ate of it so that their shame became apparent to them, and they began to cover themselves with the leaves of the garden. Thus did Adam disobey his Lord and go astray. [122]Then his Lord chose him, returned to him with forgiveness and guided him.

Analysis of the Qurʾanic Tradition

Perhaps the most obvious difference between this text and that of sura 7:10-25 is the relatively limited role Iblis/Satan plays here. Several elements are missing: (1) the explanation of why he refuses to prostrate; (2) the conversation between Allah and Satan in which the latter is cursed and then asks for a reprieve; (3) the threat by Satan to seduce Allah's faithful servants; and (4) the detailed description of how Satan is able to deceive the couple. These differences indicate that Iblis and his role in the scene are not the focus of this passage. He simply does what he has to do in order to contribute to plot development and then disappears from view. The interests of this text lie elsewhere, in the characterization of Adam and the image of humanity that is being put forward. While the key relationship in the passage from sura 7 is that between Allah and Iblis/Satan, here it is clearly the interaction between Allah and Adam that is central.

The first and last verses of the passage indicate that its key themes are human culpability and divine forgiveness, or divine forgiveness despite human culpability. Humanity is depicted as unable to sustain its commitment to the deity. "Earlier, We made a covenant with Adam but he forgot. We did not find in him any resolve" (v. 115). Despite this shortcoming on Adam's part, Allah is portrayed as compassionate and caring. "Then his Lord chose him, returned toward him with forgiveness and guided him" (v. 122). The intervening verses describe the way Adam has violated the divine/human relationship and the text leaves no doubt that, despite Satan's involvement, Adam has no one to blame but himself for the predicament he finds himself in.

The covenant language that is employed in the passage highlights this theme. The text begins with a mention of the intimate relationship that exists between humanity and deity, and Allah is shown honoring that bond. Allah's special concern for humanity is seen in the warning to avoid Iblis in verse 117 and the subsequent description of what awaits the couple if they should give in to temptation.[7] This is done not with a threat, as we see in the biblical tradition at Genesis 2:17 ("In the day you eat of it you shall die"), but in the form of a reminder of the many blessings they presently enjoy in the garden which will no longer be available to them if they should follow Satan. "For in it you will not be hungry or naked, you will not be thirsty or scorched by the sun"(vv. 118–119).[8] Even after Adam refuses to heed the deity and violates the divine prohibition Allah does not reject him. In fact, in this text we never hear of humanity being expelled from the garden or punished in any way. The response by Allah is just the opposite and summed up in the three verbs used in the last verse: "chose," "returned to him with forgiveness," and "guided." The second of these verbs is particularly interesting. The Arabic word (*tāba*) can mean, as it does here, the act of Allah turning to someone in compassion and forgiveness. But another meaning, more frequently found in the Qur'an, is that of a human being turning to Allah and asking for forgiveness. Its presence here may be an example of intentional *double entendre* in which the Qur'an is making the point that Allah is both exercising divine forgiveness and reminding Adam of the action which is required of him. In a sense, Allah is a model for the human that shows him how to behave in the context of their relationship. Throughout this text, then, the deity acts in ways that are determined by the covenant that exists with humanity.

This is not the way Adam acts at all. Perhaps the quality of humanity that is stressed most here is its free will. Adam is given a choice in the text and allowed to make whatever decision he wishes. Unfortunately, he makes the wrong choice and this error in judgment has the potential to damage his relationship with Allah. The role of Adam's free will in this passage is apparent in his encounters with both Allah and Satan. As already seen, Allah cautions Adam against associating with Satan and points out to him the benefits of the garden and the drawbacks of its alternative. He is therefore aware of the dangers, but in exercising his free will disregards this counsel and opts for the wrong choice. The brief encounter with Satan is equally damning since it does not appear that Adam is deceived in the same way he was in sura 7. Here, Satan simply asks a question ("Oh Adam, shall I show you the tree of immortality and a kingdom that does not pass away?"), once again giving the man the opportunity to exercise his free will. The choice is Adam's; he can respond with a yes or a no and decides on the former. In this passage, Adam is presented as someone who is acting with full knowledge and completely responsible for the decisions he makes. This makes his transgression a willful, intentional violation of the divine will and the text places the blame squarely on his shoulders. "Thus did Adam disobey his Lord and go astray" (v. 121). In short, he has not behaved in a way consistent with the covenant that has been established with Allah.

The difference between the divine and human partners in this relationship is brought into sharp relief at the end of the passage when Allah freely turns to and forgives Adam. It is striking that Adam never acknowledges his mistake and begs for Allah's mercy as he and the woman do in sura 7. The reader wonders if Adam is even aware of the error of his choice and whether or not he has reoriented his life. Such questions cause the reader to reach one conclusion: the restoration of the divine/human relationship at the end of the passage is due to divine initiative and Adam has had no hand in it. This points out a key distinction between human will and the divine will which is basic to Islam. While human actions can tend toward error, those of Allah are only capable of good, even to the point of instructing and guiding those who have freely chosen to disregard the divine will.

In this text Allah functions less as an authority figure and more as an adviser or companion to Adam. The deity alerts, informs, encourages, forgives and supports the man, all in the context of a passage that is heavily laden with references to and images of their covenantal bond. It is almost as if Allah is being depicted as the partner of the man here, and this may be part of the reason why the woman does not figure very prominently in the text. Allah seems to be saying in this passage, "it is not good for the man to be alone, so I will remain with him to be his helpmate." This is not to suggest that the woman is rendered irrelevant or unnecessary, but rather that it might be better to understand Adam in this passage as a symbol or representative of humanity at large rather than the first male of the species. Each person, like Adam, has a special relationship with Allah but each person, like Adam, forgets this fact from time to time. This text is a reminder to the reader that Allah does not forget.

Application to the Biblical Tradition

Reading the opening chapters of Genesis in the light of Qur'an 20:115-122 can allow us to glean additional meaning and insight from the biblical text that we might normally miss. The general tendency when reading the biblical story of the garden is to focus on the element of human sin and interpret it as a text that tries to explain the origin of our weak and corrupt nature. The Christian reader, particularly, is likely to view the narrative as the scriptural basis for a belief in the "fall" of humanity from a prior sinless state. The Qur'an text questions the tendency to see this as the sole meaning of the Genesis account by enabling us to discover often unrecognized aspects of the familiar biblical story that put it in a more positive light.

We have seen that the dominant motif of the Qur'an passage is the covenantal relationship that exists between humanity and the deity and how each partner responds to its demands. Allah is presented as a faithful adherent to the covenant who guides Adam even as he exercises his free will to violate the relationship. Similar elements are also present in the Genesis account although they are frequently overlooked. Perhaps the most basic reason for this is it is not common to think of the first few chapters of Genesis in terms of a covenant. Explicit covenant language is not used in the Bible until a bit later in the book with the story of Noah, after which point it becomes a very common part of the biblical view of the relationship between God and humanity, particularly the people of Israel. Despite the absence of specific references to a covenant, however, there is a way in which we might understand the texts that discuss the creation of humanity as laying the foundation for the concept of covenant.

Even if we acknowledge the possibility of viewing the Genesis story as somehow covenantal, it is still difficult to view it positively since it is common to understand it as an explanation or illustration of what is wrong in our relationship with God. This has often affected the interpretation of the text, particularly its depiction of the deity and the first couple. The Qur'an passage can open up the possibility of a more constructive reading of its biblical counterpart by reminding us that a covenantal relationship between humanity and the deity was established when Adam was created. If we reread the biblical text with that idea in mind it becomes apparent that this is also an important component of the Genesis material.

Many texts in Genesis hint at the divine concern for humanity. Not only is it alone made in God's image, but it is also the only part of creation that is infused with the divine breath (2:7). Similarly, the man's being placed in the garden that has been created by God to till and care for it (2:15) suggests trust and confidence toward humanity on the part of the deity. The reference in 2:18 to God's wish that the man not be alone likewise indicates concern for Adam, as does the time-consuming search to find a suitable mate. It is clear, then, that prior to their eating of the forbidden tree God expresses commitment toward and care for humanity in a variety of ways.

But this divine concern does not end with their transgression. After their offense, there is continued evidence of interest on God's part in how the couple is faring. God is absent from the scene with the serpent but reappears soon after it to ask, "Where are you?" (3:9). Rather than understand this question as their being called to account for their sin, it might indicate genuine interest in their whereabouts and anxiety over their fate. Similarly, God's subsequent questions asking who told them they were naked and whether they ate of the forbidden tree (3:11) could be an attempt to protect or help them by getting at the truth. Another obvious description of divine concern for the couple is found in 3:21 where, before they leave the garden, God makes garments of skins for them. A final manifestation of God's fidelity to the covenantal relationship with humanity occurs after their expulsion from the garden. In 3:23 it is mentioned that the man's work will be to till the ground from which he had been taken. Although it will now be a difficult occupation as a result of their violation (3:17-18) it is important to keep in mind that this is the very thing for which the man originally had been created (2:15). He will therefore still serve the same purpose he was initially given and this suggests God continues to see him playing a unique role in creation.

It would therefore be a mistake to adopt a narrow view of God's role in Genesis which focuses only on divine anger at the couple for their transgression which leads to their rejection by being expelled from the garden. These are clearly important aspects of the biblical presentation but a strong secondary theme is the persistence of divine compassion and patience despite their offense. This latter quality of God is a dominant one later on in Genesis and throughout the rest of the Bible when the covenantal relationship becomes the interpretive framework for understanding the bond between Yahweh and the people, but it is not completely missing from the opening chapters of Genesis. In the Qur'an it has a higher profile and texts like 20:115-122 can cooperate with Genesis 2–3 in making its presence there more obvious.

NOTES: CHAPTER 1

[1]The explicit reference to these natural and cosmological elements might be due to the Qur'an's attitude toward polytheism. The pre-Islamic Arabs, as well as many during Muhammad's time, identified the forces of nature and heavenly bodies as loci of divine presence and power. The Qur'an frequently challenges its audience to reject such false worship and turn to Allah, the one true God. By stating that all these things are subject to humanity, as it does here, it points out the absurdity of engaging in these practices.

[2]This is one of the places, mentioned in the introduction, where there are connections between the Qur'an and nonbiblical Jewish and Christian sources. "The Life of Adam and Eve" is a work whose roots might be as early as the first century C.E. and it describes Satan's fall in a way similar to what is found in the Qur'an.

[3]It could be argued that the reason why God is presented in this way is to highlight the role and importance of free will in human existence. By asking these questions, God is forcing Adam to exercise free choice and own up to his guilt. This interpretation has some value and does help clear up the issue of why God asks the questions, but it is still reading more into the text than is

there. On its surface level, the passage simply indicates that God does not have certain information and therefore asks the questions.

[4]There is a gap in this text since the warning about Satan being an enemy to the couple is not explicitly given. This type of omission is a fairly common feature in the Qurʾan and may be due to the fact that we often have multiple versions of the same episode. In the present case, the warning about Satan is given in the version of the scene presented in sura 20. This text will be discussed in detail later in the chapter.

[5]Each of the 114 suras in the Qurʾan but one (sura 9) begins with the words "in the name of Allah, the merciful one, the compassionate one." Its repetition of this phrase is a constant reminder to Muslims of the nature of the deity and it is also used frequently in everyday speech. It is not uncommon to hear a Muslim say, "In the name of Allah, the merciful one, the compassionate one" prior to engaging in an activity. The absence of the phrase at the beginning of sura 9 is thought to be due to suras 8 and 9 having been originally one long chapter that was later divided into two.

[6]This is also common usage in modern Arabic where human beings are frequently referred to as *banī ʾādam*, or children of Adam.

[7]This is the warning to the couple that is mentioned in 7:22 ("Did I not warn you that Satan is a clear enemy to you?") but never actually given there.

[8]Somewhat ironically, we might also interpret these two verses as a kind of "temptation" on the part of Allah. By mentioning the advantages of remaining in the garden, the deity tries to entice or tempt the couple to avoid the wiles of Satan. I owe this insight to Ms. Rachel Bozynski, a student at Rhodes College.

2

Noah

Noah is mentioned by name more than forty times throughout the Qur'an and the text is remarkably consistent in its presentation of him. In the great majority of these passages he is portrayed as a prophet of doom whose job it is to warn his people of their imminent destruction if they do not change their ways and worship Allah, the one true God. The description of his relationship with the people explains how they refuse to listen to him and accuse him of impure motives. They ultimately suffer the consequences of their faithlessness by being drowned in a flood sent by Allah while Noah and the few who heed his message are preserved in the ark which Allah commanded him to build. While in many places the outline of Noah's story in the Qur'an has a clear connection with the version of events recounted in the Bible in Genesis 6–9, there are some significant differences which allow us to better appreciate how the tradition functions for the Islamic community.

A MESSENGER FROM THE LORD OF THE UNIVERSE

A summary of the story of Noah is found in 7:60-65, a text containing all the key elements of the tradition which were mentioned above.

> [59] We sent Noah to his people and he said, "Oh my people, worship Allah, there is no other god for you than Him. Truly, I fear for you the punishment of a great day." [60] The chiefs of his people said, "Surely, we

see you to be in clear error." [61]He said, "Oh my people, there is no error in me, but I am a messenger from the Lord of the universe. [62]I bring to you the messages of my Lord and I advise you. I know from Allah what you do not know. [63]Are you surprised that a reminder from your Lord has come to you through a man among you that he might warn you so you might be pious and then be treated mercifully?" [64]But they called him a liar, so We saved him and those with him in the ark and We drowned those who rejected Our signs. They were truly a blind people.

The most distinctive feature of Noah's character in this text and throughout the Qurʾan is his role as a messenger or intermediary between Allah and humanity. The initial verse begins with Allah sending Noah whose first words indicate that he has taken his divine commission seriously. He immediately informs his audience that they are doomed unless they turn to Allah. Because they refuse to believe him, part of his message is a validation of himself as one sent from Allah. He explicitly refers to himself as "a messenger from the Lord of the universe" and informs them that because of this role he has information and knowledge which they do not possess but desperately need. The Qurʾan sees Noah as a person uniquely called by Allah who plays a special purpose in the divine plan and has been set apart from the rest of humanity.

This is an expansion of the figure of the biblical Noah. Although he has a special status in Genesis since he is the one through whom God saves humanity, the reasons for this privilege are not clearly stated. We are simply told in Genesis 6:8 that "Noah found favor in the sight of the Lord." How he has done so we do not know. He is not designated a messenger or intermediary and he does not warn his contemporaries of their coming demise. In fact, throughout his entire four-chapter career in the Bible Noah never utters a single word to anyone, God included, until the very end of chapter 9 when he curses one son and praises the other two (9:25-27). Prior to and during the flood Noah is completely silent, and this creates the impression of his being a very passive, submissive figure who simply takes orders and follows instructions. This is a far cry from the Noah of the Qurʾan who is a man with a message and not shy about delivering it. In order to understand the reason for this difference we need to consider the Islamic view of prophecy.

According to the Qurʾan, Allah has maintained communication with humanity throughout history by speaking to and through the prophets, among whom was Noah. "Truly, we have made revelation known to you (Muhammad) as we made revelation known to Noah and the prophets after him" (4:163). Among these prophetic individuals are figures like Abraham, Moses, David, and Jesus who are all familiar to Bible readers. Others mentioned in the Qurʾan, like Hūd and Ṣāliḥ, are not found in the Bible and may be examples of pre-Islamic Arabian prophets. Each of these individuals was sent by Allah to a particular people at a particular time and charged with the task of reminding his audience of its obligation to worship Allah and follow the straight path. We see an example of this idea of one prophet/one people in the text from sura 7 quoted above when, in verse 59, Allah says "We sent Noah to *his* people," and when Noah refers to himself as "a man among you" in verse 63. In the Islamic view, the message the prophets delivered to their people was identical and it is the same message found in the Qurʾan. But, according to Islamic belief, the contemporaries of these prophets typically dismissed or disregarded the message, as in the case of Noah, or sometimes even falsified and distorted it. This made a final, definitive prophet necessary who would communicate the true, untainted message and preserve it for future generations. This was Muhammad's role and the text he received, the Qurʾan, faithfully transmits the message of Allah that all previous prophets shared. A common title for Muhammad is "seal of the prophets" (33:40) which highlights the finality of his prophethood. Islam strictly adheres to the belief that after him there is no longer any need for more prophets or further revelation from Allah.

This view of history and Allah's relationship with humanity explains why the Qurʾanic Noah is presented the way he is. As the first in a series of prophetic figures whose task it is to remind his people of their commitment to Allah, he is shown as someone ready and willing to proclaim the message entrusted to him. The biblical portrait of him as an inarticulate individual who merely responds to the deity's will rather than disclosing it conflicts with the vocal, dynamic nature of Islamic prophecy. The Qurʾan therefore goes to great lengths to give Noah a voice and contains numerous examples of his prophetic pronouncements. One such place where we see an example of this is in 11:25-49 which is a detailed narrative of the flood and events prior to it.

THE FLOOD STORY

[25]We sent Noah to his people (saying), "I am a clear warner to you [26]that you worship none but Allah. I fear for you the punishment of a painful day." [27]The unfaithful chiefs of his people said, "We see you as nothing but a human being like ourselves, and we see that the only ones who follow you seem to be those who are the most vile among us. We do not consider you to be better than we are, but we think you are liars." [28]He

said, "Oh my people, do you think that if I have firm evidence from my Lord and He has granted mercy to me from Himself but it has remained unapparent to you that we should force it upon you while you are averse to it? [29]Oh my people, I do not ask you for any payment in return for it since my reward is only Allah. I am not going to drive away those who believe. Surely, they will meet their Lord. But I see you are an ignorant people. [30]Oh my people, who would aid me against Allah if I were to drive them away? Will you not remember? [31]I do not say to you that I possess the treasuries of Allah or that I know what is invisible. I do not say I am an angel, nor do I say about those whom you hold in contempt that Allah will not grant them anything good. Allah knows what is in their minds. Truly, if I did that I would be among the evildoers." [32]They said, "Oh Noah, you have argued with us long and hard. Bring on us what you threaten us with, if you are among the truthful." [33]He said, "Allah will bring it upon you, if He wishes, and you cannot escape. [34]My counsel will not be of use to you, even if I wish to advise you, if Allah wants to lead you astray. He is your Lord and to Him you shall be made to return." [35]Do they say, "He has fabricated it."? Say, "If I have fabricated it may my guilt be upon me, but I am innocent of the crimes you commit." [36]It was revealed to Noah, "None from your people will believe except those who have already believed, so do not be bothered by what they are doing. [37]Build the ark under Our eyes and Our inspiration. Do not speak to Me about those who have done wrong for they will be drowned." [38]He made the ark and whenever the chiefs of his people passed by they mocked him. He said, "If you mock us we shall eventually mock you as you are now mocking. [39]Then you will know upon whom a punishment will come that will disgrace him. A permanent punishment will settle upon him." [40]When Our command came and the fountains gushed forth We said, "Load on it (the ark) a pair of every kind and your family, except for the one against whom the word has already gone forth, and whoever believes." But only a few believed with him. [41]He said, "Get on! May its sailing and mooring be in the name of Allah. My Lord is truly the forgiving, merciful One." [42]And it made its way with them through waves like mountains. Noah cried out to his son who was standing apart, "Oh son, get on with us and do not be with the unbelievers." [43]He said, "I will take refuge to a mountain that will protect me from the water." He (Noah) said, "There is no protection today from the decree of Allah except for the one to whom He shows mercy." And a wave came between them and he was among the drowned. [44]And it was said, "Oh earth, swallow your water! Oh heavens, desist!" The water subsided and the matter was decided. It (the ark) came to rest upon al-Judi and it was said, "A curse upon the people who do wrong." [45]Noah cried out to his Lord and said, "Lord, my son is of my family. Surely Your promise is true and You are the most just of judges." [46]He said, "Oh Noah, he is not of your family for he is an unrighteous work. Do not ask me about that which you have no knowledge. I admonish you to be one of the ignorant." [47]He said, "Lord, I seek Your protection for asking You about what I have no knowledge. Unless You forgive me and show me mercy I will be among the lost ones." [48]It was said, "Oh Noah, disembark with peace from Us and blessings upon you and upon the peoples of those with you. We shall provide for (other) peoples and then a painful punishment from Us will befall them." [49]This is part of the tidings We reveal to you (Muhammad). You did not know it before this, nor did your people. Be patient, for the end is for the pious.

This text is a parallel to the biblical account of the Noah tradition but the Qurʾan's presentation of the events is different in several important ways. In the first place, the Islamic passage is much briefer than the biblical one. While Genesis devotes ninety-seven verses in chapters 6–9 to telling the story of Noah, this Qurʾan text, which is the book's longest section on Noah, runs only twenty-five verses. Secondly, the two texts emphasize different aspects of the Noah tradition. The Bible goes to great lengths to recount in careful detail the construction and dimensions of the ark (6:14-16), followed by an elaborate account of the experiences of Noah and his family during and immediately after the flood (6:17–9:17). This material comprises the majority of the biblical narrative as only thirteen of its ninety-seven verses are concerned with the period prior to the building of the ark and Noah does not figure prominently in them.

The Qurʾan's treatment shifts the focus. Noah is commanded to build the ark in verse 37, which is the midway point of the passage, and so the Qurʾan spends an equal amount of time on both the period prior to the flood and the flood itself. A third difference between the biblical and Qurʾanic versions has to do with the use and development of the characters in the story. Several key figures in the Qurʾan do not have counterparts in Genesis while a number of individuals in the biblical story are absent from the Qurʾan. Even those characters present in both, notably Noah and the deity, are portrayed somewhat differently in order to serve the purposes of each text. Just as we observed with its use of the Adam tradition, these three differences of length, focus, and characterization are due to the Qurʾan's interest in underscoring the message behind the Noah story for its Muslim audience. To appreciate this more easily we now examine the Qurʾan's handling of five aspects of the narrative.

1. Noah's Role

As noted earlier, the general view of Noah in the Qurʾan is that he is, like all prophets prior to Muhammad, sent to his own people with a message. All of these elements are found in the first verses of the present text. Allah acknowledges sending Noah to his people and then Noah proceeds to deliver his message. The bond between people and prophet is accented when Noah explicitly addresses them as "oh my people" three times in the course of the text (vv. 28, 29, 30) and they are referred to as "his" or "your" people in four other places (vv. 25, 27, 36, 38). All of these references occur prior to the flood, after which we no longer hear mention of "his people." This may be a subtle way of reminding the reader that most of Noah's people ceased to exist since they maintained their faithless ways and did not survive the flood. Noah's function as a messenger comes across clearly in his first words with his self-designation as a "clear warner" (v. 25). The warning he gives is succinct and to the point: worship only Allah or suffer dire consequences (v. 26).

If these were the only words Noah uttered in this passage they would already be more than what he says in Genesis prior to and during the flood. But this is just the beginning of a veritable verbal onslaught that will continue throughout the narrative. Noah has no fewer than six different oral encounters with his people, the chiefs of his people, those on the ark, his son, and Allah. In each case, his words are centered on his message as he reminds either his listeners or himself about the need to remain faithful to Allah. Even his cry in verse 41 as the ark gets underway falls under this heading: "Get on! May its sailing and mooring be in the name of Allah. My Lord is truly the forgiving, merciful One."

The reticent Noah of Genesis is now a loquacious spokesperson for Allah who will take every opportunity to spread his word. But this is not necessarily a completely praiseworthy quality. Two facets of the text suggest that Noah's verbosity needs to be toned down at times. In verse 33 his antagonists tell him, "Oh Noah, you have argued with us long and hard. Bring on us what you threaten us with, if you are among the truthful." In effect, they are saying to him that all his words are ultimately unpersuasive unless he backs them up with action. In other words, "Noah, it is time to put up or shut up!" A similar message might be behind Allah's admonition to him in verse 37, "Do not speak to me about those who have done wrong for they will be drowned." This curious reprimand might be an indirect way of Allah telling Noah that he cannot simply rely on his verbal skills to prove his fidelity as a messenger. The Arabic verb *kataba*, translated "speak" here, actually carries the connotation of "converse, dialogue" and its presence here might mean that Noah should not consider himself to be so privileged that he can interact with Allah in the same way he might with another person. A spokesperson is not necessarily a peer, and in Islam this is clearly the case when one is a spokesperson for Allah. These texts make the point that words alone are insufficient to be a true follower of Allah and may hint at what lies ahead for the Noah in the Qur'an. Shortly, he will be called upon to practice what he preaches in order to demonstrate his true worth as a prophet.

Despite its relative lack of narrative drama and detail the Qur'an gives us some insight into Noah's personality and character that cannot be gained from the Genesis account. This is especially true in the area of his relationship with the deity. In the Bible, Noah is obviously a good person since he finds favor in God's eyes (6:8). But because he does not speak and the text does not specify why God finds him worthy of being saved we are forced to rely on his actions to try to understand the reasons for this special treatment. A careful reading of the Genesis text suggests that perhaps the major quality that sets Noah apart from his contemporaries is his obedience. In a number of ways Genesis presents Noah as someone who listens to and follows the word of his God. The first verbs used in reference to him clearly make this point. After the detailed instructions from God on how to build the ark and what its cargo should be, the notice of Noah's reaction is brief and to the point. "Noah did this; he did all that God commanded him" (6:22). The second set of directions concludes with the same result: "And Noah did all that the Lord commanded him" (7:5). In two other places the text explains how the creatures entered the ark "as God had commanded Noah" (7:9, 16), and later Noah and his family do not leave the ark until they are told to do so by God (8:16, 18). Such a consistent portrayal of the character, particularly given the lack of any dialogue on his part, points in the direction of seeing his obedience and compliance to the divine will as the quality that distinguishes Noah and leads to his rescue from the flood.

If, in the same way, we were to try to depend on Noah's actions in the Qur'an for information on his character we would be soon frustrated. He is the subject of ten verbs in this passage and all but one describe the act of speaking. The lone exception is found in verse 38 where it is reported "he made the ark." Beyond this, Noah does nothing but talk in this text. The verbal nature of his character is stressed to such a degree that when Allah commands him to load up the ark Noah does not act, he speaks: "Get on!" (v. 41). Therefore, in order to understand who the Qurʾanic Noah is we need to examine his words, not his actions. They provide a rich source of information on his character and they show him to be a person of deep faith and unswerving commitment to the will of Allah. He is an upright, blameless, faithful human being who is responsibly executing his duty to serve as a warner and messenger to his people. His words in verse 29, "my reward is only Allah," sum up his character as well as any and explain why he is saved from the fate of the unbelievers. We are, then, confronted with a fascinating difference in the way the Bible and the Qurʾan portray the character of Noah. In the former text, he is someone who says little and does much while in the latter he says much and does little. One is a man of action and the other is a man of words, but despite this contrast the man remains the same. In both he is someone who submits himself to the will of the deity but that submission is expressed by deed in Genesis and by word in the Qurʾan.

A final aspect of Noah's role in the Qurʾan that is worth noting is the fact that he has followers who have accepted his message as true. This is mentioned twice in the text. In verse 27 his enemies refer to him and those who follow him as "liars," and in verse 40 we learn that only a few believed him and were saved in the ark. This is different from the biblical account where the only people in the boat with Noah are his immediate family. We are not told in Genesis why they are saved but one could conclude that the reason is an accidental one: they are his relatives and he has found favor with God. The people in the Qurʾan have earned their salvation by believing the message of Allah delivered by Noah and, as we shall see, this has important implications for how to interpret the text. But for now, it should be observed that the presence of the saved remnant puts the Qurʾanic Noah in a very different light than that of his biblical counterpart. In Genesis he is simply a good person whose reward is a free ticket to ride out the flood. In the Qurʾan he is an agent for Allah who has had some, if however limited, success in his role as warner to his people.

2. The Cause of the Flood

Genesis issues a blanket condemnation against humanity in identifying the reason why God was compelled to send a flood to wipe clean the face of the earth. "The Lord saw that the wickedness of humankind was great in the earth, and that every inclination of the thoughts of their hearts was only evil continually" (6:5). More or less the same idea is expressed in other places early in the Noah story to account for the coming deluge (6:11-12; 7:1). Such texts are frustratingly incomplete since they are clear about the general cause of the flood but vague regarding the precise nature of humanity's offense that called for such harsh retribution. What exactly did humankind do to deserve such a punishment? Terms like "wickedness," "evil," "corruption," and "violence" give some indication of the severity of the transgression but fall short of the specificity and precision needed to accurately answer this question. One might conclude, based on the previous discussion of Noah's role, that, unlike him, humanity was guilty of disobeying God and was therefore worthy of extinction, but this is an inference that has no obvious basis in the text.

The Qurʾan is much more helpful on this point since it not only identifies specifically the sin of humanity but it also illustrates it in action. Unlike in the biblical account where evil humanity is not personified, the chiefs of Noah's people in the Qurʾan represent humankind gone astray and are living, breathing models of depravity. The passage identifies aspects of their sinful nature by referring to them as ignorant (v. 29) and wrongdoers (v. 37), but such indefinite terms are not much different from the vague presentation in Genesis. It is in their encounters with Noah, though, that they show their true colors in all their detail. Noah's first warning to them is that they must worship none but Allah. This suggests that they are following other gods and, consequently, not acknowledging Allah's complete authority. The description of their discussions with Noah shows this to be the case. Most of their debate with Noah centers on his role since they fail to recognize him as an inspired speaker and believe him to be a liar or impostor. Their first words to him reflect this mindset. "We see you as nothing but a human being like ourselves, and we see that the only ones who follow you seem to be those who are the most vile among us. We do not consider you to be better than we are, but we think you are liars" (v. 27). Noah's defense is to try to establish his legitimacy by appealing to his special relationship with Allah (vv. 28–29), but his words fall on deaf ears. In effect, they are uncomfortable with Noah's unique status as a prophet and choose to reject him as a valid spokesperson for the deity. But in rejecting Noah they have really rejected Allah, and this is what leads to their destruction.

That their offense is primarily one of a failure to recognize Allah's legitimate intermediary, and therefore Allah, is apparent in the Arabic text. The verb *raʾā* is found three times in verse 27 where it is translated twice as "see," its most common meaning, and once as "consider." Noah's enemies are claiming that their own powers of perception allow them to see that he is not what he claims to be. They believe they can see him for what he really is and so they reject his message. Their senses and experience tell them it is impossible that a human being can speak on behalf of Allah. Their mistake is that they have relied exclusively on themselves and this error will have deadly consequences for them. Noah turns the tables on them by adopting their own strategy. Using the same Arabic verb he condemns them, "But I see you are an ignorant people" (v. 29). Their disagreement has been turned into a battle of perspectives but Noah enjoys the upper hand since his vision is informed by an obedience to the divine will which they lack. There may be a subtle wordplay to this effect in verse 37 where Noah is instructed by Allah to "Build the ark under Our eyes and Our inspiration."[1]

Noah is depicted in this text as the ideal believer and the chiefs of his people function as his foils. They personify evil humanity which has lost sight of its obligation to Allah. According to Islam, the divine will is communicated through messengers who have been chosen to convey it. When one rejects the messenger one has also rejected the One who sent the messenger. This is a common human sin in the Islamic view and it makes salvation an impossibility. The Genesis tradition lacks such specificity regarding the nature of human corruption, but by presenting a more detailed account of Noah's career prior to the flood and giving him flesh-and-blood antagonists who dispute with him the Qurʾan leaves no doubt as to its character.

Since it is a prophet's responsibility to warn his people and urge them to return to the straight path their failure to do so could be interpreted as an indication that the prophet has failed or not done his job effectively. The Qurʾan rules out such a conclusion since it maintains that each person is free to accept or reject the message, and rejection should not reflect negatively on the quality of the prophet. This idea is conveyed in verse 36 when Allah tells Noah not to take it personally if some of his audience refuse to heed his message. "None from your people will believe except those who have already believed, so do not be bothered by what they are doing." Noah should not blame himself if some do not believe because faith is ultimately a matter of free choice on the part of the individual. This reminder from Allah is important for a couple of reasons. In the first place, it maintains the credibility of the office of prophethood by not linking its validity to the approval rating of its audience. According to the Qur'an, Noah or any other prophet is a legitimate representative of Allah regardless of the reception they get from their people. Secondly, the presence of human free will points out the heinous nature of humanity's sin in the Qur'an. The message has been presented to them and they have intentionally chosen to spurn it and follow a path other than Allah's. Neither the deity nor the prophet is responsible for their ruin and they must shoulder the blame themselves. Human responsibility for their own demise is not as clearly present in the Genesis narrative and this can cause the reader to question God's motive for the flood (6:5-13). The Qur'an, on the other hand, leaves no doubt that humanity is getting what it deserves.

3. The Saved

Both the Qur'an and the Bible make mention of a small group of people saved from the flood with Noah but they do not agree on the identities of these individuals or the reason why they are preserved from destruction. According to the Genesis tradition only Noah's immediate family members are allowed to go with him into the ark, and each time they are specifically mentioned the same people are listed: Noah's wife, his sons, and his sons' wives (6:18; 7:7, 13; 8:15, 18). We have already noted that no reason is given for their inclusion and a logical assumption to make is that they are saved simply because they are Noah's relatives. Several aspects of the biblical text support this conclusion.

Only Noah is found to be righteous in God's eyes and nothing is said about the personal attributes of any of his family members prior to or during the flood. He plays the dominant role throughout the flood narrative while they fade into the background, and this reinforces the notion that their salvation is dependent upon him since they do not share in his quality of righteousness. This is convincingly brought out in 7:1 where God tells Noah, "Go into the ark, you and all your household, for I have seen that you alone are righteous before me in this generation." The English translation of this verse is ambiguous since two meanings are grammatically possible and therefore equally plausible. God might be telling Noah that both he and his household are righteous or God might be saying only Noah is righteous. The uncertainty is due to the fact that English lacks any way of distinguishing between the singular and plural forms of the second person pronoun "you." The Hebrew text does not allow for such a double meaning since it, like Arabic, has two distinct forms for the second person singular and plural. In this verse, the word "you" is singular and so God is telling Noah that only he has been found righteous upon the earth. Grammatically, his family members have been excluded from sharing in his state of righteousness.

There are other subtle indications that Noah's family are marginal characters during the flood and that only his role is central to the plot's development. At 7:16 we are told that the male and female of all flesh went into the ark and "the Lord shut *him* in." Even though the ark is crammed full of animals of every kind and seven other humans, the text speaks of God closing the door behind only Noah. Similarly, in 8:1 we are informed that "God remembered Noah and all the wild animals and all the domestic animals that were with him in the ark." What has happened to his family? Has God forgotten about them? Even the animals are mentioned, in separate categories no less, but not a word about Noah's relatives.

The absence of any explicit reference to Noah's family during their time on the ark suggests their role in the narrative is different from Noah's. He is the righteous one who is rewarded with rescue from the flood and so during this liminal period of time while the earth is cleansed and restored the focus is on him alone. The text states "Only Noah was left" (7:23), and then adds, in an aside, "and those that were with him in the ark." They are nameless passengers whose identities and activities are inconsequential. Only Noah opens the window and sends out the raven and the dove (8:6-12); only Noah knows that the water has subsided from the earth (8:11); only Noah removes the cover from the ark and sees that the ground has dried (8:13). As the rains fall and God punishes wicked humanity this is Noah's story, not his family's. But all that changes when the rain stops and the ark settles on dry land.

A turning point occurs at 8:16-17 where God commands, "Go out of the ark, you and your wife, and your sons and your sons' wives with you. Bring out with you every living thing that is with you of all flesh—birds and animals and every creeping thing that creeps on the earth—so that they may abound on the earth, and be fruitful and multiply on the earth." Once again, an analysis of the Hebrew allows us to detect an important element of this text. There are four imperative forms, or commands, in these verses. The first two, "go out" and "bring out" are singular and directed to Noah. The other two, "be fruitful" and "multiply," however, are plural and directed to Noah and his family. Once they have left the ark, the attention shifts to his entire family and Noah is no longer the focal point. Throughout the rest of the biblical story, whenever God uses the word "you" it is in the plural form as both Noah and his family are addressed simultaneously.

God's words to the family after they have disembarked furnish us with some important clues regarding the role of Noah's relatives in Genesis and why they have been saved along with him. At this point, God reassures the family that such a punishment will never be inflicted again and makes a covenant with them as a way of reestablishing a relationship with them. A statement of divine favor upon humanity is expressed in 9:1-17 in which they are told two more times to be fruitful and multiply (vv. 1, 7). In these seventeen verses, which speak of the benefits humanity will enjoy and the divine protection they will receive, the word "you" or "your" appears seventeen times and each time it is grammatically plural.

Noah's family members are addressed by God for the first time only after the flood and are told that they will play an essential role in the new creation that has been brought about. This is their function in the biblical text. If he alone were saved, Noah would not be able to repopulate the earth by himself so others are needed. These four couples are the human equivalents of the male and female pairs of animals that were loaded onto the ark, and a clever shift in wording makes this abundantly apparent. Almost every time Noah's relatives are mentioned they are listed in the same order: his sons, his wife, his sons' wives (6:18; 7:7, 13; 8:18). The only exception to this is found in 8:16, quoted above, where God says "Go out of the ark, you and your wife, and your sons and your sons' wives with you," and then instructs them to be fruitful and multiply. The order has been changed for a very obvious reason. God is identifying them as the pairs, or couples, whose responsibility it will now be to reestablish a human presence on the earth. In the biblical tradition, then, while those who share in Noah's journey on the ark are not as righteous as he is, their survival is equally necessary in order to insure the future propagation of the human species.

The Qur'an text moves in an entirely different direction since it refers to two distinct groups of people that have been spared. Allah orders Noah in verse 40, "Load on it (the ark) a pair of every kind and your family, except for the one against whom the word has already gone forth, and whoever believes." The mention of the latter group of believers indicates that some of those with Noah in the ark are not saved because of family ties but have earned this reward through their own merit. Earlier, in verse 37, Allah told Noah that those who have done wrong will be drowned. This leaves open the possibility that others, who avoid doing wrong, will be saved and that is precisely what happens as the narrative unfolds. Their numbers are not very large, as verse

40 relates ("But only a few believed with him"), but their inclusion in the ark has a significant effect on the story.

The Qurʾanic Noah, unlike his biblical counterpart, is not the only righteous person on earth. This is not the account of a sole survivor, the only one deemed worthy in the midst of total human depravity, and his lucky family who are innocent by association and pardoned from the watery fate of the rest of humankind by virtue of their relationship with him. Rather, this is the tale of a faithful remnant who are all righteous and equally deserving of divine protection. The identities of these anonymous believers is an unimportant matter for the Qurʾan. Information regarding their names or other distinguishing features is not given as all we are told about them is that they have believed Noah's message. This is the quality that sets them apart and grants them the right to ride out the storm with him and his family. But what about Noah's family? Are they, too, to be included among the ranks of the believers? The curious episode of Noah's son suggests that this question should be answered affirmatively.

According to the Qurʾan, not all of Noah's family was rescued from the flood. The tragic story of his son who stubbornly refuses to enter the ark explains why this is so. His fate is foreshadowed in verse 40 when Allah tells Noah to load his family onto the ark "except for the one against whom the word has already gone forth." Like the chiefs of Noah's people, his son should be seen as a personification of the lost ones who reject the messenger of Allah and cling to their false beliefs. The description of his end once again highlights the issue of free will and human choice. His father cries out for him to get on the boat and discloses what his refusal to do so will mean. "Oh son, get on with us and do not be with the unbelievers" (v. 42). In effect, the son is being given a choice to either believe or not believe. He opts to seek refuge on a nearby mountain rather than place his trust in Allah as his only sure haven and suffers the consequences of the other unbelievers who did not heed his father's warning.

This is an extraordinary scene which highlights the depth of human iniquity. Not even Noah's own son, the offspring of one of Allah's prophets, can make the proper choice and be spared this horrible outcome. The incident also has an effect on the reader's view of the surviving members of Noah's family. The punishment of one of their own as an unbeliever places them among the believers since they, too, would have met their own demise if they were not. The Qurʾan is therefore clearer than the Genesis account regarding the faith of the family and why they were saved. Membership in Noah's family does not guarantee salvation since only belief in Allah guarantees passage on the ark.

But Noah has a difficult time accepting this fact. In verse 45, after the water has subsided, his first words are in the form of a plea to Allah.[2] "Lord, my son is of my family. Surely Your promise is true and You are the most just of judges." He appeals to the familial relationship in a way that implicates Allah for allowing his son to drown. The deity's response to this challenge serves as both a reminder and an instruction to the grieving father. "Oh Noah, he is not of your family for he is an unrighteous work" (v. 46).[3] Allah is putting forth a new definition of family here. Shared genes or marital bonds alone are not sufficient for maintaining the ties that bind one to another; there must be a common faith. A family is not simply a biological or legal entity, it is a theological one in which belief in Allah is essential for membership. After the flood, the Qur'anic Noah has a much wider, more inclusive family than he does in Genesis. It now embraces all righteous people who put their faith and trust in Allah and is not limited to those related to him by birth or marriage.[4]

This difference between the Bible and Qur'an regarding the makeup and nature of the flood's survivors reflects a difference in the group's mission and purpose. We have seen that the family of Noah in Genesis, like the pairs of animals, has been charged with the task of repopulating the planet. The expanded family of Noah in the Qur'an has a further responsibility. They, too, will be the ancestors of succeeding generations but beyond this they are to be models of righteousness and faith in Allah for those who come after them. Their role is to be one of proclamation, not simply procreation.

4. The Result

According to Genesis, Noah's first act upon leaving the ark is to build an altar and offer animal sacrifices to God. The pleasant aroma from the altar causes the deity to make a decision regarding humanity. "And when the Lord smelled the pleasing odor, the Lord said in his heart, 'I will never again curse the ground because of humankind, for the inclination of the human heart is evil from youth; nor will I ever again destroy every living creature as I have done'" (8:21). There is an element of good news/bad news in this divine utterance. On the one hand, humanity can breathe a collective sigh of relief knowing they will never again be destroyed by their Creator. But the less encouraging side is that in God's mind human beings remain evil to the core. This is the very aspect of human nature that first turned God against humanity and led to the decision to send the flood as a remedy for human corruption and wickedness. After the deluge and complete annihilation of the human species except for Noah's family the problem still exists and God appears to be resigned to accepting the imperfection of humanity.

Violence is so endemic to human nature that God issues an edict against murder and imposes a stiff penalty on those who violate it. "Whoever sheds the blood of a human, by a human shall that person's blood be shed; for in his own image God made humankind" (9:6). Without such a deterrent, people will give in to their base instincts, allowing confusion and disorder to rule. After accepting the fact of humanity's propensity to do evil, the deity establishes a covenant with Noah and his family (9:8-17). This is a profoundly moving passage in which God once again places humanity over creation, pledges to never again destroy all living things and offers the rainbow as a sign of that promise. The divine/human relationship has been reestablished, the chaos of the flood has been replaced by order, and things are very much as they were in the beginning when God first created humanity.

But there is something deeply disturbing about this scenario. The problem is that things are more or less as they were before the flood. People were evil then and they are still evil. The flood was sent as a corrective meant to eliminate this aspect of human nature but it failed. This raises gnawing questions: Was all that death, destruction, and loss necessary? What good did sending the flood accomplish? From the point of view of humanity it achieved little, if anything. But from the deity's perspective there is a tangible result: it taught God that human nature will never change and needs to be accepted for what it is. The covenant is a symbol of that acceptance.

The Qurʾan's account of post-flood events initially centers on Noah and his encounter with Allah over the death of his son. Once the ark reaches dry land Noah does something we would not expect from one of Allah's prophets: he violates a divine command.[5] In verse 37, after giving him instructions to build the ark, Allah admonishes him, "Do not speak to me about those who have done wrong for they will be drowned." Noah soon disobeys this injunction when he challenges Allah about his son being included among those punished. True to form, the Qurʾanic Noah speaks out and makes use of his strong verbal skills, only this time he is not acting as Allah's spokesperson. The words he speaks are his own and they are directed against, not in support of,

Allah's will. The deity's response is notable. Rather than punish Noah for his transgression or comment upon the sinful nature of humanity, Allah instructs Noah about the importance of trust and the need to accept his limitations. "Do not ask me about that which you have no knowledge. I admonish you to be one of the ignorant" (v. 46). Noah immediately recognizes his error and begs to be restored to Allah's good graces. "Unless You forgive me and show me mercy I will be among the lost ones" (v. 47).

The now-repentant Noah has learned an important lesson from his son's death and has shown that even a prophet can be in need of mercy and forgiveness. He has been forced to practice what he has been preaching and submit himself to the divine will no matter the cost. Such an idea is easy to accept until it runs up against other things that are held near and dear, in this case the feelings of a father for his son. But Noah proves his worthiness and makes the leap of faith his son was unable to accomplish. "Lord, I seek Your protection for asking You about what I have no knowledge" (v. 47). The contrast between father and son could not be starker. By taking matters into his own hands and fleeing to the mountain the younger man sought refuge from the power of Allah, but by acknowledging his own limits Noah seeks refuge in the power of Allah.

With this episode of the remorseful Noah, the Qur'an treats the same issue of human wickedness that is addressed in Genesis but does so in a very different way. Noah, one of Allah's own prophets, has committed a serious offense by questioning the deity's authority. In the Islamic view of things, this is one of the gravest sins one can commit. Here, Noah personifies the common tendency to try to transcend the limits of human existence which prevents complete surrender *(islām)* to the divine will. Unlike in the biblical account, Allah's reaction to this tendency in humanity is not one of resignation or grudging acceptance that this is the way things must be. The outlook here is much more hopeful about the possibility of change and conversion of the human heart. Allah and Noah work together in bringing about this transformation, and the process whereby they achieve it can serve as a model for the believer. The Qur'an does not deny the fact of human evil, but it does not concede to it either.

Only after undergoing this change of heart by seeking Allah's mercy and forgiveness is Noah allowed to leave the ark. His relationship with the deity has been restored and this is represented by the divine favor he now receives. "Oh Noah, disembark with peace from Us and blessings upon you and upon the peoples of those with you" (v. 48). The believers who were in the ark with him now reenter the picture and these righteous ones and their offspring share in all the benefits that Noah receives. There is no explicit reference to a covenant as in the Genesis text, but the peace and blessings from Allah mentioned here are its functional equivalent since they signal a special relationship between Allah and humanity. But not all of humanity will enjoy this relationship. In another recognition of the fact that some people will continue to do evil, the text describes the fate that awaits such sinners in verse 48. "We shall provide for (other) peoples and then a painful punishment from Us will befall them." Allah does not reject such people outright since they will be taken care of for a time. But if they do not change their ways and follow the straight path they are doomed. Here we see the Islamic worldview clearly sketched out. Those who, like Noah, turn to Allah will be rewarded but those who, like his son, choose to turn from Allah must suffer the consequences.

5. The Image of the Deity

There is a somewhat harsh or stern quality to the deity's character in Genesis that is not as evident in the Qur'an. At the outset of the Noah story, God's recognition of human evil allows for a glimpse into the divine mind and the experience for the reader is somewhat unsettling. "And the Lord was sorry that he had made humankind on the earth, and it grieved him to his heart" (6:6). As disturbing as this news might be it does not prepare the reader for the shock of learning how God intends to deal with wayward humanity. Four times during the next twenty verses we hear, in God's own words, that all people will be blotted out from the face of the earth (6:7, 13, 17; 7:4). Further adding to this image of divine rage is the reference to the annihilation of other, nonhuman, forms of life. "I will blot out from the earth the human beings I have created—people together with animals and creeping things and birds of the air, for I am sorry that I have made them" (6:7). Humanity appears to deserve some type of retribution because of its corruption, but why are other living beings included as well? This lends a capricious element to God's character that creates the impression of an angry, impulsive, and unforgiving deity. This image is reinforced by the lack of any communication between God and people. The entire human species is wiped out without ever being told why or given an opportunity to explain or defend themselves.

After the flood, when the covenant is established, God's attitude toward humanity does not appear to change much. Despite the continued presence of human wickedness God decides to enter into a special relationship with people but the conditions of the pact are indicative of an ambivalent attitude on the deity's part. The only thing God promises Noah is that a flood will never again be sent to destroy the earth. This is a covenant that uses only negative language: here is what I will not do. No mention is made of what God will do or what God thinks of humanity. The only guarantee they have is that they will never again be exterminated by a flood, but such a promise could cause the leery human partner in the covenant to wonder what other means God might be tempted to use next time. Even the rainbow, offered as the sign of the covenant, might be viewed cautiously. "When I bring clouds over the earth and the bow is seen in the clouds, I will remember my covenant that is between me and you and every living creature of all flesh; and the waters shall never again become a flood to destroy all flesh" (9:14-15). This is a symbol meant as much for the deity as it is for humanity. Why does God need such a sign as a reminder not to send another flood? If the rainbow were not a cue to refrain, might the deity forget the promise and begin the search for another Noah? The covenant functions as a way of keeping in check the anger of the God of Genesis.

By beginning its account of the flood story with Allah sending Noah to warn his people the Qur'an softens the image of the deity somewhat. Humanity has been alerted and told of the punishment that is coming if they fail to change their ways. The flood is not a sneak attack that arrives without notice. In the same way, the inclusion of characters representing evil humanity, lacking in Genesis, highlights human culpability and downplays divine responsibility. The chiefs of Noah's people almost force Allah's hand and call down the flood upon themselves. In verse 32 they appear to be asking for it when they deride Allah's prophet, "Oh Noah, you have argued with us long and hard. Bring on what you threaten us with, if you are among the truthful." Similarly, their taunting of Noah in verse 38 while he is building the ark can be seen as an attempt at making a mockery of the divine message that deserves the punishment it receives. This characterization of Noah's enemies helps to establish their guilt and reduces the need to question the deity's action in sending the flood.

Allah does not wish to destroy humanity and this is why Noah has been sent. Anyone who listens to him and becomes a believer is therefore included among the ranks of those who are saved in the ark. The deity in the Qur'an has a generally hopeful and optimistic view of people but, at the same time, recognizes sin as a fact of life and so calls upon them to exercise careful judgment in determining which path they choose to take. The reference to "other peoples" in verse 48 illustrates this point well. Although a painful punishment may come upon them they are not abandoned and rejected outright by Allah but are taken care of for a time. Why does Allah provide for them? During the period prior to their punishment it is possible that some of them may heed the divine message, experience a change of heart, and turn to the straight path. Allah supports them during this interim period, giving them the benefit of the doubt. They may become believers or they may not, the choice is theirs. But Allah has not neglected them in the process of choosing.

Allah's chief quality in this Qur'an passage is mercy, a trait that is central to the Islamic understanding of the deity. Four times in the text, explicit reference is made to the mercy of Allah (vv. 28, 41, 43, 47) and each time it is found on the lips of Noah. This usage is not accidental since the prophet is the one who knows Allah best and the only other humans who have speaking parts in the story, the chiefs of his people and his son, are all unbelievers who never speak to or about Allah. But Noah knows personally the mercy of the deity and this is dramatically presented in verse 47 when he begs Allah to pardon his shortcomings. "Unless You forgive me and show me mercy I will be among the lost ones." The Arabic original of this plea is virtually identical to the one voiced by Adam and the woman in 7:23, discussed in the last chapter, after their own offense. In each case the pattern is the same: human transgression, divine instruction, human appeal for mercy and forgiveness, divine expression of mercy. The stories of both Adam and Noah, two examples for the modern believer, make abundantly clear the presence of and need for the mercy of Allah.

The end of the Qur'an story also presents a very different picture of the deity than the biblical tradition. In Genesis, God, who might still be sorry for having created people, promises not to exterminate them by a flood ever again. This pledge does not signal a close bond between the two sides and might better be understood as divine willingness to tolerate flawed humanity and coexist with them. The biblical God neither makes any positive overtures nor guarantees any divine favor in the present or the future. Allah, who has not second-guessed the decision to create humanity, treats the survivors of the flood very differently. There is no need to vow not to send another flood because all the evildoers have drowned and only true believers remain. All that remains is the granting of a sign, but this time it is not the rainbow, a symbol of punishment deferred. Rather, it is the blessing, a symbol of reward to come. "Oh Noah, disembark with peace from Us and blessings upon you and upon the people of those with you" (v. 48).

ISLAMIZATION OF THE TRADITION

It is in the presentation of the character of Noah that we see the most obvious Islamization of the story. He has all the features of a Qurʾanic prophet in this text: he is sent by Allah to his people in order to warn them of imminent disaster if they maintain their faithless ways. Being misunderstood by one's own people and the relative lack of success of one's mission are also recurring themes in the Qurʾan's view of prophecy. In order to carry out his office as a spokesperson of Allah, Noah in the Qurʾan is presented as a person capable of articulating his message despite a largely unreceptive audience and willing to debate and argue with his adversaries. All of these attributes are present to a high degree in the Islamic text but lacking in its biblical complement where Noah is a voiceless character whose relationship to his fellow humans is undefined.

In several places, the text makes use of language and terminology typical of an Islamic context. It has already been pointed out how frequently it refers to the mercy of Allah. In the Muslim view, this is the defining quality of the deity's nature and so it comes as no surprise that divine mercy is a major component of Noah's message throughout the passage. We even have the opportunity to see it at work at the end of the text when Noah asks for and receives forgiveness from Allah after questioning the divine will regarding the death of his son.

His words in verse 41 as he prepares the ark's passengers for its journey are distinctively Islamic and they cast Noah in the role of a faithful Muslim exhorting his fellow believers by extolling the goodness of Allah. "Get on! May its sailing and mooring be in the name of Allah. My Lord is truly the forgiving, merciful One." The reference to the entire trip being undertaken "in the name of Allah" is particularly meaningful. The phrase "in the name of Allah" (Arabic, *bismillāh*) is a significant one throughout the Qurʾan and it plays a prominent role in the daily life of Muslims. As was noted in the previous chapter, each sura in the Qurʾan except one begins with the same words, "in the name of Allah, the merciful one, the compassionate one" *(bismillāh al-raḥmān al-raḥīm)*. This superscription, which functions as an introduction to each sura, serves to mark off the words that follow it as divine revelation. Occasionally, individuals in the Qur'an will do or say things "in the name of Allah," as Noah does here. This is a way of expressing the idea that the activity or action about to commence is being done with Allah in mind. This practice has been carried over into everyday life and is still a very frequent part of modern Muslim experience. Today, many Muslims begin activities by reciting the phrase *bismillāh*. It might be uttered before relatively rare acts like flying in an airplane, giving a speech or taking an exam, or more commonplace ones like waking up in the morning, eating a meal or preparing to pray. The devout Muslim knows that all things begin and end in the name of Allah and will often make a statement to that effect. This is the image of Noah that is being presented in the text. By declaring that the ark's journey will be done in Allah's name he is acting as any good Muslim should.

In the last chapter it was noted how certain verses in sura 7 are directed to their Muslim audience and this has an effect on how the Adam passage should be understood. We see the same dynamic at work here when, after recounting the Noah story, Allah speaks to Muhammad in verse 49.[6] "This is part of the tidings We reveal to you (Muhammad). You did not know it before this, nor did your people. Be patient, for the end is for the pious." The deity is explaining to Muhammad why this story of Noah is included in the Qur'an's revelation. Since neither Muhammad nor his people knew about the Noah tradition previously, it was necessary to reveal it to them in its correct form. This may be a tacit criticism of prior versions of it, including the Genesis account, since the implication seems to be that even if Muhammad had come in contact with another form of the story it was not the right one. There is a clever wordplay in this verse that is lost in the English translation. The verb "we reveal" is *nūḥī* in Arabic and this is virtually identical to the Arabic form of Noah's name, *nūḥ*. This similarity of sounds creates a pun-like effect for the reader of the original text: "This story of *Nūḥ* is part of the tidings We reveal *(nūḥī)* to you."

God's mention of "your people" when speaking to Muhammad in verse 49 recalls the many references to Noah's people throughout the text and establishes a connection between the two figures that is a consistent theme of the passage. The sending of Noah, the earlier prophet of Allah, to his people prefigures the sending of Muhammad, the final messenger, to all people. But the similarities between the two men do not end there, and many Muslim commentators maintain that since it contains so many echoes of Muhammad's experiences, key aspects of the Qur'an's treatment of Noah are really a veiled depiction of Muhammad's prophetic career. Reading the passage with this possibility in mind can help explain many of the differences between it and the biblical account in Genesis.

We have observed that the chiefs of Noah's people do not have a biblical counterpart but their role is central to the plot development of the Qurʾan's text. This group, which personifies evil humanity in its inability to listen to God's spokesperson, might be meant to represent the enemies of Muhammad who did not respond positively to his message. The Qurʾan refers repeatedly to the lack of faith of the Meccan leaders who rejected Allah's will as revealed to Muhammad. "Those who did not believe said, 'This is nothing but a lie which he has forged. Other people have assisted him in it.' They have truly brought about injustice and falsehood" (25:4). In many such passages, Muhammad's opponents accuse him of deceit and dishonesty and the similarity between their charges and what Noah's foes say about him is remarkable. Note, for example, the accusation of lying that is leveled against both. In the same way, the taunting challenge hurled at Noah in verse 32 ("Bring on us what you threaten us with, if you are among the truthful"), and the reference to his being mocked in verse 38 correspond to the type of reaction Muhammad's warnings elicited from his audience.

Another problem Muhammad and the early Muslim community had to confront was the painful issue of what to do about loved ones and family members who refused to convert to Islam. The Qurʾan leaves no doubt about the only response to such a situation: the demands of faith take precedence over family ties. "You will not find a people who believe in Allah and the last day showing affection for anyone who opposes Allah and His messenger even if they are their parents, children, siblings or relatives" (58:22). The episode of Noah's son in which Allah denies the family relationship due to the younger man's refusal to believe can be understood as a dramatic example for the early Muslim of how to act in a similar situation.

A final place where we can see evidence of Islamization of the Noah tradition is in verse 35. "Do they say, 'He has fabricated it?' Say, 'If I have fabricated it may my guilt be upon me, but I am innocent of the crimes you commit.'" This verse, directed toward someone in the second person, does not fit its context well since the text before and after it is a third-person account concerned with the encounter between Noah and the chiefs of his people. If it were deleted, the narrative would flow smoother since verse 34 ends with Noah's comment that the fate of his adversaries is ultimately in Allah's hands, and in verse 36 this comes to pass when Allah tells Noah only those who already believe will be saved. How then are we to explain the presence of verse 36 if it has a disruptive effect on the story?

While it could be addressed to Noah as a way of offering him advice on how to handle the challenges of his opponents, a more likely solution is that these words are directed to Muhammad and briefly interrupt the Noah story. Two reasons make this the more attractive alternative. In the first place, there is the matter of the uneven shift from third person to second person and back to third person. While such a multiple change of perspective regarding the same character is not impossible, it is quite erratic and seems out of place in a text that has flowed smoothly and consistently up to this point. A second reason why it makes more sense to understand this verse as addressed to Muhammad is that in another Qur'an passage he receives a very similar message. In 46:8 we read, "Do they say, 'He has fabricated it?' Say, 'If I have fabricated it you could not do anything to avail me against Allah.'" In both verses the first six words of the Arabic text are identical and there is no doubt that the addressee of the verse in sura 46 is Muhammad. Throughout the Qur'an, Muhammad is frequently denounced by his enemies for inventing the revelations and this theme appears to be a part of the Noah tradition. But the ambiguous nature of the text prevents absolute certainty about the identity of its intended audience and this makes the depiction of Noah as a prototype for Muhammad all the more intriguing.

COOPERATING REVELATIONS

Another version of the Noah story is recounted in sura 71 which carries the title "Noah" and is comprised entirely of material dealing with his life and prophetic career. It shares much in common with the themes and content of the Noah tradition in sura 11 that we have been examining, but there is a shift of focus that offers new insight regarding Noah's message. When read in conjunction with Genesis 6–9, this text can illuminate certain aspects of the biblical account and contribute toward solving some of its more vexing problems. Sura 71 is translated here in its entirety.

> In the name of Allah, the merciful one, the compassionate one. [1]We sent Noah to his people, "Warn your people before a painful punishment comes upon them." [2]He said, "Oh my people, I am a clear warner to you

³that you worship Allah, fear Him and obey me. ⁴He will forgive you your sins and grant you respite until a designated time. Truly, the time of Allah, when it comes, cannot be delayed. If only you knew." ⁵He said, "Lord, I have called to my people day and night ⁶but my pleas have only made them flee. ⁷Every time I called them in order that You might forgive them they placed their fingers in their ears and put their garments over their heads, persisting in haughty pride. ⁸Then I called out loud to them, ⁹speaking to them both openly and in private. ¹⁰I said 'Ask forgiveness of your Lord for He is the forgiving One. ¹¹He sends down upon you abundant rain, ¹²increases your wealth and children, and makes gardens and rivers for you. ¹³Why is it that you do not fear the majesty of Allah? ¹⁴He created you in different forms. ¹⁵Do you not see how Allah has created seven heavens one above the other, ¹⁶making the moon a light in them and the sun a lamp? ¹⁷Allah has caused you to sprout from the earth as a growth. ¹⁸Then He will put you back into it and take you from it again. ¹⁹Allah has made the earth spread out for you ²⁰so that you might travel wide paths of it.'" ²¹Noah said, "Lord, they have resisted me and followed one whose wealth and children only add to his loss. ²²They schemed a grand scheme ²³and said, 'Do not abandon your gods, do not forsake Wadd, Suwāʿ, Yaghūth, Yaʿūq, or Nasr.' ²⁴They caused many to go astray, so do not increase the wrongdoers in anything but error." ²⁵Because of their sins they were drowned and made to enter the fire. Without Allah, they did not find any helpers. ²⁶Noah said, "Lord, do not leave a single unbeliever dwelling on the earth. ²⁷If you leave them they will lead astray your servants and they will beget only transgressors and unbelievers. ²⁸Lord, forgive me, my parents, the believer who enters my house, faithful men, and faithful women. Do not increase the wrongdoers in anything but ruin."

Analysis of the Qurʾanic Tradition

When we compare this sura to 11:25-49, it is apparent that it tells the story of the prophet Noah from an entirely different point of view. In the earlier text, the emphasis is on Noah and his role as a spokesperson for Allah. His adversaries figure prominently in the story as personifications of the unbelievers who reject his message. Much of what Noah has to say is in the form of an apology or self-defense that explains who he is and what the basis of his authority is. Sura 11 also contains a fairly detailed description of the flood itself which includes the fateful story of Noah's unbelieving son. This latter episode allows Noah to have a painful personal experience of the cost involved in following the divine will. The text is in the form of a series of conversations between

Noah and others which identify and illustrate the various possible responses to Noah's call for conversion.

These matters are not of primary concern in sura 71. Noah does not defend himself against the unbelievers, who remain anonymous and are lacking in character development. There is less interest in the flood which is only briefly alluded to in verse 25 ("Because of their sins they were drowned and made to enter the fire"), and no mention at all is made of Noah's son. We also do not have any interaction among the characters in the form of conversations or dialogue. Except for verse 1, where Allah commissions Noah to go to his people, and verse 23, which quotes the words of some unknown ones regarding the worship of false gods, Noah is the only one who speaks in the entire sura. Allah does not utter another word and we never hear from Noah's audience, enemies, family or anyone else. The focus here is more on the content of Noah's message than the reception it receives. The text from sura 11 has very little to say about Noah's actual message to his people but contains a great deal of information on their reaction to it. Here, while there is still a description of the reaction to them, it is the actual words of Noah's message that dominate the scene.

Noah is presented as a persistent messenger who refuses to give up when his audience rejects him. Even when they plug their ears with their fingers and wrap their heads so they cannot hear him (v. 7) he is not silenced but calls out to them all the louder. A chord Noah strikes repeatedly in the early part of his message to his people is on their need to ask forgiveness from Allah. He refers to the forgiving nature of the deity three times in the first 11 verses (vv. 4, 7, 10) and the third time he makes double use of the concept. "Ask forgiveness of your Lord for He is the forgiving One." This point resurfaces at the end of the sura in verse 28 when Noah asks Allah to forgive him and all faithful people. This resumption of the theme, creating a bookends effect, suggests that forgiveness is a key component of the passage and an important part of Noah's message. He is urging the people to acknowledge their sin and ask for pardon for their offenses.

The reference in verse 7 to their "haughty pride" indicates that the sin of the people is related to their arrogance and conceit. Noah's warning to them beginning in verse 11, immediately after the third of his three references to Allah's forgiving nature, points out the reason for their pride. From verse 11 to verse 20 Noah recites a litany of elements of the natural world that should remind his audience of the power and might of Allah. In quick succession, he informs them that Allah is responsible for rain, wealth, children, gardens, rivers, the heavens, the moon, the sun, birth, death, resurrection, and all human activity. The point of this inventory is to put humanity in its place by urging them to remember that Allah is the source of all that exists.

This section, particularly verses 14–18, is full of creation language and imagery. "He created you in different forms. Do you not see how Allah has created seven heavens one above the other, making the moon a light in them and the sun a lamp? Allah has caused you to sprout from the earth as a growth. Then He will put you back into it and take you from it again." This heavy stress on the creative role of Allah, coming directly after Noah's appeal to ask forgiveness, identifies the nature of humanity's sin. They are guilty of forgetting that Allah is responsible for bringing all things into existence, and therefore have a distorted view of the world and their purpose in it. This sin can be expressed in a number of ways. It might take the form of boasting of their own accomplishments so that they become too self-reliant, as the reference to their pride in verse 7 suggests. It might also be manifested in setting up false gods of their own making, as seen in the mention of their worship of Wadd, Suwāʿ, and other pre-Islamic Arabian deities in verse 23. The point being made is that human sin is connected with the inability to recognize Allah as creator of the universe and the only way to avoid the consequences of such an error is to beg for mercy and pardon. Those who fail to change will suffer greatly, and this text adds the threat of hell fire to the flood (v. 25). Such a harsh punishment might seem strange coming from a deity who is referred to throughout the sura as "forgiving," but this highlights once again the importance of human free will in the Qurʾan. Allah is always ready to absolve a sinner but only if he or she confesses the shortcomings and freely turns to Allah.

In this sura, the drama of the flood is downplayed and its cause is highlighted by presenting a verbatim account of Noah's warning to his people as the focal point of the text. Noah's message now looms large and it articulates both the character of human sin and the means of rescue from it. Humanity has a tendency to lose sight of Allah's role as creator and when this happens our relationship with the deity and the world is damaged. But the compassionate and forgiving nature of Allah offers hope and a way out of our corrupt condition. We can be saved by earnestly acknowledging our error and asking for pardon. The more detailed version of Noah's message in this text diverts attention away from Noah himself and the reception he receives and directs it toward Allah. Now the critical issue is the response to Allah, not the response to Allah's prophet. The way the sura is structured forces the reader to adopt a very personal view of the matter. Unlike the passage in sura 11 which refers to the chiefs of his people and his son, Noah's audience and detractors here are anonymous. This engages the reader more directly in the text since it allows him or her to identify personally with Noah's audience and feel as if his message is directed to them. It therefore forces the reader to consider his or her own life in light of Noah's words and ask, "Have I forgotten to recognize Allah as creator of the universe?"

Application to the Biblical Tradition

A number of times in the course of our analysis of the biblical Noah story we have identified questions or issues that the text raises in the mind of the thoughtful reader. Some of these questions can be disturbing, particularly when they ask us to consider the image of God that is being put forth in the flood story. As we read Genesis 6–9, we are tempted to try to fill in the gaps in our knowledge by asking what exactly it was that humanity had done that justified such a terrible punishment. Why didn't God warn them of the coming disaster in an effort to have them change their ways? Why is God so angry and intent on humanity's destruction? Why are all other living beings also wiped out with humanity? There are no clear answers to these and related questions, but by considering the biblical tradition in light of what the Qur'an has to say in sura 71 we are able to approach the Genesis account in a way which allows us to appreciate overlooked aspects of the biblical Noah tradition that begin to address some of these issues.

At the outset, it is important to note that the two texts tell Noah's story from entirely different points of view. In the Qur'an, the perspective adopted is Noah's. He is the one who does most of the talking and acting; he goes and preaches to the people; he complains to Allah when the people are unresponsive; he asks Allah not to spare a single unbeliever; he begs forgiveness for himself and other righteous people. As Noah complains and appeals to Allah, the deity is unresponsive so the reader wonders if Noah is being heard and what reaction, if any, Allah will have. Even when the flood is mentioned in verse 25 it is introduced in a very oblique way that does not directly indicate Allah's involvement. "Because of their sins they were drowned and made to enter the fire." Although the sin is against Allah, it is described through Noah's eyes in sura 71. This is in keeping with the Qur'an's view of Noah as a prophet sent to warn his people.

In the biblical account things are just the opposite. God is the one who does all the talking and the story, particularly as it relates to human sin and its punishment, is told through God's eyes. God sees the wickedness of humanity; God is sorry they were created; God decides to destroy them; God commands and Noah obeys. We are therefore reading the same story from two different viewpoints and the character whose perspective is not adopted remains silent throughout. In the Qur'an text Allah never speaks to Noah after commissioning him, and in Genesis Noah never speaks to God. This difference in point of view accounts for many of the questions the Bible reader is left with at the end of the text. The Qur'an tradition, told from the human point of view, is primarily concerned with explaining how and why humanity sinned and merited punishment. Its focus is on the way people respond, or fail to respond, to Allah's will. The biblical tradition, told from the deity's point of view, is interested in how God responds to humanity's rejection of the divine will. For Genesis, human corruption is a given fact that does not need to be explained or described. It is simply recognized and dealt with. But this does not mean we cannot come to a better understanding about the nature of human sin and the reasons for God's actions in Genesis. Sura 71 is very clear on these matters and there are hints and subtle indications in the biblical story that it shares a similar view.

We have seen that sura 71 identifies human pride as the fundamental sin, especially when it is expressed in ways that cause one to forget Allah's role as creator. In this text Noah goes to great lengths to remind his audience of the forgiving nature of the deity, suggesting that no sin is incapable of being pardoned. We are able to uncover these same ideas in the biblical tradition when we read Genesis 6–9 in light of its Qur'anic counterpart. Biblical scholars have frequently called attention to the important role creation language and imagery play in the Noah story. Many consider the description of the flood and its aftermath to be a narrative that depicts the destruction of God's original creation and its replacement with a new creation. They believe that portions of the flood story intentionally mirror the creation story so that righteous Noah and his family take the place of Adam and Eve as the progenitors of the human species.

In support of this view, Hebrew Bible scholars have identified a number of points of contact between the biblical stories of creation and the flood. Many of these parallels between the Noah story of Genesis 6–9 and the creation narrative in Genesis 1–3 are quite striking. The following are some of the more interesting.

(1) *Breath of life*—both sections refer to the act of God animating creation by blowing life into it (1:30; 2:7; 6:17; 7:22).

(2) *God's wind*—both sections mention God sending a wind over the waters (1:2; 8:1).

(3) *Types of animals*—both sections list various types of animals, including birds, creeping things, and fish. In Genesis 1–3 they are created while in Genesis 6–9 most are destroyed while only two of each are saved (1:20-26, 28, 30; 2:20; 6:20; 7:14, 21, 23; 9:2).

(4) *Human creation*—both sections refer to humanity as being created in God's image (1:26; 9:6). Humans are also told in both that they are to exercise dominion over the rest of creation and eat what they like of it (1:26, 28-30; 9:2-3).

(5) *A divine prohibition to humanity*—both sections contain a warning from God that limits what humans may eat (2:17; 9:4).

(6) *A divine charge to humanity*—both sections contain the identical command that humanity should populate the earth (1:28; 8:17; 9:1, 7).

The creation theme, therefore, plays a significant role in the telling of the biblical flood story just as it is an important element of sura 71. But does it function in the same way in the Bible that it does in the Qurʾan? As we have seen, in the Qurʾan it becomes identified with human sin and the tendency to forget Allah as creator. Might the same thing be said about the Genesis account? Is the heavy concentration of creation language in it somehow connected with the wickedness of humanity that has God so enraged? Although the Bible is less straightforward about this than the Qurʾan, where Noah explicitly links attitudes about creation to human sin, there is some suggestive evidence that argues in favor of seeing the same point being made in Genesis.

As in the Qurʾan, we may have another example here of the punishment fitting the crime. Because humanity does not have a correct relationship with and understanding of creation, the only way to discipline them is to bring about the end of creation, to undo it so that it might be made right. The description of the flood, depicting the unraveling of creation and the return to primordial chaos, suggests a corrective to human sin and evil. Because humanity has transgressed in its relationship with creation the only way it can be healed is through the elimination of creation as the locus of its sin. Even blameless creatures like the animals must be destroyed because the natural balance of harmony among the various components of creation has been damaged beyond repair. Reading Genesis 6–9 makes most sense when we understand it as part of the larger Genesis story and relate it particularly to chapters 1–3. Humanity was made with the purpose of ruling and exercising dominion over the rest of creation. Because it has violated that responsibility all of creation must be destroyed in order to be renewed.

There are indications in the text that, just as in sura 71, humankind's transgression in the Genesis Noah story is a result of their forgetting to recognize God as creator and trying to usurp that function for themselves. The literary context immediately prior to and after the flood is especially informative in this regard. Genesis 6:1-4, which is the section just before the Noah story, relates a strange tradition that many scholars believe to be part of a mythological story that attempts to explain certain aspects of the relationship between humanity and divinity. It relates how a group called the "sons of God" took human females as wives and children were born of the union. God responds by stating that the divine breath, or spirit,[7] will not stay in humans forever and then limits their life span to 120 years. Whatever the history or point of this curious tale might be, its presence just before the Noah story, which begins with a reference to the wickedness of humankind in verse 5, suggests there is a connection between it and humanity's sin.

This text describes the evil nature of people as they try to push beyond the bounds of their condition and attempt to become more God-like. The fixing of their lifetime at 120 years is a way of reminding them that they are nothing more than creatures and are not in control of their lives. The message of Genesis 6:1-4 is therefore very similar to that of Noah's words in the Qur'an at 71:17-18: "Allah has caused you to sprout from the earth as a growth. Then He will put you back into it and take you from it again." But the similarity between the two does not end there. Beyond the presence of the creation theme, the Genesis text also contains an implicit reference to the idea of a forgiving God, an element we have seen is central to Noah's preaching in sura 71. A suggestion of divine mercy comes out in Genesis 6:3 when, rather than destroying or physically harming humanity, God opts to limit their years. This is a relatively mild sanction which establishes divine authority without having to resort to harsher measures. God chastises them but still forgives them in the hope that they will learn their lesson. The flood can therefore be seen as a last resort which is forced upon God only after humanity has failed to respond positively to earlier, more moderate warnings.

The episode immediately after the flood also gives us a glimpse of the nature of human wickedness and it, too, identifies it with people's tendency to forget God's role in creation. Recall that one of the first things God says after Noah and his family disembark is that the human heart is "evil from its youth" (8:21). After putting all of creation under the dominion of humanity in 9:1-3, God shifts topics to treat the theme of murder and issues a legal ruling against it in 9:6: "Whoever sheds the blood of a human, by a human shall that person's blood be shed; for in his own image God made humankind." People are not to murder each other and if they do they will suffer harsh consequences. The rationale behind this prohibition is found in the last phrase of the verse which picks up the creation theme by making use of Genesis 1:26. God has created humankind in the divine image but this does not mean it is created as God's equal. Only God has the right to determine when one dies, so in the act of murdering another human being one usurps God's role.

The task decreed for humanity is not to diminish its own ranks through murder and bloodshed, but to increase its number as the divine charge immediately following in 9:7 makes clear: "And you, be fruitful and multiply, abound on the earth and multiply in it." The prohibition against murder, therefore, plays an important role in the narrative since it simultaneously reminds Noah and his family of God's supreme authority over creation and limits their own power so that it does not include control over life and death. The ground rules have now been set, and it is only at this point that God explicitly invokes the covenantal relationship with humanity in 9:8-17. The language of this latter section expresses well the qualities of divine mercy and forgiveness and this establishes another thematic link with the Qur'an text. Despite the ongoing presence of human evil, God does not reject humanity but promises to never again destroy them by a flood. In effect, God does not hold their weakness against them but accepts them for what they are.

The structure of the biblical flood narrative makes use of the literary device of *inclusio*, a bookends effect that brackets the beginning and ending of a passage with the same theme or language. The flood story commences and concludes with God commenting on the wickedness of humanity (6:5; 8:21), and in both places this is accompanied by a text that offers an example of humankind's sinful nature. At the beginning of the narrative this is done through the mythological story in Genesis 6:1-4 describing the sexual relations between the "sons of God" and human females that leads to God's fixing a limit on the human life span. At the end of the flood story the ban on murder in Genesis 9:5-6 functions in a similar way by highlighting the need to curb human depravity. Such a literary structure is typically used to identify the key theme or point of the text found within the *inclusio*, in this case the flood narrative. When we consider these two portions of Genesis in relationship to each other that theme becomes apparent. By limiting the human lifetime in Genesis 6:1-4, God is doing precisely what humanity is forbidden to do in Genesis 9:5-6 with the prohibition against murder. Only God may determine how long a person lives, and anyone who tries to do so has overstepped the bounds and intruded on God's authority. The *inclusio* helps to make clear the distinction between humanity and deity and the intervening flood story illustrates the consequences that can result when that distinction is ignored and humans try to act like God.

Reading the biblical Noah story with the Qur'an tradition of sura 71 in mind helps to bring this dimension of the narrative to the forefront and allows us to see a message behind the flood that might normally be missed. The Qur'an urges us to remember that Allah is the supreme authority and creator of all that exists. Even when we forget this fact and give in to the temptation to try to violate the limits of our human condition there is still hope for us. If we recognize our error and ask for pardon we will experience the forgiveness and mercy of Allah. As long as we maintain the proper perspective on our place in the world and our relationship with the rest of creation we will avoid divine retribution.

This is essentially the same lesson that can be learned from the Genesis flood narrative. It is not the story of an angry and vengeful God who does not give wayward humanity a chance to correct its mistakes and, in a blind fit of rage, destroys almost all of the world. When we note that the themes of creation and God's mercy are as central to the biblical tradition as they are to the Qur'an, the story can be seen in a different light. It is about a God who does not completely give up on humanity despite its unwillingness to accept the limits of its condition. It reminds people that what they need to do to remember their true place in the world is look around at the works of creation which are of God's making, not theirs. In Genesis, the flood functions as a sign of God's complete control over all that exists, despite human claims to the contrary, and the covenant is the symbol that God is always ready to forgive.

NOTES: CHAPTER 2

[1]There is an interesting connection to this idea in 7:64, discussed earlier in the chapter, which refers to those who rejected Allah's signs and were drowned as "blind people."

[2]The Arabic verb used here for "cry out" is the same one that is used to describe how Noah speaks to his son in verse 42. This indicates that Noah is feeling the same sense of helplessness and frustration toward Allah in trying to come to terms with his son's death as he did toward his son when he refused to heed his advice.

[3]Allah's words here are ambiguous in the original Arabic and Qur'an commentators have debated their precise meaning. Another possible meaning is "he is a worker of unrighteousness," but the translation proposed here ("he is an unrighteous work") seems to fit the context better.

[4]This idea is supported by other Qur'an texts that treat the Noah tradition. For example, in the passage discussed earlier in this chapter no reference is made to Noah's family at all. The text simply says those in the ark with Noah were saved without giving any indication of who they were (7:64). While most references to those saved with Noah either do not mention his family or see them as only a portion of the survivors of the flood, the Qur'an is not consistent on this point. In 37:76-77, for instance, it is said, "We saved him and his family from the great distress. We made his offspring the only survivors."

[5]In both the Bible and the Qur'an the ark comes to rest on a mountain but the two texts differ on its location. According to Genesis, it is among the mountains of Ararat in the area of eastern Asia Minor (8:4). The Qur'an, in 11:44, identifies the mountain as al-Judi, which probably refers to a prominent high point in the Arabian peninsula.

[6]The addressee of this verse is ambiguous in the Arabic original and it is possible that these words are a continuation of Allah's words to Noah. But many translators understand it to be a comment directed toward Muhammad, and that is how it is taken here. This type of shift of addressee within the middle of a passage is a fairly common occurrence in the Qur'an and several other examples of it will be seen in later chapters.

[7]The Hebrew word found here, *rūḥ*, can mean both "breath" and "spirit."

3

Abraham

*A*braham plays a very visible and central role in the Qur'an. He is explicitly mentioned in twenty-five different suras and only the name of Moses appears more frequently in the text. Despite this high profile, however, the Qur'an does not offer the same detailed presentation of the character of Abraham that emerges from the pages of the Hebrew Bible. Genesis 11–25 is an extended narrative that describes the experiences of Abraham as he journeys far and wide. He leaves his homeland in Mesopotamia for the land promised him by God only to continue on to Egypt when a famine breaks out. He eventually returns to Canaan where he settles and dies. Along the way we read of his encounters with many others, including God, his wife Sarah, Sarah's servant Hagar, his sons Ishmael and Isaac, his nephew Lot, Pharaoh, other foreign kings, three mysterious visitors, and the elders of the city of Hebron.

The Qur'an's treatment of Abraham is much more streamlined as it centers on just a few incidents in his life and then, as it typically does elsewhere, recounts several different versions of these episodes. But these various accounts of these few moments in Abraham's life all work together to create a singular vision of his character that points out for the reader his important place in Islam. Throughout the Qur'an, Abraham is recognized as the first true believer and the prototypical Muslim.

A GOOD EXAMPLE FOR YOU

Islam understands Abraham to be, like Noah, one of a series of prophets who received special revelation from Allah for the benefit of humanity. "Say, 'We believe in Allah, what has been revealed to us, what was revealed to Abraham, Ishmael, Isaac, Jacob, and the tribes, and what was given to Moses, Jesus, and the prophets from their Lord. We do not make a distinction among any of them and to Him we submit'" (3:84). This is an important text for appreciating the Islamic concept of revelation. It is in the form of a command instructing Muhammad and his community to profess that the message from Allah they have received is identical to that given to the prior prophets and they are not to consider any one of these messengers to be preeminent over the others. In other words, Abraham is a link in a chain that extends into their own day since the God of Abraham is also the God of Ishmael, Moses, Jesus, Muhammad, and the other prophets.

We see the same idea expressed frequently in the Hebrew Bible where Abraham enjoys a similar status as the one who initiated the covenantal relationship with God that was then passed on to succeeding generations. For example, a frequent designation of the God of Israel is "the God of Abraham, the God of Isaac, and the God of Jacob" (Exod 3:6, 15, 16; 4:5), and this phrase affirms the continuity of revelation in much the same way the Qur'an passage does. According to the Qur'an, Abraham possessed certain qualities that set him apart and marked him as a true believer, but many who came after him did not fully understand who he was or how they should relate to him. A key passage that addresses this theme is 3:65-67.

> [65]Oh people of the book! Why do you argue among yourselves about Abraham when the Torah and the Gospel were not revealed until after him? Will you not understand? [66]You are those who argued about that of which you had knowledge. Why do you argue about that of which you have no knowledge? Allah knows and you do not know. [67]Abraham was not a Jew or a Christian, but he was an upright person who submitted and was not one of those who associate.

The first thing in this text that deserves comment is its audience. It is addressed to the "people of the book," which is a very common phrase in the Qur'an that refers to other peoples who received written revelation prior to the time of Islam. Scholars debate the precise identity of these groups but all would include Jews and Christians as people of the book and many would add to them Zoroastrians and adherents of other pre-Islamic religions of the Near East. In the present text, the mention of the Torah and Gospel and the reference to Abraham being neither a Jew nor a Christian suggest we should adopt a more narrow definition here and see it as a designation for members of the Judeo-Christian tradition.

Throughout the Qur'an, the "people of the book" are viewed both positively and negatively. On the one hand, they enjoy a special status since they have been recipients of the divine word and so are viewed more favorably than other non-Muslims who engage in polytheism or other forms of false worship. On the other hand, some texts adopt a very critical tone when discussing the beliefs and practices of the people of the book. In general, if they conduct themselves in a way that is consistent with the divine revelation they have received they can attain salvation. "If the people of the book had believed and been pious We would have granted pardon for their offenses and allowed them to enter the gardens of comfort. If they had followed the Torah and the Gospel and what was sent down to them from their Lord, they would have eaten (of good things) from above them and from under their feet. Among them are some people who are moderate, but many of them do evil" (5:65-66).

One of the criticisms leveled against the people of the book is that they argue among themselves concerning Abraham. Each group tries to claim him as one of their own, but the Qur'an reminds them that Abraham predates both Judaism and Christianity and it is therefore anachronistic to identify him with either religion. In the Qur'an Abraham is neither a Jew nor a Christian but is superior to both. He is consistently portrayed throughout the text as a practitioner of a type of monotheism which existed prior to both Judaism and Christianity that was free of the errors that, in the Islamic view, infiltrated and came to dominate those later faiths.

The Arabic word used to describe someone who adopts this pure monotheism is *ḥanīf*, a term that is found twelve times in the Qur'an. In eight of those occurrences Abraham is described as a *ḥanīf* and he is the only individual who is ever explicitly designated as such in the entire Qur'an. The word comes from the Arabic root *ḥanafa* which carries the basic sense "to incline," and outside the Qur'an *ḥanīf* has the meaning "to incline toward a right state or tendency."[1] In Islamic usage, it refers to the pure faith of radical monotheists like Abraham and it is translated in 3:67 as "upright person." As a *ḥanīf*, Abraham was an individual of high moral and spiritual quality which enabled him to have a special relationship with Allah. This is the reason why he is referred to elsewhere as "friend of Allah" (4:125), another title that is unique to Abraham in the Qur'an.

After telling us what Abraham is, the passage in 3:65-67 goes on to tell us what he is not. As a *ḥanīf*, he is incapable of engaging in *shirk*, the gravest sin imaginable to a Muslim. The word comes from an Arabic root that means "to associate or participate," and the term *mushrik* refers to someone who associates someone or something with Allah. In the Islamic view, such a person has committed an unforgivable sin because the divine nature has been violated. It is forbidden to associate some aspect of the created order with Allah since this infringes upon the unity and oneness of Allah which is at the heart of the Islamic understanding of the deity. Such associating can take a variety of forms but the most common is idolatry, which ascribes divinity to a statue, image or some other created object that does not partake of the divine essence.

According to 3:67, Abraham is not one of those who associates and, as we shall see, much of his energy in the Qurʾan is directed against those who engage in idolatrous activity as he tries to convince them to reject their false worship. The Qurʾan contrasts the faith of the *ḥanīf* with that of the *mushrik* whenever it can. In eleven of the twelve texts where the word *ḥanīf* appears a reference to the *mushrik* is found soon after it. When the passage refers to Abraham's upright faith, as in 3:67, it quickly adds that he was not one of those who associated. When the text is a more general appeal to believers to adopt the way of the *ḥanīf*, an admonition against associating comes right after it. In this way, the virtue of Abraham, the model *ḥanīf*, is juxtaposed with the vice of the quintessential sinner and his character is elevated beyond reproach.

The Qurʾan does more than simply praise Abraham for his virtue by drawing a distinction between his faith and that of the Jew and Christian. It also equates his religion with Muhammad's and thereby understands it to be an earlier form of Islam. This makes sense in light of the Islamic belief, mentioned above, that no distinction is to be made among the various prophets since they all carried the same message to their people. According to Muslim doctrine, the difference with Muhammad is that, unlike in Judaism and Christianity, his followers did not distort or change the message after they received it. Muhammad and the Qurʾan, therefore, preserve the original and authentic form of Abraham's religion that the other two monotheistic faiths lack. In 6:161 Allah commands Muhammad, "Say, 'Truly, my Lord has guided me to a straight path, a true religion, the religion of Abraham, an upright person who was not one of those who associate.'" In this verse the religion of Muhammad, which is called the "straight path," is equated with the religion of Abraham since the nature of the latter's faith was virtually identical to that preached by Muhammad centuries later.

According to the Qur'an, Islam is not a religion that began in the Arabian peninsula of the seventh century C.E. with the coming of the prophet Muhammad. Its roots are much deeper than that since it was already being lived by Abraham and other earlier people. This is the basis for the Islamic view of Abraham as the prototypical Muslim, an idea which the text frequently supports in subtle ways. We see an example of this in 3:67 where Abraham is described as an upright person *(hanīf)* who "submitted." The Arabic original of this last word is *muslim*, a term used commonly in describing Abraham and other pre-Islamic figures that must be interpreted carefully. We should not understand its use as implying that Abraham shared the beliefs and adopted all the practices of later day Muslims. Rather, it is a way of explaining how Abraham possessed the quality of submission *(islām)* to the will of Allah which is essential for true belief. His importance for those who come after him is spelled out in 16:120-123.

> [120]Truly, Abraham was a model of virtue, obedient to Allah, upright, and not one of those who associate. [121]He was thankful for the favors of Him who chose him and guided him to a straight path. [122]We bestowed good upon him in the world and he will truly be among the righteous in the hereafter. [123]Now We have revealed to you (Muhammad) to follow the religion of Abraham as an upright person. He was not one of those who associate.

Abraham is the ideal believer who should be emulated by anyone wishing to enjoy the rewards he received. Even Muhammad is instructed in this text to imitate Abraham by following his religion and being an upright person *(hanīf)* just as he was. At this point, the connection between the two figures could not be stated more bluntly. The prophet of Islam is being urged by Allah to adopt the way of Abraham, his predecessor in faith. The distinction between the *hanīf* and the *mushrik* is once again evident in this passage as it is repeated twice that Abraham was not among those who are guilty of associating something with Allah. But this time the point is made more cleverly through the use of a wordplay. Immediately after the first mention of Abraham not being an associator in verse 120 we are told at the beginning of verse 121 that he was thankful. The two words used here sound alike in Arabic since they contain the same root letters in a slightly different order. As we have seen, the verb "to associate" comes from the root *sharika* and the noun form that describes the sin of association, *shirk*, comes from it. The verb "to thank" comes from the root *shakara* which is identical in form except for the transposition of the second and third root letters. Words built on these two roots follow one right after the other in the Arabic text as verse 120 ends with a word from *sharika* and verse 121 begins with one formed on *shakara*. Through this witty use of the similarity between the two words the Qur'an makes its point more memorable: Abraham was not guilty of *shirk* (association) because he practiced *shukr* (thankfulness). The way to insure that one remains on the straight path and under Allah's guidance is to be ever thankful for the favors one has received from Allah.

In the Qur'an, Abraham functions as the paradigmatic believer for Muhammad and the Islamic community. He is the prototypical Muslim and, in order to reach the straight path, one's belief and behavior must be patterned on his. In other words, every person must strive to be a *ḥanīf* and avoid the temptation to be a *mushrik*. As 60:4 reminds them, all Muslims, including the prophet himself, are exhorted to see Abraham as their model and conform their lives to his standard. "Truly, there is a good example for you in Abraham."

MESSENGERS FROM ALLAH

As noted earlier, the Qur'an's treatment of Abraham lacks the scope and detail of the biblical story as it narrates a limited number of events in his life that are recounted in several versions. While Genesis attempts to present a more or less chronological account of his life that describes what happened to him from the time he was called by God until his death, the Qur'an prefers to narrow the focus. This is in keeping with the Qur'an's interest in its message that was noted earlier. Unlike the Bible, the Qur'an does not offer a comprehensive and sequential retelling of history. Rather, it relates individual, purportedly historical, events that help to illustrate or validate the point it is attempting to make at a given time.

We have seen that the Qur'anic Abraham functions as an example and model for believers. Most of the episodes from his life depicted in the text attempt to illustrate this aspect of his character by highlighting his faith and presenting him as a person worthy of emulation. Some of the Abrahamic traditions found in the Qur'an have biblical parallels and others do not. We will first examine one that is also found in Genesis and then consider some that are unique to the Qur'an. A tradition it holds in common with the Bible is found at 11:69-82 which describes a visit to Abraham by divine messengers.

> [69]Our messengers came to Abraham with good news. They said, "Peace." He answered, "Peace," and did not delay in bringing a roasted calf. [70]But when he saw that their hands did not reach for it he became suspicious of them and felt afraid of them. They said, "Do not fear. We have been sent to the people of Lot." [71]His wife, standing by, laughed when We gave her the good news of Isaac and, after Isaac, Jacob. [72]She said, "Alas! Shall I bear a child when I am old and this husband of mine is an old man? Truly, this is something strange!" [73]They said, "Do you wonder at Allah's command? The mercy of Allah and His blessings are upon you, oh people of the house. He is praiseworthy and glorious." [74]When the fear had left Abraham and the good news came to him he disputed with Us about the people of Lot. [75]Truly, Abraham was mild, tender, repentant. [76]"Oh Abraham, stop this. Your Lord's command has gone forth and there is surely coming to them a punishment that cannot be turned back." [77]When Our messengers came to Lot he was troubled for them and he did not know how to give them protection. He said, "This is a difficult day!" [78]His people, long used to committing transgressions, hastened to him. He said, "Oh my people, these are my daughters. They are purer for you. Fear Allah and do not disgrace me in my guests. Is there not a reasonable man among you?" [79]They said, "You know we have no right to your daughters. Truly, you know what we want." [80]He said, "If only I had power over you or I had refuge in some strong support." [81]They said, "Oh Lot, we are the messengers of your Lord. They shall not reach you. Depart with your family during the night and may none of you turn around except your wife. What befalls her will also befall them. Truly, their appointed time is the morning. Is not the morning near?" [82]When our command came to pass we made its top its bottom and rained upon it layers of clay stones.

The biblical parallel to this passage is found in Genesis 18–19 and the basic outline of the two texts is quite similar. In each, Abraham receives divine messengers for whom he prepares a meal. They announce the news that the elderly couple will have a son, and this elicits a reaction from Abraham's wife which leads to a response from the messengers. In the course of the encounter the visitors make known their intention to go to the place where Lot is living in order to destroy it. After Abraham responds to this information, the messengers journey to Lot's town where they convince him to flee with his family before destroying the area. Despite this similarity of plot, however, the two traditions disagree considerably on some of the details and this results in

two distinct stories which serve different agendas. The contrast between the passages is most clearly seen when we consider two aspects
of the story: the content of the divine message and the characters' reactions to that message.

The Divine Message

The biblical passage of Genesis 18–19 is only properly understood
when we keep in mind the surrounding narrative which furnishes us
with important background information. Genesis 17 is particularly
crucial in this regard. In that chapter God initiates a covenant with
Abraham and his descendants forever. "I will establish my covenant between me and you, and your offspring after you throughout their generations, for an everlasting covenant, to be God to you and to your
offspring after you" (Gen 17:7). At this point in the narrative, Abraham
already has a son in Ishmael through Hagar, the maidservant of his wife
Sarah. But God goes on to tell him that Sarah herself will conceive and
have a son, Isaac, who will be the offspring of the covenant. In effect,
God chooses one of the sons of Abraham and excludes the other from
the covenant. Therefore, when the messengers announce in Genesis 18
that Sarah will bear a son the reader knows that this is the promised
child who will initiate the covenantal relationship between God and
Abraham's offspring. In this way, the message from the visitors is intimately linked with the divine promise made in the previous chapter.

This is not the way the story is presented in the Qurʾan. While there
is an announcement to Abraham's nameless wife of the birth of Isaac
the text does not identify the child with a covenant. This view is maintained throughout the entire Qurʾan where covenantal language is rare
in the Abraham traditions and there is no hint of the biblical notion of
a chosen people set apart to enjoy a special relationship with Allah. In
the Muslim view, Allah does not play favorites but desires all people to
embrace Islam and thereby establish an intimate and special bond with
the deity. The covenant context of the biblical passage has been replaced by something different: the motif of "good news." The text from
sura 11 begins with an explicit reference to the purpose of this visit to
Abraham by stating that the messengers are bringing him good news.
This is followed by two other mentions (vv. 71, 74) of the good news
which first his wife and then Abraham receive. This triple reference to
divine good news has an ironic quality given its presence in a text that
will end with the destruction of Lot's people. But this juxtaposition

makes the Qurʾan's point all the more emphatic. Those who obey and follow the will of Allah will be rewarded with good news, but those who violate the divine will must suffer punishment.

While the message from the biblical visitors is connected to the covenantal promise, the visitors in the Qurʾan highlight a different aspect of the deity's character. When Abraham's wife questions them in the Qurʾan the messengers do not adopt a wait and see attitude as they do in the biblical account. In Genesis, after Sarah expresses her doubt, Abraham is told, "Is anything too wonderful for the Lord? At the set time I will return to you, in due season, and Sarah shall have a son" (18:14). This response suggests that the only way Sarah will be convinced is to wait until her son is born. Such is the nature of a promise. It can only be verified when what has been pledged is realized and experienced. The visitors cannot persuade or force Sarah to believe the promise since its legitimacy is tied to its realization.

But good news is of a different nature since one can be convinced to accept or believe it. The divine messengers of the Qurʾan attempt to do this to Abraham's wife through a subtle shift of focus. After she initially balks at their birth announcement they respond by asking "Do you wonder at Allah's command?" (v. 73). The "good news" from Allah is not a promise but a command and, as such, demands an immediate response. In effect, the messengers are telling Abraham's wife to make up her mind now on whether or not she believes the divine word. In an attempt to persuade her to respond affirmatively they then remind her of the beneficence of the deity as a way of indicating why the divine command must come to pass. "The mercy of Allah and His blessings are upon you, oh people of the house. He is praiseworthy and glorious" (v. 73).

The message Abraham and his wife receive from the visitors in the Qurʾan, while seemingly similar to that conveyed to their biblical counterparts, is radically different in tone and intent. By presenting the divine word as a command from Allah the Qurʾan text stresses the all-powerful, authoritative nature of the deity and portrays the human recipients of the message as individuals who must respond immediately and faithfully. That this is a dominant theme of the Qurʾan's version of the episode becomes apparent when we recognize its presence as the scene shifts to the people of Lot.

Both Genesis 18–19 and sura 11 link the episode of the divine messengers who visit Abraham with the story of Lot and the destruction of the people among whom he is living. In each text Abraham is told of the coming punishment of Lot's people, but the way this message is communicated to the patriarch in the two versions varies considerably. The biblical account (Gen 18:16-21) describes an encounter between God and Abraham during which the deity considers whether or not to divulge to Abraham the fate of Sodom and Gomorrah. God finally determines that Abraham should have this information and the reason given for this decision is connected to the covenant and the special status of the chosen people. The reader is given a privileged glimpse of the innermost thoughts of the divine mind when God muses, "Shall I hide from Abraham what I am about to do, seeing that Abraham shall become a great and mighty nation, and all the nations of the earth shall be blessed in him? No, for I have chosen him . . ." (vv. 17–19). God then informs Abraham of the consequences of the great sin of Sodom and Gomorrah.

This scene occurs when the visitors, having resumed their journey, are on their way to Sodom and Gomorrah and it is the first time Abraham is told of the imminent destruction of the two cities. There then follows the description of a curious exchange between God and Abraham in which the latter appeals to the deity not to destroy Sodom if some of its population is found righteous (Gen 18:22-33). Abraham begins with the hypothetical scenario that fifty good citizens are present in Sodom and works his way down to the point that God agrees to spare the city even if only ten such individuals are found. This bargaining scene indicates that the destruction of Sodom and Gomorrah is not a forgone conclusion for God, and this idea is reinforced by God's own words in 18:21 where the possibility is raised that the cities are not as guilty as imagined. "I must go down and see whether they have done altogether according to the outcry that has come to me; and if not, I will know." The reader, therefore, does not know what will happen to Sodom and Gomorrah and this lack of knowledge reflects divine ignorance on the matter as well. Only in 19:13 is it explicitly stated that the place is about to be destroyed because "the outcry against its people has become great before the Lord."

No such uncertainty is possible in the Qurʾan's version of events since at the outset Abraham and the reader are apprised of what will happen. Sensing his initial concern at their reluctance to eat the food he offers, the visitors reassure Abraham, "Do not fear. We have been sent to the people of Lot" (v. 70). This remark identifies the mission of the strangers as one that will strike fear into people's hearts. The Qurʾan text therefore begins on a much more ominous note since in Genesis the strangers' destination and purpose are not revealed until after their visit to Abraham and Sarah and even then, as we have seen, not definitively stated until after their arrival in Sodom. In the Islamic text, the purpose of their visit is stated in their first words and this gives the deity a quality of resolve or certainty that is lacking in Genesis. This is reinforced by a second reference to the "command" of Allah in verse 76. After Abraham attempts to reverse the divine decision to annihilate the people of Lot, he is rebuked, "Your Lord's command has gone forth and there is surely coming to them a punishment that cannot be turned back." Unlike the biblical account, the Qur'an does not indicate any hesitancy or indecision on Allah's part and the only thing Abraham can do is accept the divine will. Because Allah has commanded the ruin of Lot's people negotiation is pointless and so the Islamic text does not include the scene in which Abraham bargains with the deity over the fate of the city.

The designation "Lot's people" is an interesting one and highlights the distinctive role this figure plays in Islam. He is mentioned by name more than twenty-five times in the Qur'an and in most of these texts he is linked with a specific people identified as his own. He is sent to warn them of the need to change their ways and follow the straight path, but they refuse to do so and suffer the consequences of their unbelief. The identification of them as Lot's people is particularly interesting in light of Genesis 19:9 where they refer to him as an "alien" among them, indicating that his relationship with them in the Bible is markedly different from that of the Qur'an. The cities of Sodom and Gomorrah are identified as the area that is destroyed in Genesis but the location remains unnamed in the Qur'an.

In Genesis 13 Lot is linked with the divine promise of the land to Abraham when he separates himself from the patriarch and settles in the well-watered plain of the Jordan. In a certain sense, he is a counterpoint to Abraham in that he chooses to reside in the part of the land that is not blessed, and the destruction of Sodom and Gomorrah highlights the error of his choice. The last time we hear mention of Lot in the Bible he is described in a most unflattering way that casts his legacy to the biblical tradition in a negative light and makes him the antithesis of his uncle Abraham. In Genesis 19:29-38 he engages in sexual relations with his two daughters while he is in a drunken state, and the offspring of those unions become the eponymous ancestors of the Moabites and Ammonites, who are frequently depicted in the Bible as enemies of the Israelites. Lot suffers no such humiliation in the Qur'an where he remains the paradigmatic believer and is consistently portrayed as someone who faithfully follows Allah's will. Due to the lack of any reference to a chosen people or the promise of a land in Islam's text these elements are not a part of the Lot tradition and the dominant motif is one of Lot as a messenger sent to warn his people.[2]

Another aspect of the Islamic Lot tradition that deserves some brief consideration is the reference to the fate of his wife. This episode is described in a slightly different form than the Hebrew Bible in a way that is more in line with Allah's image in the Qur'an. In Genesis 19:26 Lot's wife looks back toward Sodom and Gomorrah and is immediately turned into a pillar of salt. The text understands this as a punishment due to her willful violation of the divine command given nine verses earlier when Lot and his fleeing family were told not to turn around. The Qur'anic version of events removes the elements of human responsibility and accountability by presenting her death as mandated by Allah. As the messengers instruct Lot to escape with his family they tell him, "Depart with your family during the night and may none of you turn around except your wife. What befalls her will also befall them" (v. 81). The emphasis here is on the divine, not human, will. Allah's messengers are stating what will happen rather than warning them about what might happen, and this recalls the theme of the "command" of Allah that has already been mentioned explicitly twice in the narrative. The Qur'an scene consequently rehabilitates the memory of Lot's wife in a dramatic way. Rather than being the quintessential unbeliever who disobeys the word of God knowing full well it will cost her her life, she personifies the ideal believer or "muslim" who submits herself to Allah and whose death is the fulfillment of the divine will.

The Human Response

The Bible and Qur'an passages also differ considerably on the reception the divine message receives. A striking feature of the Genesis account is the way in which God and the messengers are challenged or second-guessed throughout the narrative as each of the major characters at one time or another expresses resistance to God's will. This is seen in Genesis 18:22-33, already discussed, where Abraham successfully attempts to negotiate with God in order to spare Sodom. While the divine willingness to withhold punishment from the city can reasonably be interpreted as reflecting the boundless mercy of God, on another level the episode is equally indicative of the qualities Abraham's character possesses. His non-stop interrogation comes close to badgering the deity and the reader is left with the uneasy feeling that Abraham does not trust God's judgment regarding the fate of Sodom and feels the need to intercede in order to insure the proper outcome.

A similar position is adopted by Sarah, albeit in a more toned-down form. She speaks twice in the passage and both times her words suggest a certain defiance toward God. In 18:12, after hearing the divine announcement that she will bear a son, she questions this news, "After I have grown old, and my husband is old, shall I have pleasure?" Her doubt turns to insolence three verses later when, after being confronted by God, she disavows laughing at the news with the blanket denial "I did not laugh," to which the deity responds, "Oh yes, you did laugh." The reader is forced to side with God in this dispute since verse 12 explicitly states "Sarah laughed to herself" and this establishes her as an argumentative figure who is somewhat antagonistic toward God.

Lot, too, exhibits reluctance to follow the divine will, and this hesitancy is reflected in the narrative's repeated references to his obstinate refusal to do as God's messengers command him. We get a hint of things to come in the description of his first encounter with the strangers when, in Genesis 19:2-3, he invites them to spend the night at his house but they decline, preferring to sleep outdoors in the square. The text then recounts Lot's unwillingness to take no for an answer. "But he urged them strongly; so they turned aside to him and entered his house" (19:3). Although this response can be interpreted as an expression of Ancient Near Eastern hospitality which required that guests be treated respectfully, Lot's subsequent interactions with them suggest that this initial meeting between them might also be highlighting his stubbornness as an important element in their relationship.

His uncooperative nature is described at three different moments in the story. Prior to the destruction of Sodom, the visitors urge Lot to warn his family when they say, "Have you anyone else here? Sons-in-law, sons, daughters, or anyone you have in the city—bring them out of the place" (Gen 19:12). This verse is unusual because of the order in which Lot's relatives are listed. Normally, we would expect to find the father's biological offspring mentioned first, beginning with his sons and followed by his daughters, with the latter's husbands, if any, after that. But this verse has the sons-in-law in the unexpected first position and the list is made even more awkward by inserting the sons between the daughters and their husbands, grammatically separating the sons-in-law from the very people who make possible their familial relationship with Lot.

This unorthodox sequence identifies the sons-in-law as significant actors in the plot, and this is born out in Genesis 19:14-15 when Lot unsuccessfully attempts to warn them to flee and they think he is jesting. It is striking that Lot is not shown warning his own children of the coming danger or repeating his admonition to his sons-in-law. This indicates an element of half-heartedness on his part since he does not explicitly alert two of the three parties he has been told to inform and he appears to just go through the motions of warning his sons-in-law, the very first ones he is told to notify. This also puts the final scene of Lot's life recorded in the Bible in a new light. Thinking the rest of humanity has been destroyed, his daughters decide to engage in an incestuous relationship with him because "there is not a man to come in to us after the manner of all the world" (Gen 19:31). The men who would normally fill this role, their husbands, cannot do so because they have been killed in the conflagration at Sodom. But Lot is partly responsible for their demise since he did not fully carry out the command of the Lord's messengers by convincing them to flee. Ironically, the indignity that he and his daughters experience is partly his own fault.

A second narrative moment that highlights Lot's reluctance is found in Genesis 19:15-16. As the day appointed for Sodom's demise dawns, he is instructed by the angels, "Get up, take your wife and your two daughters who are here, or else you will be consumed in the punishment of the city." In a response that echoes that of his unbelieving sons-in-law, Lot tarries and does not take seriously the messengers' words. "But he lingered; so the men seized him and his wife and his two daughters by the hand, the Lord being merciful to him, and they brought him out and left him outside the city." The reference to the Lord being merciful to Lot is particularly notable since it points to the fact that he has failed miserably in his response to the divine message and deserves to be left behind with the other faithless inhabitants of the city.

There immediately follows a final example of the biblical Lot's obstinate nature when he once again refuses to follow the instructions of God's messengers. After they remove Lot and his relatives from the city, the messengers urge them to run away to the hill country where they will be safe from the divine wrath. But Lot, true to form, balks at this plan and proposes an alternative escape route. "Oh, no, my lords; your servant has found favor with you, and you have shown me great kindness in saving my life; but I cannot flee to the hills, for fear the disaster will overtake me and I die. Look, that city is near enough to flee to, and it is a little one. Let me escape there—is it not a little one?—and my life will be saved!" (Gen 19:18-20). Once again, Lot second-guesses the divine command in the belief that he knows better than God's spokespersons. They agree to his plan and allow him to flee to the "little city," but, in an ironic twist to the story which suggests the messengers were right all along, Lot continues on from there to settle in the very hills he refused to journey to earlier and it is there that he engages in sexual relations with his daughters.

As this analysis of his character indicates, Lot is consistently depicted as reluctant to follow God's command since every time he is told to do something he is either halfhearted in his attempt to carry it out or he ignores the directive entirely. This same perspective is also adopted by the other two major human characters in the story, Sarah and Abraham, and, if we understand the fate of Lot's wife to be the result of her disobedience of the divine order not to turn around, she exhibits the same quality. Genesis paints a very negative picture of the response to the divine message and the attitude of these people toward God.

In the Qur'an, however, the situation is the opposite as the command of Allah is consistently followed and all the characters are quick to obey the divine will. Unlike his talkative biblical counterpart, in this sura Abraham says only one word. His single utterance, "peace," echoes the greeting of the messengers and its brevity is remarkable in light of the fact that in Genesis he speaks fifty-five words before they say anything. The Qur'an alludes to, but does not describe, Abraham's discussion with Allah regarding the fate of Lot's people and it presents a very different image of the patriarch's character in that encounter.

Abraham does not annoy and pester God to reconsider his punishment until he gets his way as he does in Genesis. There is a reference to Abraham disputing with Allah, but this is quickly followed by a positive assessment of his character that identifies three admirable qualities he possesses. "Truly, Abraham was mild, tender, repentant" (v. 75). These three adjectives contrast greatly with the way his character is presented in the Bible where his aggressive and assertive nature is emphasized. In a similar way, the deity is hardly the compliant and submissive figure described in Genesis who acquiesces to Abraham's demands. In the Qur'an, Allah abruptly cuts off Abraham before he can argue his case by putting him in his place. "Oh Abraham, stop this. Your Lord's command has gone forth and there is surely coming to them a punishment that cannot be turned back" (v. 76). The focus then quickly shifts to Lot as if to suggest that Abraham was unable to counter this reprimand from Allah and was left with no choice but to surrender himself to the divine will. In this scene, then, Abraham accepts Allah's decision more readily than he does in the Genesis account and the deity comes across as a more authoritative figure who is clearly in charge of the situation.

In a similar way, the response of Abraham's wife to the divine message is softened somewhat in the Qur'an. There is mention of her laughing and pointing out her own and Abraham's advanced ages as Sarah does in Genesis 18, but her verbal reaction to the news of her pregnancy does not contain the same element of doubt that is found in the biblical account. Here she refers to the news as "something strange" (v. 72), a translation of the Arabic term ʿajīb which is a word conveying a sense of wonder or joy at an unusual or unexpected occurrence. She is therefore not displaying skepticism about the reliability of the information she has received but is marveling at its miraculous nature. The reply of the messengers highlights this same element by using a verb from the same Arabic root to ask her, "Do you wonder at Allah's command? The mercy of Allah and His blessings are upon you, oh people of the house" (v. 73). By using words that stress the "command" of the deity, they point out for her that it is the power and beneficence of Allah that has enabled such a remarkable event to occur, simultaneously removing her confusion and instructing her in authentic faith. While the biblical story ends on a negative note with God pointing out the fact that Sarah has lied about laughing, the Qur'anic parallel is less critical about her character since it presents her in a more positive light.

Lot in the Qur'an is equally compliant to Allah's will and lacks the quality of stubbornness that characterizes him in Genesis. He does not challenge or override divine authority and is not depicted second-guessing the messengers. In fact, in the Qur'an he never speaks directly to them and when they tell him to depart with his family the reader is to assume that is exactly what he did, no questions asked. In an interesting difference with the biblical tradition where they leave at the first light of morning, in the Qur'an Lot is told to flee during the night and the resulting image of him and his family journeying in the dark to parts unknown underscores a degree of trust on his part that is missing from the biblical account.[3]

Perhaps the most important indication of his different relationship with the deity is found on Lot's own lips. Unlike his biblical counterpart, he does not have all the answers and this is strikingly demonstrated in the fact that two out of the three lines of dialogue he speaks show him in an exasperated state not knowing what to do. His very first words in the text are, "This is a difficult day!" (v. 77), implying a certain frustration and inability to respond to the situation at hand. This same state of mind is behind the last words he speaks when he acknowledges his helplessness to his people who wish to treat his guests dishonorably.

"If only I had power over you or I had refuge in some strong support" (v. 80). The Lot of Genesis is able to change and manipulate the divine will as revealed to him through God's messengers, but the Lot of the Qur'an is a powerless individual who cannot even control his own people. It is only at this point, when he recognizes his own frailty, that the messengers step in and reveal themselves as sent from Allah. Lot then realizes that Allah is the "strong support" he has cried out for and that only obedience to the divine command can save him from his hopeless predicament.

The "command" of Allah is the dominant motif throughout the Qur'an passage and serves to link together the lives and experiences of the three major human characters. The word itself is found three times in the text, once each in the sections treating Abraham's wife (v. 73), Abraham (v. 76) and Lot (v. 82). Each of them is asked to acknowledge and accept the divine command even though it conflicts with the laws of nature (pregnancy for Abraham's wife) or their own wishes (the destruction of the city for Abraham and Lot). They do not challenge or alter Allah's word as their biblical counterparts do and this has a profound effect on the reader's attitude toward both them and the deity. They come across as submissive figures who model perfectly the attitude of the ideal believer, and Allah is the omniscient, omnipotent presence who is totally in charge of events and deserves such submission.

ISLAMIZATION OF THE TRADITION

The Qur'an text shares a great deal with the Genesis account in terms of their similar cast of characters and common plot outline. Consequently, the Bible reader who picks up this passage unaware of its origin would find nothing unusual about it and might reach the conclusion that it is simply a variation or retelling of the more familiar story found in Genesis 18–19. The only clear clue to its derivation are the references to "Allah" which identify its Islamic context. But if these several occurrences of the Arabic term for the deity were replaced by "God" or "the Lord," any questions about the text would disappear and the Bible reader would be hard-pressed to find anything objectionable about this version of the tradition.

The same thing could be said for a Muslim who might read the Genesis version unaware of where it came from. On the surface level, then, we appear to have two very similar stories that are more or less interchangeable. But the more detailed analysis undertaken above shows that, in fact, these two texts are quite different and, on some points, hard to reconcile with each other. We have seen that the Qurʾan's portrayal of the human and divine characters of the story conveys certain theological points that are often radically different from those which can be drawn from Genesis. We can best understand this difference as due to the purpose of the Qurʾan story within the framework of Islamic belief and practice.

As noted above, in the Qurʾan Abraham is not identified as the ancestor of a chosen people who are given special status and set apart from the rest of humanity. This is different from his role in the Bible where he is the progenitor of the Israelite community due to the covenant that is established with him and the guarantee of the Promised Land to his descendants forever. The biblical election of Abraham through the line of his son Isaac highlights the divine preference for some people over others. The Qurʾan is devoid of all such language and imagery since Allah is the God of all nations and every individual is expected to express his or her faith in Allah through acts of obedience and reverence. Because Islam maintains that all people are born Muslims ("submitters" to the divine will), it is impossible for Allah to randomly choose some for salvation while excluding the rest. The Qurʾan therefore claims to set the biblical record straight by presenting Abraham as a more universal ancestor who is not just the proto-Israelite but the ideal person of faith whom all should emulate.

This more submissive portrait of Abraham is expressed well by his subdued manner in the Qurʾan. When in the presence of Allah's messengers, he only speaks one word and does nothing to prevent the realization of the divine command. Similarly, when the text mentions his dispute with Allah over the people of Lot he accepts his chastisement passively and is presumed to have learned from his mistake. In short, he is the perfect "muslim" who humbly surrenders himself to Allah's will. The three adjectives used to describe him in verse 75 ("mild, tender, repentant") might well describe anyone who has embraced Islam and seeks to follow its straight path.

Likewise, the character of Lot has been redefined in a way that stresses his affinity with the Islamic tradition. In the Genesis account he and Abraham are relatives and, at times, his success appears to be the result of the divine covenant established with his uncle rather than due to anything he himself has done. In the Qurʾan no such family ties exist between the two men and Lot is presented as an independent individual whose fortunes rise or fall on his own merits. But he is more than simply that. As one of a long line of prophets that the Qur'an asserts have been sent to humanity to warn specific groups of the need to change their ways, Lot plays a vital role in the divine plan. As this text makes clear, like all such figures he has his own "people" who, through no fault of Lot's, refuse to heed his warning and suffer the dire consequences. Elsewhere in the Qur'an Lot himself acknowledges his divinely ordained vocation when he says to his people, "Will you not fear (Allah)? Truly, I am a faithful messenger for you. So fear Allah and obey" (26:161-163).

It is clear, then, that the human characters in the Qur'an text are meant to serve as models of faith for the members of the Islamic community. The latter day believer is invited to read this text and take both Abraham and Lot as examples of faithful living who can guide the modern Muslim through the challenges and temptations of daily life. This function also extends to their wives, although in very different ways. Abraham's suddenly pregnant wife personifies the believer who wonders at the ways of Allah and does not question or doubt the divine power to bring about anything, no matter how unexpected or unusual. She responds in joy and humility to the surprising blessings that have come her way, ever mindful of their source.

Lot's wife, on the other hand, exemplifies another type of believer. She typifies the one who experiences the more mysterious, unsettling aspects of Allah's authority. She is no less submissive and open to the divine will than Abraham's wife, but she experiences inexplicable misery rather than unaccountable bliss. She silently, anonymously accepts her death which the text presents as nothing other than the realization of the divine will. Her life, too, is a model for Muslims, particularly those who experience the mysterious pain and suffering that is a part of human existence and who are urged to accept such moments as equally a part of Allah's will. The cessation of life for Lot's wife is no less indicative of divine power and might than is the inception of life within Abraham's wife.

As on earth, so too in heaven. We have seen that the role and image of the deity in the Qur'an text is quite unlike what is found in the biblical parallel and this, too, can be understood as a function of its Islamic context. In the Muslim text, Allah is always in charge of the situation and is the clear authority figure. All that happens in the story is a direct result of the divine will and the human characters never influence or determine the course of events. The biblical account departs from this pattern significantly as human beings are constantly at odds with the divine plan and disrupt it in a variety of ways. Each biblical character, in his or her own way, succeeds in rebelling against divine authority by putting their desires and hopes ahead of God's. In the Qurʾan, the deity possesses a determined and uncompromising quality that is absent from Genesis, and this resolve is in keeping with the Islamic understanding of the nature of Allah. According to the Muslim view, it is impossible to change the deity's mind or somehow interfere with the divine will because this would infringe upon Allah's supremacy and ultimate authority. A line from Qurʾan 2:284 succinctly summarizes this viewpoint: "Allah has power over all things." Throughout the pages of the Qurʾan there is a consistent call to be ever-mindful of Allah's controlling presence. As we have seen, the primary way the idea is expressed in this version of the encounter between Abraham and the divine messengers is through repeated reference to the command of Allah and its inevitable realization.[4]

ABRAHAM THE *ḤANĪF*

The Qurʾan contains a number of Abrahamic traditions that have no biblical counterparts. Such texts are best understood within the context of the Qurʾan's portrayal of Abraham as the prototypical *ḥanīf*, or pure monotheist. These passages depict him as a follower of the one true God who, as a prophet in the Islamic mold, tries to warn his faithless contemporaries and urges them to return to the straight path. They give a detailed account of his efforts to sway his people from polytheism to monotheism and to institute a proper system of worship. At times, it appears that Abraham is being presented as the first Muslim in these texts since many aspects of his preaching and faith life strongly resemble the beliefs and practices of Islam.

It is a particularly striking feature of many of these passages that the themes they address and situations they describe closely resemble those of key moments in Muhammad's life. The general outline of the faith lives of both figures as recorded in the Qurʾan is very similar and focuses on two main themes. The first is their complete rejection of the religion of their contemporaries as nothing but paganism and idol worship. The second theme is their setting up an alternative religious system which allows for the expression of true and proper worship. This similarity has led some scholars to propose that such Abrahamic texts played a very important double function within the early Muslim community since they served to legitimate Muhammad's mission in the eyes of his contemporaries while offering him strength and support in his more difficult moments.[5]

Out with the Old

A Qurʾan passage which shows Abraham criticizing the religion of his contemporaries is found at 19:41-50.

> [41]Mention Abraham in the book. Truly, he was trustworthy and a prophet. [42]He said to his father, "Oh my father, why do you worship what does not hear, does not see, and cannot help you in anything? [43]Oh my father, a knowledge has come to me that has not come to you. So follow me and I will guide you on a proper path. [44]Oh my father, do not worship Satan. Truly, Satan is disobedient to the Merciful. [45]Oh my father, I fear that a punishment from the Merciful will come upon you and you will become a friend to Satan." [46]He said, "Are you forsaking my gods, oh Abraham? If you do not stop this I will stone you. Leave my presence for a while!" [47]He (Abraham) said, "Peace be upon you. I will ask forgiveness from my Lord for you. Truly He is kind to me. [48]I will separate myself from you and from what you call upon that is not Allah and I will call upon my Lord. Perhaps in calling upon my Lord I may not be in distress." [49]So when he separated himself from them and from what they worshiped that is not Allah We gave to him Isaac and Jacob and We made each of them a prophet. [50]And We gave to them of Our mercies and granted them true and high renown.

This text is one of several versions of the same story in the Qurʾan that all relate how Abraham criticized and rejected his father's religion.[6] It shows him imploring his father to give up false worship and embrace true faith. The insistent and impassioned way he tries to do this is conveyed through the repetition of the words "oh my father" that begin four consecutive verses of the text. This mode of address expresses both the urgency of the son's appeal and the nature of the relationship between the two men. Abraham is concerned not least of all because he is speaking to his own father who he does not want to suffer the harsh consequences of his misguided ways.

The older man's response in verse 46 is similar to, yet painfully different from, Abraham's words. He, too, makes use of the vocative mood ("oh Abraham"), but not to highlight the bond that exists between the two. Rather than echo Abraham's term of endearment by saying "oh my son" or something similar, he chooses to address him by his name. This signifies a sense of distance that is only intensified by the father's next words. After threatening to stone his son, he tells him to leave his sight. At this point the differences between the two could not be drawn any more sharply. While Abraham requests a reconciliation by urging his father to follow him so that they might journey the road of life together in faith, his father desires further estrangement by commanding Abraham to get out of his sight. The cause of this fractured relationship is clearly identified in the passage. The wedge that has driven apart this parent and child is their religious differences.

There is much in this text that conforms to Muhammad's situation, particularly early in his prophetic career. He was orphaned at a young age since his father died before he was born and his mother passed away when he was a child. This means that the Qurʾan's description of Abraham disagreeing with and ultimately separating himself from his father is not an experience that Muhammad could have had. Nonetheless, numerous passages refer to the problems he encountered in trying to spread his message among the Meccans of the time and the often unfavorable reception he received. The text frequently depicts these individuals as enemies of Muhammad who were incapable of accepting him as a prophet and unwilling to embrace his ideas as authentic expressions of divine will.

According to the Qurʾan, his enemies charged Muhammad with being a fraudulent pretender and refused to believe him on a number of grounds. Included among these are his being a liar (25:4-6), the piecemeal nature of the Qurʾan's revelation which was not sent down to him all at once (25:32), the fact that he did not perform signs (17:90-93) and their belief that he was insane or possessed (34:46). This last possibility was one that, according to early Muslim tradition, even Muhammad himself entertained early on. When he first began to receive his revelations he thought he was losing his mind, but his wife Khadija convinced him that he was no madman and, with the help of her Christian cousin, enabled him to overcome his self-doubt. At times, the Qurʾan attempts to reassure the prophet of his legitimacy while censuring his critics, and such texts, like 68:2-8, underscore the sometimes tense nature of life in Mecca during the period.

> [2]By the grace of your Lord, you (Muhammad) are not possessed. [3]But, truly, for you there is a gracious reward. [4]Truly, you possess outstanding moral character. [5]You will see and they also will see [6]which of you is afflicted with madness. [7]Your Lord surely knows who strays from His way, and He knows those who follow guidance. [8]So do not comply with those who lie.

The identity of Muhammad's early antagonists and the reasons for their disagreement with him are issues that have been discussed frequently by scholars. There is no universal agreement on these matters but it is safe to assume that the prophet's message was considered to be a threat to certain social and religious aspects of Meccan society, and the people who were closely involved with those areas of life would have been most resistant to him and his ideas. More likely than not, Muhammad's claim to be a prophet had far-reaching political implications and his preaching against polytheism had significant economic and religious ramifications that caused many in positions of power to reject him.[7]

When read with this background in mind, the Qurʾan's tradition of Abraham and his father can be seen as addressing the same issue. Just like the prophet of Islam, the earlier messenger experienced rejection due to the inability of those close to him, here represented by his own parent, to put aside their idolatrous ways and worship the one true God. The link between the two is also made in other texts where we are told that just as Abraham's father threatened to stone him if he did not remove himself, so also Muhammad had to endure potential danger to his safety and well-being. "Remember how the unbelievers plotted against you (Muhammad). They tried to confine you or kill you or expel you. They plotted and Allah plotted, but Allah is the best of plotters" (8:30). In this way, the Qurʾan develops the theme we have already observed of placing Muhammad's career within the context of the other messengers that had been commissioned previously by Allah. Like Abraham, Muhammad was sent to his own people, many of whom refused to believe him and ultimately rejected him. But also like Abraham, Allah was with him and he eventually overcame the hatred and threats of his enemies to establish true worship. Each man, in keeping with his role as a *ḥanīf*, began his mission with a critique of the old idolatrous way in order to introduce pure monotheistic faith.

Another important connection with Muhammad is seen in the reference in verses 48-49 to Abraham separating himself from his father's people and from what they worship that is not Allah. The patriarch is forced to withdraw from his native place due to its inhabitants' unwillingness to respond positively to his preaching and this closely mirrors a similar event in Muhammad's life. As noted in this book's introduction, a turning point in the early history of the Islamic community was the *hijra*, or migration, which occurred in 622 when Muhammad and a small group of Muslims left Mecca for the city of Yathrib located about two hundred miles to the north. Muhammad had been invited to this oasis area to function as an arbiter or judge who would settle disputes that arose among the local tribes. Earlier, some of the people of Yathrib had come in contact with Muhammad and his followers in Mecca and had converted to Islam. When they were looking for someone to help them maintain order in their own city he was a logical choice. Eventually, the name of the city was changed to Medina ("city" in Arabic) and it became the administrative center of the early Muslim community which Muhammad lived in for the remaining ten years of his life.

The parallel with the Abraham tradition should be apparent. In both cases, a prophet who has been sent by Allah to warn his people is forced to withdraw from his homeland due to the lukewarm, potentially violent, reception he encounters. But the end result for each man is positive as Allah continues to bless and reward them. For Muhammad this divine support is seen in the success he enjoys among the Medinans as his community continues to grow and develop. Similarly, Abraham is rewarded after he leaves his father's people through offspring who continue his prophetic office. "We gave to him Isaac and Jacob and We made each of them a prophet" (v. 49).[8] By understanding Muhammad's life story within the pattern of rejection and vindication that Abraham and the other prophets experienced, the Qurʾan affirms the legitimacy of his prophethood and offers support to him in his more difficult moments. This underscores the vital role Abraham plays as a forerunner or prototype for the final prophet of Islam.

Although there is no exact biblical parallel to the Qurʾan episode between Abraham and his father there are some interesting thematic and structural similarities that connect the two. Abraham's role as a warner or preacher among his people is not a part of the biblical tradition, but several aspects of the beginning of the Abraham story in Genesis 12:1-9 correspond to the account in the Qurʾan we have been examining.[9] God's first words to the patriarch in Genesis summarize the plot that is laid out in the Qurʾan text. "Go from your country and your kindred and your father's house to the land that I will show you." While the Bible does not make mention of a religious disagreement between Abraham and his father like that found in the Qurʾan, it nonetheless describes a clean break from his surroundings that moves from the general to the specific. Abraham is ordered to leave his land ("country"), relatives ("kindred") and nuclear family ("father's house") as he journeys in faith to an uncertain future, and this captures well the result of the dispute with his father in the Qurʾan. Similarly, in each case the deity is the cause of Abraham leaving his homeland. In the Islamic text his fidelity to the religion of Allah causes him to withdraw from his father's people, while in Genesis he responds to God's command to uproot himself and travel to parts unknown.

A more subtle, but extremely important, similarity between the two texts relates to a theological point each makes that has to do with the belief that the deity is not limited to a particular land or locale. In Genesis, God speaks to Abraham in Haran in Mesopotamia and tells him to travel to the Promised Land of Canaan, a distance of several hundred miles. But before he settles there, Abraham is forced to journey further south to Egypt due to a famine (Gen 12:10-20). The text explains how God continues to be with Abraham while he is in Egypt and this further reinforces the idea of the deity's presence and involvement in events outside the Promised Land. This theme becomes a critical one later on in the biblical story when, in the sixth century B.C.E., the Israelites lose the land during the period known as the Babylonian Exile and this experience raises many questions about the relationship between God and the land. We see the answers to many of those questions anticipated here in the Abraham story where God's power and influence is not limited to Canaan.

This same theme is present in the Qur'an text which explains how Allah is not tied to a particular place or area but can be worshiped anywhere. Abraham had been a devotee of Allah among his father's people, but when they refused to heed his call to conversion he left them for someplace else where he could continue to follow the straight path. This is in agreement with Muslim understanding of the nature of the deity. As the supreme authority and power in creation, Allah is not confined to one people or limited to one place and this Abrahamic tradition illustrates that belief.

In with the New

Critiquing the false worship of his people is only one aspect of Abraham's role in the Qur'an. He is also frequently depicted as instituting the proper religious belief and practice that are meant to take the place of a polytheistic, idolatrous system. In these passages, he is once again presented as the prototypical Muslim, functioning as a model for all later-day believers who struggle to maintain their Islamic identity in the face of social and religious forces that oppose their faith. As we have already seen, his role as reformer is one that Muhammad also shared and so it is not surprising that we find a great deal of overlap between the two figures in terms of the changes they introduce and the reasons behind them. In fact, in some texts the resemblances between the two are so strong that one could substitute Muhammad's name for that of Abraham and, except for minor details, the scene would fit perfectly well in the later context.

In the passage just considered from 19:41-50, Abraham withdraws from his father's people to avoid their idolatrous faith. Unlike in the biblical tradition, we are not told in that text where he journeys and eventually settles. This lack of information is undoubtedly due to the Qur'an's primary concern with the message or point of the passage and its relative lack of interest in what is considered to be secondary detail. But there are other texts which do give an indication of Abraham's destination and describe what he did upon arrival there. One such text is found in 14:37 where, after asking Allah to preserve him and his children from worshiping idols, Abraham discusses his new surroundings. "Our Lord, I have settled some of my offspring in a barren valley near Your sacred house in order that they might pray. So make the people's hearts incline toward them and provide for them from the fruit of the earth so that they may be thankful."

Several elements of this verse are significant but, unfortunately, they are not elaborated upon or explained. One is the reference to Abraham's settling near "Your sacred house" which seems to indicate a particular location that might be well known. A second interesting feature in this verse is the somewhat vague mention of prayer that raises some questions. What type of prayer is this? Is it a new form of worship? Is it done in or near the sacred house? Third, the reference to Abraham's offspring is an intriguing comment that also needs some answers. Who are these offspring? Why have only some been settled in the barren valley? Why does Abraham ask that the people's hearts be inclined toward them? These are all important issues that must be considered in order to properly understand Abraham's character in the Qur'an, but this verse is much too brief to adequately address them. Fortunately, 2:122-133 presents an expanded account which allows us to more fully understand this crucial episode in Abraham's life.

[122]Oh children of Israel! Remember My grace which I bestowed upon you, and that I set you above all creatures. [123]Beware a day when no soul shall compensate for another, nor shall any recompense be received from it, nor shall any intercession benefit it, nor shall they be aided.

[124]His Lord tested Abraham with commands and he fulfilled them. He said "I am making you a leader for humanity." And he said, "And from my offspring?" He (Allah) said, "My covenant does not apply to evil-doers." [125]We made the house a sanctuary and security for the people. Take the place of Abraham as a place of prayer! We made an agreement with Abraham and Ishmael to purify My house for those who circum-ambulate, the devout, and those who bow and prostrate. [126]Abraham said, "Lord, make this land secure and provide fruit to its inhabitants who believe in Allah and the last day." He (Allah) said, "I will make the unbeliever prosper for a while then I will lead him to the punishment of fire. How wretched will that fate be." [127]Abraham and Ishmael raised the foundations of the house saying, "Our Lord, accept it from us. You are the all-hearing one, the all-knowing one. [128]Our Lord, make us submis-sive to You and make of our offspring a community submissive to You. Show us our forms of worship and mercifully turn to us for You are the often-returning one, the merciful one. [129]Our Lord, send forth to them a messenger from among them who will recite Your revelations to them and teach them the book and wisdom so that he may purify them. You are truly the mighty one, the wise one." [130]Who but a fool would shun the community of Abraham? We chose him in this world and, surely, in the world to come he will be among the righteous. [131]When his Lord said to him, "Submit!" he said, "I have surrendered to the Lord of all crea-tures." [132]Abraham commanded his sons, as did Jacob, "Oh my sons, surely Allah has chosen the true religion for you, so remain in submis-sion until you die." [133]Were you witnesses when death came to Jacob and he said to his sons, "What will you worship when I am gone?" They said, "We will worship your God, the God of your fathers Abraham, Ishmael and Isaac, the one God. We submit ourselves to Him."

This is an important text for understanding the nature of the reform which the Qurʾan says Abraham introduced in the place of previous idol-atrous practices. A careful analysis of the vocabulary, themes, and char-acterization of the scene indicates that this religious system shares much in common with Islam and that, once again, Abraham is being presented as a precursor to Muhammad since his life's experiences adhere closely to those of the later prophet. A consideration of the three elements identi-fied above—place, prayer, and progeny—will make this connection clear.

1. Place

In this text Abraham, along with his son Ishmael, builds and puri-fies what is referred to as the "house of Allah." It is meant to be a sanc-tuary and place of security for those who walk around it, the devout, and those who bow and prostrate (v. 125). This has commonly been understood to be a reference to the Kaʿba, a cube-shaped structure in Mecca which has been the spiritual and geographic focal point of Islam virtually throughout its entire history. Today it is located in the center of the great mosque in Mecca, and all Muslims throughout the world are required to face in its direction at five prescribed times throughout the course of each day as they fulfill their prayer obligation. The Kaʿba also figures prominently in the pilgrimage ritual which all Muslims are encouraged to complete. Each year during the month of pilgrimage millions of pilgrims journey to Saudi Arabia to participate in these activities which include circumambulation around the Kaʿba and other rituals within the great mosque at Mecca.

The Kaʿba building has undergone modifications over the centuries and its exact age is unknown, but it is generally agreed that its reputation as a sacred space and pilgrimage site predates Islam considerably. There are many traditions and legends about the polytheistic nature of worship at the place prior to the coming of Islam, and one well-known story claims that 360 different idols were associated with the Kaʿba. Toward the end of his life Muhammad returned to Mecca in order to bring its inhabitants into the growing Islamic fold and the early biographies and other accounts describe in dramatic detail how he destroyed all the pagan statues in the Kaʿba and dedicated it to the worship of Allah. Despite his rejection of the gods of the Meccans, Muhammad still incorporated a number of their practices and rituals into Islam and the pilgrimage appears to be a prime example of this. Many scholars believe the Muslim form of pilgrimage is modeled very closely on the pre-Islamic one and contains many elements of the earlier ritual. Muhammad's decision to maintain close ties with a place and practices that were so clearly identified with polytheism may strike us as a strange one given the radical monotheism he preached and this may well have been a controversial issue for the early community.

It is in light of this controversy that we might best be able to understand the connection the Qurʾan draws between Abraham and the Kaʿba. His role in erecting the shrine gives the site an undeniably monotheistic origin that, according to Islam, was abandoned during the centuries of idolatrous worship but eventually was retrieved with the coming of Muhammad. Viewed from this perspective, Muhammad's preservation of the pilgrimage and other practices connected with the Kaʿba is not only understandable but necessary since by doing so he was able to restore them to their proper form and dignity.

Abraham's role in the history of the Kaʿba therefore serves to explain and legitimate the building's importance for Islam. This point is made in the text in verse 125 which says, "Take the place of Abraham as a place of prayer!" This command was interpreted literally by the Muslim community, and even today there is a location near the Kaʿba called the "place of Abraham" *(maqām ibrāhīm)*, which is a small building containing a stone upon which is the impression of two human feet. Abraham is believed to have stood on this stone while building the Kaʿba and the outline of his feet was miraculously preserved on it. The legitimating function of Abraham for later Islamic practice is also seen in the mention of those who will circumambulate and prostrate at Allah's house. These actions are part of the pilgrimage ritual at Mecca, and the reference to their existence during Abraham's time indicates that they were practiced much earlier, and in a more proper fashion, than they were during the polytheistic period prior to Muhammad. Indeed, elsewhere in the Qurʾan Allah explicitly commands Abraham to "proclaim the pilgrimage to people" (22:27). Undeniably, the Qurʾan's description of Abraham's role in the establishment of the house of Allah has had a profound impact on Islamic belief and practice.

2. Prayer

The Qurʾan understands the house of Allah to be a place of prayer, and the references to bowing and prostrating, which are essential components of Muslim prayer, as well as the mention of the circumambulation around the Kaʿba that is a part of the pilgrimage ritual all reinforce this connection. But this text does more than simply theoretically discuss the importance of prayer at the Kaʿba. It also explains what true prayer is by citing examples of it on the lips of important individuals. The passage contains two explicit prayers and a third statement of faith that functions as a type of prayer. A careful reading of these sections reveals the vital purpose they serve for the Muslim community.

The first prayer mentioned is that of Abraham in verse 126, "Lord, make this land secure and provide fruit to its inhabitants who believe in Allah and the last day." Here, the patriarch calls upon the deity to protect the area of Mecca and certain of its inhabitants. This petition is made immediately after the reference to Abraham and his son purifying the house of Allah for proper worship, and this cleansing action bears a similarity to what Muhammad did upon reclaiming Mecca and the Kaʿba for Islam. By destroying all idols and removing every vestige of paganism from the area, Muhammad purified the site by eliminating the obstacles that prevented faith in Allah. We see Abraham under-taking the same activity here in a way that once again establishes him as Muhammad's prototype. This link is made more obvious by the way Abraham limits divine protection to only Meccans who believe in Allah and the last day. These are central articles of faith for all Muslims, and the two topics of Allah and the last day were frequent themes of Muhammad's message, particularly early in his career as he sought to convert Mecca. This prayer continues the pattern of tracing the roots of these basic Islamic principles back to the time of Abraham.

The same thing is found in a more obvious and detailed way when we examine the second, lengthier, prayer which is uttered by Abraham and Ishmael in verses 127–129. This prayer is actually three separate petitions, each with the same three-part structure. Each petition begins with the identical address ("our Lord"), followed by the appeal or re-quest that is being made, and concluding with a statement of faith in Allah that identifies two qualities of the divine nature. For our pur-poses, the middle section which expresses the heart of the petition is the most important element, but a recognition of the overall structure of the passage can contribute to an appreciation of the literary artistry of the Qurʾan. In outline form, with the object of the request in bold type, the pattern is the following:

	First Petition (v. 127)	Second Petition (v. 128)	Third Petition (v. 129)
Address	Our Lord	Our Lord	Our Lord
Request	Accept **it** from us	1) Make **us** submissive 2) Make **them** submissive	Send **them** a messenger
Statement of Faith	the all-hearing one the all-knowing one	the often-returning one the merciful one	the mighty one the wise one

We can discern a clear movement within this set of requests in terms of their intended object or beneficiary. The first petition is con-cerned with the Kaʿba itself. After building the structure, Abraham and Ishmael desire that it be deemed acceptable by the deity and so they humbly implore that Allah look favorably on their work. With the sec-ond petition we see a shift of focus to the human as Abraham and his son ask that first they themselves, and then their offspring, be made submissive to Allah. The third petition concerns their offspring exclu-sively and requests that a messenger be sent to them so that they might be instructed and purified through divine revelation.

The structure of this triple petition is quite interesting in that Abraham and Ishmael are in the pivotal middle position as the focus shifts from the Ka'ba, through them, and to their descendants. We might say that their offspring are the equivalent of the Ka'ba since they, like the building, are the "work" of Abraham and his son. Just as the two pray that the inanimate work of their hands, the Ka'ba, be acceptable to Allah as a place of worship, so they also pray that the animate fruit of their labor, their offspring, be an equally suitable locus of faith. The reference to the offspring being "purified" is especially interesting in this regard since that is precisely what Abraham and Ishmael were instructed to do to the Ka'ba in order to make it ready (v. 125).

A very important aspect of this second prayer is the high concentration of Islamic language and themes that it employs. We see this, for example, in the third part of each petition where two attributes of Allah are identified. The Qur'an contains many such titles for the deity, each of which acknowledges some quality that Allah possesses perfectly. In Muslim piety and practice, these titles have been identified with what are called "the names of Allah" in several places in the Qur'an. "Allah, there is no god but He. His are the most beautiful names" (20:8). Over time, a tradition developed that Allah possesses ninety-nine beautiful names and many of them, including the six mentioned in this passage, are taken from the Qur'an. A very popular practice among Muslims is the recitation of these divine names, and it is common in the Islamic world to see someone fingering their prayer beads while quietly invoking Allah's names. This passage has Abraham and his son engage in this very practice of calling upon Allah's names in their prayer and gives them the appearance of pious Muslims.

Several other obvious allusions to Islamic thought are found in the second and third petitions of Abraham and Ishmael. In verse 128 they ask that they and their offspring might be made submissive to Allah. The words translated "submissive" come from the Arabic verb ʾaslama which, as we have already seen, is the verb from which the words "islam" and "muslim" are derived. In effect, Abraham and his son are requesting that they and their descendants might become adherents to Islam and this is seen especially clearly in the supplication regarding themselves where they literally ask to be made "muslims." Read in this light, verse 131 might be understood as a description of Abraham's conversion as a *ḥanīf* when he adopted the monotheistic faith centering on submission to the divine will that predated Islam.

Their third petition in verse 129 is fascinating since it is obviously an allusion to the coming of Muhammad. Abraham and Ishmael plea that a messenger possessing divine revelation be sent to their offspring to teach them the book and wisdom. No person fits this job description better than Muhammad, and when we keep in mind the Meccan location of the scene and the reference to the messenger coming from "among them" the identity of the individual is beyond doubt. The role that Abraham plays in legitimating and affirming the prophetic career of Muhammad could not be any more obvious than it is in this verse. Centuries before the emergence of Islam, Abraham, desiring himself to be a "muslim," is at the Kaʿba in Mecca praying that Allah will send Muhammad as a messenger.

The third text to consider (vv. 132–133), which contains a statement of faith rather than a prayer, maintains this same focus while addressing the situation of later generations. It recounts how both Abraham and Jacob urge their offspring to submit themselves to the religion of Allah and how the younger generation willingly accepts this charge. "We will worship your God, the God of your fathers Abraham, Ishmael and Isaac, the one God. We submit ourselves to Him." It, too, makes use of vocabulary that is built on the Arabic verb *ʾaslama* and concludes with the sons of Jacob proclaiming themselves "muslims." In this way, the passage informs the reader that the prayer of Abraham and Ishmael in verse 128 that their offspring might be a community submissive to Allah was heard and answered affirmatively. The faith statement of Jacob's offspring therefore conforms well to the pattern established by the two prayers of Abraham and Ishmael as an expression of submission to and faith in Allah.

3. Progeny

Abraham is venerated as an ancestor by adherents of all three monotheistic religions. The Jewish community reads the biblical account of his life found in Genesis 12–25 with particular emphasis on the covenant God established with him and the promise of the land as a visible sign of that covenant. For them, Abraham is the one to whom God first revealed the election of Israel as a chosen people and he is consequently the one to whom they trace their origin. The Hebrew Bible supports this by presenting the early history of the community as the story of one family. The twelve tribes of Israel are named after the twelve sons of Jacob/Israel, who himself was Abraham's grandson. Christians also claim to be of Abraham's lineage, but they understand their connection with him to be primarily one of faith rather than due to any direct genealogical descent. In his willingness to accept and believe God's word that he would be the father of many despite his and Sarah's advanced ages, and in his unswerving obedience in offering Isaac as a sacrifice to God (Gen 22:1-19), Christians see a model and prototype for their own faith lives. This idea is summed up well in Galatians 3:6, "Just as Abraham believed God and it was reckoned to him as righteousness so, you see, those who believe are descendants of Abraham."

Muslims likewise view Abraham as an ancestor, and the text we have been studying makes this point very clearly. The Qurʾan presents him as someone who played a vital role in the history and development of Islam because he built the Kaʿba in Mecca, called the people to pilgrimage there, and prayed for the coming of Muhammad. Similarly, his desire to be one who submits himself completely to Allah makes him someone worthy of emulation. But the text does not limit Abraham's influence to the Islamic community alone. In verse 124 Allah tells him, "I am making you a leader for humanity." The Arabic word for "leader" here, *imām*, refers to someone who is to be not only followed, but imitated, because he or she possesses outstanding qualities. Abraham is designated an exemplar whose influence is universal and not the exclusive property of one group or people.

But widespread significance does not necessarily mean widespread acceptance. The passage is quick to point out that not all people have chosen to embrace Abraham as the standard to be followed. According to Islam, all are called to submit themselves to Allah as he did, but not all respond affirmatively to that call. Only those who do so are the true offspring of Abraham. That is why when Abraham queries Allah about his descendants the deity tells him, "My covenant does not apply to evildoers" (v. 124). This is an important text for understanding Islam's notion of covenant, which is not the same as that found in the Hebrew Bible where God establishes a special bond with the people of Israel that will never be broken. In verse 122 Allah addresses the children of Israel and tells them to remember "that I set you above all creatures." This sounds very much like the biblical theme of the election of Israel as God's chosen people, and this text suggests that the Qurʾan does allow for the possibility of such a special status. But when we interpret it in light of Allah's words to Abraham that the covenant does not apply to evildoers we see that it does not impart a permanent or immutable special status. According to the Qurʾan and Islamic belief, the children of Israel, like all people, can enjoy the rewards of a covenantal relationship with Allah but this is possible only when they live their lives in conformance with Islam. Because Jews and Christians do not submit themselves to Allah and fail to heed divine revelation as it was originally transmitted to their prophets, they are not truly offspring of Abraham.

Abraham's descendants in faith are not the only progeny mentioned in this text since it makes explicit reference to his biological offspring when it identifies his son Ishmael in several places. He is, of course, also a biblical figure of some importance but the trajectory of his life and career is presented in markedly different ways in the two texts. A consideration of some of these differences can tell us much about this intriguing character's importance for Islam.

In 14:39 Abraham expresses thanks to Allah for the birth of his two sons. "Praise be to Allah who has given to me, in spite of old age, Ishmael and Isaac." As in this text, whenever the two sons are mentioned together in the Qur'an, Ishmael is given pride of place as the first one named (2:133, 140; 3:84; 4:163). This superiority is reflected in the fact that he plays a more prominent role throughout the text than Isaac does. Isaac is mentioned by name some fifteen times in the Qur'an, but many of these passages simply refer to him as one member in a list of other important figures or explain how Allah gave him to Abraham and his wife. He is never explicitly depicted as a significant actor in a way that is comparable to Ishmael. Ishmael plays a more dominant role than his brother in helping their father establish authentic monotheism and this is vividly portrayed by his contribution in building the house of Allah.

This portrayal is notably different from the way in which the story of the two brothers is related in the Hebrew Bible. In Genesis, and in the Judeo-Christian tradition generally, Isaac, not Ishmael, is the true heir who takes up his father's mantle. Their Qur'anic situation is reversed as Ishmael is the more marginal figure who leads a somewhat shadowy existence and the story becomes Isaac's. According to the biblical account, Ishmael has a very ambiguous position in the family from the outset since his mother is the maidservant of Abraham's wife Sarah. Even before he is born, his pregnant mother Hagar is forced to temporarily flee into the wilderness to escape the anger of her mistress (Genesis 16). This is a foreshadowing of the permanent separation that occurs when Sarah convinces Abraham to banish Hagar and her son after the birth of Isaac, the child of the covenant (Gen 21:8-21). The Bible reader is left with the impression that Ishmael, the son not chosen, was cut off from the family and led a nomadic existence. The text goes on to recount how he lived in the wilderness and became an expert with the bow and arrow (Gen

21:20). The only time we are told of any contact between him and his family occurs in Genesis 25:9 when Ishmael returns to perform his filial duty and, with Isaac, buries their father Abraham.

These elements are not found in the Qur'an which gives no hint of this fractured family history. Later Islamic tradition and commentary does discuss the expulsion of Hagar but with an interesting twist. Abraham does not send her and Ishmael into the wilderness alone, but accompanies them as far as Mecca where he leaves them in order to return to his family obligations. These sources go on to recount several subsequent visits to Mecca by Abraham, including one in which he and Ishmael erect the Ka'ba. But these expansions of the tradition are due to contact with Jewish sources and are not based on any evidence from the Qur'an.[10] No reference to Ishmael's mother is found anywhere in the text and it does not report any rift or estrangement between Ishmael and Isaac. This last point is particularly important because it highlights the different ways the two brothers' relationship functions in the Qur'an and the Bible. In the latter text, they give rise to two separate and distinct groups of people as Isaac becomes the ancestor of the Israelites while Ishmael is the father of the Ishmaelites, or Arabs. Eventually, the division was interpreted religiously as Isaac became identified with the Jewish/Christian line of Abraham's family and Ishmael with the Muslim line. But such distinctions are not warranted by the Qur'an since it never even remotely suggests that the sons of Abraham gave rise to an ethnic or religious divide. Rather, as we have seen, the two brothers are united in the Qur'an through their common faith and their family identity as sons of Abraham.

Whereas Genesis presents the story of Abraham's progeny as one in which God makes a choice for one side of the family (Isaac's) which automatically excludes the other (Ishmael's), no such divine favoritism is depicted in the Qur'an. In the Islamic text, the choice is up to the individual, not Allah. Abraham is sent as a leader for all humanity and each person must freely choose to accept his message and surrender to the divine will. Those who do so are offspring of Abraham and those who do not will join the ranks of the unbelievers.

For Islam, membership in the covenantal community has nothing to do with genealogy and everything to do with faith. This point is dramatically brought home when we compare the biblical and Qur'anic versions of the last words of Jacob, the grandson of Abraham. Genesis 49 describes Jacob on his death bed surrounded by his twelve sons, the ancestors of the twelve tribes of Israel. The purpose of this gathering is for information only. Jacob is about to announce what the future will hold for each of the twelve. "Gather around, that I may tell you what will happen to you in days to come" (Gen 49:1). One by one, he informs each of his fate as some will be rewarded and others punished. Throughout the entire scene not one of the sons ever responds or says a word to his father. Why bother, when things are already decided and there is no room for negotiation? The future of Jacob's family tree is in the hands of God and it has already been determined which branches will flourish and which will wither.

The parallel scene in the Qur'an presents a completely different picture in a much briefer form. "Were you witnesses when death came to Jacob and he said to his sons, 'What will you worship when I am gone?' They said, 'We will worship your God, the God of your fathers Abraham, Ishmael and Isaac, the one God. We submit ourselves to Him'" (2:133). Here, Jacob poses a question that initiates a conversation. Rather than telling his sons what the future is going to be he asks them what they intend to make of the future. That future is not a birthright, but a choice. He reminds them that they are the ones who are ultimately responsible for their own fate and that their response to his question will determine the course of their lives. Their answer to his question is equally revealing. Unlike their biblical counterparts, these brothers have a common future since they all respond together as a group united in their faith. By identifying the object of their faith as the God of their ancestors Abraham, Ishmael and Isaac they recognize that it is primarily that shared belief which makes them members of the same family. Their response expresses well the nexus between faith and family that is at the heart of Islam and helps to instill within it a strong sense of community. It is a community which traces its roots back to the time of Abraham the *ḥanīf* and continues to flourish through the faith of his progeny.

COOPERATING REVELATIONS

Perhaps the most well-known event in Abraham's life for Bible readers is his near-sacrifice of Isaac which is described in Genesis 22. That scene has been the subject of countless works of art which have attempted to capture the drama and intensity of the moment. Its function as an episode which provides insight into Abraham's character has also been cited frequently by preachers and teachers who try to interpret the text's relevance for modern audiences and explain how its message might be applied in their daily lives. It would not be an exaggeration to claim that this may well be one of the most famous scenes in all of biblical literature. Abraham's near-sacrifice of his son has been equally influential within Islam and an account of the event is given in the Qur'an at 37:100-112.

> [100](Abraham prayed,) "My Lord, grant me one from among the righteous." [101]So We gave him the good news of a mild-tempered son. [102]When he was old enough to work with him he said, "Oh my son, I have dreamed that I should sacrifice you. What do you think of that?" He said, "Oh my father, do what you have been commanded. If Allah wills, you will find me patient." [103]When they both submitted and he threw him face down [104]We called to him, "Oh Abraham, [105]you have fulfilled the dream. Thus do We reward those who do good." [106]Truly, that was a clear test [107]and We ransomed him with a great sacrifice. [108]Through the succeeding generations we left upon him the salutation: [109]"Peace be upon Abraham!" [110]Thus do We reward those who do good. [111]Truly, he was among our believing servants. [112]And We gave him the good news of Isaac, a prophet from among the righteous.

Analysis of the Qur'anic Tradition

This text, while clearly a parallel to the account given in Genesis 22, presents a distinctively Qur'anic version of the event. A relative lack of narrative detail is something we have come to expect in the Qur'an and this passage does not disappoint us in that regard. Several of the features which make the biblical tradition such a compelling story and help it achieve a sense of drama and tension are not present here. We are not told, for example, where the near-sacrifice occurs or if the father and son have to journey to get to the location. The Genesis description of Abraham cutting the wood, loading the donkey, bringing his servants and wielding the knife over his son all contribute to the power of the biblical account but are not found here. Once again, this difference is best understood in light of the Qur'an's primary interest in the message or meaning of a text, its preference for purpose over plot.

Perhaps the largest gap in the reader's knowledge involves the identity of the son since the text does not tell us his name or clearly distinguish him. The resulting ambiguity has led to much discussion among commentators throughout history since, as we have seen, both Ishmael and Isaac play prominent roles in the Qur'an as Abraham's sons. Early on, most scholars favored the view that Isaac was the intended victim but, over time, more came to hold the position that it was Ishmael and this is the dominant view in Islam today. The text itself offers no help in solving the problem although verse 112 might furnish a key to interpretation.

There are at least two possible ways of understanding how this verse is related to what comes before it. If we read the entire passage sequentially, then the reference to Allah announcing the birth of Isaac would come after the near sacrifice and Ishmael would have to be the intended victim. If, on the other hand, verse 112 is not meant as a coda or conclusion to the story but somehow summarizes it, then Isaac is the likely candidate as the anonymous son. One clue which might favor the latter alternative is found in verse 100 when Abraham prays for a child who will be "righteous" and Allah responds with the news of a son. This adjective is the identical one used to describe Isaac in verse 112 and this echo is an argument in support of seeing him as the intended sacrifice. As interesting as this question might be, it should not be a major concern for us. The Qur'an has chosen not to name the son and its silence on the matter suggests that his identity is not an important factor in uncovering the meaning of the passage.

A possible reason for the Qur'an's reticence in identifying the intended victim is that he does not have the same theological function in the Qur'an that he does in the Bible. We have seen that a major theme in the biblical treatment of Abraham's sons is the divine choice of Isaac over Ishmael as the one who continues the covenantal relationship. In Genesis, Abraham is being asked to sacrifice the chosen son, the one through whom he has been told the promise will be realized. This aspect is expressed several times, both before and after the near-sacrifice, when Isaac is referred to as "your son, your only son" (Gen 22:2, 12), and when God restates the covenant to Abraham after he has passed the test (22:15-19). Because neither son is the sole heir of the promise in the Qur'an and Allah does not prefer one over the other, this is not an element of its version of the event. Both Ishmael and Isaac are esteemed equally in the Qur'an and each is held up as a model of faith for the reader, so it is inconsequential which one was almost killed by his father. The important thing for the Qur'an is that Abraham almost did it, not the identity of the one he almost did it to.

Although we do not know who he is we do know certain things about the son which are important to the plot and make him a focal point in the development of the story. The most important piece of information is found in verse 102 where we are told he was old enough to work with his father. The Arabic word for this concept, *sa'ya*, is a rich one that can have a number of possible meanings. A very common one is "to be active or busy" and a meaning related to this is "to be able to engage in an occupation or activity with energy." This idea is the basis of the translation proposed here, but there is another well-attested meaning which emphasizes more the mental, even moral, capacity of a person. The word can also mean "to occupy oneself according to one's own judgment, discretion or free will," and this sense may also be operative in the description of Abraham's son in this text. If we focus on this latter meaning, the word *saʿya* might indicate that the son has reached the age of reason and is able to evaluate things for himself. In other words, the verse is saying he has not only developed physically enough to be able to work with and assist his father, but he also possesses the intellectual maturity necessary to be able to think for himself, judge his situation and reach reasonable conclusions in a way comparable to Abraham.

The son exhibits this very quality when his father tells him about the dream he has had and then asks him his opinion on it. In effect, Abraham wants him to reflect on this dream and consider its significance. An interesting aspect of this scene is we are not told exactly when Abraham had this dream. Is this a recent experience for him or one he had long ago? This is quite different from the biblical version where God commands the patriarch to sacrifice Isaac and Abraham wakes up early the next morning to carry out his charge (Gen 22:1-3). In the Qurʾan, there might have been a period of time between the dream itself and Abraham's mention of it, and this lag makes sense if we keep in mind the double meaning of the word *saʿya*. The text might mean that when his son had reached the age of reason Abraham asked his opinion on a dream he had had some time ago. His son's answer to the question is immediate and unambiguous: since Allah has commanded the sacrifice it must be carried out. This response highlights the role the son's faith plays in informing his rational power. He is thinking as one who has truly surrendered himself to the will of Allah. Abraham then takes his son's lead as the text goes on to say that "they both submitted."

This passage is as much about the son's faith as it is about Abraham's. Beyond that, it suggests that the father's faith is dependent upon the son's. Abraham has had a dream which he finds difficult to understand and impossible to carry out so he turns to his son for assistance in making sense of it. His son's direct and faithful response becomes a catalyst for the father that enables him to accept the divine will as readily as his offspring has. It is no coincidence that they both submit only after his son has answered Abraham's question. The reader cannot help but wonder if Abraham would have been able to carry out the near-sacrifice without his son's faith. In this way, Abraham's question "What do you think of that?" serves to call forth first the faith of the son and then his own.

The Qur'an agrees with the Bible on the idea that the near-sacrifice is some kind of divine test but this theme is presented in a different way here. The reader of Genesis is told in the very first verse that God is about to test Abraham (22:1), while the Qur'an does not divulge this information until after the scene has been described (v. 106).[11] But who is being tested in the Qur'an? The text never makes this clear. Most likely, the reader is expected to come to the realization that both father and son have been tested. Abraham experiences a troubling dream that torments him as a parent and a believer in Allah, but in the end he is able to meet the challenge and demonstrate his trust in the deity. But this expression of faith would not have been possible if his son had not first passed his own test. By accepting his father's invitation to consider and evaluate his dream and by interpreting it as a command from Allah, Abraham's son took the initial leap of faith that allowed both of them to respond as ideal Muslims and submit themselves entirely.

Application to the Biblical Tradition

The Qur'an's version of the scene of the near-sacrifice invites us to reread the biblical account through Isaac's eyes in order to better understand what his role is in Genesis. The main theme and focus of the Islamic text raise several interesting questions about the Hebrew Bible story. Is this a testing of both Abraham and Isaac? Does Isaac somehow help bring his father to faith? Does the Genesis story tell us anything about the son's faith? Such questions are important ones but are often not asked by Bible readers who reflect on the significance of Genesis 22.

The reason for their lack of attention to these components of the text is at least partly due to the way the story is recounted. We have already observed how the biblical description, as is typical, contains a great deal of narrative detail that is absent from the Qur'an's version. Almost all of this detail concerns the character of Abraham as it is explained what he says, does, sees, hears and learns. The plot unfolds primarily from his perspective, with the result that the reader views this as a story about Abraham and rarely stops to consider the purpose or perspective of the other characters. In Genesis, we have very little idea of what Isaac thinks or feels about the events as they unfold and, consequently, he tends to retreat into the background as a figure who is necessary but nondescript. But such a limited view of Isaac's character causes us to miss certain elements of the biblical tradition and this can ultimately prevent us from appreciating the richness and complexity of its presentation. A consideration of the biblical story with the Qur'anic tradition in mind helps to bring Isaac out of the shadows and underscores his vital function in Genesis 22.

The Bible does not tell us Isaac's exact age when he is almost sacrificed by his father but he is clearly no toddler. An indication of the degree of his physical development is seen in his ability to walk some distance with a load of firewood after journeying several days with the traveling party (Gen 22:4-6). The Qur'an also draws attention to this aspect of the character but, as we have seen, uses a word that also connotes a level of intellectual maturity that allows the son to use his reasoning power and this ability proves crucial for himself and his father. Is the same thing operative here in Genesis? Does Isaac act as a catalyst for his father's faith? A careful reading of the text suggests that he does indeed, and a comparison with the Qur'an's version of the scene points out some intriguing similarities between the two regarding how his son assists in Abraham's spiritual development.

We noted how the linchpin of the Qur'an episode is Abraham's question to his son, "What do you think of that?," regarding the dream he has had that he is to offer his offspring as a sacrifice. The son's answer simultaneously expresses his own faith in Allah and challenges his father to adopt the same posture of trust and confidence. This is the only conversation between the two that the text relates. Interestingly, Genesis 22 also reports only one verbal encounter between father and son and it, too, is in the form of a question and answer. Only this time it is Isaac who asks the question while Abraham responds. "Isaac said to his father Abraham, 'Father!' And he said, 'Here I am, my son.' He said, 'The fire and the wood are here, but where is the lamb for a burnt offering?' Abraham said, 'God himself will provide the lamb for a burnt offering, my son'" (vv. 7–8).

We should not mistake this exchange for small chitchat as the two make their way to the place of sacrifice. Rather, it offers us an important glimpse into the characters of both father and son. This is the only time Isaac speaks in Genesis 22, and his words inform the reader that, just as in the Qur'an, he is able to evaluate his situation through exercising his powers of reason. As he hauls the wood, he observes that his father is bringing the fire and knife, and he realizes that something essential, the sacrificial victim, is missing. We also learn much about Abraham through his response to Isaac's question. Though he speaks several other times throughout the chapter and the scene is described primarily from his perspective, this is the only time we find an explicit articulation of his faith in God on his own lips.

Once again, his son says something that enables Abraham to respond in faith. In the Qurʾan, it is the son's response to Abraham's question that makes this possible. Here it is Isaac's question that causes Abraham to publicly profess his trust in God. When reading the biblical account it is easy to miss this point since the narrative is slowly building toward the climax when Abraham will kill his son. The reader is caught up in the growing tension and drama as that horrible outcome is anticipated. But reading Genesis with the Qurʾan's account as background allows us to stop and ponder the importance of Isaac's question and the implication of his father's answer. This enables us to recognize the profound point being made and the fascinating connection between the two traditions: Isaac's question has served as the catalyst to bring his father Abraham to faith.

A critique of this last statement is possible. It could be said that, even if there has been no explicit acknowledgment of it, Abraham must already possess faith prior to this point since he has responded affirmatively to God's command and has not wavered in obeying the divine will. The text seems to support this reading but it also contains some clues which suggest that Abraham's faith after Isaac's question is different than what it was before. In verse 5 Abraham instructs the young men traveling with him, "Stay here with the donkey; the boy and I will go over there; we will worship, and then we will come back to you." His statement that he and Isaac will return together after worshiping is a curious one given Abraham's knowledge of what is supposed to happen on the distant hill. After sacrificing his son how could he possibly return with him? There are at least two ways of interpreting Abraham's words here. On the one hand, they could be indicative of a belief that God will not allow him to kill his son, but will intervene before the act can be completed. In other words, Abraham might be anticipating an outcome that is identical to the one that is found in the text. In that case, his words would be a statement of complete and total trust in God. On the other hand, we can also understand his words to mean that Abraham thinks he will find it impossible to carry out the divine command to sacrifice his son. As much as he might desire to obey God's will, he believes he will be unable to do so and will return with his son to the others in the traveling party. In that case, his words would be a statement of his lack of faith and inability to completely trust God.

If we adopt the latter alternative, that at this point in the narrative Abraham is still struggling with the divine order to kill Isaac, then his response to his son's question indicates a change within him and a movement toward trust and faith in God. Isaac's question then becomes the critical point at which Abraham is forced to respond one way or another to the difficult task with which he has been charged. Without that call to accountability on his son's part, Abraham might not have found the faith needed to raise the knife to Isaac's neck.

Following this interpretation, what occurs at the scene of sacrifice takes on added meaning. In verse 9 we are told that Abraham bound Isaac prior to placing him on top of the wood. There are several possible reasons behind the action of binding his son, perhaps the most logical being that he did not want Isaac to run away or escape his fiery fate. If so, Abraham is here expressing such supreme trust in God that he does not even want to take the chance of Isaac's natural instinct for survival preventing the realization of the divine will. The description of Abraham binding Isaac comes immediately after the statement of faith that responds to his son's question and might therefore be understood as an expression or illustration of that complete faith. By fettering his son, Abraham acknowledges that the lamb God will provide might, in fact, be his own son and he accepts that possible outcome.

Without doubt, the biblical account of Abraham's near-sacrifice of his son is a story about his faith, but attention to Isaac's function in the scene helps us see that Abraham's is an evolving, developing faith. The key moment is Isaac's question to his father regarding the intended victim, and this query leads to the chapter's only unequivocal statement of faith on the patriarch's part. Prior to this we can discern hesitancy on his part to carry out the divine command, but after he answers Isaac's question and publicly expresses his trust in God he does all he can to insure the realization of the divine will. This dimension of the biblical story might easily escape our notice were it not for its high profile in the version found in the Qurʾan.

NOTES: CHAPTER 3

[1] There is some evidence to suggest that prior to adopting the name "Islam" the religion of Muhammad was called *hanifiyya*. This underscores the close connection, to be explained below, between the faiths of Abraham and Muhammad.

[2]An interesting exception to this is seen in 21:71, which states that Abraham and Lot were delivered to the land which Allah had blessed for the peoples.

[3]As we have seen, an important component of the biblical passage is the discussion between Lot and the messengers over where he should flee. The Qur'an passage does not recount that scene, but there is an intriguing connection with it nonetheless when the messengers ask Lot "Is the morning not near?" (v. 81). This echoes his comments to them regarding the city to which he wishes to escape in Genesis 19:20: "Look, that city is near enough to flee to, and it is a little one. Let me escape there—is it not a little one?—and my life will be saved!"

[4]The visit from the messengers is an episode which is recounted in several different versions in the Qur'an. See, for example, 15:51-77 and 51:24-37, for other texts that tell the same story in slightly different form. The latter text is particularly interesting for the way it Islamizes the tradition. There, the general plot is the same as that of sura 11 but Lot is not mentioned by name and in verse 36 his family is referred to as the only house in the city in which "submitters" lived. The Arabic word used to describe them is *muslimūn* ("muslims") which, of course, creates a direct link between the faithful family of Lot and the later Islamic community.

[5]Fazlur Rahman discusses this phenomenon when speaking of other prophetic figures in his *Major Themes of the Qur'an* (Chicago: Bibliotheca Islamica, 1980) where he states, "Not only were the points and lessons of those stories (of other prophets) transformed through revelation but often their content as well. Shu'aib is represented as admonishing his people against fraudulent forms of commerce—which was Muhammad's problem at Mecca; Noah is seen rejecting the demands of the powerful in his community that he dissociate himself from his socioeconomically weak followers before the powerful would join his religion—a situation which, of course, Muhammad himself was facing in Mecca. And so on" (136).

[6]Other passages that treat the theme are found in 6:74-84, 21:51-75, and 26:69-104. Each of the texts is slightly different from the others and contains details on such matters as the type of idol worship engaged in, the people's reaction to Abraham, and Abraham as the quintessential good Muslim.

[7]For a concise treatment of Muhammad's Meccan enemies and the opposition he encountered there see W. Montgomery Watt, *Muhammad at Mecca* (Oxford: Oxford University Press, 1953) 100–36.

[8]The reference to both Isaac and Jacob in this verse has generated some discussion among commentators regarding the degree of relationship between them. In several other suras which, like this one, are from the earlier, Meccan period they are also mentioned in a way which might suggest they are both sons of Abraham (6:84; 11:70; 21:71; 29:27). This goes against the biblical view

which presents them being from three different generations with Jacob as Abraham's grandson.

[9]Certain features of the description of Abraham and his message in the Qurʾan bear a striking resemblance to the later biblical prophets. In the present text, his admonition to his father in verse 41 against worshiping something that cannot see, hear or help in any way is reminiscent of similar messages found in the writings of the prophets as seen, for example, in Isaiah 44:9-20.

[10]Despite the lack of any support for it in the Qurʾan, the tradition of Hagar and the child Ishmael being abandoned in Mecca has been very influential in Islam. A required component of the pilgrimage ritual calls for each participant to run back and forth seven times between two locations and this is meant to recall the actions of the panic-stricken Hagar in the desert as she searched for water for herself and her son. Similarly, tradition has it that the well of Zamzam, located near the Kaʿba, first sprung up when the child Ishmael scratched on the ground while his mother looked for water.

[11]The translation understands the statement "Truly, that was a clear test" as a comment addressed to the reader, but it is also grammatically possible that it continues Allah's words to Abraham which would then extend through verse 107.

4

Moses

M oses is the most frequently cited individual in the Qurʾan, and the description of his life there shares much in common with that of the other biblical figures we have already considered. He is presented as a special person who enjoyed a unique relationship with Allah and who can serve as a model of faith for others. Similar to Noah and Abraham, the Moses of the Qurʾan is sent by Allah to confront his unbelieving contemporaries and, like theirs, his warnings and admonitions fall on deaf ears. One important difference with Moses is that the Qurʾan contains more narrative on him than it does for the other biblical figures. This can be both helpful and confusing for the Bible reader. On the one hand, the text contains a great deal of information on events in Moses' life which parallels the biblical account. This creates an impression of familiarity with the material since the Bible reader is acquainted with large portions of it. On the other hand, the differences with the biblical tradition are profound enough to be unsettling for the reader who is accustomed to that version of the story. In places, the Qurʾan's presentation of the life of Moses is frustratingly incomplete in comparison with the one in the Hebrew Bible. Elsewhere, the presence of multiple versions of the same episode in the Qurʾan can leave the Bible reader wondering what the relationships among these various narratives are. This fascinating mix of familiarity and foreignness makes the work of sorting through and understanding the Qurʾan's portrait of Moses all the more complex and exacting.

A PROPHET WITH A BOOK

A brief summary of some of the key elements of the Moses figure in the Qur'an is found in 19:51-53. "Remember Moses in the book. Truly, he was a chosen one, a messenger, a prophet. We called him from the right side of the mount and drew him near in communion. We gave him, out of Our mercy, his brother Aaron, a prophet." In this text, we have an explicit reference to Moses' status as a prophetic messenger and this puts him squarely in the line of other such figures in the Qur'an like Abraham and Noah. In addition, other aspects of this passage conform well to the biblical account of Moses' life. Specifically, the mention of the mount recalls the prominent part that the giving of the Law at Mount Sinai plays in the Hebrew Bible. Similarly, the idea that Moses and Allah communed privately is consistent with the recurring biblical theme that God's will for the Israelites was often disclosed to Moses through intimate encounters with the deity that were off-limits for the rest of the people. Also, the reference in this text to Aaron being involved in Moses' career is analogous to his function in the Hebrew Bible where Aaron is frequently depicted as a partner in his brother's activities.

Throughout the pages of the Qur'an we find references to and descriptions of some of the key events in Moses' life and many of these have biblical counterparts. One such episode which is cited frequently in the Islamic text and is central to the Bible is the Exodus during which Moses led his people out of the land of Egypt.

> [5]And We sent Moses with Our signs (saying), "Bring your people out of the darkness into the light and remind them of Allah's days." Truly, in that there are signs for every patient and thankful person. [6]And Moses said to his people, "Remember Allah's graciousness upon you when He rescued you from Pharaoh's people who brought upon you evil punishment, killing your sons but letting your women live. In that was a great trial from your Lord" (14:5-6).

Many events connected with the Exodus, from Moses' initial confrontation with Pharaoh to his people's eventual safe passage, are described in the Qur'an in dramatic, gripping narratives. We will consider these and many other texts in this chapter as we attempt to understand the way Moses' character is drawn in the Qur'an and the reasons why the text presents him the way it does.

Perhaps the most important aspect of Moses' life in the Qur'an, one which sets him apart from the biblical figures we have studied up to this point, is his special status as the recipient of divine revelation which he communicated to his people in the form of a book. "We gave Moses the book and We made it a guidance for the children of Israel that they should not take a protector apart from Me" (17:2). According to the Qurʾan and Islamic theology, a small number of prophets have been entrusted with a written text that expresses a divine message which must be accepted as authoritative by the messenger's community. As this passage indicates, the book is to serve as a guidance for the people that instructs them on how to live their lives in accord with the divine will. Moses is one of these rare individuals who was called to be a messenger and, consequently, the Qurʾan pays a great deal of attention to the theme of the book and the reception it receives by the Israelites.

In order to facilitate our study and give some order to the many Moses traditions scattered throughout the Qurʾan we will adopt a chronological approach in this chapter by beginning with the narrative recounting Moses' birth and then moving on to treat other key moments in his life in the order in which they are found in the Hebrew Bible. Many of these texts are isolated passages no longer than a few verses in length, but there are some lengthier portions of the Qurʾan which present a sequential account of Moses' life. The reader interested in perusing one such longer text which contains virtually the entire story of Moses should refer to 20:9-99, portions of which are found in this chapter.

BIRTH

A Qurʾan text which narrates some important events connected with the birth of Moses is found in 28:3-13.

> [3]We relate to you in truth a story of Moses and Pharaoh for a people who believe. [4]Truly, Pharaoh was master over the land and divided its people into different groups. He weakened one group of them by slaying their sons and allowing their women to live. Truly, he was one of the evildoers. [5]We wished to show favor to those who were weakened in the land, to make them leaders and heirs [6]and to establish them in the land to make Pharaoh, Haman and their legions see from them that which they feared. [7]We announced to Moses' mother, "Suckle him, and if you fear for him toss him into the river. Do not fear or grieve, for We will restore him to you and make him one of the messengers." [8]Pharaoh's family picked him up and he became an enemy and cause of sorrow for them. Truly, Pharaoh, Haman and their legions were sinners. [9]Pharaoh's wife said, "He will be a joy for me and for you. Do not kill him. Perhaps

he will be of some use to us or we may take him as a son." They were not aware (of what was going to happen). [10]Moses' mother became anxious and she was about to reveal it had We not strengthened her heart in order that she might be a believer. [11]She said to his sister, "Follow him!" So she watched him from a distance and they were unaware. [12]We had already caused him to refuse the wetnurses so she said, "Shall I direct you to a household who will raise him for you and take care of him?" [13]Thus We returned him to his mother so that she might have joy and not grieve and in order that she might know that Allah's promise is true, although most do not know.

There is much here that agrees with the biblical account of Moses' birth found in Exodus 1:8–2:10. Among the most obvious similarities are the Egyptian setting, a ruthless Pharaoh, the river as the vehicle of the child's survival, the child's rescue by members of Pharaoh's family, and the return of the child to his mother through the agency of his sister. There are, however, some interesting differences in the details of the two texts. In the Qurʾan, it is Pharaoh's wife who plays a critical part in having the baby Moses accepted into the royal household, but in Exodus his daughter fills this role. His daughter's involvement in the story is further diminished in the Qurʾan when it says in verse 8 that Pharaoh's family rescued the child from the river. In the Hebrew Bible it is his daughter who finds and saves the child while she is bathing at the river. Similarly, the version of the story in Exodus describes Moses' mother returning the child to Pharaoh's daughter after he grows up, and the Egyptian woman taking him as her son.[1] The Qurʾan does not mention this detail in its account.

An intriguing difference between the biblical and Qurʾanic narratives is the presence of a character called Haman in the latter. He is mentioned by name twice in this text and four other times in the Qurʾan (28:38; 29:39; 40:24, 36) and in all of these occurrences he is associated with the figure of Pharaoh. He appears to function as a type of counselor or advisor for the Egyptian monarch, and this text with its reference to the "legions," or armies, of Pharaoh and Haman suggests a military dimension to his office. Fascinatingly, while he is absent from the Moses tradition in the Bible there is a figure of some importance with the same name in the book of Esther. There, Haman is a minister of the Persian king Ahasuerus and a mortal enemy of the Jews. In Esther 3:7-11 he convinces the king that all Jews living in the kingdom deserve to die due to their disobedience to royal authority. The connection between this figure and the Haman referred to in the Qurʾan has been the subject of some debate, and many scholars favor the view that the two texts are talking about the same individual but placing him in two different places and time periods.

The Haman texts of 28:38 and 40:36 in the Qurʾan illustrate a similar phenomenon since they appear to locate a biblical episode in a completely different context. In these passages there is a probable allusion to the tower of Babel tradition found in Genesis 11:1-9. "Pharaoh said, 'Oh nobles, I know of no other god for you except myself. So, oh Haman, burn for me clay (bricks) and make for me a tower so that I might ascend to the god of Moses, for I think he is a liar'" (28:38). The references to the clay bricks, the tower and the desire to climb up to see the deity are all reminiscent of what occurs in the Genesis text, but here they are relocated to the Moses story and it is Pharaoh, rather than humanity at large, who wishes to scale the tower's heights. These apparent instances of confusion with the biblical tradition in connection with the character of Haman have caused many scholars to question this figure's portrayal in the Qurʾan.[2]

A more important difference between the biblical and Qurʾanic versions of Moses' birth is the prominent role the deity plays in the latter text while being virtually absent from the former. While God is never explicitly mentioned in the Exodus story, in the Qurʾan all things occur at Allah's initiative or order. A consideration of how and why the baby Moses ends up in the river in each text makes this point clear. According to Exodus 1:21, Pharaoh issues a command that all newborn Hebrew boys are to be thrown into the river. A few verses later we are told that Moses' mother hides her infant son among the reeds of the river in a small papyrus basket in order to protect him. She appears to act on her own initiative in doing this since the text gives no indication that she is obeying a divine order or has been contacted by God in any way.

The Qurʾan version of events differs in some significant ways. There is no directive from the Egyptian king to throw all newborn males into the river. Rather, the text simply says the sons were slain, without specifying the method of murder. Nonetheless, the outcome for the child Moses is the same since he finds himself in the river due to a command. Only this time his watery experience is the result of an order from Allah. "Suckle him, and if you fear for him toss him into the river" (v. 7). In words that evoke the horror of the biblical Pharaoh's edict, Allah asks Moses' mother to do two contradictory things. On the one hand, she is encouraged to fulfill her maternal duty by feeding the child who is dependent on her for his survival. At the same time, she is ordered to act in a most unparental way by abandoning her child to certain death in the relentless forces of the river. The contrast between her actions in the two texts is striking. Her placement of the child in the relative safety of the basket which floats upon the water in Exodus is at odds with the Qur'an's image of her casting her son into the river where he will be quickly swallowed.

But the text does not let us dwell too long on this unpleasant outcome since Allah goes on to explain to her why she should follow the divine command. "Do not fear or grieve, for We will restore him to you and make him one of the messengers." Moses' mother is being asked to place all her trust in Allah and she is up to the task. She does not abandon her son to the forces of nature but surrenders him to the power of Allah. In this way, the presence and role of the deity in the Qur'an, lacking in the biblical account, allows the reader to interpret her actions within the context of her faith. In Exodus, she hides him in a basket hoping he might be saved by another person, but in the Qur'an she tosses him into the river believing he will be saved by Allah.

The presence of the deity is even more obvious in the latter part of the text when the mother experiences momentary anxiety and Allah strengthens her heart so she might become a believer (v. 10). She immediately orders her daughter to follow the child, and this command can be understood as an expression of her strengthened heart and deepened faith. This element of the story is not present in the Exodus account where the sister follows at a distance to see what the outcome will be (2:4). Because her mother has not instructed her to do so, the younger woman's motivation in the Hebrew Bible is left unexpressed. It might be that she is genuinely concerned about the fate of her little brother, but it is equally plausible that she is merely curious about what will happen to him. No such ambiguity is possible in the Qur'an's version of events because her mother has charged her with the task of pursuing the baby. She is therefore acting out of obedience to her parent who, herself, is responding to the will of another. The mother's shout "Follow him!" coming after the mention of her heart being strengthened by Allah, is evidence of her trust in Allah and her firm belief that her son will survive. Consequently, the actions and words of both women have been informed by the divine will in a way that is not explicitly described in the Bible.

When Moses' sister tracks him down she discovers that Allah has been involved in the scene prior to her arrival. "We had already caused him to refuse the wet nurses" (v. 12). This reference to the deity's control over the child's eating habits dramatically illustrates the degree to which Allah has been involved in the course of events surrounding Moses' birth. It also underlines the profound difference between the Qurʾanic and biblical versions of the tradition since, in the latter, God's name is never mentioned and there is not a single reference to divine involvement. In verse 7 Moses' mother is promised two things by Allah: "We will restore him to you and make him one of the messengers." The first of these pledges is fulfilled when he is returned to his mother who will raise him. The second promise that he will be one of the messengers is yet to be realized but will come to pass in other passages from the Qurʾan that describe Moses' prophetic career.

THE INITIAL ENCOUNTER WITH ALLAH

The Qurʾan, like the Hebrew Bible, describes the first meeting between Moses and God as one in which Moses is commissioned as a representative and spokesperson for the deity. The most detailed account of the scene is found in Qurʾan 20:9-36.

> [9]Has the story of Moses come to you? [10]When he saw a fire he said to his family, "Wait here. I see a fire. Perhaps I will bring an ember from it to you or I might find guidance at the fire." [11]When he came to it he was called, "Oh Moses, [12]truly I am your Lord, so take off your shoes for you are in the holy valley of Ṭuwā. [13]I have chosen you, so listen to what is revealed. [14]Truly, I am Allah and there is no god but I, so worship Me and observe prayer in order to remember Me. [15]Truly, the hour is coming and I am keeping it hidden so that each soul might be rewarded for what it endeavors to do. [16]So do not let the one who does not believe in it and who follows his own inclinations turn you away from it so that you perish. [17]What is that in your right hand, oh Moses?" [18]He said, "It is my staff. I lean upon it, beat leaves with it for my flock and have other uses for it." [19]He said, "Throw it down, oh Moses." [20]So he threw it down and it became a writhing serpent. [21]He said, "Grab it and do not fear! We will return it to its previous state. [22]Put your hand under your armpit. It will come out white without any disease. Another sign [23]so that We may show you some of Our greater signs. [24]Go to Pharaoh! He has exceeded all bounds." [25]He said, "My Lord, lay open my heart [26]and make easy for me my task. [27]Untie the knot of my tongue [28]that they might understand my speech. [29]Give to me as an assistant from among my family, [30]Aaron, my brother. [31]Strengthen my weakness by him [32]and make him share in my task [33]so that we might glorify You much [34]and remember You much. [35]You are truly watching over us." [36]He said, "You are granted your request, oh Moses."

The general setting and outline of the scene is similar to that found in Exodus 3:1–4:17 but, as is typical, the Qurʾan's version lacks much of the narrative detail of its biblical counterpart. The Exodus passage is commonly referred to as the episode of the "burning bush" which is not consumed by the fire, but this would be an improper designation for the text in the Qurʾan since it does not explicitly mention a bush. Also missing from the Islamic account is a reference to Mount Horeb as the place of revelation (Exod 3:1)[3] and to the angel of the Lord as the agent of revelation (Exod 3:2). Interestingly, while Moses is alone with his father-in-law's flock in Exodus, he is accompanied by his family in the Qurʾan, and they play a key role in the plot without uttering a word. The biblical Moses approaches the bush primarily because he is curious about the strange spectacle he observes. He is therefore acting in his own self-interest. "I must turn aside and look at this great sight, and see why the bush has not burned up" (Exod 3:3). But Moses in the Qurʾan has a different motive. "Wait here. I see a fire. Perhaps I will bring an ember from it to you or I might find guidance at the fire" (v. 10). He hopes to gain something from the experience that can help him and those with him. From the outset, he entertains the possibility of some practical (an ember) or theoretical (guidance) benefit from the fire that can improve their lives. What he ends up getting is much more than he anticipated.

Most interpretations of this scene stress the importance of the act of divine self-disclosure. The primary purpose of the encounter between Moses and the deity, in the view of many commentators, is that it allows Moses to learn who God is from God's own lips. According to this analysis, the act of self-revelation on the part of the deity enables Moses to better understand the divine plan for humanity. This reading of the text has a long history among Jews, Christians and Muslims and it highlights one of its most important elements. But it is an incomplete reading because it fails to consider the dialogic, even conversational, aspect of the encounter. In this passage God does not do all the talking. Moses, too, has much to say. There is a back and forth, give and take dimension to the exchange which allows each partner to learn a great deal about the other. What we have here is not a one-sided self-disclosure from God to Moses but, more properly, a mutual exchange of self-disclosures, from God to Moses and from Moses to God, during which the true nature of each partner is revealed to the other. While this conversational form is present in both the Bible and the Qurʾan, the content and tone of the dialogue is strikingly different in the two texts. When we compare the two accounts with attention to this contrast, two distinct portrayals of both the deity and Moses emerge.

From God to Moses

It takes the Hebrew Bible a much longer time to relate this scene than it does the Qur'an. A word count of the two texts makes this abundantly clear. While the Qur'an uses some 330 words to narrate Moses' encounter with the deity, the Exodus passage needs approximately 1200 words to tell the story. The reason for this difference is Moses' hesitancy in Exodus. In the Bible, he is a reluctant envoy and it takes a long time for God to convince him to undertake the task that has been set before him. God's first revelation does not persuade Moses and this forces the deity to begin a series of subsequent revelations which disclose other aspects of the divine nature bit by bit. Each time, Moses expresses some reservation in the form of a statement or action which God must address. Seven such exchanges occur which can be outlined as follows.

(1) *God*: I am the God of Abraham, Isaac, and Jacob (Exod 3:6).
    Moses: Hides his face, afraid to look (Exod 3:6).

(2) *God*: I hear the cry of the people and send you to tell them I will deliver them (Exod 3:7-10).
    Moses: Who am I to go to Pharaoh and lead the Israelites? (Exod 3:11).

(3) *God*: I will be with you and you will worship me on this mountain (Exod 3:12).
    Moses: What if the Israelites ask me your name? (Exod 3:13).

(4) *God*: I am who I am and I will bring them out. I will strike Egypt (Exod 3:14-22).
    Moses: What if they do not believe me? (Exod 4:1).

(5) *God*: Turns Moses' staff into a serpent and turns Moses' hand leprous (Exod 4:2-9).
    Moses: I am slow of speech and slow of tongue (Exod 4:10).

(6) *God*: I will be your mouth and teach you what to say. Go to them! (Exod 4:11-13).
    Moses: Lord, send someone else! (Exod 4:13).

(7) *God*: Your brother Aaron will go with you and be your mouth (Exod 4:14-17).

This seven-step structure which alternates divine self-disclosure with Moses' reluctant responses lengthens the story in Exodus considerably and suggests a gradual, almost piecemeal, revelation on God's part. Given the repeated pattern of God's words followed by Moses' reply, the encounter ends rather abruptly. We assume the dialogue will continue and expect to hear Moses' reaction to God's plan to send Aaron, but his response to this final portion of the divine revelation is not described. God responds affirmatively to Moses' request to send another but not in the way Moses wishes. Rather than replace him, his brother is to accompany him. Try as hard as he might, Moses cannot get himself off the hook! It is as if he finally realizes this is a debate he cannot win since God has an answer for every objection he raises, so he grudgingly concedes defeat and returns to his father-in-law Jethro (Exod 4:18). Has he accepted his commission willingly or simply grown tired of this game of cat and mouse and resigned himself to his fate?

The Qurʾan does not allow for the latter possibility because it lacks the element of Moses' hesitancy which is central to the biblical story. He does not have the opportunity to express his doubt, or any other reaction for that matter, because the deity does not engage in the same type of give-and-take dialogue. Allah begins the encounter by offering a revelation of the divine nature that is not interrupted until its end with the double sign of Moses' staff and hand (vv. 17–23). It is only at that point that Moses is allowed to respond to what he has heard. A consideration of Allah's words of self-disclosure in the Qurʾan reveals some key differences between it and the account in Exodus.

A common self-designation of the deity in the biblical passage is "the God of Abraham, the God of Isaac, and the God of Jacob," a title found several times in the story (Exod 3:6, 15, 16; 4:5). The linking of God with the patriarchs functions in a way that establishes a connection between the covenant made with these ancestors and the action that God is about to undertake, through Moses, of freeing the Israelites from their Egyptian bondage. Their entry into the promised land will be the realization of the promise made to Abraham and passed on through his descendants (3:16-17). In this way, a great deal of emphasis in the biblical story is placed on what God will do, and this stress on divine activity is reflected in the deity's self-revelation to Moses.

The Qurʾan focuses on a different aspect of the deity. Rather than emphasize what Allah will do, the text highlights what Allah is and the effect that divine identity has on what Moses and others should do. The very first words Moses hears identify the deity in a way that implies human subordination. "Oh Moses, truly I am your Lord so take off your shoes for you are in the holy valley of Ṭuwā" (v. 12). The authority of the deity is further reinforced by the next words Allah utters, "I have chosen you so listen to what is revealed" (v. 13). In striking contrast to his biblical alter ego, here Moses is being told to reflect rather than react, to consider rather than contend. After alerting Moses to the importance of listening to what is being revealed, the deity then offers another statement of self-identification that is both simple and bold: "Truly, I am Allah and there is no god but I" (v. 14). The logical conclusion for Moses and all of humankind then follows: "So worship Me and observe prayer in order to remember Me" (v. 14). The cause and effect relationship of these last two statements could not be any clearer. Allah's identity has been firmly established and the only possible response on the part of a person is complete faith. Whereas the Exodus tradition is interested in what God will do as an expression of divine power and fidelity to the covenantal promise, the Qurʾan is primarily concerned with what Allah is and the consequent implications for humanity. As Moses listens in obedient silence in the Qurʾan he learns that his reaction should be one of devotion, not doubt. Only after this lesson is learned does Allah then commission him to go to Pharaoh (v. 24). Because the Qurʾan first underscores the supreme authority of the one issuing that commission, Moses is in no position to refuse it or attempt to circumvent it.

From Moses to God

In both the Bible and the Qurʾan, Moses responds to the deity's message but, as we have seen, the way in which he does so is different in the two texts. While his response in Exodus is actually a series of responses in the form of an ongoing exchange between himself and God, in the Qurʾan Moses does not reply until Allah's revelation is complete and he has been commissioned to go to Pharaoh. But it is not only the manner and timing of his reply that differ in the two texts. More importantly, the content of his response varies greatly as well. As the following lists show, each text reports six distinct reactions on Moses' part to what he hears from God.

Bible	*Qurʾan*
(1) Moses hides his face, afraid to look (Exod 3:6).	(1) Lay open my heart (v. 25).

(2) Who am I to go to Pharaoh? (Exod 3:11).

(2) Make easy my task (v. 26).

(3) What if the Israelites ask me your name? (Exod 3:13).

(3) Untie my tongue (v. 27).

(4) What if they do not believe me? (Exod 4:1).

(4) Give me an assistant (v. 29).

(5) I am slow of speech and slow of tongue (Exod 4:10).

(5) Strengthen my weakness (v. 31).

(6) Lord, send someone else! (Exod 4:13).

(6) Make him share my task (v. 32).

In the Exodus account, Moses does all he can to get out of his situation as he adopts every avoidance strategy at his disposal. The story reads like a textbook case of how to evade responsibility as he employs such means as averting his eyes (no. 1), speaking in a self-deprecating manner (nos. 2, 5), and posing hypothetical scenarios (nos. 3, 4). When all this fails, he is forced to go on the offensive and boldly demand that God choose another person (no. 6). This command, grammatically imperative in Hebrew, expresses both Moses' frustration at his inability to dodge the task that is being set before him and his arrogant pride in thinking that he can somehow manipulate and control the divine will.

In the Qurʾan, similarly, Moses speaks to the deity in the imperative but not as a last resort. In fact, all six of the verbs that begin each of his responses in the Qurʾan are grammatically imperative in Arabic. But note how different in tone they are from the Bible's "Lord send someone else!" Moses is not trying his best to elude Allah's call, but doing all he can to insure he will be able to carry it out. He accepts his task but also makes demands on the deity to help him realize his mission. His requests to Allah to open his heart, make his task easy, untie his tongue, give him an assistant, strengthen his weakness and make Aaron share his task are not efforts to shirk his duty as Allah's spokesperson but appeals for help in carrying out the demands of that office. In Exodus, Moses' command to God is an explicit refusal to cooperate with the divine plan, but in the Qurʾan his commands are more like pleas which ask the deity to cooperate with him in bringing about the divine plan. In other words, rather than rebelling against God's authority as his biblical counterpart does, Moses in the Qurʾan acknowledges his complete dependence on the deity.

In a certain sense, Moses' response to Allah in the Qurʾan is patterned on the deity's revelation to him. A high concentration of imperative forms is also found in Allah's message as the following list indicates.

(1) Take off your shoes (v. 12).
(2) Listen to what is revealed (v. 13).
(3) Worship me (v. 14).
(4) Observe prayer (v. 14).
(5) Throw down your staff (v. 19).
(6) Grab the serpent (v. 21).
(7) Do not fear (v. 21).
(8) Put your hand under your armpit (v. 22).
(9) Go to Pharaoh (v. 24).

In Exodus, God commands Moses to do some of the same things found in the Qurʾan including take off his shoes (3:5), go to Pharaoh (3:10), worship (3:12), throw down his staff (4:3), seize the serpent (4:4), and put his hand in his cloak (4:6). But Moses' responses each step of the way, which stress his reticence and hesitancy, create the impression that he is an unwilling, at best reluctant, partner in this encounter. In the Qurʾan, on the other hand, Moses' responses are modeled on the words of Allah. Just as the deity has asked certain things of Moses so now he, too, requests that Allah respond in kind by agreeing to his demands. In this way, the Qurʾanic encounter has an element of cooperation and collaboration absent from the biblical account. Each side is able to express its own needs and concerns in a spirit of openness and trust. But this should not be misunderstood as a meeting between equals. The fact that Moses speaks in the imperative to Allah does not mean they are peers. The content and tone of his requests tell us this is not the case. These petitions are an admission of Moses' inability to carry out his task on his own and an expression of his total reliance on Allah to realize the divine will.

Both the Bible and Qurʾan make reference to Moses' inability to speak well, but this shared aspect of the tradition functions very differently in the two texts. In Exodus, he uses his lack of verbal skills as an excuse to decline the call to be God's agent. "O my Lord, I have never been eloquent, neither in the past nor even now that you have spoken to your servant; but I am slow of speech and slow of tongue" (4:10). Even when he is assured that God will be with his mouth and teach him what to say he flatly refuses and asks that another be sent in his place (4:11-13). Ironically, for someone who claims to lack eloquence he is never at a loss for words when it comes to refuting God's choice of him as a prophet. In the Qurʾan, too, he acknowledges his problem with speaking but does so in a way that highlights his faith and trust in the deity rather than his desire to avoid the divine commission. "Untie the knot of my tongue that they might understand my speech" (vv. 27–28). Here, Moses wants Allah to fix the problem rather than accept it as a sign of his incompetence making him unfit for the task he has been charged with. In this way, Moses in the Qurʾan already knows what he has to be reminded of in Exodus: power over the ability to speak ultimately resides with the deity. "Who gives speech to mortals? Who makes them mute or deaf, seeing or blind? Is it not I, the Lord?" (Exod 4:11).

We see a similar thing in the way Aaron is introduced in the two texts. In the Bible, after Moses asks that someone else be sent, God becomes angry with him (Exod 4:14) and includes Aaron in the mission to serve as a spokesperson between Moses and the people. The sending of Aaron is therefore God's idea and is done in response to Moses' reluctance. But in the Qurʾan the inclusion of Aaron is Moses' idea, and his involvement is meant to support and strengthen Moses in his prophetic role. Whereas in Exodus Moses wants God to send someone else in his place, in the Qurʾan he requests an assistant to make his work more effective. Once again, in the Islamic text Moses appeals to the deity in order to embrace his call rather than escape from it.

The two stories end on a very different note. In the Bible, Moses never responds directly to God's last words which give him Aaron as a spokesperson and tell him to take the staff with which he will perform signs (Exod 4:15-17). The next we hear of Moses he is on his way back to his father-in-law Jethro in Midian. We have already noted how this lack of an explicit reply on his part might indicate a grudging acceptance of his call after he has exhausted all his options to refuse it. God gets the last word and Moses' slowness of tongue finally catches up with him. In the Qurʾan, things are different since it is Allah, rather than Moses, who acquiesces. After listening to Moses' list of demands the deity's response is immediate and simple. "You are granted your request, oh Moses" (v. 36). The word "request" is the key here. Moses has just unleashed a heavy barrage of imperatival forms at Allah which might easily be interpreted as orders or commands directed toward the deity. But this would be a misconstrual of Moses' intent. He is petitioning the deity and appealing for help in fulfilling the responsibility that has been entrusted to him. The argumentative, contentious Moses who is reduced to silence at the end of the Exodus account has been replaced by a responsive, solicitous figure who knows the dialogue must continue. By referring to Moses' words as a "request," Allah understands their respectful tone and agrees that their conversation will indeed go on.

It should be clear that more is going on in these texts than simply God's self-disclosure to Moses. The dialogic nature of the encounter underscores the fact that Moses, too, reveals a great deal about himself. In other words, God learns as much about Moses as Moses learns about God. And the picture of Moses that emerges from the Hebrew Bible is quite a bit different from that found in the Qur'an. In Exodus, Moses appears resistant to God's plan for him as he tries to counter each part of the revelation with a question or objection that will free him from his divinely ordained responsibility. The resulting image of their meeting is one in which God is compelled to subdue Moses' instinct to challenge the divine will and force him to enter into a relationship with the deity he does not want. The Qur'an presents a more positive assessment of the scene. Moses is a receptive partner who willingly accepts his call. He sees his mission as a cooperative venture between himself and Allah, and so feels comfortable to ask the deity for the assistance he needs in realizing it.

PHARAOH AND HIS MAGICIANS

The next episode from Moses' life to be considered is his confrontation with Pharaoh, which is described a number of times in the Qur'an. Here we will discuss the version that is presented in 20:41-73.[4]

> [41]"I have chosen you (Moses) for Myself. [42]Go, you and your brother, with My signs and do not neglect to remember Me. [43]Go to Pharaoh for he has transgressed. [44]Speak to him gently. Perhaps he will remember or fear." [45]They said, "Our Lord, we fear that he might do something evil to us or transgress." [46]He said, "Do not fear. I am with you both. I hear and I see. [47]Go to him and say, 'We are messengers of your Lord so send the children of Israel with us and do not punish them. We have come to you with a sign from your Lord. Peace be upon the one who follows the guidance. [48]Truly, it has been revealed to us that punishment will be upon the one who rejects and turns away.'" [49]He (Pharaoh) said, "Who is the Lord of you two, oh Moses?" [50]He said, "Our Lord is the One who gave every thing its own form and then guided it." [51]He (Pharaoh) said, "What is the state of the previous generations?" [52]He said, "Knowledge of them is with my Lord in a book. My Lord does not make a mistake or forget." [53]It is He Who made the earth an expanse for you, made paths upon it for you, and causes rain to come down from the sky by which We bring forth different types of vegetation. [54]Eat and pasture your cattle. Truly in this there are signs for those with understanding. [55]We made you from the earth, We will return you to it and We will bring you out from it a

second time. [56]We showed him (Pharaoh) all of Our signs but he rejected and refused them. [57]He said, "Did you come to us to drive us out of our land with your magic, oh Moses? [58]We shall surely bring you magic just like it. So at a convenient place set up a meeting between us and you that neither of us shall fail to keep." [59]He (Moses) said, "Your meeting will be on the day of the feast. Let the people be gathered at mid-day." [60]So Pharaoh turned away and drew up his strategy and then returned. [61]Moses said to them, "Woe unto you! Do not forge a lie against Allah for He will destroy you with a punishment. The one who forges a lie is disappointed." [62]They debated their situation among themselves and discussed things privately. [63]They said, "Truly, these two are magicians who seek to drive you out from your land with their magic and do away with your exemplary way of life. [64]Organize your strategy and then come in a group. Whoever is superior shall succeed today." [65]They said, "Oh Moses, either you throw first or we will be the first to throw." [66]He said, "No! You throw!" Then their cords and staffs seemed to him to be set in motion by their magic. [67]Moses felt fearful within himself. [68]We said, "Do not fear! You will be the superior one. [69]Throw what is in your right hand and it will seize what they have made. They have concocted a magician's deceit but a magician does not succeed, whatever he does." [70]The magicians fell down prostrate saying, "We believe in the Lord of Aaron and Moses!" [71]He (Pharaoh) said, "Do you believe in Him before I give you permission? He must be your chief who taught you magic. I will surely cut off your hands and feet on alternate sides and crucify you on trunks of palm trees. You will come to know which of us has a harsher and more lasting punishment." [72]They said, "We do not prefer you to the clear signs that have come to us or to the one who has created us. Decree what you wish to decree. But you can only decree concerning this present life. [73]Truly, we believe in our Lord so that He might forgive our sins and the magic you forced us to practice. Allah is the best and most lasting."

There are some similarities between this text and the biblical account of the series of plagues which God, through Moses, visits on Egypt in Exodus 7–11, but the divergences between the two stories are more obvious. In the first place, there is no explicit mention of plagues in the Qur'an while this element, with its descriptive and detailed references to frogs, flies, boils, locusts, and other calamities, tends to dominate the biblical plot. There may be a subtle allusion to the plagues in the signs from Allah which Pharaoh rejects (vv. 42, 56), but this can only be inferred and a great degree of ambiguity remains regarding the nature of these signs.[5] The focus here in the Qur'an is not on the mighty works of Allah, but rather on the response that individuals make to the power and presence of the deity in their lives. This is most clearly seen with Pharaoh's magicians, but there is also a great deal of interest in the response of the Egyptian monarch himself. Another interesting difference between the biblical and Qur'anic accounts is that, in the latter, the theme of letting the Israelites go, which is central to Exodus and frequently repeated there, is only mentioned once very early in the text (v. 47). This indicates that the episode serves a further purpose in the Qur'an beyond explaining how the problem of the Israelites' experience of bondage in Egypt will be resolved.

The physical dynamics of the two texts also differ a great deal. In the Bible, Moses and Aaron constantly shuttle back and forth as they go into and out of the Pharaoh's presence. No less than seven times they are instructed by God to go to Pharaoh in order to deliver a message or perform a work designed to persuade him to release the Israelites (Exod 7:15; 8:1, 20; 9:1, 10, 13; 10:1). Five other times they are told by Pharaoh to leave his presence in order to engage in worship of one form or another (8:8-15, 25-32; 9:27-35; 10:16-20, 24-29). We never hear of Pharaoh initiating an encounter by coming to Moses but, interestingly, he himself initiates a number of encounters between Moses and God by asking Moses to intercede for him. The overall impression we get of the Pharaoh is in line with the high social status he enjoyed in Egypt. As the most powerful person in the land who sits at the epicenter of authority, all things revolve around Pharaoh and everyone is at his beck and call.

Things are not like that in the Qur'an. As in Exodus, Moses and Aaron are sent to the Egyptian king by the deity, but this time they are not dismissed by him and hold their ground. Rather, it is the Pharaoh who is on the move. He departs by "turning away" from Moses to prepare for their contest and returns after he has determined his strategy (v. 60). This subtly shifts the focus of power from the monarch and creates a more even-handed situation between him and the two messengers from Allah. His own words also support this change in the relationship. Unlike in the Bible, where their interactions always take place in his world and on his terms, giving him the "home court advantage," Pharaoh in the Qur'an levels the playing field by inviting Moses to determine where and when they will meet. He declares, "Set up a meeting between us and you at a convenient place that neither of us shall fail to keep" (v. 58). The Arabic word translated "convenient" here can also convey the sense of "equidistant" or "midway point" which lends an air of neutrality to the location of the encounter that is not present in Exodus.

Another interesting difference is the order of events regarding who goes first when the two sides engage in their contest of supernatural powers. In the Qur²an, Moses declines the Egyptian magicians' offer to lead off by telling them to be the first to cast their spell. This is unlike the biblical story where the Egyptian magicians' feats, whenever they are attempted,[6] are always in response to and try to mimic some act already accomplished by Moses and/or Aaron. This change in order might be done for a theological reason since it makes it clear that it is the Egyptians, not Allah, who have introduced the theme of magic into the debate. When Moses responds by casting his own spell at Allah's command he is engaging in the battle on their terms and answering their challenge in like manner. In order to better appreciate this aspect of the text, a brief discussion of the Qur²an's attitude toward magic is necessary.

Magic in the Qur²an

Two key terms in this passage are *siḥr* (sorcery, magic) and *sāḥir* (sorcerer, magician), each coming from the Arabic root *saḥara*. The verbal forms of this root carry the general sense of "to enchant, fascinate" and this is frequently extended to mean "to deceive, delude, beguile." The noun *siḥr* has as a basic meaning the act of turning something from its proper state to another state, and this is most often understood in a negative way as producing what is false in the form of truth. The related noun *sāḥir* refers to one who engages in *siḥr* and typically denotes anyone who produces falsehood by practicing enchantment due to being possessed by *jinn* or some other evil spirit.

The two terms appear a total of fifty times in the Qur²an with the number of occurrences of each almost evenly divided in the text. The passage under discussion contains their highest frequency of occurrence as the two words are found ten times in 20:57-73. Their presence in a passage connected with Moses reflects a pattern that runs throughout the Qur²an since more than 60 percent of the usages of these two terms are in texts that discuss Moses' encounter with Pharaoh and his magicians. The great majority of the other examples of *siḥr* and *sāḥir* are found in contexts that discuss Muhammad and the reception he received from his fellow Meccans as he tried to convert them to Islam. An example of this is seen in 38:4 where they consider the prophet to be a sorcerer. "They are surprised that a warner has come to them from among themselves. The unbelievers say 'This is a magician, a liar.'" This follows the tendency in the Qur²an that has already been noted of recounting the lives of earlier prophets in a way that highlights the similarities between their experiences and those of the prophet of Islam. In this case, the text often points out how both Muhammad and Moses were unfairly accused of being magicians by those who were opposed to their message and mission.

The Qurʾan understands magical abilities and acts to be dependent upon supernatural powers. We have already seen in our discussion of the encounter that Adam and his wife have with Iblis in the garden that there is a distinction between good angels and bad angels in Islam. Both types can interact with humanity, and when bad angels influence human behavior they can cause a person to rebel against the divine will. One of the ways this estrangement from Allah can be expressed is through involvement in sorcery and other improper activities. According to the Qurʾan, humanity was taught *sihr* by the two fallen angels Harut and Marut. "They (evil people) follow what was chanted by the devilish ones against Solomon's kingdom. Solomon did not disbelieve, but the devilish ones did disbelieve and taught people sorcery (*sihr*) and what was revealed to the two angels in Babylon, Harut and Marut" (2:102). In the Qurʾanic view, then, the magicians of Pharaoh's court are individuals who have opted to follow the guidance of demonic forces and have rejected Allah's help. This is what makes their conversion at the end of the story so dramatic and theologically powerful.

Although Moses is frequently considered to be a magician by his opponents in the Qurʾan this text explicitly rejects that title for him. In verse 69 Allah tells him that a magician is doomed to failure in whatever he does. This is the fate of the Egyptians when their magical feat is trumped by Moses and they end up renouncing their life as Pharaoh's puppets. But this is not a battle of magicians. Moses does not emerge victorious because he possesses a special brand of sorcery that renders theirs impotent. Were he, too, a magician he would fail as miserably as they because, as the deity reminds him, failure is the lot of all magicians. Moses succeeds rather than fails because he is a messenger and no magician. What he performs is not the feat of a wizard but the sign of Allah. It is not a deed he has conjured up on his own, but a miracle he is empowered from on high to perform. This is the difference between him and them that they come to grasp but which continues to elude Pharaoh. The monarch mistakenly thinks his magicians have served as apprentices under Moses. "He must be your chief who taught you magic" (v. 71). The unbelieving Pharaoh thinks the divine sign Moses performs is no different than magic, but the believing exmagicians recognize that only the sign is authentic because of Allah's involvement in it.

After this initial overview of the passage and a consideration of its magical background we are now in a position to discuss some of its details. By examining how each of the characters is presented in the Qur'an and comparing them with their biblical counterparts we can better appreciate the purpose and function of the Islamic text.

1. Moses/Aaron

Both Moses and Aaron are mentioned by name in this Qur'an passage, but Moses is the more dominant figure since his brother does not speak or engage in any activity on his own. This is in marked contrast to the story in Exodus where Aaron, while still silent, is an equal partner with Moses in bringing about the plagues which God sends on the Egyptians. The commission they receive is likewise presented in different ways. In the Qur'an, Moses and Aaron are told to go to Pharaoh and speak to him "gently" in the hope that he will remember or fear (v. 44). The Arabic text literally reads "Speak to him a tender word." Allah asks the brothers to be kind and considerate when they face the Egyptian leader since this type of approach is more likely to achieve the desired result of having him acknowledge his mistake. It appears that their primary purpose is to mildly nudge Pharaoh into a proper relationship with Allah through their well-chosen and discerning words.

In the Bible, the brothers are also ordered to speak to Pharaoh but they are further told that their message will fall on deaf ears. After directing them to talk to Pharaoh, God informs them, "But I will harden Pharaoh's heart, and I will multiply my signs and wonders in the land of Egypt. When Pharaoh does not listen to you, I will lay my hand upon Egypt and bring my people the Israelites, company by company, out of the land of Egypt by great acts of judgment" (Exod 7:4-5). Here, the brother's words, which are doomed to failure from the start, take a back seat to the awesome signs and wonders that God will bring about in leading the Israelites out of bondage. This raises a potentially troubling theological question since it appears that, in hardening Pharaoh's heart, God has given the Egyptian little, if any, opportunity to respond favorably to Moses' and Aaron's words. This issue will be discussed in detail below when we consider the characters of Pharaoh and the deity.

In the Qur'an, Pharaoh's fate primarily hinges on what the brothers say, but in Exodus it rests on what God does. This distinction is critical for understanding how the stories unfold. It is a striking feature of the biblical text that Moses never waits for a reply from Pharaoh after delivering the divine message to let the Israelites go. Rather, each time but one,[7] he and Aaron immediately bring about the next plague which God has commanded. On several occasions Pharaoh then goes on to agree to release the Israelites or to appeal for help, but this is always in reaction to the plague itself and not to Moses' spoken words. This lack of an explicit reply on Pharaoh's part reinforces the idea that it is the acts of God, rather than the words of Moses, which are the focal point of the plot.

This makes the presence of a conversation between Moses and Pharaoh in the Qur'an all the more interesting. They engage in a discussion about the identity and nature of Allah in which Moses tries to teach the Egyptian leader a theological lesson. After being told that the brothers have been sent as emissaries of their Lord and that whoever rejects their message shall be punished (vv. 47–48), Pharaoh asks, "Who is the Lord of you two, oh Moses?" (v. 49). The question leads to a reply by Moses in the form of a statement of faith. "Our Lord is the One who gave every thing its own form and then guided it" (v. 50). This response leads to a further query by Pharaoh and rejoinder by Moses. "He (Pharaoh) said, 'What is the state of the previous generations?' He (Moses) said, 'Knowledge of them is with my Lord in a book. My Lord does not make a mistake or forget'" (vv. 51–52).

In this exchange, Pharaoh seems to be trying to understand who Moses' Lord is, and his questions are attempts to get at the truth and clear up his uncertainty. Moses assists him in the process by instructing him about Allah's nature and relationship to the created order. This dialogue gives Pharaoh a voice that is missing in Exodus and highlights the critical role the Egyptian monarch plays in his own fate. He is given the opportunity to respond affirmatively to Moses' words and come to belief in Allah but is unable to make that leap of faith. Only after Moses has first identified the deity in whose name he comes and Pharaoh has had the chance to accept the message does Allah send the signs which are then rejected and refused (v. 56). This missed opportunity by the Egyptian, coupled with the lack of reference to the biblical theme of the deity hardening his heart, creates the impression that it is Pharaoh himself, more than anyone else, who is responsible for his fate. By failing to hear the "tender word" spoken to him by Moses and Aaron he turns his back on Allah.

2. The Egyptian Magicians

In both the Qur'an and the Bible, the Egyptian magicians come to recognize the authority of the God of Moses, but this development is presented in different ways in the two texts. It is a more gradual, drawn-out process in Exodus where their magical abilities are rendered increasingly less effective until they are completely powerless before the God of Israel. The first three times the magicians are mentioned they can, without difficulty, recreate the works that Moses and Aaron perform as they turn their staffs into snakes (Exod 7:11-12), change the river's water into blood (7:22), and bring frogs upon the land of Egypt (8:7). But from this point on they are not able to keep up with God's messengers.

When they attempt to duplicate the next feat of producing gnats they are unable to do so and their reaction to this unexpected change is telling. Rather than make excuses or attempt to explain away their sudden incapacity, the magicians acknowledge a power greater than their own. "The magicians tried to produce gnats by their secret arts, but they could not. There were gnats on both humans and animals. And the magicians said to Pharaoh, 'This is the finger of God!'" (8:18-19). While not an explicit articulation of faith in the God of Moses, their cry is nonetheless a recognition of God's authority and their own relatively inferior status. The Egyptian magicians never attempt to reproduce any of the subsequent wonders that Moses and Aaron enact, and their absence from the rest of the story suggests that they have been put in their place. The last time we hear of them they are pathetic figures whose impotence makes them objects of pity. "The magicians could not stand before Moses because of the boils, for the boils afflicted the magicians as well as all the Egyptians" (9:11). Not only have their powers been found wanting in comparison to those of God, they have been inflicted with bodily reminders of God's control over them.

The magicians in the Qur'an undergo a similar transformation, but theirs is more properly a conversion in which they come to have explicit faith in Moses' God. It is also a change that occurs more quickly since it lacks the development and progression of the biblical account. This text does not narrate each of the various plagues but lumps them all together in verse 56. "We showed him (Pharaoh) all of Our signs but he rejected and refused them." The Qur'an passage does not describe the magicians attempting to duplicate the signs of Moses and Aaron. Rather, they are introduced into the story after the signs as those who engage in a grand competition with Moses to determine whose powers are superior.

The contest is very similar to their first encounter in the Bible. In Exodus 7:8-13 the magicians reenact Aaron's feat by throwing down their staffs which quickly change into snakes. Aaron's staff then swallows up theirs in a demonstration of his superior power. The Qur'an relates a similar episode that differs in several ways. Moses, not Aaron, plays the key role as the magicians' cords and staffs are seized by his (v. 69). Another difference is that the order is reversed in the Qur'an with the Egyptians going first and Moses responding to their act of magic. The most important difference between the two texts is seen in the reaction this contest elicits from the Egyptian magicians. Exodus does not describe any response on their part but mentions Pharaoh's reaction, or lack thereof. "Still Pharaoh's heart was hardened, and he would not listen to them, as the Lord had said" (7:13). It is only after several further encounters with Moses and Aaron, culminating in their inability to reproduce the plague of gnats, that the magicians will explicitly acknowledge God's power and presence (8:19).

In the Qur'an the magicians' reaction is immediate and unambiguous: "We believe in the Lord of Aaron and Moses!" (v. 70). This is much more than the simple recognition of Moses' deity that they voice in Exodus. It is a statement of faith that implies a conversion and acceptance of that God as their own. In the Bible, there is still some question regarding what precisely the Egyptian magicians think about the God of Moses when they exclaim "This is the finger of God!" But there is no such uncertainty in the Qur'an because their words are in the form of a creedal statement that is a blunt declaration of belief. At this point the plot thickens considerably. The magicians do not have much time to savor their conversion experience since their newfound faith is straightaway put to the test. Pharaoh's response is as immediate as their own when he tells them he will not tolerate their shift of allegiance and threatens them with execution, thinking this will remind them that he is to be feared more than the God they have just accepted. "You will come to know which of us has a harsher and more lasting punishment" (v. 71). Their reaction to this warning is a remarkable expression of both the depth of their faith and their recognition of Pharaoh's true nature as a man and no god. They willingly face death at Pharaoh's hands knowing he has no control over matters of ultimate significance. "Decree what you wish to decree. But you can only decree concerning this present life. Truly, we believe in our Lord so that He might forgive our sins and the magic you forced us to practice. Allah is the best and most lasting" (vv. 72–73).

Their comment that Pharaoh had forced them to engage in magic is an interesting one that has no parallel in the biblical tradition. It has the double effect both of creating sympathy for the magicians who have been coerced into practicing their craft and of placing Pharaoh in an even more negative light as the reason why the magicians initially embarked on the misguided life they have now abandoned. The reader's final evaluation of this group of characters is quite different in the Bible and the Qurʾan. In the former text, the magicians are tragic, impotent figures who have recognized the presence of the deity but still lack explicit faith and, consequently, suffer from the painful physical ailments with which they and all the Egyptians have been afflicted. In the Qurʾan they have a more heroic quality. They not only recognize God's power, but respond to it with a faith that is so deep they are willing to put their lives on the line for it. They, too, have been marked but not with the boils and sores that their biblical counterparts share with their fellow Egyptians. The magicians in the Qurʾan have been marked internally with the sign of faith in Allah that sets them apart from unbelievers like Pharaoh.

3. Pharaoh

In both texts, the Egyptian monarch is a villain who plays the antagonist to Moses' hero. As we have seen, in the Qurʾan he and Moses initially engage in a conversation during which Pharaoh asks questions about Allah, indicating an interest or curiosity about the God of Moses. "Who is the Lord of you two, oh Moses?" (v. 49). This causes the reader to evaluate Pharaoh's character somewhat positively since he appears to be someone who is trying to learn about Moses' God. This assessment abruptly shifts and becomes more negative seven verses later when we are told that Pharaoh rejected and refused the signs of Allah. At the end of the text, Pharaoh's vile nature is confirmed when he threatens to kill his magicians after they express their faith in the God of Moses and Aaron. This presentation is a bit different than the biblical one where Pharaoh's hostility to God is evident the first time he opens his mouth. "Who is the Lord, that I should heed him and let Israel go? I do not know the Lord, and I will not let Israel go" (Exod 5:2). Once again, Pharaoh begins with a question, one very similar to that in the Qurʾan, only this time it is of a more rhetorical nature meant to express his complete unwillingness to accept the presence or authority of God. While Pharaoh in the Qurʾan does not know anything about Allah but makes an attempt to learn something, in Exodus he says he does not know, and does not *want* to know, anything about Moses' God.

There is a reason for Pharaoh's disinterest in the Bible that has nothing to do with the man himself. In the previous chapter it is reported that God is behind this obduracy when Moses is told, "When you go back to Egypt, see that you perform before Pharaoh all the wonders that I have put in your power; but I will harden his heart, so that he will not let the people go" (Exod 4:21). The hardening of Pharaoh's heart is a recurrent motif in the biblical story of the plagues that has a profound effect on the plot. Fourteen times in Exodus 7–11 the hardening of his heart is mentioned. In eleven of those texts God is responsible for the hardening,[8] and the remaining three say Pharaoh hardened his own heart. But even in those latter cases the reader assumes divine involvement since the first time the topic is brought up in Exodus 4:21 God claims responsibility for the hardening.

This element of the story affects the reader's view of both the deity and Pharaoh. Throughout these chapters in Exodus, Moses repeatedly visits the monarch with the request to release the Hebrews. On a number of these occasions Pharaoh is on the brink of complying but his heart is hardened and he denies them permission to leave, thereby bringing the next plague on Egypt. This pattern continues right up until the end of the story when the drowning of the Egyptian forces is a result of divine intervention. God commands Moses, "But you lift up your staff, and stretch out your hand over the sea and divide it, that the Israelites may go into the sea on dry ground. Then I will harden the hearts of the Egyptians so that they will go in after them" (Exod 14:16-17). While such texts underscore the supreme power of Moses' God over Pharaoh and Egypt, they also raise some troubling theological questions. Why does God harden Pharaoh's heart, thereby rendering him incapable of letting the Hebrews go? Is God, rather than Pharaoh, responsible for the suffering and death the plagues bring upon Egypt? Why does God harden the hearts of the Egyptian forces after the Hebrews have safely passed through the waters? The attentive reader cannot help but ask these and related questions about the deity's motives and actions in an attempt to understand the story's message.

God's hardening of Pharaoh's heart makes the Egyptian leader a tragic, almost sympathetic, figure in the Bible. The reason for his refusal to comply with Moses' requests lies outside himself and he is someone who has very little control over his situation and fate. This quality of his character comes to the fore in those scenes where he acquiesces momentarily to Moses' demands but then reverses himself once his heart is hardened. In a number of places he appears to be genuinely contrite and even seems to be moving toward an initial, if not yet fully formed, faith in Moses' God. After one plague Pharaoh cries to Moses, "This time I have sinned; the Lord is in the right, and I and my people are in the wrong. Pray to the Lord! Enough of God's thunder and hail! I will let you go; you need stay no longer" (Exod 9:27-28). But each such instance of recognition of God's authority on Pharaoh's part is short lived since there always immediately follows a description of the divine response. "So the heart of Pharaoh was hardened, and he would not let the Israelites go, just as the Lord had spoken through Moses" (Exod 9:35). The portrait of Pharaoh that emerges from these passages is that of a figure who is more an instrument than an individual, one upon whom the divine will acts but is never really given the opportunity to react freely to God of his own will.

In the passage from the Qur'an, this aspect of the tradition is missing since there is no reference to Pharaoh's heart being hardened.[9] In fact, it might be said that rather than harden Pharaoh's heart, Allah wishes to soften it and make it receptive to the divine message. When they are commissioned in the Qur'an, Moses and Aaron are told to speak gently to Pharaoh in the hope that he will remember or fear (v. 44). Allah desires that the Egyptian leader change his ways and be converted to true faith, and Moses and his brother are to try to facilitate this process. How different their purpose and the expected outcome are in the Bible, where God's hardening of Pharaoh's heart has guaranteed from the outset that no matter what Moses and Aaron might say to him their words will fall on deaf ears.

Since Allah is not responsible for Pharaoh's rejection of the divine message and signs in the Qur'an the fault can rest with only one person: Pharaoh himself. The lack of the hardening of the heart motif therefore plays a critical role in how we evaluate the characters of both the deity and the Pharaoh in this story. In Exodus, the Egyptian's hands are tied since God has prevented him from doing anything but reject Moses' requests to let the people go. The spotlight is on the marvelous powers of God as expressed in the hardening of Pharaoh's heart and the series of plagues which humble Egypt. We have already seen how this can cause the reader to feel sympathy for the Pharaoh and wonder about God's actions and motives. Such an evaluation is not possible in the Qur'an since Pharaoh is a free subject who speaks and acts on his own, not manipulated by the deity. The focus here has shifted from the mighty works of Allah to the human response to divine power. Pharaoh has been spoken to gently in order to bring him to faith and he has chosen of his own free will to cut short the conversation, thereby sealing his own fate. In the Qur'an, this is a story about human response and responsibility, not divine might and control.

Pharaoh's personal fault is expressed in the Qur'an through some interesting choice and use of vocabulary. In verse 43 Moses and Aaron are told what the nature of Pharaoh's offense is when Allah informs them that he has "transgressed." Two verses later when they express some reluctance about their task they voice concern that the Egyptian leader might do something evil to them or transgress. Both times the word "transgress" is found it translates the Arabic verb *ṭaġā*. This word carries with it the sense of exceeding or going beyond the limit of what is proper, normal or acceptable in a way that exalts oneself. Its use here in relation to Pharaoh suggests that his problem is one of an inflated sense of self-importance which causes him to act in ways that transcend and violate the bounds of his office. In other words, he is infringing on areas in which he has usurped the authority of another, namely Allah.

His personal responsibility for this distorted view of himself is dramatically captured through another use of repetition in the text. In verse 48, Moses and Aaron tell Pharaoh that punishment will befall the person who rejects Allah and "turns away." The same Arabic verb is found later on when, after the arrangements for the encounter between Moses and the Egyptian magicians have been made, Pharaoh "turns away" to formulate his strategy. These are the only two times the verb is found in the passage and the second time we hear it we look both back to its earlier occurrence and ahead to the end of the story. We realize that Pharaoh is the one Moses spoke of who "turns away" and we expect him to behave in such a way that he will merit the punishment promised to one who does so. In other words, by the very act of turning away and not continuing his discussion with Moses, Pharaoh has damned himself and become one of the lost ones. This is a particularly apt action to symbolize Pharaoh's break with Allah since it highlights the personal, willful nature of Pharaoh's violation which is central to the Qur'an's understanding of his character. Pharaoh turns away of his own accord; he is not turned around by Allah.

4. The Deity

It has already been seen how the deity's character is drawn in different ways in the two texts. Of primary importance is the presence of the hardening of the heart theme in the Bible, making God directly involved in Pharaoh's negative response to Moses' requests and therefore influencing the outcome of the story. The Qur'an lacks this element and offers the more compassionate image of Allah desiring the Egyptian leader's conversion and using Moses and Aaron to try to bring this change about. In both cases, then, the deity is concerned about Pharaoh's fate but works toward realizing opposite results in the two accounts.

Perhaps the main reason for this contrast is the presence of different understandings of the nature of the relationship between the deity and humanity in the two versions of the story. The Exodus text reflects the common biblical view that Israel enjoys a special status in the eyes of God that is not shared by any other people. The covenantal relationship between God and the Israelites consequently becomes paramount in the world of the biblical text. Those who are not a part of the chosen people are considered to be outsiders and automatically excluded from the possibility of a proper relationship with the deity. The Qur'an, on the other hand, adopts a more universal perspective by expressing the belief that Allah is the Lord of all and does not favor one group over others. A consideration of how the deity is referred to in the two texts underscores this difference.

In Exodus, God is consistently understood to have a special relationship with Moses and his people. When the deity refers to the Israelites, a very common designation for them is "my people," a term which excludes as much as it includes and indicates that God's favor has been limited or restricted to this particular group of people (8:1, 20; 9:1, 13, 17; 10:3). The implication is clear: if the Israelites are God's people then the Egyptians and all others are not. Elsewhere, we see a similar use of selective terminology when the deity is referred to as the "God of Israel" or, more commonly, the "God of the Hebrews" (5:2-3; 7:16; 9:1, 13; 10:3).

But the divine preference for Israel over all others extends beyond these relational titles and other statements of partiality. Elsewhere in the story, God's choice of Israel is concretely expressed in action. Several times, God makes a distinction between the Egyptians and the Israelites in order to protect the latter from the distress and suffering of the plagues. When the flies swarm upon the Egyptians, the Israelites are miraculously spared (8:22-23). When Egypt is forced to endure the death of its livestock due to a deadly pestilence, the animals of Israel go unharmed (9:3-4). When hail falls throughout the land causing damage to property and life, only the area where the Israelites live escapes unscathed (9:25-26). When the entire country is thrown into darkness for three days, the Israelites alone have light (10:22-23). And, of course, in what is undoubtedly the most dramatic and, in some ways, troubling expression of divine favoritism, the final plague entails God's striking dead the first born of all Egyptians while those of the Israelites celebrate the first Passover with their families and escape with them through the parted waters.

Things are very different in the Qur'an text where no such distinction between one group and another is made. Allah is accessible to and interested in all people regardless of their prior history or present state. This becomes plainly obvious when we pay attention to the way the deity is designated in the text. "Allah" and "Lord" are the two titles used to refer to the deity in this passage and there is a dramatic difference in the frequency of their occurrence. While "Lord" is found nine times, "Allah" appears only twice, and this disparity is probably no coincidence. "Allah" is a more generic term which simply means "the deity" in Arabic, but the title "Lord" carries a relational sense. To call Allah "Lord" is an expression of faith which implies a relationship between oneself and the deity. If we pay attention to whose relationship to Allah is being identified whenever the word "Lord" is used in the Qur'an, the network of connections is clarified and we are able to uncover the image of the deity that is being put forward there.

All nine times the word "Lord" appears in this text its relational aspect is to the fore since it is never found by itself but is always part of the expression "the Lord of so and so." In fact, at one point or another in the story Allah is identified as the Lord of each of the characters. Tracing the use of the expression in the plot and paying attention to how it shifts from character to character helps us appreciate the centrality of this key theological component.

The first time it is used is in verse 45 when Moses and Aaron begin their prayer "our Lord" as they seek protection and guidance in their mission to Pharaoh. The next two occurrences are found in the following verse when Allah responds and tells them what they are to say to the Egyptian leader. Both times the word is used the deity is identified as Pharaoh's Lord: the two brothers are messengers of his Lord who bring a sign from his Lord (v. 47). This designation sets in high relief the difference between this account and the biblical one where Yahweh is never called the Lord or God of Pharaoh but, rather, takes measures to insure such a relationship will remain impossible. The next time the word is mentioned in the Qur'an is when Pharaoh disavows any connection to their God by referring to the deity as the Lord of Moses and Aaron. "Who is the Lord of you two, oh Moses?" (v. 49). With this question, he implicitly rejects the invitation to be included among Allah's people and chooses not to establish a relationship with the deity. Once again, the distinction between this situation and the biblical one is obvious. There, the lack of affinity between God and Pharaoh is due to the deity's hardening Pharaoh's heart, while here it is the Egyptian's own fault. In the Qur²an, Allah wishes to establish a proper relationship with Pharaoh but is prevented from doing so by the latter's unwillingness to recognize the deity as his Lord.

The next three times the title "Lord" appears it has been reclaimed by Moses and Aaron when Allah is referred to by Moses once as "our Lord" (v. 50) and twice as "my Lord" (v. 52). Its use here suggests that Moses is acknowledging Pharaoh's distancing of himself from Allah and his unwillingness to entertain the possibility of entering into a relationship with the deity. Things have returned to square one as Allah is once again identified as the Lord of the two brothers.

But this reversal is only a temporary setback which sets the stage for the most dramatic use of the title when it is found two final times on the lips of the Egyptian magicians. In verse 70 they fall on their faces and utter their statement of faith, "We believe in the Lord of Aaron and Moses!" This is an interesting declaration in that Allah is still identified as the Lord of the two brothers, but now the magicians are including themselves as somehow sharing in that relationship. This articulation of faith on the part of his magicians leads Pharaoh to rebuke them and threaten them with execution, and this results in the most extraordinary use of the title when, in the face of certain death, the magicians call upon Allah as their own Lord. "Truly, we believe in our Lord so that He might forgive our sins and the magic you forced us to practice" (v. 73). Once again, the issue of human free will is to the fore as the Egyptian magicians choose to embrace Allah as their Lord in a way that their leader finds impossible to do. Through this fascinating use of the title "Lord" the Qur²an sounds its characteristic note of universality. Allah is the Lord of all people and each character in the story is given the opportunity to accept or reject that truth.

THE EXODUS

The Qur²an makes reference to the Exodus tradition by describing the Israelites' escape from Egypt and journey to a new land under Moses' leadership. Some of the elements of its telling of these events are shared with the biblical account and others are unique to the Islamic text. As is frequently the case, the Qur²an contains a number of versions of this story, each with its own particular emphasis and point to make. We will study several of these texts as we first consider descriptions of the Israelites crossing the sea and then study some passages that re-count the journey to their new land.

Crossing the Sea

As does the Hebrew Bible, the Qur'an understands the Israelite ex-perience in Egypt as primarily one of oppression under the heavy hand of Pharaoh. The Egyptian leader is described as unwilling to acknowl-edge the power and authority of the Israelite God revealed through the signs and wonders that Moses and Aaron work, and this results in a final act of divine intervention that sets free the people. Allah parts the waters of the sea which allows the Israelites to escape and puts Pharaoh in his place. The version of these events found in sura 26 follows the biblical story closely.

> [52]We revealed to Moses, "Journey by night with My servants, for you will be pursued." [53]And Pharaoh sent people into the cities announcing, [54]"These are truly a small group of people [55]but they have enraged us, [56]we who are numerous and vigilant." [57]And We removed them from gardens and springs, [58]treasures and noble dwellings. [59]Thus We gave them as an inheritance to the children of Israel. [60]They pursued them at sunrise. [61]When the two groups were within sight of each other Moses' companions said, "We are caught!" [62]He said, "No! My Lord is with me and He will guide me." [63]We revealed to Moses, "Strike the sea with your rod." It parted and each side was like a great mountain. [64]Then We brought near the others. [65]We saved Moses and all those with him, [66]then We drowned the others. [67]Truly, in that there was a sign but most of them did not believe.

This text agrees with the account in Exodus 14 that the deity is be-hind everything that occurs in the story. In the Bible, God issues orders to Moses regarding where to position the Israelites (vv. 2–4), how to di-vide the sea (vv. 15–16), and how to make the waters flow back to their original location (vv. 26–27). Without this divine assistance, Moses would be at a loss about what to do as he watches the advancing Egyp-tian forces with his back to the sea. It is God who formulates the escape plan and gives Moses the ability to carry it out. The deity's direct involvement in the outcome is explicitly stated several times. An angel of God leads the Israelites (v. 19) and a pillar of fire and cloud protects them from the Egyptian army (v. 24). When Moses stretches out his hand over the waters, it is the Lord who drives back the sea (v. 21). When the Egyptians are unable to flee from the returning waters, it is because the Lord has clogged the wheels of their chariots (v. 25). In addition, twice in this chapter mention is made of God's hardening the hearts of Pharaoh and his army to explain why they foolishly pursue the Israelites (vv. 8, 17).

The biblical text therefore goes to great lengths to show that the Israelites have been saved as a result of divine intervention and to demonstrate that God, not Moses, is the main actor. The final two verses of Exodus 14 make this point clear. "Thus the Lord saved Israel that day from the Egyptians; and Israel saw the Egyptians dead on the seashore. Israel saw the great work that the Lord did against the Egyptians. So the people feared the Lord and believed in the Lord and in his servant Moses" (vv. 30–31).

The passage from the Qurʾan communicates the same message about the divine role. Allah instructs Moses twice (vv. 52, 63) regarding what he is to do. As in Exodus, Moses in the Qurʾan calls upon the deity for guidance and support (v. 62). Allah claims explicit responsibility for bringing the Pharaoh's forces to the sea (v. 64), saving the Israelites (v. 65), and drowning the Egyptians (v. 66). There may also be an indirect reference to divine involvement in the comment that the Israelites are a small group of people (v. 54). This is contrary to the biblical tradition which states in Exodus 12:37 that the escaping Israelites numbered approximately six hundred thousand, not counting women and children. By envisioning a smaller group, the Qurʾan highlights the relative helplessness of Moses and his followers. The text suggests that such a mismatch can only be overcome with the help of Allah.

This Qurʾan passage contains another interesting break with the story in Exodus in the way it concludes. They both highlight the theme of faith but in very different ways. Whereas the biblical tradition mentions the faith that is engendered by God's miraculous work at the sea, this passage from the Qurʾan refers to the lack of faith on the part of many despite that miracle (v. 67). Each presents the story in a way that underscores the deity's role in controlling and determining the action, but each reaches different conclusions about the human response to that divine activity. Exodus understands the event as one that leads to faith in God and Moses, while the Qurʾan interprets it as yet another squandered opportunity for people to express their belief in Allah.

Another version of the story in the Qurʾan stresses more strongly this theme of lack of faith in Allah. In 7:134-140 it is the death of the unbelieving Egyptians, rather than the salvation of the Israelites, that is the focus of attention. It begins with a reference to the Egyptian reaction to the lice, frogs, blood, and other signs which Allah, through Moses, visited upon them.

> [134]When the punishment came upon them they said, "Oh Moses, call upon your Lord for us according to what He has promised you. If you will remove the punishment from us we will believe you and we will send the children of Israel with you." [135]But when We removed the punishment from them for a time so that they might accomplish this they broke their promise. [136]So We took revenge on them and drowned them in the sea because they considered Our signs to be lies and they were unmindful of them. [137]And We caused the people who were oppressed to inherit both the eastern and the western parts of the land which We blessed. The good word of your Lord came to pass for the children of Israel because they were steadfast. And We destroyed what Pharaoh and his people had made and what they had built. [138]We brought the children of Israel across the sea and they came to a people who were devoted to their idols. They said, "Oh Moses, make for us a god like their gods." He said, "Truly, you are an ignorant people. [139]These people are involved in something that will be destroyed and all they do is in vain." [140]He said, "Should I seek for you a god other than Allah who has exalted you above all others?"

In this version, the sin of the unbelievers is to the fore. The Egyptians manipulate Allah's power by convincing Moses to relieve their suffering but they fail to honor their promise to believe Moses and release the Israelites. In effect, they have taken advantage of the mercy and forgiveness of Allah in order to meet their own selfish needs. The outcome for them is the same as in the previous text, but this passage lacks the narrative detail and plot development found there. Here the parting of the sea is not mentioned at all and there is only one brief reference to the drowning of the Egyptians. This time the emphasis is on the reason for the drowning rather than the act itself as the text illustrates the depth of Egyptian unbelief and disrespect for the authority of Allah. In contrast, the Israelites are rewarded for their patience and endurance by being delivered from their oppression. The reference to the fulfillment of the "good word of the Lord" (v. 137) points out the distinction between the deity and the Egyptians. While the latter do not keep their word and are quick to violate the agreement they make with Moses, Allah remains ever faithful to the divine word and rewards the Israelites for their steadfastness.

But it would be a mistake to think that the purpose of this text is to contrast the lack of belief on the part of the Egyptians with the true faith of the Israelites. Moses' people, too, fall short when they desire to be like the idol worshipers they encounter on the other side of the sea. If anything, the contrast in this story is not between the Egyptians and the Israelites but between the Israelites themselves prior to and after Allah brings them across the sea. In asking Moses to make a god for them they are rejecting Allah's role as the one true God by engaging in *shirk* through trying to associate something in the created order with the uncreated deity. This is a striking about-face for a people who, in the previous verse, were rewarded for their dedication and devotion to Allah.

This Qur'an text reminds the reader that the temptation to wander from the straight path is always present and even a group like the Israelites, who have just experienced their miraculous rescue by Allah, can succumb to it. Their petition to Moses to create a god for them mirrors that of the Egyptians at the beginning of the text when they ask Moses to intercede to Allah on their behalf. But the reader disapproves more of the Israelite request because theirs is an outright rebuff of the deity who has just come to their aid, while the Egyptians at least acknowledge, if only implicitly and for their own selfish reasons, Allah's authority and control over their lives.

So this passage contains a curiously ambiguous evaluation of the Israelites. On the one hand, the image of them is a very positive one that comes close to the biblical concept of their being the chosen people of God. Due to their fidelity and faithfulness, the good word of their Lord comes to fruition and they are led out of Egypt to inhabit a land which Allah has blessed. Similar to their status in the biblical view, they have been "exalted above all others" (v. 140). On the other hand, they are, in the words of Moses, "an ignorant people" (v. 138) whose faith is easily swayed by the lure of false gods and empty promises. This ambiguity regarding the people of the book is a common theme throughout the Qur'an. It both expresses the high regard in which Jews and Christians are held by virtue of their special relationship with Allah and explains how they violated that relationship thereby making necessary the coming of Muhammad and Islam.

Perhaps the major difference between the biblical and Qur'anic accounts of the crossing of the sea is the lack of any reference to the Passover tradition in the latter text. In the Bible, God decides to inflict a final plague on the Egyptians as the firstborn of all humans and livestock are killed (Exodus 11), and it is this major loss of life which convinces Pharaoh to let the Israelites go free (Exod 12:29-32). This sets them off on their escape from Egypt which culminates in the parting of the sea after the Egyptians reconsider and decide to give chase in pursuit of the fleeing Israelites. In the biblical telling, then, the crossing of the sea is closely connected to, indeed dependent upon, the Passover killing of the firstborn of Egypt.

Another important aspect of the Passover tradition is that it functions as an etiology, a story which explains the origin of some practice or belief. On the night they flee from Egypt, the Israelites partake of a ritual meal which is to be reenacted in the future during the annual commemoration of their escape from Egypt. Large sections of Exodus 12 and 13 are legalistic texts which establish the feast of Passover for future generations of Israelites and lay down the cultic details of the celebration. Several times throughout these chapters the binding nature of the command to reenact this Passover ritual is stressed. "This day shall be a day of remembrance for you. You shall celebrate it as a festival to the Lord; throughout your generations you shall observe it as a perpetual ordinance" (Exod 12:14).

The Qur'an lacks any reference to the Passover, the killing of the firstborn, or Israelite ritual, and it does not attempt to link the flight of Moses' people with the death of Egyptians. This is primarily due to the Muslim understanding of Allah as a merciful, universal deity who is the Lord of all and not just interested in the welfare of a select group of people. The Bible indicates that the death of the Egyptian offspring, just as the other plagues described in Exodus 7–11, is an expression of divine favoritism for Israelites over Egyptians. "Every firstborn in the land of Egypt shall die, from the firstborn of Pharaoh who sits on his throne to the firstborn of the female slave who is behind the handmill, and all the firstborn of the livestock. . . . But not a dog shall growl at any of the Israelites—not at people, not at animals—so that you may know that the Lord makes a distinction between Egypt and Israel" (Exod 11:5, 7). Such a bald statement of divine partiality would be completely out of place in the Qur'an given its consistent emphasis on Allah's concern for all humanity. As we have seen, texts like 7:140, which refers to Allah's exalting the children of Israel over others, can be cited in support of the idea that the children of Israel enjoy a special status in the Qur'an, but this still falls well short of the exclusive, privileged position they enjoy in the biblical text.[10]

A final point on which to compare the crossing of the sea tradition in the Bible and the Qur'an concerns Pharaoh's character. In Exodus, it appears that he does not lead his forces into the parted waters and share their watery grave. In listing the Egyptian casualties, the text speaks of

Pharaoh's horses, chariots, chariot drivers, and army but never mentions the man himself. "The waters returned and covered the chariots and the chariot drivers, the entire army of Pharaoh that had followed them into the sea; not one of them remained" (Exod 14:28). The poetic hymn celebrating the Exodus in chapter 15, which many scholars believe to be a much older text, similarly makes no reference to Pharaoh's demise in the sea. "Pharaoh's chariots and his army he cast into the sea; his picked officers were sunk in the Red Sea" (Exod 15:4). If the biblical tradition thought Pharaoh was among the drowned, one would expect to find some explicit reference to this, so the text probably wants us to imagine him as a spectator or eyewitness to the miracle at the sea rather than a victim of it.

The two Qur'an texts we have been discussing agree with the biblical account on this point since they do not claim that Pharaoh drowned with the other Egyptians and they give no indication that he even attempted to cross the divided sea. However, there are other passages in the Qur'an which describe him leading his army through the parted waters in hot pursuit of the Israelites. "Pharaoh followed them with his troops but they were engulfed by the sea. Pharaoh led his people astray and did not properly guide them" (20:78-79). The last phrase of this text is a nice example of *double entendre* as it allows for both a spiritual and physical interpretation. Pharaoh failed to properly guide his people through both his rejection of the God of Moses, which led to their spiritual destruction, and his plunging headlong into the sea as he chased the Israelites, which resulted in their physical demise.

There is another passage from the Qur'an at 10:90-92 which also describes Pharaoh entering the sea with his army but this time there is a completely different outcome.

> [90]We brought the children of Israel across the sea and Pharaoh and his troops followed them wickedly and maliciously until, as he was about to drown, he cried out, "I believe that there is no god but the one Whom the children of Israel believe in and I am among those who submit." [91]What? Prior to this you were rebellious and one of the corrupt. [92]Today, We will save you bodily so that you may be a sign for those who come after you. Truly, many people do not heed Our signs.

Here, Pharaoh is saved after making an explicit confession of faith in the God of Moses. His choice of words is characteristically Islamic since he refers to himself as one of the "muslims," those who surrender themselves to the will of Allah. In this case, we have a clear example of how two contrasting traditions can be found in the Qur'an and each be equally valid due to the different points they attempt to convey. Rather than drowning and being the cause of his people's destruction as in 20:78-79, in this text Pharaoh is rescued so that he might help bring about the salvation of later generations. The latter scene is interesting in light of the biblical account where a similar confession of faith is uttered but to no avail. In Exodus 14:25, after God clogs the wheels of their chariots the Egyptians exclaim, "Let us flee from the Israelites, for the Lord is fighting for them against Egypt." Unlike in the Qur'an, this cry falls on deaf divine ears since the next verse goes on to recount the Lord's command to Moses, "Stretch out your hand over the sea, so that the water may come back upon the Egyptians, upon their chariots and chariot drivers." Despite their recognition of God's presence, the Egyptian army in the Bible does not enjoy the act of divine mercy that is extended to their leader in the Qur'an.

Journeying to a New Land

In both the Bible and the Qur'an, the Israelites leave Egypt with a particular destination in mind. They are to travel to a place that has been divinely set aside for them where they can live as an independent people free to worship their God. Prior to arriving there, however, they experience some obstacles which complicate their passage and hinder their relationship with the deity. The biblical tradition presents a much more detailed and developed account of the Israelite journey, but some Qur'an passages, like 5:21-26, share some of its basic elements. It begins with Moses addressing the people.

> [21] "Oh my people, enter the holy land which Allah has decreed for you. Do not turn back in retreat for you will go astray." [22]They said, "Oh Moses, a powerful people is there and we will not enter it until they leave. If they depart from it we will enter." [23]Two men from among those who feared, on whom Allah granted favor, said, "Enter the gate against them; if you enter it you will surely be victors. Place your trust in Allah if you are believers." [24]They said, "Oh Moses, we will never enter it as long as they are there. You and your Lord go and fight. We will stay here." [25]He said, "My Lord, I have no one except myself and my brother, so separate us from these disobedient people." [26](Allah) said, "It (the land) is forbidden to them for forty years while they wander the earth. So do not grieve for the disobedient people."

The Promised Land motif is central to the Hebrew Bible and plays a key theological role throughout the text. It is linked to the covenant made to Abraham who, at God's command, traveled from his ancestral home to a new land given to him and his offspring forever. Even before they took full possession of it, that land was seen as a sign of the special relationship existing between God and the Israelite people. Centuries after they gained control of it, the land was lost when it was invaded first by the Assyrians (eighth century B.C.E.) and then by the Babylonians (sixth century B.C.E.), which brought about the period known as the Exile (586–38 B.C.E.). This experience of loss of control of the Promised Land raised profound theological questions for the community as they struggled to make sense of how such a thing could happen. Many scholars believe large portions of the biblical material were given final form within the context of the Exile, and so it is possible that the experience of the loss of and return to the land has had a significant impact on the way the biblical story is presented.

A great deal of attention in the Bible is devoted to explaining how the Israelites were able to gain access to the Promised Land. Virtually all of the books of Exodus, Leviticus, Numbers, Deuteronomy, Joshua, and Judges are, in one way or another, concerned with describing the Israelites' experiences as they made their circuitous way to Canaan and then encountered the people already inhabiting the land. This is the central episode of the Hebrew Bible since all prior events point toward it and all subsequent events flow from it. The close connection between the land and the covenant is highlighted by the dominant presence of the Law as the focal point of this portion of the text. Moses' encounter with God on the mountain, where he is given the Law by which Israel is to live, occurs within the context of the journey and establishes the covenantal obligations the people must accept if they wish to live in the Promised Land.

In the Qur'an, the idea of a Promised Land for Israel carries nowhere near the importance or weight it does in the Bible. One reason for this is the common tendency to downplay such expressions of divine preference which run counter to Islam's more universal attitude toward both faith and the deity. In the Muslim view, the true religion for all people is Islam because it does not draw distinctions among people and set some over or against others. In the same way, Allah does not play favorites by establishing special relationships with some groups that are unavailable to others. Such beliefs are difficult to reconcile with the biblical notion of a Promised Land and a people set apart. Nonetheless, the Qur'an does agree, in a limited way, with this aspect of the biblical tradition, and the above text is a case in point since it speaks of a holy land that has been decreed for Israel by Allah (v. 21). So, while the Promised Land motif is downplayed considerably in the Qurʾan, it is not completely lacking.

This Qurʾan text presents a negative picture of the Israelite people as it shows them unable to place all their faith and trust in Allah. It begins with Moses telling them that the land he is asking them to enter is a holy place that Allah has set apart for them and if they choose not to enter it they will go astray (v. 21). The Arabic verb "to turn back" *(tartaddū)* could be understood in two different ways and so might be an example of the use of an intentionally ambiguous word with a double meaning. It can refer to being lost in the physical sense of wandering about and it can also carry a more spiritual meaning referring to one who has turned away from true faith to follow a false religion. Both meanings fit the literary context here and contribute to the interpretation of the passage. In turning back and not entering the land, the people express their spiritual waywardness through their inability to believe that Allah has given the land to them despite the presence of the powerful people presently living there. Similarly, their refusal to enter the land leads to their physical wandering since their punishment is that they are forced to roam the earth for forty years (v. 26).

These two possible meanings express the physical and spiritual consequences of the Israelite lack of trust in Allah. Their rejection of the deity is graphically expressed in their response to Moses in verse 24, "Oh Moses, we will never enter it as long as they are there. You and your Lord go and fight. We will stay here." As noted earlier, the word "Lord" has a relational sense, and this helps us appreciate the depths of the Israelite lack of faith in the text. Rather than saying "our Lord," they disavow any connection to Allah here and refer to the deity as Moses' Lord. There might be an element of sarcasm in their response indicating they do not think it is possible that even with Allah on his side Moses can be victorious. Their words might also be expressing their overwhelming fear in the face of the perceived threat of the people in the land as they prefer to sit back and observe the outcome from a safe distance. In either case, their statement is a self-incriminating expression of lack of faith since they have just been urged to believe and reminded of the implications if they fail to do so. "Enter the gate against them; if you enter it you will surely be victors. Place your trust in Allah if you are believers" (v. 23). Their refusal to place their trust in Allah is a way of saying "We are not believers."

The biblical story which is most similar to this Qurʾan passage is found in Numbers 13–14, a text describing a reconnaissance mission into the Promised Land. At God's instruction, Moses sends twelve men, one from each tribe, into Canaan to gather information about the place and its inhabitants. After a forty-day foray they return to report to Moses that the place is appealing but its occupants present a problem. "We came to the land to which you sent us; it flows with milk and honey, and this is its fruit. Yet the people who live in the land are strong, and the towns are fortified and very large; and besides, we saw the descendants of Anak there" (Num 13:27-28). Fearing that they might be asked to invade the land, some of the traveling party then fabricate a tale about the Canaanites that they spread among the Israelites. "The land that we have gone through as spies is a land that devours its inhabitants; and all the people that we saw in it are of great size. There we saw the Nephilim (the Anakites come from the Nephilim); and to ourselves we seemed like grasshoppers, and so we seemed to them" (Num 13:32-33).

Before the Israelites can begin to enact their plan of mutiny to return to Egypt, two of the spies, Joshua and Caleb, attempt to calm them down by reminding them of their relationship with God. But their words go unheeded.

> "The land that we went through as spies is an exceedingly good land. If the Lord is pleased with us, he will bring us into this land and give it to us, a land that flows with milk and honey. Only, do not rebel against the Lord; and do not fear the people of the land, for they are no more than bread for us; their protection is removed from them, and the Lord is with us; do not fear them." But the whole congregation threatened to stone them (Num 14:7-10).

This causes God to refuse the people entry into the land. They are punished by being forced to wander forty years in the wilderness where they will die, a fate that only Joshua and Caleb are saved from. "And your children shall be shepherds in the wilderness for forty years, and shall suffer for your faithlessness, until the last of your dead bodies lies in the wilderness. According to the number of days in which you spied out the land, forty days, for every day a year, you shall bear your iniquity, forty years, and you shall know my displeasure" (Num 14:33-34).

There are some interesting points of contact between the Qur'an passage and the account in Numbers 13–14. Joshua and Caleb appear to function in a way similar to the two unnamed men in the Qur'an who have been granted favor by Allah and unsuccessfully attempt to convince their comrades to enter the land by appealing to their faith. A second intriguing connection concerns the Arabic word for "powerful" in verse 22. Among other things, this term (*jabbār*) can refer to some-one who is proud, bold, or insolent, but other attested meanings include "tall" and "giant." This latter sense coheres well with the biblical narrative in which the spies make exaggerated claims about the immense size of the Canaanites.

The two texts agree on seeing the forty-year period of wandering as a penalty for the Israelites' lack of trust and faith in the deity, but in the biblical story this is a negotiated settlement that results from Moses' unwillingness to accept God's initial punishment which was much harsher. According to Numbers 14:11-12, God's first reaction is to totally annihilate the Israelites and start over with a new chosen people, under Moses' leadership, who will be more faithful. "I will strike them with pestilence and disinherit them, and I will make of you a nation greater and mightier than they." Moses manages to circumvent this outcome by convincing God to spare the people, thereby rerouting their journey into the wilderness and extending it to forty years. But this only delays their inevitable demise in the desert banned from their Promised Land. Here we are once again confronted with an image of the deity that is not at home in the Qur'an, and this difference is reflected in the contrasting ways the two stories end. The Islamic tradition softens the deity's role somewhat by avoiding any reference to divine wrath and vengeance that permanently bans them from the Promised Land. Rather than speak of their death in the wilderness, the Qur'an refers to their being forbidden from the land for forty years. This is a more hopeful conclusion since it implies the possibility that they might one day be allowed to enter the land after they have paid the price for their lack of faith.

In their accounts of the Israelite wandering in the wilderness, the Bible and Qur'an both describe key events which define the parameters of the divine/human relationship and highlight the essential role of Moses as an intermediary between the deity and the people. A succinct summary of some of these episodes is offered in the Qur'an at 2:57-61.

[57]We caused clouds to overshadow you and sent down to you manna and quails, saying, "Eat the good things We have provided for you." They did not wrong Us but they wronged themselves. [58](Remember) when We said, "Enter this town and abundantly eat whatever you wish in it. Humbly enter the gate and say, 'Forgive us!' We will forgive your sins and give increase to those who do good." [59]But the wrongdoers perverted what was said to them and We sent down on them a punishment from

heaven because they disobeyed. [60](Remember) when Moses prayed for water for his people and We said, "Strike the stone with your rod." Then twelve springs flowed out from it and each people knew their drinking place. Eat and drink from the provision of Allah and do not act wrongfully in the land, spreading corruption. [61](Remember) when you said, "Oh Moses, we will not be satisfied with one type of food. So pray to your Lord for us that He might bring forth for us what the earth grows of its herbs, cucumbers, grain, lentils and onions." He said, "Do you wish to replace that which is good with that which is worse? Go down to a town since what you ask for is there." They were hit with humiliation and abasement and incurred Allah's anger because they rejected Allah's signs and unjustly killed the prophets. That was how they disobeyed and transgressed.

The people's inability to be thankful and appreciate all that Allah has done for them is the thematic focus of these five verses. Three times Allah acts in a way that shows concern for the Israelites, and the people snub each of these expressions of divine largesse. The manna and quails which are a provision from Allah do not lead them to deeper faith but result in their wronging themselves. When they are instructed regarding what to do upon entering a town they do the opposite and are punished from on high. After being blessed with water in a miraculous way, they complain about their monotonous and bland diet, thereby rejecting the heavenly provisions that have sustained them up to that point. These are a people who want things on their own terms and are uncomfortable with submitting themselves to the divine will. Although the text does not contain their answer to Moses' question in verse 61, it could only be an affirmative response since they are depicted as consistently preferring that which is bad for them over that which is good.

The mention of the twelve springs of water (v. 60) is reminiscent of the biblical text at Exodus 15:27 which says the Israelites camped by the waters of Elim, an oasis area with twelve springs of water and seventy palm trees. The Qur'an passage goes on to say that each group knew its drinking place, giving the impression that the people were divided into twelve sections. This calls to mind the biblical idea of the twelve tribes of Israel which is referred to in several places in the text of Islam. In 5:12-13, for example, there seems to be a clear allusion to this tradition.

[12]Allah made a covenant with the Israelites and We raised from them twelve chiefs and Allah said, "Truly, I am with you. If you engage in prayer, offer almsgiving, believe in my messengers and assist them, and

lend to Allah a good loan then I will forgive your evil and bring you into gardens with running streams. Whoever among you disbelieves after that has surely strayed from the right path." [13]Because they broke their covenant, We cursed them and made their hearts hard. They pervert words out of their context and have forgotten a portion of what has been mentioned to them. You will always find all but a few of them to be deceitful. But pardon them and bear with them for Allah loves those who do good.

In texts like this one the Qur'an shows familiarity with the biblical theme of Israel being divided into twelve tribes, each organized around its own leader. But even these tribal chiefs lack true faith and ultimately violate the covenant Allah establishes. They may know their proper drinking places but they do not know their place in relation to the deity. The previous text from sura 2 illustrates this waywardness by showing their rebellion in action as they repeatedly do what they want rather than what Allah wants. The reference to distorting words in verse 13 of the text above is a criticism of the people of the book and their tendency to distort the divine revelation that has been given to them. According to this passage, such misrepresentation and falsification of Allah's word is their own fault and a result of their violation of the covenant.

Another aspect of the text from sura 2 deserving some comment concerns a word in verse 61. When the people gripe to Moses about the lack of variety in their meals, he says, "Go down to a town since what you ask for is there." The word "town" *(miṣr)* can also carry the meaning "Egypt," and many English editions of the Qur'an translate it as such. This is another example of an ambiguous word with a double meaning, each of which can fit the context and contribute to the text's meaning. If it is rendered as "town" Moses is highlighting the people's inability to put all their trust and faith in Allah. The wilderness is a harsher environment than a town and in order to survive in it one needs to acknowledge one's dependence on the deity. A town will meet their physical cravings and desire for a varied menu, but taking refuge in such a place will signal their inability to carry out Allah's will and their replacement of what is good with what is worse. The same might be said if the word is translated as "Egypt," but in this case the theological implications for the Israelites are even more serious. If Moses is telling them to return to Egypt, he is not simply suggesting a temporary respite from their uncomfortable situation as the translation "town" might suggest. Retracing their steps to the land they are fleeing would, in effect, completely sever their ties with Allah since it would reverse and negate all that the deity had done for them. A town is a haven where they might recuperate before resuming their journey, but back-tracking to Egypt would be a permanent about-face.

The scenes in this Qurʾan passage of Allah providing food and drink for the Israelites in the wilderness have biblical counterparts which are presented in somewhat different form there. Early in the Bible's account of their journey, we read of God sending manna and quails for the Israelites to eat. Soon after they leave the oasis town of Elim and enter the wilderness of Sin, the people begin to complain to Moses about their harsh conditions and empty stomachs. "If only we had died by the hand of the Lord in the land of Egypt, when we sat by the fleshpots and ate our fill of bread; for you have brought us out into this wilderness to kill this whole assembly with hunger" (Exod 16:3). God then responds to their cries by sustaining them with manna in the morning and quails in the evening (Exod 16:4-36), but the emphasis in this passage is clearly on the manna. The quails are mentioned only once (v. 13), and then not referred to again as the text explains the elaborate instructions the Israelites are to follow in gathering the manna to insure that they do not violate the Sabbath prohibition against work. The Qurʾan contains none of this information on the Sabbath, but that should not be surprising since it tends to avoid any explicit discussion of practices and rituals that are uniquely Jewish or Christian.

The Bible contains another version of this scene in which the quails figure more prominently. Numbers 11:4-35 explains how manna was the only thing the Israelites originally had to eat but, after they complained about this to Moses, God sent quails to supplement their diet. Before they were able to eat the meat, God became very angry with them because of their craving and sent a plague upon them. This is different from the story in the Qurʾan in which Allah encourages the Israelites to eat of the manna and quails (v. 57) but the people still end up wronging themselves. The biblical account in Numbers 11 can cause the reader to question God's motives and actions. Why does God choose to send a plague after sending the quails? The text indicates it is due to the people's selfish desire for other food, but why does God first provide different food and then become enraged? Is God unsure of how to respond to their complaints? God and Moses also engage in a heated discussion in this chapter, which further puts the deity in a negative light and raises questions about the divine character. Such concerns are not present when reading the Qurʾan since Allah is a more consistent character whose relationship with Moses and the other prophets is on firmer ground.

Despite this important difference between the two texts they do share much in common. One subtle, but intriguing, agreement is the presence of the divine cloud motif in both. In verse 57 of the Qurʾan text, Allah sends clouds which overshadow the people prior to the sending of the manna and quails. We see a similar phenomenon in both the biblical texts that are parallel to it. In Exodus 16:10 the Israelites see the glory of the Lord appear in a cloud prior to God's telling Moses that the manna and quails will be sent. Similarly, in Numbers 11:25, the Lord comes down in a cloud and speaks to Moses after he gives the people the divine message about the quails. In the Bible, the cloud is often a symbol of divine presence and protection,[11] and its use in the Qurʾan suggests Islam shares a similar understanding. Another interesting connection between the two traditions is the way both texts have the Israelites complain about the lack of variety in their diet as they longingly recall the sumptuous delights previously available to them in Egypt. This similarity even extends to the details as several of the foods on the lists, like cucumbers, onions and garlic, are found in both (Num 11:5; Qurʾan 2:61).

The Bible also contains two versions of the water from a rock story, and both times Moses is the one who performs the feat. The first takes place early in the account of the Israelite sojourn in the wilderness. The text immediately following the manna and quails episode in Exodus 16 describes the Israelites, camped at Rephidim, quarreling with Moses over their lack of water (Exod 17:1-7). Their complaint is very similar to the one they voiced in the previous chapter when they were hungry. "Why did you bring us out of Egypt, to kill us and our children and livestock with thirst?" (v. 3). At God's instruction, the staff that was used to hold back the waters of the sea is now used by Moses to produce water by striking it on a rock. The only notable difference between this text and the one from the Qurʾan in sura 2 is the latter's specification that twelve springs flowed out from the rock after Moses struck it.

There is a similar story in Numbers 20:2-13 but this one has profound, indeed dire, results for Moses and the people. Once again, they complain about their lack of water and Moses is instructed by God to take his staff and draw water from the rock. But this time, after the people drink, the deity has some harsh words for Moses and Aaron. "Because you did not trust in me, to show my holiness before the eyes of the Israelites, therefore you shall not bring this assembly into the land that I have given them" (Num 20:12). God punishes the brothers for their lack of trust and forbids them from entering the Promised Land.

Scholars have debated long and hard over the nature of Moses' and Aaron's sin. What did they do to merit such a stiff penalty? How did they fail to show God's holiness before the eyes of the Israelites? Suggested answers to these questions have included the following: (1) Moses hit the rock twice but was not told by God to do so; (2) he lost his temper with the Israelites; (3) he doubted God's power; (4) he claimed for himself the ability to work the wonder. However one chooses to understand why God punishes Moses, the interesting thing for our purposes is that this part of the tradition is not found in the Qur'an. As a faithful messenger of Allah, it would be impossible for Moses or any other prophet to receive such a strict censure from the deity. Here, we touch on a key difference between the way Moses is presented in the Bible and the Qur'an. His character possesses a somewhat tragic quality in the Hebrew Bible as he dies on Mount Nebo, close enough to the Promised Land that he can see it, but prohibited from setting foot in the place that was the destination during his forty-year odyssey (Deut 32:49-52; 34:1-8). The Qur'an lacks this element entirely as we are not told how Moses dies and can only assume that he succumbed after a long and faithful career as Allah's messenger.

MOSES ON THE MOUNTAIN

The Qur'an makes reference to an encounter between Moses and Allah on a mountain, but this tradition does not play the dominant role that it does in the Bible. The biblical account of Moses' life presents the story of his meeting with God on Mount Sinai[12] as the high point of the deity's relationship with Israel because it is there that the Law is given to the people and their covenantal obligations are clearly spelled out. It is also a dramatic moment which is described in great detail with an emphasis on the overpowering, awesome presence of God. The Qur'an, in its telling of the event, also highlights the divine/human relationship and the power of Allah but does so in a more subtle way. Its version is much briefer and is not presented as the pivotal event in the community's life that it is in the Bible. The two main scenes connected with this tradition in the Qur'an describe Moses' sojourn on the mountain and the people's sin while he is absent.

Moses' Sojourn on the Mountain

According to Qur'an 20:80 a mountain is the place at which the covenant between Allah and the Israelites was sealed. "Oh children of

Israel, We rescued you from your enemies, established a covenant with you on the right side of the mountain, and sent down to you manna and quails." The name of the mountain is unexpressed in the Qur'an but the use of the definite article before it ("the" mountain) suggests this is a particular place that might be familiar to the people. Its mention between their being rescued from their enemies and being provided for by Allah in the wilderness indicates the mountain was located somewhere along their journey from Egypt to the land Allah had given them. The text lacks any information on what the covenant entailed, how it was ratified, and who was involved in its establishment. If one were to read only this passage, it would not be unreasonable to conclude that many, maybe all, of the members of the Israelite community were present on the right side of the mountain when the event occurred. But this is not the only reference to the episode in the Qur'an. Another more lengthy text at 7:142-146 describes an encounter between Moses and Allah on a mountain which might be a fuller account of the one referred to in sura 20.

> [142]We promised Moses thirty nights and We added ten more to them. Thus was completed his Lord's appointed time of forty nights. Moses said to his brother Aaron, "Take my place among my people. Act properly and do not follow the way of the corrupt." [143]When Moses came at Our appointed time and his Lord spoke to him, he said, "Show Yourself to me that I might look upon You." He replied, "You may not see Me, but look at the mountain. If it remains in its place you shall see me. When his Lord appeared on the mountain He leveled it and Moses fell down unconscious. When he came to, he said, "Praise be to You! I repent to You and I am the first of believers." [144]He said, "Oh Moses, I have chosen you from all people by My messages and My word. So take what I have given to you and be among the thankful." [145]And We wrote about everything for him upon the tablets, exhorting and explaining all things. "Take them firmly and urge your people to follow the best of them. I will show you the dwelling place of the unrighteous. [146]I will turn away from My signs those who are unjustly proud on the earth. If they see all the signs they will not believe them. And if they see the way of rectitude they will not take it. That is because they considered Our signs to be lies and did not heed them."

When we compare this passage with its counterpart in the Bible we are immediately struck by the lack of accompanying narrative in the Qur'an. Virtually all of the second half of the book of Exodus, from chapter 19 through chapter 40, takes place on or near the mountain, and much of this material has no Qurʾanic parallel. Exodus 19–20 recounts several trips by Moses up the mountain to converse with God while the people are commanded to stay below. This is followed, in Exodus 21–23, by a collection of laws which God sets down for the Israelites. Exodus 24:1-11 describes several ritual activities as Moses returns to the people, writes down the divine message, erects twelve pillars, offers sacrifices, and dashes sacrificial blood on both the altar and the people.

It is not until Exodus 24:12-18, when Moses is called by God, told he will be given the tablets of stone, and spends forty days and nights on the mountain far removed from the people, that we can discern a connection with the Qurʾan text. But much of the Qurʾanic passage has no equivalent in Exodus 24. In particular, Moses' request to see Allah and the subsequent miraculous leveling of the mountain does not have a biblical parallel. We have to make our way through eight more chapters in Exodus before we come across material that is even remotely related to this component of the Qurʾan text. Prior to that, Exodus 25–31 describes, in painstaking detail, God's orders regarding the dimensions and construction of the ark, tabernacle, altar, priestly vestments, and other cultic objects. Exodus 31 ends with a reference to God giving Moses two tablets containing the law written by the divine finger, and this immediately leads to the golden calf episode in Exodus 32 which will be discussed below.

It is at this point that the biblical and Qurʾanic versions begin to converge again. Exod 33:18-23 describes an event that is similar to the Qurʾan passage when Moses asks for a face-to-face encounter with God.

> [18]Moses said, "Show me your glory, I pray." [19]And he said, "I will make all my goodness pass before you, and will proclaim before you the name, 'The Lord'; and I will be gracious to whom I will be gracious, and will show mercy on whom I will show mercy. [20]But," he said, "you cannot see my face; for no one shall see me and live." [21]And the Lord continued, "See, there is a place by me where you shall stand on the rock; [22]and while my glory passes by I will put you in a cleft of the rock, and I will cover you with my hand until I have passed by; [23]then I will take away my hand, and you shall see my back; but my face shall not be seen."

The next morning Moses returns to the mountain and is given two new tablets as the Lord passes before him (Exod 34:1-9). His response is to bow down and pray, "If now I have found favor in your sight, O Lord, I pray, let the Lord go with us. Although this is a stiff-necked people, pardon our iniquity and our sin, and take us for your inheritance" (v. 9).

There are some obvious similarities between the traditions in the Bible and Qur'an describing Moses' sojourn on the mountain, but the differences are more notable. In both texts, Moses is alone on the mountain for forty days, requests to see the deity, is denied that request, expresses his remorse, and receives the tablets containing divine instruction. But the pace and manner in which these events unfold vary greatly from text to text. The Qur'an tells it all in the space of five verses, with each episode occurring on the heels of the previous one. But the Bible takes sixteen chapters, and almost five hundred verses, to relate the story of Moses and God on the mountain. The bulk of the extra material is in the form of legal texts and cultic instructions written specifically to and for the Israelite community. Beyond this difference in sheer volume, however, the Bible and Qur'an also diverge regarding the content and focus of their respective texts. This is most clearly seen when we study the scene in which Moses asks to see the deity.

In both texts, Moses' desire to see the deity is met with the response that he will be permitted to see something other than what he has requested. In Exodus 33:23 he is told that he will be allowed to see God's back but he may not gaze upon the divine face. The terms "back" and "face" are examples of anthropomorphism, the use of human attributes or qualities to describe the deity. This is a technique that is fairly common in the Bible, where God is regularly spoken of as having hands, eyes, ears, feet, and other body parts. The passage under discussion makes heavy use of this literary device. Moses is told that he will stand near God on the rock (Exod 33:21), as if the deity is right next to him like another person might be. God will put him in a cleft of the rock, cover him with the divine hand and then take away the hand so Moses can see God's back (Exod 33:22-23). All these anthropomorphic terms contribute to creating a very intimate and personal scene in which Moses is being looked after and provided for by God.

Such language is not the norm in the Qur'an where Allah is rarely depicted in anthropomorphic terms. Here, Moses does not ask to see the deity's face but says, "Show Yourself to me that I might look upon You" (v. 143). There is a general avoidance of anthropomorphism in the Qur'an because of the Islamic belief that Allah is unknowable and transcends human experience. In the Muslim view, depicting or understanding the deity in human terms might violate the absolute unity and oneness of Allah, and possibly lead to the sin of *shirk* through association of what is created with the uncreated source of all that exists. This is not to say that there are no examples of anthropomorphism in the Qur'an.

The book contains occasional references to Allah's feet, hands, hearing, seeing and other aspects of the divine nature drawn from human experience, and these texts have been the subject of much debate throughout Islamic history. The most commonly accepted interpretation Muslim scholars give to these elements is to take them as metaphors which should not be understood literally, but as attempts to express qualities of Allah that are beyond human comprehension and experience.

What Moses sees in the Qur'an is quite different from what he sees in the Bible. Rather than catch a glimpse of the deity from behind as in Exodus, he witnesses a miracle as the mountain he has been told to look at crumbles before his eyes (v. 143). This is an expression of Allah's supreme power and authority that is meant to humble Moses. His response on observing this wonder is dramatic in its own way: he is overcome by what he has seen and faints. Upon regaining consciousness, his first words are both a statement of belief and request for mercy. "Praise be to You! I repent to you and I am the first of believers." In the biblical account, Moses does not see the mountain leveled and he does not faint. But he does respond submissively by bowing down and offering a prayer to God. "If now I have found favor in your sight, O Lord, I pray, let the Lord go with us. Although this is a stiff-necked people, pardon our iniquity and our sin, and take us for your inheritance" (Exod 34:9). Interestingly, Moses in the Qur'an repents only for his own shortcomings while in Exodus he asks forgiveness for the sin of the people and includes himself among their ranks. The former text stresses more his personal relationship with Allah as he acknowledges his own weakness, whereas the Bible highlights his role as intermediary between God and the people. Since he has found favor with the deity he can now petition on behalf of the Israelites.

The Qur'an's description of the encounter on the mountain is much briefer since it lacks the legal and cultic material that is specific to the Israelite community. Nonetheless, the two texts understand the scene in similar ways. For both, this is an experience in which Moses is set apart from his people and humbled by the incredible power and authority of the deity. It is also the context in which Moses receives the tablets containing the divine instruction which he is to communicate to the people. This agreement notwithstanding, however, it is important to keep in mind that the Qur'an does not consider Allah's meeting with Moses on the mount to be the central and defining encounter between the deity and humanity that it is in the Bible. The primary reason for this difference is a simple one: the Qur'an sees itself functioning in that capacity. As the only authentic guidance for all who seek to follow the divine will, it cannot be superceded by what happened to Moses on the mountain or by any other event in history.

The People's Sin

In sura 7, there immediately follows a description of what went on among the Israelites while Moses was communing with Allah on the mountain.

> [148]During his absence, Moses' people made from their ornaments a calf, a shape which made a lowing sound. Did they not see that it did not speak to them and it did not guide them? They took it (for worship) and were transgressors. [149]When they repented and realized they had gone astray they said, "If our Lord will not have mercy on us and forgive us our sins, we will surely be among the lost ones." [150]When Moses, angry and grieving, returned to his people he said, "What you have done in my absence is evil! Are you so quick to bring on your Lord's judgment?" He threw down the tablets and grabbed his brother by the hair, pulling him toward himself. He (his brother) said, "Son of my mother, the people overtook me and were about to kill me. Do not let the enemies rejoice over my misfortune and do not include me among the transgressors." [151]He (Moses) said, "My Lord, forgive me and my brother and bring us into Your mercy, You who are the most merciful of all." [152]Anger from their Lord and humiliation in the present life will come to those who took the calf. Thus do We reward those who invent falsehood. [153]But for those who do evil and then repent and believe, truly your Lord is forgiving and merciful after that. [154]When Moses' anger had subsided, he took the tablets. In their writing is guidance and mercy for those who fear their Lord.

This passage is the Qur'an's account of the events described in Exodus 32, the so-called "golden calf" story in the Bible. The general outline of the plot is identical in the two texts which describe how Moses returns from the mountain to find the Israelites have constructed a calf from their ornaments and becomes enraged over their lack of faith. In both texts, Moses' brother Aaron, who is unnamed in the Qur'an passage, is singled out for special attention. As is often the case, the Bible and Qur'an have little more in common than this shared outline. When we move to the level of details and theology we note some profound differences between the two versions. We can uncover some of those differences by considering the way each character, or set of characters, responds to the making of the calf.

1. The Israelites

The Israelites in the Qur'an respond in a way that underscores their regret and repentance. Their personal responsibility is identified at the outset when it is stated that they made the calf (v. 148). In other words, they have no one but themselves to blame for the situation they are in. In the very next verse, they acknowledge their error and beg for divine compassion. "If our Lord will not have mercy on us and forgive us our sins, we will surely be among the lost ones" (v. 149). We are not told what leads to their change of heart, but the outcome is clear: they realize they have made a serious mistake in constructing the calf and now desire to repair their fractured relationship with the deity. Since Moses has not yet come down from the mountain, it appears that they have reached this conclusion on their own and it is not the result of any threats or rebukes that he, or anyone else, directs toward them. In the Qur'an, they reflect on their actions and become aware of the consequences, and this brings about their conversion.

In the Bible, there is not a hint of regret or repentance on the people's part. As in the Qur'an, they do not have much to say, but their words in Exodus suggest a very different relationship with the deity than the one depicted in the Islamic text. The biblical Israelites do not express sorrow or contrition. Rather, their only two lines of dialogue in Exodus 32 indicate their complete rejection of and break from their God. In verse 1 they appeal to Aaron, "Come, make gods for us, who shall go before us; as for this Moses, the man who brought us up out of the land of Egypt, we do not know what has become of him." With these words, they reveal their total lack of understanding about how they were rescued from Egypt. They believe it was Moses who brought them out when, in actuality, it was God who made their safe passage possible.

Their sin is compounded and intensified in verse 4 with their only other words. On seeing the calf they exclaim, "These are your gods, O Israel, who brought you up out of the land of Egypt!" They have now moved a further step away from Yahweh. It is no longer Moses, the legitimate agent of God, who is responsible for their freedom from Egypt but the calf, an inanimate, impotent object of their own making. The Exodus account highlights their unrepentant depravity and debauchery by referring to their sacrifices, revelry and unchecked celebrating (vv. 6, 25). Even when Moses tries to appeal to their faith by asking who will join him on the Lord's side, only the Levites respond to the call (v. 26). This is quite different from the version in the Qur'an where the people express their sorrow and beg mercy as a group, undivided and without any external prompting.

2. Aaron

Aaron's role in the calf incident is foreshadowed in the Qurʾan text we considered earlier when Moses gives his brother some last-minute instructions. In 7:142, prior to Moses' encounter with Allah at the mountain, he says, "Take my place among my people. Act properly and do not follow the way of the corrupt." Aaron does not heed this advice very well since he appears to bear at least indirect responsibility for the building of the calf. Upon Moses' return, after questioning the people about the calf, he unleashes his anger on his brother by grabbing him by the hair and pulling him near. The Qurʾan does not record Moses' words, but Aaron's reply suggests he has just been interrogated regarding his involvement in the building of the calf. "Son of my mother, the people overtook me and were about to kill me. Do not let the enemies rejoice over my misfortune and do not include me among the transgressors" (v. 150).

As a way of exercising damage control, Aaron engages in a bit of blame-shifting by explaining to Moses how he was overpowered by the people and unable to take control of the situation as he would have liked. He appeals to family loyalty ("son of my mother") and fraternal solidarity to escape punishment, and the strategy works when Moses prays to Allah on behalf of himself and his brother (v. 151). Aaron's words further the idea that the people are the ones primarily responsible for making the calf, and this notion is supported by the lack of any explicit reference to Aaron being involved in the process. Since the text plainly states that the Israelites were the ones to build the calf (v. 148), it is reasonable for the reader to assume that Moses is upset with his brother not because he had a hand in the calf's construction, but because he did not do more to try to prevent its being built. Aaron's sin is one of omission, not commission, in the Qurʾan.

In Exodus 32, things are just the opposite since the calf is Aaron's handiwork. The people gather around him and request that he make gods for them (v. 1), and he does not appear to have any qualms about doing so since he immediately asks for their gold (v. 2). A description of the design and production of the calf then follows in which Aaron is identified as the one who both conceptualizes and executes the artistic plan. "He took the gold from them, formed it in a mold and cast an image of a calf" (v. 4). But Aaron's contribution to the project does not end there. He goes on to construct an appropriate setting for his work and calls for a fitting way to celebrate its presence among the Israelites. "When Aaron saw this, he built an altar before it; and Aaron made proclamation and said, 'Tomorrow shall be a festival to the Lord'" (v. 5). In case the reader has somehow failed to grasp Aaron's involvement in all this, the final verse of the chapter removes all doubt by pointing the finger directly at him as the one responsible for the calf. "Then the Lord sent a plague on the people, because of the calf—the one that Aaron made" (v. 35).

In his conversation with Moses, the biblical Aaron, like his counterpart in the Qurʾan, tries to defend himself by shifting the blame onto the people. "Do not let the anger of my lord burn hot; you know the people, that they are bent on evil" (v. 22). He paints himself as a victim who has been coerced by the crowd and should not be held accountable for their sins. His declaration of innocence borders on the ludicrous when he attempts to explain to his brother how the calf came to be. "So I said to them, 'Whoever has gold, take it off'; so they gave it to me, and I threw it into the fire, and out came this calf!" (v. 24). The reader is able to see right through Aaron's desperate attempt to get himself off the hook since we are aware of his involvement in designing and making the calf, building an altar for it and proclaiming a feast in its honor (vv. 4–5).

This has a profound influence on how we evaluate his character. In the Qurʾan, his assertion that the people overpowered him and forced him to act against his better judgment has a ring of truth to it since nothing in the text argues against it. But in Exodus the Israelites never threaten him or put any undue pressure on him to do anything. In fact, he seems to be in charge of them rather then vice versa. This comes out clearly in verse 25 which contains a parenthetical comment on Aaron's authority over the people. "For Aaron had let them run wild, to the derision of their enemies." Consequently, Aaron's character in the Bible has a negative, or questionable, quality that is not found in the Qurʾan. In Exodus, he is willing to distort the truth, even lie, rather than acknowledge his own involvement and culpability.

3. Moses

Moses' character undergoes a transformation in the course of the Qurʾan narrative, from an initial feeling of anger toward his people and alienation from them, to an eventual cooling of his rage which allows for the continuation of his relationship with the Israelites. When he returns from his encounter with Allah, he angrily lashes out at the people and accuses them of bringing divine judgment on their heads. He then throws down the tablets he received from Allah and turns on his brother, pulling him by the hair (v. 150). After Aaron's words to him, there is a discernible shift in Moses' demeanor. No longer furious and irate, he adopts the demeanor of a pious, sincere believer as he turns to Allah and begs forgiveness for himself and his brother (v. 151). This is an interesting prayer that raises some important questions. Why are his people not included in it? Are they not deserving of Allah's mercy and forgiveness? Is Moses disavowing his relationship with them?

If we keep in mind the fact that the Israelites have already recognized their sin and repented, the purpose of Moses' prayer becomes clear. He is praying for himself and his brother because they have failed in their responsibility to keep the people on the straight path. As Allah's agents, it is their duty to act as models of proper living, and they have not lived up to that task. Nonetheless, the people have been able to correct themselves by acknowledging their mistake and expressing their own desire for forgiveness. Moses sees their recommitment to Allah and concludes that he and his brother, rather than the people, are the ones who are in need of divine mercy. The last reference to Moses in the text tells us that at the end of the passage all the relationships have been restored and things are as they should be. In verse 154 we read, "When Moses' anger had subsided, he took the tablets. In their writing is guidance and mercy for those who fear their Lord." By picking up the tablets he had earlier cast aside and making them available to his people, Moses performs his task as Allah's messenger. The tablets' contents will enable the people to follow the divine will and avoid succumbing to temptation in the future. The end result in the Qurʾan, therefore, is a positive one since Moses' anger has abated and he is able to resume his function as Allah's prophet.

In the Bible, things move in the opposite direction. Moses initially defends and supports the people despite their offense, but gradually becomes more angry and disillusioned with them until he resorts to violent measures to punish them. When we first encounter Moses in Exodus 32, he is still on the mountain with God and the deity informs him that the people are about to be destroyed because they have made the calf (vv. 7–10). Moses quickly comes to their defense by asking God to remember the Exodus event and to recall the promises that were made to Abraham, Isaac and Jacob (vv. 11–14). This strategy works as God reconsiders and decides not to carry out the plan to destroy the

Israelites. In this early part of the chapter Moses speaks out on behalf of the people, but this will change once he makes his way down the mountain and is able to see their sin for himself.

Upon returning to the people, Moses' anger is expressed in three different actions, none of which has an exact parallel in the Qur'an. His first response is to smash the tablets at the foot of the mountain (v. 19). This is similar to his reaction in the Qur'an but with one important difference. In the Islamic text, he throws down the tablets but they do not break since, at the end of the passage, he is able to pick them up again and give them to the people. His shattering them in Exodus indicates the seriousness of their sin and symbolizes the fracturing of the divine/human relationship which the people have violated. Unlike in the Qur'an, Moses will not be able to retrieve the tablets later on and the story ends without a reconciliation. Two chapters later, in Exodus 34, God will instruct Moses to cut two more tablets that will replace the ones that were smashed.

Moses' second action follows immediately after he destroys the tablets. In verse 20 he burns the calf, grounds it to powder, scatters it on water and makes the Israelites drink it. The significance of this unusual sequence of events is hard to uncover. It could be a way of expressing the idea of the complete destruction of a false god or, as some biblical scholars have suggested, it might be a type of trial by ordeal similar to that described in Numbers 5:11-31. Regardless of its precise meaning, this action clearly indicates Moses' extreme displeasure at the Israelites and his desire to somehow hold them accountable for what they have done in making the calf.

Moses' final reaction is the most violent and extreme of the three. He asks all those on the Lord's side to join him at the gate of the camp. When the Levites step forward he commands them to arm themselves with their swords and go out among the people killing "your brother, your friend, your neighbor" (vv. 25–29). The text reports that three thousand people were killed in the ensuing bloodbath that day. This is quite a dramatic turnaround from the Moses on the mountain who was defending the Israelites from God's wrath earlier in the chapter. His fury has now reached such a fevered pitch that he feels compelled to order the murder of a large number of his own people. The difference from the Qur'an text could not be any plainer. While that passage ended with the subsiding of Moses' anger and the unification of his community in faith, the one in Exodus 32 concludes with a massacre that divides the people as a result of his escalating rage.

4. The Deity

The mercy and forgiveness of Allah is a major theme throughout this Qur'an text. The people have just committed one of the worst sins imaginable to the Muslim mind by making an image which they then worship as divine. But their words of repentance express their confidence that Allah is able to pardon even such a serious offense. "If our Lord will not have mercy on us and forgive us our sins, we will surely be among the lost ones" (v. 149). They do not assume that divine forgiveness is guaranteed, but they trust in the deity's mercy and recognize that only Allah has the power and authority to remove their guilt. We see a similar idea echoed in Moses' prayer when he requests forgiveness for himself and his brother and refers to Allah as the "most merciful of all" (v. 151). All of the human characters in this text have fallen short in one way or another and are in need of mercy and all of them call upon Allah, convinced that relying on the deity is the only sure way out of their dilemma.

The latter section of the passage also treats this theme by discussing the two options available to every person who has sinned. In verses 152–153 we read, "Anger from their Lord and humiliation in the present life will come to those who took the calf. Thus do We reward those who invent falsehood. But for those who do evil and then repent and believe, truly your Lord is forgiving and merciful after that." If one chooses, like those who worshiped the calf, to cling to false ways there will be punishment in this world and in the world to come. But if a sinner turns to Allah in faith, forgiveness and mercy will follow. The latter choice is the one that is made by those in this text and the final outcome is a happy one for all concerned. In this way, the golden calf episode in the Qur'an is used to illustrate the Islamic belief in a merciful, forgiving deity.

In the biblical account, God's character is associated more with death and destruction than with mercy and forgiveness. On the mountain, the deity informs Moses of the people's offense and then expresses the desire to do away with them and start over again with a new community under Moses' leadership. "I have seen this people, how stiff-necked they are. Now let me alone, so that my wrath may burn hot against them and I may consume them; and of you I will make a great nation" (Exod 32:9-10). When Moses dissuades God from carrying out this plan it is only a temporary postponement because large numbers of Israelites eventually do suffer and die, and the text makes it clear that these incidents are forms of divine punishment. The slaughter of the three thousand at the hands of the Levites is presented as the fulfill-ment of a divine command. In verse 27 Moses instructs them, "Thus says the Lord, the God of Israel, 'Put your sword on your side, each of you! Go back and forth from gate to gate throughout the camp, and each of you kill your brother, your friend, and your neighbor.'" But the resulting carnage does not satisfy God's desire to punish the people. The chapter concludes with the mention of yet another expression of divine retribution. "Then the Lord sent a plague on the people, because they made the calf—the one that Aaron made" (v. 35).

Throughout the biblical account, God appears to be more inter-ested in mayhem than mercy, but this should not lead us to the hasty conclusion that it and the Qur'an therefore present two completely un-related images of the deity. The two can be reconciled when we realize that each is discussing a different side of the same coin. The Hebrew Bible shares the Qur'an's belief that people are confronted with the choice to do good or evil and one's choice determines one's destiny. Those who choose good will be rewarded while those who choose evil will be punished. In their accounts of the golden calf tradition, each text focuses on the implications of one particular choice. The Qur'an explains what happens to those who opt to obey the divine will even if they temporarily choose to do wrong. For this reason, it highlights the compassionate, merciful side of the deity. Exodus 32, on the other hand, explores the significance and consequences of the other choice and so discusses what the divine response is toward those who choose to do evil. Because they are related to the issue of human choice and free will, these two images of the deity are complementary, not diver-gent, and need to be held in tension.

The Qur'an contains another version of the golden calf story in 20:86-98. It shares much in common with the account in sura 7, but there are some interesting differences which deserve some comment.

[86]Moses, angry and grieving, returned to his people and said, "Oh my people, did your Lord not promise you a good promise? Did the time seem too long for you? Or did you want your Lord's wrath to come upon you, that you broke your promise to me?" [87]They said, "We did not break your promise of our own accord, but we were made to carry loads of the people's ornaments and throw them (into the fire) and the Samiri did the same." [88]Then he (the Samiri) brought forth for them a calf, a shape which made a lowing sound, and they said, "This is your god and the god of Moses whom he has forgotten." [89]Could they not see that it re-turned no answer to them and that it had no power to bring them either

harm or benefit? [90]Earlier, Aaron had said to them, "Oh my people, you have been misled by it (the calf). Truly, your Lord is the merciful One, so follow me and obey my command." [91]They had replied, "We will not cease our devotion to it until Moses returns to us." [92](Moses) said, "Oh Aaron, what hindered you when you saw them straying, [93]that you did not follow me? Did you disobey my command?" [94]He said, "Son of my mother, do not seize me by the beard or the head. I feared that you might say, 'You have divided the children of Israel and did not wait for my word.'" [95](Moses) said, "What do you have to say, Samiri?" [96]He said, "I saw what they did not see. I took a handful of dust from the messenger's trail and threw it away. This is what my mind commended me to do." [97](Moses) said, "Begone! For all your life you will say, 'Do not touch me!' and there is an appointed time awaiting you that will not be unfulfilled. Look at your god whom you devotedly worship. We will surely burn it and scatter it on the sea. [98]Your God is only Allah and there is no god but He. His knowledge embraces all things."

The most intriguing difference between this text and the one in sura 7 is the presence of a new character here. According to sura 20, a person identified as "the Samiri" is the one responsible for making the calf and leading the Israelites astray. This is the only place this figure is mentioned in the Qurʾan and several things about him make him a somewhat mysterious individual. The description of the construction of the calf is quite similar to that in sura 7, and Exodus 32 for that matter, since it speaks of the use of the people's ornaments, or jewelry, as the primary ingredient which is then melted in a fire. When Moses confronts the Samiri regarding his involvement he responds that he had special knowledge which the people lacked. "I saw what they did not see" (v. 96). What exactly he saw has been the object of some debate within the Islamic community because the Samiri's words are vague and ambiguous. He refers to taking a handful of dust from the messenger's trail and throwing it away (v. 96). This verse leaves several questions unanswered. Who is the messenger? What or where is the trail? How is the action of throwing away the dust related to the making of the calf? Muslim tradition has identified the messenger as the angel Gabriel, who plays an intermediary role between Allah and humanity in Islamic theology. The trail is understood to be a reference to the tracks of the hooves of Gabriel's horse. The most widely accepted interpretation of the passage is that the Samiri is justifying his actions to Moses by claiming he has been privileged with a special message from Allah, through Gabriel, that was not made available to the community.

According to verse 97, the Samiri is reprimanded in several ways for making the calf. In the first place, he is expelled from Moses' presence and made to utter the phrase "Do not touch me!" throughout his life. In other words, he will try to avoid interaction and close physical contact with other people. Second, he is told that a day of reckoning, or "appointed time," awaits him which he will not be able to escape. The third way he is reproved is when Moses informs him that the calf he has been worshiping will be burned and its ashes dispersed in the sea. This action is vaguely reminiscent of Moses' response to the people's idolatry in the Bible when he burns the idol, grounds it to powder, scatters it on water and makes the Israelites drink it (Exod 32:20). In both cases, we have an incineration of the calf and a sprinkling of its remains over water. After explaining to the Samiri the price he will have to pay for his sin, Moses then proceeds to instruct him about true faith and the nature of Allah. "Your God is only Allah and there is no god but He. His knowledge embraces all things" (v. 98).

It is generally agreed by scholars that the Samiri is meant to personify a particular group of people, the Samaritans. Besides the obvious etymological connection between his name and the word "Samaritan," several elements of the Qur'an text make the link with the group fairly obvious. The Samaritans are a community whose precise origin is debated, but at an early point they separated themselves from Judaism due to cultic and theological differences. To this day, a small group of Samaritans celebrate their ancient traditions and rituals that have been passed down for centuries. Mount Gerizim, located north of Jerusalem near the modern city of Nablus, continues to be their primary place of worship. As many such groups do, they have tended to shun unnecessary contact with those outside their circle, and this may be what is behind the Qur'an's reference to the Samiri saying "Do not touch me!" The text is another example of an etiology since it attempts to explain the origin of the Samaritan practice of avoiding contact with other people.[13] It understands their segregation to be a punishment whose roots can be traced back to the time of Moses when one of their group disobeyed the divine will by making the calf.

The Samaritan connection can also help explain a curious element of the calf tradition that is found in both suras 7 and 20. Unlike its biblical counterpart, the calf in the Qur'an possesses the ability to make a sound and it is referred to as lowing, or mooing. It has often been noted that the people's comment upon seeing the calf in Exodus 32:4 ("These are your gods, O Israel, who brought you up out of the land of Egypt!")

is identical to what king Jeroboam says in 1 Kings 12:28 about the two golden calves he set up at the northern and southern borders of the northern kingdom of Israel. According to the Talmud, a compilation of religious literature from the sixth century C.E. that is a basic source for Jewish law and life, one of Jeroboam's calves was able to talk. This idea of a talking calf might have been linked with the story of the Samiri in the Qurʾan due to the geographical connection between the Samaritans and Jeroboam. When king Solomon died, the united kingdom, which had been established by his father David, died with him. From this point on, there were two separate monarchies in the land. The one in the south, known as Judah, carried on the Davidic line, and the one in the north, known as Israel, established a line of rival kings. The first of the kings of the north was Jeroboam, and when it came time for him to set up a capital he chose the city of Shechem, the ancient name for Nablus, which was the cultic center of the Samaritans. The talking calf motif's link with Shechem, the city of the Samaritans, might help explain the presence of the lowing calf in the Qurʾan.

The Bible reader might be tempted to find the two distinct accounts of the golden calf story in the Qurʾan troubling or suspicious, especially given the high profile of the Samiri in one and his complete absence in the other. But this reaction would be an improper one that would be the result of reading the Qurʾan with biblical eyes. We have frequently observed how the Qurʾan does not share the Bible's concern with presenting an ordered, chronological narrative of events. Rather, the emphasis is on the message or meaning of the text, and in the double telling of the golden calf story we have a clear example of this at work.

We should not understand these two versions of the story as being in competition with each other because the question then becomes which one is right. Did the Samiri make the calf or didn't he? In the Muslim view, they are both right because they complete and complement each other. The version in sura 7 takes as its starting point the mercy and forgiveness of Allah, and the entire story is told with that belief in mind. That text seeks to show how those who sin (the people) or those who fail to execute their divinely appointed responsibilities (Moses and Aaron) can still turn to the deity in confidence that their request for pardon will be heard.

The version in sura 20 explores another aspect of the divine/human relationship. It attempts to explain what happens when people fail to acknowledge their sin and try to justify or defend their evil actions. The Samiri is not yet at the point where the people and Moses/Aaron are in sura 7 since he is unable to acknowledge his fault and ask for mercy. So this text discusses the implications and consequences of such unreflective behavior and headstrong attitudes. If a person should continue in sin, there will be a terrible price to pay. But the text in sura 20 does not end on that pessimistic and hopeless note. It concludes with a chance for the Samiri to turn his life around by admitting his sin and calling on Allah. This is the point behind Moses' final words to him. He does not reject the Samiri due to his false belief in a god of his own creation, but invites him to have faith in the God of all creation. "Your God is only Allah and there is no god but He. His knowledge embraces all things" (v. 98). The text does not tell us what became of the Samiri and whether or not he took up Moses' invitation. But it allows for the possibility that he, like the people in sura 7, repented and realized he had gone astray.

* * *

A final chapter in the life of Moses which we will discuss occurs just prior to his first encounter with the deity in both the Bible and the Qur'an. It is comprised of two scenes which describe the events surrounding Moses' sudden departure from Egypt. In the first scene, he kills a man and is then forced to flee for his life when he discovers the deed has been found out. The second scene explains what happens to him when he arrives at Midian and settles down as a resident among the people there. A careful examination of each of these scenes, murder and Midian, shows that the Bible and Qur'an can be understood as cooperating revelations since the Islamic text enables us to appreciate important aspects of the biblical story that are easily overlooked. The Qur'an text is found in 28:14-28 and its biblical counterpart is in Exodus 2:11-22.

COOPERATING REVELATIONS: MURDER

[14]When he had reached maturity and attained manhood, We gave him wisdom and knowledge. Thus do We reward those who do good. [15]He entered the city at a time when its inhabitants were heedless and found two men fighting there, one from among his own group and the other from his enemies. The one from his group sought help against the one who was of his enemies, so Moses struck him and killed him. He (Moses) said, "This is the work of Satan. He is truly an enemy, a certain misleader." [16]He said, "My Lord, I have wronged my soul, please forgive me." So He forgave him for He is truly the forgiving one, the merciful

one. [17]He said, "My Lord, because You have so favored me, I will never be a helper of those who do wrong." [18]The next morning in the city he was afraid and watchful. Suddenly, the man who had asked his help the day before cried out again in need. Moses said to him, "You are indeed a troublemaker!" [19]And when he was about to seize the man who was their enemy he said, "Oh Moses, do you wish to kill me as you killed a person yesterday? You want nothing but to be a tyrant in the land and do not wish to be a peacemaker." [20]Then a man came running from the far side of the city and said, "Oh Moses, the leaders are deliberating against you to kill you! I advise you to get away from here!" [21]So he left the city afraid and watchful saying, "My Lord, deliver me from unjust people!"

Analysis of the Qur'anic Tradition

The text opens with a reference to Moses entering the city and ends with him leaving it. In the course of his brief stay, he learns a great deal about the city's inhabitants, himself and Allah. The first two sentences draw attention to Moses' physical and intellectual maturity which is seen as a gift from Allah. The people of the city are described in less flattering terms as heedless or neglectful (v. 15). In other words, they are the antithesis of Moses whose maturity makes him mindful, thoughtful and careful. This quality comes out after the murder when he is able to evaluate his action as the work of Satan and beg his Lord's forgiveness. It is also seen when he calls for his Lord's protection upon leaving the city (v. 21). More than anything, Moses is mindful of Allah's power and authority over his life in a way that the heedless inhabitants of the city are not.

And yet, despite his superior qualities, Moses acts in ways that suggest that he, too, can be heedless and forgetful. Upon arriving in the city he comes to the defense of a comrade by murdering another man they consider to be an enemy. He immediately expresses his regret for doing this and begs Allah's mercy after coming to the realization that it is Satan, and not other human beings, who is the true enemy of a person. He then goes on to express a firm resolve to never again engage in such behavior. "My Lord, because You have so favored me, I will never be a helper of those who do wrong" (v. 17). He breaks this vow on the very next day when he comes to the aid of the same individual, whom he describes as a "troublemaker." The only thing that prevents Moses from repeating the killing of the previous day is the arrival of the messenger bearing the news that the city leaders are plotting Moses' own death. Moses comes very close to committing murder twice in this text, and the reason he is prepared to kill a second time is that he forgot the lesson he learned the day before.

The heedless nature of the city's inhabitants has begun to rub off on Moses and it is as if he has been poisoned by this environment and those in it. Note the two terms used to describe Moses both the morning after the murder (v. 18) and the moment he leaves the city (v. 21). He is "afraid and watchful" because he realizes he is in a dangerous place and needs to be on guard to protect himself from the perils it poses. This is a place of murder and death, and he has been drawn into its circle of violence, acting in ways that are not in line with the wisdom and knowledge that have been divinely bestowed on him. He recognizes this change in his character, asks forgiveness of Allah and flees for his life.

Application to the Biblical Tradition

The biblical parallel to this Qur'an text is found in Exodus 2:11-15a which contains a similar overall structure to the scene.

> [11]One day, after Moses had grown up, he went out to his people and saw their forced labor. He saw an Egyptian beating a Hebrew, one of his kinsfolk. [12]He looked this way and that, and seeing no one he killed the Egyptian and hid him in the sand. [13]When he went out the next day, he saw two Hebrews fighting; and he said to the one who was in the wrong, "Why do you strike your fellow Hebrew?" [14]He answered, "Who made you a ruler and judge over us? Do you mean to kill me as you killed the Egyptian?" Then Moses was afraid and thought, "Surely the thing is known." [15]When Pharaoh heard of it, he sought to kill Moses. But Moses fled from Pharaoh.

There are some obvious differences between the two versions of the story. While the Qur'an account takes place in a city, the location here is identified only as Egypt, although the references to the sand and lack of eyewitnesses to the murder might indicate the desert or some other remote area. The identities of the combatants in each of the two fights differ as well. The Qur'an says the first confrontation was between one of Moses' people and an enemy, while the Bible is more specific in referring to them as a Hebrew and an Egyptian. The second altercation in the Qur'an involves the same member of Moses' people and another of their enemies, but in the Exodus version there are now two Hebrews fighting and it does not appear that either of them was also involved in the previous day's dispute. Another element of the biblical story that is not in the Qurʾan is Moses' burial of the corpse after he kills the man. Prior to disposing of the body Moses looks around nervously to see if anyone has seen him commit the murder, and this expression of fear or anxiety recalls the Qurʾan's description of him being "afraid and watchful."

We have observed that a dominant theme of the Qurʾan passage is the very violent nature of the city and its inhabitants. This quality exerts a negative effect on Moses' actions and attitudes, tempting him to kill a second time. In departing from the city, he chooses to leave this corrupt, unhealthy environment and he asks for Allah's protection from such people in the future. Is this same thing present in the Exodus narrative? Is the idea of the total corruption of the place found here as it is in the Qurʾan? A close reading of Exodus that pays careful attention to the details suggests that this is the case, although the theme is not as prominent there as it is in the Islamic text.

We see a subtle, but significant, shift in perspective when we consider how the Bible identifies those who engage in the two disputes. Both times in the Qurʾan the fight is between one of Moses' comrades and "an enemy." Exodus envisions the same thing for the first encounter with its designations "Egyptian" and "Hebrew," but not for the second one. This time, two Hebrews are engaged in fisticuffs. In effect, brother is fighting brother in a way that fragments society even further. Not only are Egyptians and Hebrews unable to get along, as seen in the first confrontation, but a group that should be united has become divided as its members attempt to destroy each other. This fragmentation is also expressed in the fact that Moses' murder of the Egyptian becomes public knowledge as even Pharaoh comes to know about it, leading to Moses' flight. There is only one way this information could have been spread. The Hebrew whose life Moses saved must be the responsible party since Moses looked "this way and that" and saw no one prior to killing the Egyptian. In plain language, Moses' fellow Hebrew squealed on him. Brother fighting against brother. Brother informing on brother. This situation is comparable to and, in some ways, worse than, that envisioned in the Qurʾan.

The corruption of Egyptian society is further reflected in the forced labor which the Egyptians inflict on the Hebrews. The passage begins by mentioning that Moses went out one day and saw the forced labor of his people. We are not told if this is the first time he was exposed to Hebrew slavery but, if it was, this would help explain his strong and violent reaction to the sight of one of his own people being abused by an Egyptian. But we can not be sure about exactly who or what Moses is, or thinks he is, at this point in the story. This text clearly identifies him with the Hebrews, who are referred to as "his people" and "his kinsfolk" (v. 11). Similarly, in choosing sides, he assists the Hebrew by killing his assailant rather than allowing him to continue to beat the man, and this gives an indication of where his allegiance lies. But this passage, as the first that describes Moses as an adult, comes immediately after his birth story, in which he is taken by Pharaoh's daughter who gives him an Egyptian name and raises him as her son (Exod 2:5-10). What happened during those intervening years until he went out one day and saw an Egyptian beating a Hebrew? Was he raised as an Egyptian? Was he aware of his true identity as a Hebrew? The biblical text does not tell us so we do not know if he thought of himself as a Hebrew, an Egyptian, or both.

This theme of Moses' self-understanding will continue to be important when we turn to the scene at Midian but, for now, it is interesting to observe how the question of his identity affects our interpretation of what happens in this prior scene. Do the other characters think of Moses as an Egyptian or a Hebrew? If the first Hebrew believed him to be an Egyptian, that would help explain why he was so ready to spread the word about what Moses had done. An Egyptian prince killed another Egyptian! On the other hand, if he thought of Moses as a fellow Hebrew, he acted as a traitor when we would have expected him to express appreciation for what Moses did for him. When the two Hebrews fight the next day, they could be relating to him either as one of their own or as an Egyptian. The choice the reader makes determines how we understand their response to him. Finally, Pharaoh's desire to kill Moses will be evaluated differently depending on whether the reader believes the Egyptian leader thinks of him as a Hebrew or an Egyptian.

The biblical text understands him to be a Hebrew even if he is not yet ready to think of himself in those terms. As the scene unfolds, we and Moses come to realize it is not easy to be a Hebrew in this place owing to its corrupt nature which is expressed in several ways. The Hebrews are treated as inferiors by the Egyptians who exercise their control over them by forcing them to work against their will. This externally imposed hardship is also reflected within the community where division and discord are also present. Hebrew fights against Hebrew and Hebrew betrays Hebrew in ways that threaten the survival of the group. Before coming to the defense of his kinsman, Moses looks both ways and sees "no one," assuming it is safe to kill the Egyptian antagonist. Ironically, someone, an enemy, was there but Moses never thought he needed to fear the fellow Hebrew who later exposed him.

In Exodus, Moses flees from a decadent place in which corruption has run rampant. But this fact is easily overlooked owing to the way the biblical story is told. The Qur'an's account of the tradition assists the Bible reader in recovering this aspect of the plot and raising it to the surface. In the Islamic text, the wicked, misguided nature of the city and its inhabitants is to the fore and a rereading of the biblical version with that theme in mind helps identify its presence there as well. When Moses flees in Exodus he is not only escaping Pharaoh's wrath but, as in the Qur'an, he is rejecting the environment that Pharaoh and others like him have created. Had the Bible recorded his parting words they would probably be similar to what he says in the Qur'an upon leaving the city. "My Lord, deliver me from unjust people!" (v. 21).

COOPERATING REVELATIONS: MIDIAN

> [22]When he turned in the direction of Midian he said, "Perhaps my Lord will guide me to the right way." [23]When he arrived at the waters of Midian he found a group of people watering their flocks and two women holding back (their flocks). He said, "What is the matter with you two?" They said, "We cannot water our flocks until the shepherds leave. Our father is an old man." [24]So he watered their flocks and then he turned aside to the shade saying, "My Lord, I am in need of whatever good you might send down to me." [25]Then one of them shyly walked over to him and said, "My father invites you in order to reward you for having watered our flocks." When he came to him and told him the story, he said, "Do not fear, you have escaped from the wicked people." [26]One of them said, "Oh my father, hire him! Truly the best man to hire is a strong, trustworthy one." [27]He said, "I wish to marry you to one of these two daughters of mine provided you be in my service for eight years. But if you complete ten years, it is of your own will. I do not want to be hard on you. Allah willing, you will find me to be one of the upright." [28]He (Moses) said, "It is between me and you. Whichever of the two terms I fulfill there will be no injustice done to me. May Allah be the witness over what we say."

Analysis of the Qur'anic Tradition

In both the Qur'an and the Bible Moses flees in the direction of Midian, where he eventually marries and settles. The name "Midian" refers to an area in the northwest area of the Arabian peninsula. Archeologists have recently uncovered evidence of a very sophisticated society there, complete with walled cities, irrigation systems and mining operations, which must have played an influential role in the region at one time. It would therefore be wrong to assume that the shepherding lifestyle described in this text would have been typical of the majority of the local population. Such seminomadic groups were a relatively small part of the more settled political/cultural system of Midian. The Midianite people spoke a language that was an ancestor to Arabic and almost every Midianite name mentioned in the Bible has been found in pre-Islamic Arabic inscriptions.

As Moses sets out on his journey he begins with a prayer which voices his desire for divine assistance. "Perhaps my Lord will guide me to the right way" (v. 22). This sets the tone for the events that are about to unfold and encourages the reader to think of them as occurring under Allah's influence and guidance. Moses' reception at Midian is the antithesis of his experiences in the city from which he has just fled. He is warmly received in a way that suggests Allah has answered his prayers and has led him on the "right way." After watering the sisters' flocks he utters a second prayer, again expressing his faith and trust in Allah. "My Lord, I am in need of whatever good you might send down to me" (v. 24). As if in response to this prayer, one of the women immediately comes over to Moses and extends their father's offer of recompense for Moses' kind act. In this text, Moses is being presented as a devout follower of Allah who calls on his Lord for help and unselfishly assists others. The contrast with the previous scene is striking. There, the aid he provided to one of his own resulted in the murder of one person and the near murder of another. Because of this "act of kindness" he was forced to escape from the city in order to avoid his own death. Here, he performs a very different act of kindness for complete strangers that leads to the opposite outcome. Rather than having to run away for his life, he is invited to enter more deeply into the lives of these people.

The father's first words further highlight the difference between the city and Midian. After Moses recounts his previous experiences, the father replies, "Do not fear, you have escaped from the wicked people" (v. 25). The man's subsequent actions and words convince Moses that he has indeed left behind the corruption of the city and that the inhabitants of this new place are good. The man wishes to reach an agreement whereby Moses will marry one of his daughters, but goes to some length to reassure him that this will be a reasonable and fair arrangement. "I do not want to be hard on you" (v. 27). The father concludes his proposal by seeking divine assistance in carrying out his end of the agreement. "Allah willing, you will find me to be one of the upright" (v. 27). The older man is portrayed as a pious, fair individual who acknowledges his dependence on the deity. When he calls upon Allah for guidance, Moses knows he is in the presence of a kindred spirit and seals the deal with a similar expression of faith. "May Allah be the witness over what we say" (v. 28).

As we will see shortly, the Bible does not make any reference to an arrangement with the father according to which Moses must work for him for a set period of time before taking the man's daughter as his wife. But we do find this motif elsewhere in the Hebrew Bible. Genesis 29 describes how Jacob reaches an agreement with Laban whereby he works for him for seven years in exchange for the hand of Laban's daughter, Rachel. Laban eventually tricks Jacob by substituting his other daughter Leah for Rachel, causing Jacob to labor an additional seven years. What makes the relationship between this tradition and the one in the Qurʾan particularly intriguing is the fact that in both a well is the place where the future spouses first meet. In a scene that is strongly reminiscent of Moses' experiences in the Qurʾan and Exodus 2, Jacob encounters Rachel at a well where he rolls away a stone and waters her flocks. The Qurʾan version contains elements found in the biblical stories of both Jacob and Moses. Each of them encounters his future wife at a well, but only Jacob has to work a set number of years for her father in the Bible as Moses does in the Qurʾan.

When we next hear of Moses in the Qurʾan he is married to one of the man's daughters and about to have the initial experience of his prophetic career. "When Moses had completed his term and was traveling with his family, he observed a fire on the side of the mountain" (28:29). This is the fire out of which Allah's voice will first speak to him and commission him as a messenger to Pharaoh. The connection the Qurʾan makes between Midian and this experience is no coincidence. Here, in the midst of a people who take him in as one of their own, Moses comes to know who he is. Here, as an outsider who marries into a people with whom he feels a certain solidarity, Moses comes to know what he is called to become. In the city, among his "own people," all he experienced was death and rejection. In Midian, among the people to whom Allah has guided him, he finds peace and acceptance. In the Qurʾan, this is a story of Moses' self-discovery. After he loses sight of who he is in the city, he finds himself among the people of Midian.

Application to the Biblical Tradition

Exodus 2:15a-25 is the biblical parallel to the Qur'an text under discussion.

> [15]He settled in the land of Midian, and sat down by a well. [16]The priest of Midian had seven daughters. They came to draw water, and filled their troughs to water their father's flock. [17]But some shepherds came and drove them away. Moses got up and came to their defense and watered their flock. [18]When they returned to their father Reuel, he said, "How is it that you have come back so soon today?" [19]They said, "An Egyptian helped us against the shepherds; he even drew water for us and watered the flock." [20]He said to his daughters, "Where is he? Why did you leave the man? Invite him to break bread." [21]Moses agreed to stay with the man, and he gave Moses his daughter Zipporah in marriage. [22]She bore a son, and he named him Gershom; for he said, "I have been an alien residing in a foreign land." [23]After a long time the king of Egypt died. The Israelites groaned under their slavery, and cried out. Out of the slavery their cry for help rose up to God. [24]God heard their groaning, and God remembered his covenant with Abraham, Isaac, and Jacob. [25]God looked upon the Israelites, and God took notice of them.

When we compare the Exodus 2 passage with the Qur'an we discover some differences on certain matters of detail, such as the mention of the name and priestly status of the father, the number of daughters he has, the name of Moses' wife, and the reference to the birth and naming of Moses' son. But, underneath such superficial divergences, the Exodus account makes more or less the same point that the Qur'an one does. Moses settles in and makes his home here among the people of Midian, and his new father-in-law embodies many of the qualities lacking among Moses' own people in the previous scene. He is an honest, peaceful man with whom Moses can confidently enter into a relationship.

Moses is accepted by these people even though he is a foreigner. In fact, his foreign status is given more attention in the biblical version than it receives in the Qur'an. When the sisters are questioned by their father, they refer to Moses by his nationality. "An Egyptian helped us against the shepherds" (v. 19). Their certainty in using this designation to label Moses is interesting in light of the more ambiguous nature of his affiliation that was observed in the previous biblical scene. There, we noted that it was difficult to determine how the other characters understood Moses' background and that it was impossible to even know whether Moses thought of himself as Egyptian, Hebrew or some combination of the two. There is no such hesitancy here since the seven sisters all identify him as an Egyptian.

The foreigner motif is also highlighted in the name that Moses gives his son, Gershom, to which he relates the meaning "I have been an alien residing in a foreign land" (v. 22). It is common for the Bible to offer this type of interpretation of a newborn's name and, depending on the example, it may or may not have some solid etymological support. In this case, the first part of the name (Ger) is identical to a Hebrew word meaning "stranger, sojourner, foreigner," and this is the basis for the meaning Moses assigns the name. His interpretation of the name indicates that, at one time, Moses considered himself to be living in an alien land. But which land is he talking about? He could be referring to Midian, to which he came as a foreigner but now, with his marriage and the birth of his son, has become his home. In other words, he might be saying, "I used to think of myself as a foreigner in Midian, but not any more." Or, he might be referring to Egypt as the foreign land. In that case he would be saying, "The entire time I lived in Egypt I felt like a foreigner." This would imply that Midian is his home and he is rejecting his previous life in Egypt.

If we keep in mind the way both the Qur'an and Bible make a sharp distinction between the previous scene and this one, the latter alternative should be preferred. In Egypt (or, according to the Qur'an, the city) Moses did not fit in. He found himself in a violent, dangerous environment from which he eventually fled. Upon his arrival at Midian, everything is different. He is welcomed by its inhabitants despite the fact that he is not from there, and is even encouraged to marry and settle down in the area. When it comes time to name his son, Moses realizes that Midian is his true home and Egypt was more like a foreign country to him.

This part of the biblical Moses story contains an interesting use of *inclusio*, or bookends effect, that supports the idea he is rejecting his Egyptian background and upbringing. The only other naming in Exodus up to this point takes place in 2:10, immediately prior to the material we have been studying, when Moses himself is named. "When the child grew up, she brought him to Pharaoh's daughter, and she took him as her son. She named him Moses, 'because,' she said, 'I drew him out of the water.'" This is an adoption scene in which Moses becomes part of Pharaoh's family and takes on an Egyptian identity. The naming of Moses' son in 2:22 invites us to recall the similar scene with Pharaoh's daughter and its significance. When Moses says "I was an alien in a foreign land" he is, in effect, rejecting his adoption and disavowing any connection to Egypt. It therefore appears that the portion of the Exodus story we have been studying is concerned with the question of Moses' identity. It is preceded by a naming scene that makes him an adopted Egyptian and ends with another naming scene that repudiates the Egyptian connection and makes him an adopted Midianite. The reader knows that, actually, Moses is neither and anxiously waits for him to discover the truth about himself.

In short, Moses undergoes an identity crisis as a result of what happens to him in Egypt and Midian, unsure of who or what he is. The double scenes of murder and Midian describe his separation from his previous way of life and explain how it is that he comes to renounce his Egyptian roots. The murder episode exposes him to the utter depravity of life in Egypt, where his people are oppressed and Hebrews fight and betray each other. Not wanting to be a part of this and fearing for his life, he runs away, leaving behind his dual identity as an Egyptian and a Hebrew. The Midian episode allows him to begin to recover a sense of self as he attaches himself to a community and starts a family, signaling a clean break from his past with the naming of his son.

But Moses is not quite home yet. As in the Qurʾan, it is among the Midianites that he will have his first encounter with God and learn of the plans the deity has for him. Immediately after the naming of Gershom, in Exodus 2:23-25, we are told that the Israelites cry out in their slavery and God hears and takes notice. This leads right into the burning bush episode in Exodus 3 where Moses is charged by God to return to Egypt to lead his people to the Promised Land. Earlier in this chapter, we saw how reluctant Moses is to take up that charge, using every means possible to avoid returning to Egypt and confronting Pharaoh. He comes across as a defiant figure who refuses to accept and follow the divine will, and this raises troubling questions about his character. But if we keep in mind what has happened to him just prior to this, his response is more understandable. He has recently severed his ties with Egypt, where he had been a foreigner, and believes he has found his proper place in Midian. No longer struggling with his status as part-Egyptian, part-Hebrew, he is free and at peace. It is at this point that God enters his life for the first time and asks him to return to the very place he has renounced, to the very people he has disowned. Thus begins the final stage of his identity crisis, a stage during which he must reestablish ties with his true people and come to realize that only he, with God's help, can save them from the violence and death of Egypt and deliver them to the land of the covenant.

Key aspects of the Exodus story can be easily missed because the text does not make an explicit connection between the situations Moses confronts in Egypt and Midian. But the Qurʾan makes that link by underscoring the difference between the wicked people of the city and the good people of Midian. When we reread the biblical material with that idea in mind we are able to gain added insight into this familiar text and to uncover new facets of Moses' character. In particular, the Qurʾan cooperates with the Bible in allowing us to appreciate that an important component of the Moses story is his journey of self-discovery as he gradually comes to understand and accept God's will for him.

NOTES: CHAPTER 4

[1]The biblical tradition adds the further detail in Exodus 2:10 that Pharaoh's daughter named him Moses and it offers an explanation of the name's etymology. This act of naming is a way of expressing the fact of adoption since, in the Bible, it is an activity typically reserved for a child's parents.

[2]While such skepticism about the reliability of an account is a legitimate conclusion to reach when critically evaluating a text, it should be remembered that the Qurʾan's portrayal of Haman is a problem only for the Bible reader, not the Muslim. According to Islam, the Qurʾan is the definitive word of Allah which serves as a corrective to prior texts. For the Muslim, any contradiction between it and the Bible is due to the flawed nature of the biblical text.

[3]The location of the encounter is identified as the "sacred valley of Ṭuwā" in verse 12. Some commentators have attempted to locate this valley in the Sinai but this is not supported by the text. Alternatively, others have suggested that the word Ṭuwā is not a name but an adjective meaning "twice done," possibly referring to a place twice blessed. The Qurʾan explicitly refers to Mount Sinai in 23:20 and 95:2.

[4]Other texts which describe this encounter are 7:103-137, 10:75-89, and 26:16-51. While the details of the episode differ considerably in these passages, they all follow the same general outline.

[5]In a number of other places the Qurʾan is clearer in seeing a link between the signs and the biblical plagues. For example, in 43:47-48 the chastising nature of the signs is apparent as is their ascending degree of severity. "When he (Moses) came to them with Our signs they laughed at them. Each sign We showed them was greater than its (preceding) sister and We seized them with punishment so that they might return." Elsewhere, a direct correlation between some of the plagues of Exodus and the signs of the Qurʾan is made. "We

sent to them the storm, the locusts, the lice, the frogs and the blood—clear signs. But they were proud and a sinful people" (7:133).

[6]Exodus refers to the Egyptian magicians on five occasions, and the first three explain how they were able to duplicate Moses'/Aaron's feats by transforming their staffs into snakes (7:11), changing the water in the river into blood (7:22), and bringing forth frogs (8:7). They are less successful the next time (8:18), when they are unable to produce gnats as Moses and Aaron had previously done. The last time we hear of them they are not capable of even attempting to recreate the work of Moses and Aaron because they are incapacitated by the boils Yahweh's messengers have inflicted on them (9:11).

[7]The lone exception is found with the plague of locusts (Exod 10:1-20), when Moses and Aaron are brought back into Pharaoh's presence after making the appeal to release the Israelites and then departing. This episode will be discussed in detail later in the chapter.

[8]In some of these cases God's responsibility is implied, rather than explicitly stated, through the use of a verbal form commonly referred to as the divine passive in which the precise subject of the verb is left unexpressed. When these texts say "Pharaoh's heart was hardened" the only logical conclusion for the reader to reach, in light of Exodus 4:21, is that God is behind this development.

[9]The hardening of the heart theme is found elsewhere in the Qur'an. In 10:88 Moses prays that Allah intervene against Pharaoh and his followers, "Our Lord, destroy their riches and harden their hearts. They will not believe until they see the painful punishment." Allah responds, "Your petition is answered."

[10]Another possible reason why the Qur'an does not refer to the Passover is the desire to avoid acknowledging or validating such a uniquely Jewish belief and practice. Exodus 12:43 makes clear the exclusive nature of the feast, "This is the ordinance of the passover: no foreigner shall eat of it." Again, this is at odds with the Qur'an's more universal sense of the deity and worship of Allah.

[11]A clear example of the cloud motif from the New Testament is seen in the accounts of the Transfiguration of Jesus, a tradition found in all three Synoptic Gospels (Matt 17:1-9; Mark 9:2-10; Luke 9:28-36). In each case a cloud envelops Jesus and his companions and God's voice comes from within it announcing Jesus' divine sonship.

[12]The mountain has two names in the biblical text since it is also referred to as Mount Horeb (Exod 3:1; 17:6; 33:6). Most scholars believe this is an argument in favor of seeing different sources behind the Pentateuch. One or more sources knew the location as Mount Sinai while others were familiar with a different name for it. It is common practice to refer to it by the former designation and that is why it is adopted here.

[13]A well-known reference to the Samaritans in the New Testament can be found in John 4, which contains the story of Jesus' encounter with a Samaritan

woman at a well near Mount Gerizim. Several elements of that text reflect the tension between Samaritans and Jews and the Samaritan tendency toward segregation.

5

Mary

$\mathcal{T}$he majority of the biblical figures mentioned in the Qur'an come from the Hebrew Bible. Very few New Testament characters are found in the pages of Islam's text and some of the most important ones are completely absent. For example, the Qur'an does not mention by name Peter, Judas, Mary Magdalene, or any other of Jesus' disciples. Similarly, it makes no reference to Paul, Timothy, Lydia, or any of the other people the New Testament identifies as responsible for the early spread and development of Christianity. In fact, the only two people from the New Testament who are discussed at any length in the Qur'an are Mary and her son Jesus, who play prominent roles in the text and have been very influential in Muslim piety. The final two chapters of this book will consider their place in the Qur'an and Islam.

Mary is the only woman named in the Qur'an and the book devotes more space and attention to her than to any other female. Some seventy verses refer explicitly to her and sura 19, titled "Mary," is named after her. Among all figures in the Qur'an, only the names of Moses, Abraham and Noah are cited more frequently than Mary's. As in the New Testament, her importance stems from the fact that she is Jesus' mother but, interestingly, Mary and her son are rarely found together in the same scene in the Qur'an. This, too, is similar to the situation in the New Testament where, once she gives birth to Jesus, she recedes into the background and the story becomes his.[1] The bulk of the material on Mary in the Qur'an is concerned with explaining how she comes to be

Jesus' mother. Consequently, the scenes of the annunciation, or the announcement to her of Jesus' conception, and the birth itself comprise most of the Qurʾan's treatment of Mary.

In keeping with its generally lean narrative style which avoids the accumulation of great detail, the passages in the Qurʾan about Mary tend to be somewhat sparse in comparison to the biblical accounts. In a number of places, gaps in the reader's knowledge or textual ambiguity can leave key aspects of the story vague and unresolved. Muslim commentators throughout history have addressed this problem by trying to offer their own interpretations of what happened based on careful study of and reflection on the texts. In the same way, early Islamic history saw the development of extra-Qurʾanic Islamic traditions centered on Mary. This material attempts to fill in some of the gaps and contribute to the formation of a more cohesive and complete story around the figure of Mary.

As has been the case with the other biblical figures studied thus far, the Qurʾan's presentation of Mary often differs greatly from that of the Bible. At the same time, scholars have frequently noted some intriguing similarities between the Qurʾan's version of events and those found in some of the extracanonical texts, gospels, and other early Christian writings that are not part of the canon of the New Testament. These affinities have raised some important and fascinating questions about both the relationship between Islam and Christianity and the role of these extracanonical texts.[2]

We will examine how the Qurʾan depicts three key events in Mary's life: her birth and seclusion, the annunciation, and the birth of Jesus.

BIRTH AND SECLUSION

The only reference in the Qurʾan to Mary's birth is found in 3:35-36.

> [35]ʿImrān's wife said, "My Lord, I have vowed to You that what is in my womb will be dedicated to Your service. Accept it from me, for You are the one who hears, the one who knows." [36]When she brought forth the child, she said, "My Lord, I have brought forth a female,"—but Allah knew what she had brought forth, for the male is not like the female— "and I have named her Mary. I place her and her offspring under Your protection from Satan, the cursed one."

While Mary's mother is unnamed in this passage, her father is identified as ʿImrān, the person after whom sura 3 ("The Family of ʿImrān") is named. The New Testament has nothing to say about Mary's birth or her life prior to becoming the mother of Jesus, and so it does not give the name of either of her parents.[3]

Despite the mother's anonymity, the story of Mary's birth is told from her perspective. By offering two prayers in this brief text, she comes across as a woman of deep faith. Each prayer concerns the future of the child, as she first dedicates it for divine service and then places it under the protection of her Lord. The content of her prayer therefore tells us as much about her child as it does about the woman herself. This baby is destined to have a very special and close relationship with the deity that has been established even before she is born. This has an important effect on how the reader understands Mary's character. She is someone who, while still in the womb, has been specially set apart and, after birth, will be divinely preserved from harm. This account of her birth has contributed to the high status Mary enjoys within Islam. At times, her elevated position comes close to what we find in some Christian circles. For example, some Muslim theologians have argued for the sinlessness of Mary, a belief somewhat analogous to the Catholic doctrine of the Immaculate Conception which holds that Mary was conceived without original sin. This has never become a widely accepted view within Islam, but the discussion about it gives an indication of the very privileged place Mary holds in the religion.

The mother's second prayer gives us a hint of what is to come when she requests divine protection for her daughter's offspring. These words point ahead to the pregnancy and motherhood of her newborn daughter and anticipate the special status of any children she might have. In effect, Jesus' grandmother is praying for him here and insuring that he, too, will be safeguarded. Consequently, this is a prayer that has implications that span three generations of this family. Like mother, like daughter: the woman's first prayer guarantees that, like herself, her child will have an intimate relationship with Allah. Like mother, like son: her second prayer makes sure that, just as his mother, her future grandson will experience divine protection. In just two short verses, the Qur'an is able to assert and establish Jesus' impeccable lineage.

The next scene goes on to narrate the realization of the mother's prayers. In 3:37-41 we discover the degree of Mary's dedication to Allah and the type of divine protection she receives.

> [37]So her Lord accepted her graciously. He caused her to grow up well and gave her into the care of Zachariah. Every time Zachariah came to

see her in the chamber he found her with provisions. He said, "Oh Mary, where do you get this?" She answered, "It is from Allah. Truly, Allah provides for whomever He wishes without measure." [38]Then and there, Zachariah called upon his Lord saying, "My Lord, grant me good offspring from Yourself. Truly, You hear all prayers." [39]Then the angels called to him while he stood praying in the chamber, "Allah gives you the good news of John, who will confirm a word from Allah. He will be noble, chaste, and a prophet from among the righteous." [40]He said, "Oh Lord, how is it that I might have a son when I am old and my wife is barren?" He (an angel) said, "Thus it is. Allah does what He wills." [41]He said, "My Lord, make for me a sign." He said, "Your sign is that you will not be able to speak to a person for three days except by gestures. Remember your Lord much and praise Him in the evening and in the morning."

Zachariah is another of the very few New Testament characters who are mentioned by name in the Qurʾan. His biblical presence is limited to the first chapter of Luke where he plays an important role as the father of John the Baptist, the details of whose birth are described at the beginning of Luke's Gospel. In that book, a genealogical link between Jesus and Zachariah's family is established since Mary is a relative of Elizabeth, the wife of Zachariah (Luke 1:36). In the Qurʾan, no such relationship is claimed and Zachariah's wife is never identified by name. Nonetheless, despite the lack of an explicit family connection, Zachariah does have a special tie to Mary in his capacity as her custodian.

According to this Qurʾan passage, Mary has been given over into the care of Zachariah who is responsible for raising her and meeting her needs. Where is she living? The only clue we have to go on is the Arabic term *miḥrāb*, which is the place Zachariah comes to visit Mary and is here translated as "chamber" (vv. 37, 39). This word can have several different meanings, including the upper end of a room, a high place of honor, a room accessible by stairs, and a private chamber. The word *miḥrāb* is also used as a technical term in Islam to refer to the niche in a wall of every mosque that indicates the direction of Mecca, enabling all worshipers to be properly oriented during prayer. Some English translations, perhaps influenced by this last meaning, translate the word in this passage as "temple" or "shrine," but this is to impose a sense on it which cannot be supported.[4] More likely, it is meant to indicate a special room or chamber set aside for Mary's use while she lives with Zachariah. Even though he himself prays in the *miḥrāb* (v. 39), the word does not require a cultic or overtly religious connotation. Whatever its precise meaning, it appears that Mary is not free to come and go as she pleases but remains in the chamber. Zachariah's surprise on finding her with provisions whenever he comes to visit her suggests she is more or less confined to the room (v. 37), unaccustomed to leaving it or receiving visitors. But we should not conclude that Mary is some kind of prisoner who is being held against her will. Rather, her living arrangement with Zachariah is probably meant to express the realization of her mother's prayer. She has been dedicated to Allah and is now living a life of seclusion in a way that expresses her singular devotion and commitment to that calling.

Mary's mother also prayed that her daughter be protected by Allah and this request, too, is met in the *miḥrāb*. Every time Zachariah comes to attend to Mary he finds that she has already been taken care of. We are meant to envision Zachariah regularly coming to the chamber with the food, drink and other things he assumes Mary will need only to discover, time and again, that he is too late. In other words, someone else is doing Zachariah's job for him. As her caretaker, it is his duty to look after his young charge and provide for her, but his efforts to do so are repeatedly preempted. In frustration, he asks her how this is happening and is informed of the source of this mysterious assistance. "It is from Allah. Truly, Allah provides for whomever He wishes without measure" (v. 37). Allah, not Zachariah, is Mary's true keeper!

The word Mary uses to explain what Allah has done for her is an important one in the scene and has a powerful effect on Zachariah's response to what he hears. The verb translated as "provides" is *razaqa*, and from this same Arabic root the word for "provisions," found earlier in verse 37, is derived. It is a verb which, as here, often has Allah as its subject and it refers to the deity's capacity to provide or grant the means of subsistence to a person. It can refer to the divine bestowal of food, property or offspring, and this last possibility is particularly relevant for our purposes. Zachariah questions Mary about the inexplicable appearance of food and drink in her quarters and she responds by identifying Allah as the source of these things but uses a verb which implies that the deity is able to provide much more than simply food. Zachariah, in turn, responds to Mary's words but does not respond to Mary. Rather, he immediately voices a prayer in which he implores Allah to provide him with offspring. The first Arabic word of verse 38, here translated "then and there," expresses well both the spontaneity of Zachariah's supplication and the cause/effect relationship between what Mary tells him and the prayer he utters.

The miraculous gift of food serves a double function in the story. In the first place, it is a tangible expression of the divine protection

Mary receives as a result of her dedication and devotion to Allah. Second, it functions as Zachariah's springboard to deeper faith and trust in the deity. In the process, there has been an interesting reversal of roles between Zachariah and Mary. What he provides for her, the superfluous food and drink he brings to the *miḥrāb*, is unnecessary for her survival. But what she provides him, a much-needed lesson about the power of Allah, is indispensable for his. Sequestered in the solitude of the *miḥrāb*, she has become his caretaker.

The latter part of the text centers on Zachariah when Allah, through the angels, responds to his prayer. Although she is not mentioned, we should assume that Mary is still on the scene, observing and listening to the exchange between the heavenly messengers and Zachariah as they discuss his future child. The biblical account of this episode in Luke 1 has some similarities with the Qur'an version but there are also some key differences. Mary plays no role in the Luke text where Zachariah is alone and has a one-on-one encounter with the angel Gabriel (Luke 1:8-20). Luke's episode takes place in the Temple in Jerusalem as Zachariah fulfills his priestly duties (v. 9). When Zachariah is struck dumb in Luke, the condition lasts for Elizabeth's entire pregnancy and not just three days as in the Qur'an (vv. 20, 64). Despite such differences in detail, however, there is a general structural agreement between the passages in the Qur'an and Luke which is quite clear. Biblical scholars have long noted a common pattern to scenes of angelic visitations in both testaments which comprises the following six steps:

(1) *Appearance*—The angel appears to the human subject.
(2) *Fear*—The person responds in a way that expresses fear.
(3) *Assurance*—The angel assures the person that there is no need to fear.
(4) *Message*—A message from the deity is delivered by the angel.
(5) *Objection*—The person objects to some aspect of the message.
(6) *Sign*—The angel gives a sign which validates the authenticity of the message.

Typically, angelic appearance stories in the Bible do not contain all six of these steps but most of them will be present. When we examine the Qur'an passage with this outline in mind, we observe that it possesses all but two of the steps and, in general, it follows very closely the order and structure of its biblical counterpart in Luke 1. Both texts begin with an angelic appearance. In Luke it is one angel who stands at the right side of the altar of incense (v. 11), and in the Qur'an there are several angels who call to Zachariah while he prays (v. 39). Steps two and three are not found in the Qur'an where Zachariah expresses no fear toward the heavenly visitors. But he is terrified in Luke and needs to be reassured and comforted by the angel (vv. 12–13). Since the purpose of such visitations is to deliver a message from the deity, the fourth step is an essential element of the pattern that is always present. In the Qur'an and Luke, the message is identical as the angels inform Zachariah that his prayer has been answered and that he and his wife will have a child. In both, the child's name is given as John and some information about his personal qualities and the role he will play is provided. But the Qur'an is much briefer on these points than Luke is. In the Islamic text, John will confirm a word from Allah and be a noble, chaste prophet (v. 39). Luke includes material on the reaction his birth will elicit, his avoidance of alcohol, and the effect he will have on other people (vv. 14–17). Zachariah's objection in the two texts is virtually identical as he questions the angelic message for two reasons, his own advanced age and his wife's inability to bear children (Qur'an, v. 40; Luke, v. 18). The two texts end with a sign meant to validate the message and it is the same sign in each. Zachariah is struck dumb in both but, as noted above, the period of time this state lasts varies. In the Qur'an, he will regain his power of speech after three days (v. 41), while in Luke he will remain speechless for the entire nine months Elizabeth carries John (v. 20).

THE ANNUNCIATION

In the Qur'an, there are two scenes depicting the annunciation to Mary when she learns of her pregnancy and is told about the child to be born to her. The first, found in 3:42-47, follows immediately after the passage we have just been studying that describes the encounter Zachariah has with the angels.

[42]The angels said, "Oh Mary, Allah has truly chosen you and purified you. He has chosen you above all other women. [43]Oh Mary, be obedient to your Lord. Prostrate yourself and be among those who bow down." [44]This is part of the hidden news We reveal to you. You were not with them when they cast lots to see which of them would take care of Mary, nor were you with them when they disputed among themselves. [45]The angels said, "Oh Mary, Allah gives you the good news of a word from Him. His name will be the Messiah Jesus, the son of Mary, who will be

eminent in this world and the next, and will be one of those brought near (to Allah). [46]He shall speak to people from the cradle and in his later years, and will be one of the righteous." [47]She said, "My Lord, how can I have a child when no man has touched me?" He said, "Thus it is. Allah creates what He wills. If He decrees something, He only need say 'Be!' and it is."

It is difficult to determine the precise relationship between this scene and the one just before it involving Zachariah. Do they occur in rapid succession, one right after the other? Does this encounter between Mary and the heavenly messengers take place in the *miḥrāb*? Are the angels mentioned here the same ones who just spoke to Zachariah and informed him of the birth of John? These questions cannot be answered with any certainty, but the lack of any indication of a shift in location or time and the common theme and structure the two scenes share argue in favor of taking them as occurring in close chronological sequence.

The angels begin by stressing the qualities that set Mary apart and make her worthy of the high honor about to be bestowed on her. "Oh Mary, Allah has truly chosen you and purified you. He has chosen you above all other women" (v. 42). The two things that make her special are her purity and her being chosen by Allah. Although the angels refer twice to her being chosen, it is actually Mary's purity that dominates their message. They use the word *iṣṭafā* twice in this verse where it is translated as "chosen." The root this Arabic verb comes from (*ṣafā*) has as its primary meaning "to be clear or pure," and most of its derived forms are related to this basic sense. Implied in the verb used twice in this verse is the idea that something, or someone, has been chosen because it possesses a clear or pure quality that distinguishes it from others. There are other Arabic verbs meaning "to choose" that are well attested in the Qurʾan and could have been used here. But by opting for this one, the text is able to underscore Mary's predominant characteristic which makes her unique, her purity. The syntax of the verse clearly drives home this point. In the original Arabic, the three verbs follow one right after another, separated only by the copulative "and." If the passage were to be rendered into a semantically and syntactically exact, if somewhat stilted, English translation it would read, "Allah chose you (due to your purity), and purified you, and chose you (due to your purity) above all women." This bookends effect has a profound impact on the reader's evaluation of Mary's character. Above all, it is her pure nature that makes possible the miraculous event about to be revealed to her.

The angels also include some words of advice on how Mary should conduct herself. "Oh Mary, be obedient to your Lord. Prostrate yourself and be among those who bow down" (v. 43). While not overtly suggesting that Mary is a Muslim, this verse uses terminology that has an Islamic flavor and thereby conforms her faith life to the ideal expressed in the Qur'an. Prostration and bowing are the quintessential actions of Islamic prayer, and the Qur'an makes frequent reference to the importance of these movements when urging people to worship properly. Mary is being exhorted to do the same. The intention behind this, as we have seen with other biblical figures found in the Qur'an, is to remind the reader that the attitude of submission at the heart of Islam is not something that came into existence only with the arrival of Muhammad. Many virtuous people, like Mary, fully submitted themselves to the divine will centuries prior to the emergence of Islam.

In verse 44, the text briefly shifts focus and directly addresses Muhammad. This kind of interruption is common in the Qur'an, and it is not unusual to experience frequent, at times jarring, switches of addressee in a text. This one is an aside to the prophet meant to explain to him the nature of this revelation ("hidden news") and the reason why it is being communicated to him now. Because he was not actually on the scene when these things happened, he is being told about them now so that he, and his community, might understand the background to Mary's story. The reference to the men casting lots to determine which of them would become Mary's caretaker has no biblical parallel, but this is one of those areas, mentioned earlier, where we see a connection with an extracanonical Christian text. The Protoevangelium of James, written in the mid-second century, describes a scene in which the widowers of the area are all gathered together by Zachariah the priest to draw lots and see who will take Mary as his wife.

The thread of the narrative is picked up again in verse 45 as the angels resume their message to Mary. She is told that they are bringing her the good news of a "word" from Allah. What is this word they refer to? Is it the message they are now giving her, or might it be a reference to Jesus himself? The idea of Jesus as the "word of God" is an important one in the New Testament (John 1:1-18), and it is possible that we may have an echo of this same notion here in the Qur'an. Interestingly, the angels also refer to a word from Allah in 3:39 when Zachariah is given the news of John's birth. "Allah gives you the good news of John, who will confirm a word from Allah." John is to confirm a "word" from Allah and, again, the ambiguity regarding this term is frustrating. Is it an oblique reference to Jesus, who will be validated by John? The Qur'an contains no detail on the relationship between John and Jesus and it does not designate the former by the title "the Baptist," so these particular texts do not allow us to reach a concrete conclusion on the matter.

But there is another passage which is more explicit and clearly refers to Jesus as Allah's word. In 4:171 we read, "The Messiah Jesus, son of Mary, was Allah's messenger and His word He sent to Mary." When we consider the annunciation scene in light of this text, it is reasonable to conclude that the angels are referring to Jesus when they speak to Mary of the good news of a word from Allah. The Qur'an does, therefore, understand Jesus as a "word," but how are we to interpret this notion? Sensitivity to the beliefs and attitudes of Muslims requires that we be very cautious on this matter and not flippantly assert that the Qur'an refers to Jesus as the word of Allah in the same way that Christians use the term. In Christianity, the idea of Jesus as the word is tied in with the incarnation, God's taking on human form. The prologue to John's Gospel has been very influential in the development of this belief. It begins with a statement of the divine nature of the word. "In the beginning was the Word, and the Word was with God, and the Word was God" (1:1). But the word does not remain an abstract, theoretical concept for John. In 1:18, an incarnational theology is expressed as the divine word enters human history. "And the Word became flesh and lived among us." So, for Christians, to speak of Jesus as the word of God is to implicitly speak of his divinity.

There are some problems with this from the Muslim point of view. In the first place, Islam does not accept the idea that Jesus, or any other person, can be divine. Second, the concept of the word of Allah already has a precise significance for Muslims. In Islam, the Qur'an itself is most worthy of that designation since it is the only faithful, accurate account of the deity's will for humanity. This idea is central to Muslim belief and has itself been the subject of much debate and discussion within the community. Throughout history, theologians have attempted to articulate what it means to hold the Qur'an to be the word of Allah. Lengthy and divisive arguments raged over the question of whether the Qur'an, as Allah's word, is created or uncreated and intellectual heavyweights lined up on both sides of the issue. To claim that the Qur'an sees Jesus as Allah's word in the same way that Christians do would be to raise a host of theological problems that would prove even more difficult to resolve. In what way can a human being be considered Allah's word? Would this not be a violation of the divine unity that would result in *shirk*, the association of an element of creation with the uncreated deity? In light of the Qur'an's own vagueness on the matter, and respecting the beliefs of Muslims, it is important to avoid a simple correlation between the two beliefs. What Muslims mean when they speak of Jesus as the word is very different from what Christians mean.

In verses 45–46, the angels give Mary additional information about her child, including that his name will be "the Messiah Jesus, Son of Mary." As we will see in the next chapter, the title "Messiah" is a frequent designation in the Qur'an for Jesus and it indicates his exalted status in the text and within Islam generally. "Son of Mary" is also a very common way of identifying him. More than twenty times in the Qu'ran he is referred to as "Son of Mary" and these titles account for more than one-half of the occurrences of her name in the text. The angels go on to tell Mary that he is someone who will enjoy prominence both during this life and in the afterlife and will be among the privileged ones who are brought near to Allah. Note the complete lack of any terms or ideas that could lead to the belief that this child will share in the divine nature. The angels describe Jesus as a human being, nothing more. Perhaps his most remarkable quality is the ability to speak while an infant, but this still falls well short of ascribing divinity to him. As we will see below, elsewhere in the Qur'an Jesus is shown actually engaging in conversation with people from his crib.

The New Testament text that is the clearest parallel to this Qur'an passage is Luke 1:26-38, an angelic appearance story which describes the annunciation to Mary.[5] A comparison of the two texts shows that they each follow the outline of the standard angelic visitation that was discussed earlier.

(1) *Appearance*: We noted that there is some support for the view that in the Qur'an this scene occurs immediately after Zachariah's encounter with the angels. If so, this explains why there is no reference to the appearance of the angels to Mary. They are already in the *miḥrāb* and she has witnessed the exchange between them and her caretaker. Luke, on the other hand, has a well-developed description to the appearance in which he explains where Mary is from and her marital status and includes the words of salutation, "Greetings, favored one! The Lord is with you" (vv. 26–28).

(2) *Fear*: As with the Zachariah scene, the Qur'an makes no reference to Mary being afraid at the angels' words. Consequently, this and the next step are not found in the Islamic text. In Luke, she is troubled

by this unexpected visitor as she ponders his greetings and is perplexed by his words (v. 29).

(3) *Assurance*: The angel's next words in Luke highlight the fear element which was not explicitly expressed in the previous step and explain why she need not be afraid. "Do not be afraid, Mary, for you have found favor with God" (v. 30).

(4) *Message*: The general content of the message is identical in both passages as it is explained to Mary that she will conceive and bear a son. In each text, she is told what the child's name will be and is given some further information on his role in society. As we have already seen, in the Qur'an this latter material is of a more general nature, referring to his eminence in this world and the next and his status as one of the righteous ones who will be brought near to Allah (vv. 45–46). Luke is more specific on Jesus' future, and the angel's words in verses 32–33 are more heavily laden with theological and political implications. "He will be great, and will be called the Son of the Most High, and the Lord God will give to him the throne of his ancestor David. He will reign over the house of Jacob forever, and of his kingdom there will be no end." The title "Son of the Most High" does not necessarily imply divine status, but it suggests a uniqueness to the relationship between Jesus and the deity that is absent from the Qur'an text. Similarly, there is a political element in this biblical description not found in the other passage. Jesus is to have a kingdom and he is linked with the throne of David and the house of Jacob. The use of such references to specific figures and images that are central to Israelite history and identity is Luke's way of defining Jesus' role within the context of the traditions of his people. The Qur'an adopts a much broader perspective since it avoids singling out one particular group and defining Jesus' role in relation to them.

(5) *Objection*: Mary's complaint is identical in the Qur'an (v. 47) and Luke (v. 34). She does not understand how it is possible that she can become pregnant without having engaged in sexual relations.

(6) *Sign*: In each case, the sign that is meant to authenticate the message is related to the power of the deity. The angel in the Qur'an appeals to the divine will (v. 47) and reminds Mary that whatever Allah wishes will come to pass. "Thus it is. Allah creates what He wills. If He decrees something, He only need say 'Be!' and it is." We see a clear link between this scene and the previous one involving Zachariah. The first two sentences spoken to Mary are virtually identical to the response Zachariah receives in verse 40 when he asks how it is possible that he

will have a son: "Thus it is. Allah does what He wills." The supreme power and authority of Allah is being emphasized here as the angel tells Mary that the divine ability to do anything is the only sign she needs to accept her pregnancy. In Luke, we have a double sign, with the first one similar to that found in the Qur'an. Mary is told, "The Holy Spirit will come upon you, and the power of the Most High will overshadow you; therefore the child to be born will be holy; he will be called Son of God" (v. 35). Here, we have a repetition of the Son of God theme used earlier by the angel (v. 32) and a reference to the Holy Spirit's role in the conception of the child. This is similar to the Qur'an's statement on Allah's will being realized. The angel is telling Mary that the power of God is what is ultimately behind her pregnancy. But the messenger goes on to offer another sign to convince Mary of the legitimacy of the message. Her relative Elizabeth, who is beyond normal childbearing age, is well into her own pregnancy (v. 36). Luke then describes Mary's acceptance of what she has heard as she utters her well-known obedient response. "Here am I, the servant of the Lord; let it be with me according to your word" (v. 38). The Qur'an does not record a similar final reaction to the message on Mary's part, but there is no reason to doubt she did anything but submissively and humbly accept it as true.

The other annunciation scene in the Qur'an is found in the sura named after Mary at 19:16-21.

> [16]Remember Mary in the book. When she withdrew from her family to a place in the east [17]and took cover from them, We sent to her Our spirit which appeared to her in the form of a normal person. [18]She said, "I take refuge in the merciful one from you if you fear Him." [19]He said, "I am only a messenger from your Lord, to give you a righteous son." [20]She said, "How can I have a son when no man has touched me and I have not been unchaste?" [21]He said, "Thus it is. Your Lord said, 'It is easy for Me. We will make him a sign for people and mercy from Us.' It is an accomplished fact."

This passage is not as tightly connected to the Zachariah/John tradition as the one in sura 3. There, Mary is visited by Zachariah in the *miḥrāb* where he appeals to Allah for a child after learning from Mary that the deity can provide a person with whatever one desires. The present text does not weave together the stories of Mary and Zachariah in the same way. He is mentioned at the beginning of the sura where he is shown praying for a child (vv. 2–11), but Mary is not present and there is no indication that he is her caretaker or has any other relationship to her. Similarly, there is no description of or reference to Mary's birth here and her parents are not mentioned. On the other hand, after this scene there follows an account of Jesus' birth (vv. 22–29), the details of which will be discussed below.

It appears that Mary is alone in this scene since Zachariah is not with her and she is no longer with her family, whom she has left to go to a place in the east (v. 16). The exact location of this place is something of a mystery and Qur'an commentators have identified it differently. Some say it is a private room or area in the eastern part of her house. Others take it to mean she set off on a journey eastward with no precise destination in mind. Still others have linked it to the temple in Jerusalem or some other place of worship. It is even possible to relate it to the text in sura 3 and see it as a reference to Mary leaving her family to go and live with Zachariah. The passage states that Mary "took cover from" her family (v. 17), suggesting she is trying to flee from them or avoid them for some reason. It cannot be that she is running away because she is afraid her pregnancy will be discovered since she will not learn about it for another two verses. Rather, the terminology of the verse suggests that it is probably an allusion to Mary's being secluded and devoted exclusively to Allah, similar to the way she is confined to the *miḥrāb* in sura 3. The Arabic word translated "cover" here is *hijāb*, which can refer to anything which conceals, covers or protects something or someone. Whatever its exact meaning, the general sense is that Mary is cut off from her family and is now on her own.

She does not remain alone for long. As in sura 3, she experiences an angelic visitation, only this time it is one messenger and not several. It is referred to as a spirit from Allah in human form (v. 17). This is a term that needs to be interpreted carefully to avoid giving it a meaning that would be incorrect. The Arabic word *rūḥ*, which is translated "spirit" in this verse, should not be identified with the Holy Spirit as that term is understood in Christian thought. As we will see in the chapter on Jesus, the Qur'an does make reference to "holy spirit," but the concept designates something very different than it does in Christian theology. One of the primary meanings of the word *rūḥ* is "wind, breath," and this idea should inform our interpretation of what is happening to Mary. She is being visited by the breath of Allah in human form, and this breath, or spirit, will contribute to bringing about her pregnancy. This connection between spirit and breath is brought out well in another text. In 66:12, the Qur'an refers to "Mary, the daughter of ʿImrān, who guarded her chastity, so We breathed into her Our spirit *(rūḥ)*."

This text includes all six of the standard steps commonly found in an angelic visitation narrative. It begins with a direct reference to the angel's appearance and the added detail that it took the shape of a human being (v. 17). The second step follows with the mention of Mary's fearful response to this unexpected visitor. Her reaction is one that expresses both her apprehension and her faith as she acknowledges that her only source of protection is Allah (v. 18). "I take refuge in the merciful one from you if you fear Him." The angel's reassurance is found in the first part of verse 19 when he informs her, "I am only a messenger from your Lord." This is an attempt to calm her down by letting her know he has come only to communicate a divine word to her. The fourth step, the message, is very brief and contained in the second half of verse 19. The angel has come to give Mary a righteous son. With these words, he appears to claim a more involved role for himself than simply delivering a message and, as we shall see, this raises some interesting issues about the text.

His message leads to an objection on Mary's part as she asserts the absurdity of the scenario he has just put forth. "How can I have a son when no man has touched me and I have not been unchaste?" (v. 20). This is actually a double objection since she posits two reasons why a pregnancy is an impossibility for her: she is both a virgin and not unchaste. The latter Arabic term *(bağī)* often refers to illicit sexual activity like prostitution and adultery. In effect, Mary is maintaining that she has not engaged in any relations, legal or illegal, that could result in pregnancy. The sign the angel offers (v. 21) is similar to the one given in 3:47 in that it stresses the divine will and Allah's power to do anything. Rather than perform or initiate an action meant to persuade Mary of the truth of the message, the angel simply reminds her of Allah's authority. The messenger's final words succinctly express the finality of the matter from the divine point of view. "It is an accomplished fact."

With the addition of the second and third steps of the pattern, which are not found in the account in sura 3, the structure of this text is remarkably similar to the one in Luke which also contains all six steps. But there are some important differences. This Qur'an passage, like the earlier one, lacks any reference to a final response on Mary's part and this is a key element of the New Testament text. Similarly, the description of Jesus here is exceedingly brief as the angel communicates to the mother-to-be only one quality her son will possess: he will be righteous. We have seen that Luke goes into much more detail regarding both the child's personal traits and the effect he will have on other people (1:31-33). In fact, the angel in this Qur'an passage is so reticent that, unlike in the other one, he does not even tell Mary the name of her future offspring.

The most distinctive element of the annunciation scene in sura 19 is the human form of the messenger. This raises some complex issues about the text, perhaps the most fundamental of which is the purpose this detail plays in the narrative. Is it somehow related to the message about Mary's pregnancy? To get right to the heart of the matter, is the messenger's human appearance meant to suggest that this was not a virginal conception? Generally, Qur'an commentators have not considered the question of whether Mary and the messenger engaged in sexual relations, but several aspects of the text suggest this is a legitimate matter to address. The word *sawī*, translated as "normal" in verse 17, can, when referring to a man, denote one who is full grown or mature. This could be a way of expressing the idea that he not only had the appearance of a man but was able to function like a man in every way, including sexually.

The text's setting might also lend support to the idea of this being a sexual encounter. The group of angels in sura 3 is now a single figure who looks human. The text gives the impression that he and Mary are alone, and this sense of isolation is heightened if we understand the reference to her withdrawing from her family in verse 16 as implying an actual physical distancing of herself from them. Mary's initial reaction to the stranger, in which she "takes refuge" from him (v. 18), might be her own acknowledgment of the potential for a man to take advantage of a young woman in such a situation. Similarly, her self-designation as "not unchaste" could be a way of informing him that she has never engaged in illicit sexual relations and has no plans to do so now or in the future. Finally, the content of the angel's message could be understood as an indication of the sexual nature of his visit. He describes his mission as "to give you a righteous son" (v. 19), which might mean that he himself, in his now-human form, will help to bring about this pregnancy in the normal way. Alternatively, one might argue that there is an unexpressed direct object in the sentence that is meant to be understood and he is really saying "I come to give you (the good news of) a righteous son," which would correspond to the angelic message in sura 3.

Evidence like this could be cited in an attempt to propose a sexual reading of the episode, but such an interpretation has not met with approval in the Islamic community. Muslims hold that the Qur'an speaks of Mary's virginal conception of Jesus and this has become a widely accepted article of Islamic faith. Throughout history, Qur'an commentators and Muslim theologians have attempted to explain this mystery of their faith just as their Christian counterparts have attempted to do the same. While Matthew's Gospel lacks the narrative drama and detail of Luke's on the question of Jesus' conception, it agrees with Luke in seeing Mary's condition as due to the working of the Holy Spirit (Matt 1:18, 20). Ultimately, any attempt to explain or logically prove how such an event could occur is doomed to failure. Christians must accept on faith the truth of such texts, acknowledging their own limitations and their inability to comprehend the transcendent power of God.

Islam adopts a similar approach of submissive assent to this unexplainable miracle, and the texts in the Qur'an themselves form the basis for this attitude. We have observed that when Mary expresses her objection in the Islamic passages she is not given a tangible sign that is meant to convince her, as happens in Luke. In the New Testament, she is told that her kinswoman Elizabeth is also pregnant and she then runs off to see this for herself in order to verify the truth of the angel's words (Luke 1:36-56). No such thing happens to Mary in the Qur'an. In both texts, the response to her words of objection is more words. In both suras 3 and 19 Mary's protest is initially met with an angelic response so concise and terse that it comes close to being an admonition. The angel informs her "thus it is," an English phrase that is one word in the original Arabic (3:47; 19:21). Imagine Mary's frustration at receiving this reply after asking how it is she will become pregnant. She must have experienced all the insight and satisfaction of a child whose question is addressed with a parental "Because I said so!" Luckily for Mary, this is not the end of the conversation. In both texts, the messenger goes on to explain to her the reason behind the "thus it is," and in each case the emphasis is on the supreme authority and power of the divine will. Mary will become pregnant because this is what Allah wants to happen. The lack of a palpable sign in the Qur'an means that Mary is being asked to have a level of faith that even exceeds that required of her in the Bible. Without an Elizabeth to run off to for validation, Mary becomes the perfect model for the Muslim believer who is asked to trust in Allah's word in the same way she herself was required to do.

The Qur'an's lack of detail regarding the mode of Mary's pregnancy is offset by the contributions of commentators who attempt to explain how such a thing might have happened. Many of their interpretations draw upon the meaning "breath, wind" for the Arabic term *rūḥ* as they propose a method of conception that requires an exchange of breath between the angel and Mary. One such idea is that the messenger breathed into Mary's mouth and when his breath reached her belly she conceived.

Related views hold that the messenger blew into her sleeve, pocket or a tear in her blouse and she became pregnant when his breath came in contact with the skin covering her womb. A variation of this scenario maintains that Mary had removed her garment to bathe and the angel blew into it while it was on the ground. After finishing her bath, she put her garment back on and immediately became pregnant. These and other interpretations by Qurʾan commentators, as well as the material on Mary that is found in Islamic traditions, help to fill in some of the gaps of the Qurʾan passages, allowing Muslims to more readily recognize the uniqueness of Mary and her special role in history.[6]

THE BIRTH OF JESUS

The only explicit reference to Jesus' birth in the Qurʾan is found at 19:22-29. It occurs immediately after the annunciation text and includes a scene that describes how Mary's people react to the birth of her son.

> [22]She conceived him and withdrew with him to a distant place. [23]The birth pangs led her to the trunk of a palm tree where she cried, "Oh, if only I had died before this and had been forgotten, unremembered!" [24]Then (a voice) called out to her from below her, "Do not grieve. Your Lord has placed a stream beneath you. [25]Shake the trunk of the palm tree and it will drop fresh ripe dates upon you. [26]Eat, drink and be consoled. If you should see another person say, 'I have vowed a fast to the merciful one and will not speak to anyone today.'" [27]She carried him (Jesus) to her people who said, "Oh Mary, you have done something strange! [28]Oh sister of Aaron, your father was not wicked nor was your mother unchaste." [29]Then she pointed to him. They said, "How can we talk to a child in the cradle?"

This text opens in a way similar to the annunciation scene earlier in sura 19 with a reference to Mary distancing herself yet further from her family and familiar surroundings. The Arabic verb used here (*intabadat*) is the identical form found in verse 16 and this repetition, combined with the identification of her destination as a "distant place," adds to the sense of isolation and seclusion that is an important part of the Mary tradition in the Qurʾan. The passage offers no clue on the precise location, but Muslim commentators have proposed a number of possible candidates, including Jerusalem, Bethlehem, and Egypt. The text appears to have in mind a desolate, remote area since Mary finds herself all alone, thirsty and hungry, wishing she were dead.

Her cry in verse 23, a heartfelt complaint in which she laments her situation, raises some interesting questions about her character. Is this a reaction to the physical pain she is experiencing as her birth pangs intensify? Is it due to the mental anguish she undergoes as she struggles to understand the reasons for and implications of her unexpected pregnancy? Perhaps it is a combination of both of these things. Commentators have frequently reflected on the possible theological significance of her words. An issue of particular interest has been whether or not Mary's desperate cry is meant to express her unwillingness to accept the angel's message and submit herself to the divine will. In other words, is Mary somehow being disobedient to Allah in preferring death to her present state? Given Mary's role within Islam as a paragon of faith and virtue, it should come as no surprise that this idea has found little support among Muslims. Consequently, most of the explanations of the cause of her anguish extend beyond herself, like her concern that others might mistakenly call Jesus the son of God, rather than understand it as due to lack of belief or some other personal flaw on her part. Whatever its precise cause, there is an ironic element to her prayer that can be easily overlooked. The image of Mary praying that she be unremembered and obliterated from history strikes the reader as incompatible with the high profile and exalted status she has come to hold within both Islam and Christianity. Against her wishes, she certainly was not forgotten! In this sense, Mary's prayer was not answered.

But in another sense, it was. No sooner have her words left her lips than she hears a voice from beneath her offering advice and support. It tells her she will be given sustenance in the form of a stream provided by Allah and fruit from the nearby tree (vv. 24–25). It also instructs her to avoid interaction with other people by claiming to be engaged in a fast that does not allow her to speak (v. 26). This guidance appears to be asking Mary to do two contradictory things. On the one hand, she is to eat and drink her fill. At the same time, she is to tell anyone she encounters that she is fasting and prevented from speaking. How does one fast and eat at the same time? Is the voice asking Mary to lie? Commentators have addressed this seeming inconsistency by maintaining that the fast Mary undertakes is one that entails abstaining from speech only and does not refer to eating or drinking.

One of the mysteries of this text is the origin of the voice. Who speaks to Mary here? This is another place in which we are confronted with a frustrating silence in the Qur'an on a matter of some interest and importance. The desire to understand exactly what is going on in the story encourages the reader to be curious about the source of this disembodied voice. Once again, what the Qurʾan lacks, commentators have attempted to supply. Some scholars have understood this to be the angel's voice, while others maintain that it is the voice of Jesus who tries to console and assist his mother in this difficult moment. Those who opt for this latter view, which is the more preferred interpretation among Muslims, see the scene as an account of the first of the many miracles Jesus will perform in the course of his lifetime. If we take this as the voice of the infant, the miraculous nature of the event is obvious. Not only does he possess the ability to speak as a newborn, he speaks with knowledge and authority that are far beyond his years. In particular, the tone of his discourse underscores this element of the text. In verses 24–26 he issues six orders to his mother, all grammatically imperative, and these serve to establish him as her superior, thereby laying the groundwork for their future relationship.

The Qurʾan lacks any reference to the birth itself as the setting abruptly shifts to Mary's return to her people (v. 27). This is an interesting action on her part in light of her earlier movements. After twice distancing herself from her family and those close to her (vv. 16, 22), she now rejoins them. Carrying the baby in her arms, she returns to her community where she experiences a chilly homecoming. "Oh Mary, you have done something strange! Oh sister of Aaron, your father was not wicked nor was your mother unchaste" (vv. 27–28). Why does Mary decide to return at this point? Perhaps Jesus' birth signals an end to her period of seclusion and she is now able to reintegrate herself back into society. Both suras 3 and 19 understand her encounter with the angel, during which she is told about her pregnancy, as occurring while she is isolated and far-removed from familiar surroundings. Now that the child is born and the angel's message has come to pass, it is time for her to resume her previous way of life among her own people.

The phrase "her people" has some provocative connotations. It is mentioned both at the beginning of this passage when she leaves "her people" (v. 16), and here at its end with her return to "her people" (v. 27). In the intervening verses, she receives a divine revelation that is affirmed with the birth of her child. In verse 21 she is told that Allah will make Jesus a "sign for people" and a mercy for them. In order for this part of the revelation to be fulfilled, she must bring the child back to her community so they can see the sign and experience divine mercy. Her return is therefore an attempt to fully realize the divine message she has received.

Mary functions here exactly as the prophetic figures in the Qurʾan do. As we have seen, Noah, Abraham, Lot, and Moses each has "his people," to whom he is sent to deliver a divine message. Mary does a similar thing. She temporarily leaves her people and then comes back to them with a message meant to strengthen their faith in the power of Allah. The affinity between Mary and prophecy is further highlighted when we note how Islam identifies the angel who speaks to Mary. He is traditionally understood to be Gabriel, the voice to the prophets *par excellence*, through whom Allah revealed the Qurʾan to Muhammad.[7] The difference with Mary is that, unlike in the case of the male prophets, the message is not in the form of mere words. This time, it is a flesh and blood human being, miraculously conceived, whom she carries in her arms. If we think of Jesus in this way, then the Qurʾan's use of the term "word of Allah" to describe him (3:45; 4:171) takes on added meaning. He is the word, or message, that Mary is to communicate to her people in a way analogous to the verbal message Noah and the other prophets communicate to their people. We see a further connection between Mary and the male prophets in the reception they receive from their people. Just as in the case of the other prophets, Mary's people refuse to accept the divine source of the word she brings to them and they consider it to be illegitimate.

Despite the similarity between her experience and theirs, the idea of Mary as one of the prophets has not been accepted by the majority of Muslims. This is primarily due to the Islamic belief that prophethood is an office that is reserved exclusively for men. This position has been supported by appeal to the general content of the Qurʾan, which only speaks of men as prophets, and to particular texts like 12:109, which specifies those sent by Allah as being male in gender. "We sent only men before you (Muhammad). We gave revelation to them who were from among the people of the towns." Such arguments to the contrary must be respected, particularly by non-Muslims, but they do not fully address the many striking correspondences that exist between Mary and those who are explicitly identified as prophets in the pages of the Qurʾan.

Several further elements of this scene deserve some brief comment. The title "sister of Aaron" (v. 28) used for Mary is a curious one that has been interpreted in a number of ways. Some commentators, mostly non-Muslims, have argued that it is an indication of confusion between Mary, the mother of Jesus, and Miriam (Mary's name in Arabic), the sister of Moses and Aaron in the Bible. On the other hand, those who desire to maintain the accuracy of the text claim that it might be a reference to an individual named Aaron who was close to Mary, perhaps her own brother. Mary's mother and father are mentioned at the end of the passage in sura 19 (v. 28), which is different from what we saw in sura 3 where they, her mother in particular, play a prominent role at the beginning of that text (vv. 35–36). Despite this different placement, however, the way their characters are presented is consistent in the two passages. The emphasis in both is on their admirable qualities as good, faithful people. This comes out clearly in the mother's case. In sura 3, she dedicates her child to Allah and requests divine protection for Mary and her offspring. Sura 19 contains less detail but identifies a negative trait each parent does not possess. Mary's father is referred to as "not wicked" and her mother as "not unchaste." This latter term is the very same one (*bagī*) Mary uses in reference to herself when she raises her objection to the angel's news of her pregnancy earlier in sura 19 (v. 20). The mention of this attribute shared by the two women points out for the reader the grave error Mary's people commit in their haste to condemn her. They implicitly accuse her of being unchaste, a quality she has already explicitly rejected for herself.

The passage ends with Mary silently pointing to the child Jesus rather than mounting a verbal defense against her accusers. This response may be related to the voice's order that she not speak with anyone she might meet (v. 26). If so, it shows her complete obedience to that voice, even at a moment when she is being unfairly denounced and is strongly tempted to cry out and clear her name. If, as discussed above, the voice belongs to Jesus, Mary's silence reflects her compliance with his will, despite his tender age. Whatever its motivation, Mary's lack of speech and pointing gesture shift the attention to her child who, as we will see in the next chapter, becomes the focal point of the story. Mary's son will open his mouth and display his eloquence in a way that underscores the folly of her people's question, "How can we speak to a child in the cradle?" (v. 29).

When we compare the Mary material in the Qur²an with that found in the New Testament it is clear that the Islamic text places greater emphasis on her being alone at key moments in her life. In particular, the absence of Joseph, the man to whom she is betrothed in the Bible, is a striking feature of the Qur²an. Joseph plays an important supporting role in Luke where he is with her at Jesus' birth in Bethlehem (2:4-7), present at the manger when the shepherds visit (2:16), accompanies her to Jerusalem when they bring the baby to the Temple (2:22-38), and returns with her and Jesus to Nazareth (2:39). In Matthew's Gospel, Joseph has an even higher profile since the story is primarily told from his perspective as he is the one who receives the angelic messages and is the primary actor in the plot. In fact, Mary never utters a single word in Matthew's infancy narrative, which is in sharp contrast to the loquacious nature of her character in Luke.

Joseph is never mentioned in the Qurʾan and nowhere does it give the impression that Mary is engaged to be married at the time she is told of her pregnancy. According to the text, she is a young woman, a girl by modern standards, who is all alone when she conceives and gives birth to Jesus. But this does not mean that Muslims are unfamiliar with Joseph. As commonly occurs, nonscriptural Islamic traditions expand on the Qurʾan story and Joseph plays an important role in this material as someone who assists and takes care of Mary. He is often presented as her companion in devotion, a pious, spiritual man who shares her deep faith in Allah. There is a general tendency to avoid presenting their relationship as a sexual one. According to some traditions, for example, Joseph is Mary's cousin who comes to look after her when Zachariah gets too old and can no longer perform his duties as her guardian. Such references to Joseph lend an air of familiarity to the Mary tradition for the Bible reader, but it must be kept in mind that Joseph is not a part of the story in the Qurʾan and this has implications for how we should understand what happens to Mary. Our discussion of the two texts as cooperating revelations will now suggest that Joseph's absence from the Qurʾan has a significant effect on how we should evaluate his presence in the New Testament.

COOPERATING REVELATIONS

We have seen that in 3:35-47 the Qurʾan weaves together the Mary/Jesus and Zachariah/John annunciation stories in a way the New Testament does not. Luke is the only gospel that contains the Zachariah tradition and it presents it as a separate story from that of Mary. The gospel opens with an account of Zachariah's encounter with the angel Gabriel in the Temple in Jerusalem (1:5-25). After this, the setting shifts to Nazareth where Gabriel notifies Mary of her pregnancy (1:26-38). Nowhere in Luke, or anywhere else in the New Testament, do Mary and Zachariah speak to each other and they are never even shown together in the same scene. Sura 3, on the other hand, brings them together and envisions a close relationship between them. We will now consider several aspects of this text in an attempt to see how it can help us appreciate elements of the biblical story that might be overlooked. For the sake of convenience, 3:35-47 is translated here in its entirety.

[35]ʿImrān's wife said, "My Lord, I have vowed to You that what is in my womb will be dedicated to Your service. Accept it from me, for You are the one who hears, the one who knows." [36]When she brought forth the child, she said, "My Lord, I have brought forth a female"—but Allah knew what she had brought forth, for the male is not like the female— "and I have named her Mary. I place her and her offspring under Your protection from Satan, the cursed one." [37]So her Lord accepted her graciously. He caused her to grow up well and gave her into the care of Zachariah. Every time Zachariah came to see her in the chamber he found her with provisions. He said, "Oh Mary, where do you get this?" She answered, "It is from Allah. Truly, Allah provides for whomever He wishes without measure." [38]Then and there, Zachariah called upon his Lord saying, "My Lord, grant me good offspring from Yourself. Truly, You hear all prayers." [39]Then the angels called to him while he stood praying in the chamber, "Allah gives you the good news of John, who will confirm a word from Allah. He will be noble, chaste, and a prophet from among the righteous." [40]He said, "Oh Lord, how is it that I might have a son when I am old and my wife is barren?" He (an angel) said, "Thus it is. Allah does what He wills." [41]He said, "My Lord, make for me a sign." He said, "Your sign is that you will not be able to speak to a person for three days except by gestures. Remember your Lord much and praise Him in the evening and in the morning." [42]The angels said, "Oh Mary, Allah has truly chosen you and purified you. He has chosen you above all other women. [43]Oh Mary, be obedient to your Lord. Prostrate yourself and be among those who bow down." [44]This is part of the hidden news We reveal to you. You were not with them when they cast lots to see which of them would take care of Mary, nor were you with them when they disputed among themselves. [45]The angels said, "Oh Mary, Allah gives you the good news of a word from Him. His name will be the Messiah Jesus, the son of Mary, who will be eminent in this world and the next, and will be one of those brought near (to Allah). [46]He shall speak to people from the cradle and in his later years, and will be one of the righteous." [47]She said, "My Lord, how can I have a child when no man has touched me?" He said, "Thus it is. Allah creates what He wills. If He decrees something, He only need say 'Be!' and it is."

Analysis of the Qurʾanic Tradition

The two verses prior to this text serve as an introduction to it that asserts a connection between Mary's family and important prophetic figures of the past. "Truly, Allah chose Adam, Noah, the family of Abraham, and the family of ʿImrān above all others as descendants of one another. Allah is the one who hears, the one who knows" (3:33-34). The use of the term "descendants" to refer to the individuals cited indicates that this is a type of genealogy which establishes their familial relationship. ʿImrān, the father of Mary, continues the line that began with Adam and is traced through Noah and Abraham. Whether or not the Qurʾan assumes an actual biological relationship among these figures is unclear, and it may be that the connection is due to their common faith or prophetic role rather than being a result of genetic lineage. Since ʿImrān is his grandfather, this is also Jesus' genealogy and it helps to legitimate his position as a prophet and messenger from Allah.

Matthew and Luke, the only two gospels with narratives on Jesus' conception and birth, are also the only ones that contain genealogies for him. Matthew's genealogy is found at the beginning of the gospel, prior to Jesus' birth, while Luke's occurs in chapter three, after his baptism as an adult by John the Baptist. The unusual placement of Luke's genealogy will be discussed below, but the key point to note for the moment is that both gospels trace Jesus' lineage through Joseph, the husband of Mary (Matt 1:16; Luke 3:23). The Qurʾan, which lacks any mention of Joseph, moves in the other direction by identifying Jesus in relation to his maternal family tree. Jesus' family history is not established through a man to whom his mother Mary is married. Rather it is her father, her own blood relative, who determines his ancestry. Note how this subtly shifts the focus of attention onto Mary. Her son's pedigree is not understood in relation to her husband. She does not even have a husband in the Qurʾan. Rather, it is Mary's own line which defines her son's identity. And what a line it is! Jesus' forebears include such notables as Adam, Noah and Abraham. In the Qurʾan, therefore, the spotlight is on Mary as a single parent who establishes Jesus' lineage. This is quite different from the New Testament where her family history is unknown and her primary role is to conceive and give birth to Jesus, not to give him a bloodline he can be proud of. The mini-genealogy in the Qurʾan which highlights Mary's importance sets the stage for the way she remains independent and free of male control throughout the story.

In verse 37, Zachariah is put in charge of Mary and made her caretaker. The syntax of the sentence makes it clear that Allah is behind this development since the deity is the subject of the Arabic verb which is here translated as "to give (someone) into the care of someone else." The authority and power that Allah exercises over Zachariah in making him Mary's guardian foreshadows their relationship as the story unfolds. Zachariah is not able to properly discharge his duties because whenever he comes to the *miḥrāb* to bring Mary what she needs he finds that Allah has already been there before him. Allah appoints Zachariah to be Mary's provider but then renders that role redundant by responding to Mary's needs before Zachariah can address them. A key theological point is being made here. Mary is not dependent upon any man, including the one who has been divinely designated as her keeper. Her true caretaker, and the only one on whom she is dependent, is Allah alone. This same idea is expressed in the version of the annunciation and birth of Jesus that is found in sura 19, where we read of Mary twice distancing herself from her own people, those upon whom she should depend and who should provide for her. After she has secluded and isolated herself from those caretakers, Allah enters her life and offers her protection by responding to her needs.

The absence of Joseph and the ineffectiveness of Zachariah as Mary's provider make apparent her total dependence on Allah in the Qurʾan. Even her family surrenders its caregiving role when Mary's mother dedicates her to the deity and sends her off to live with Zachariah. What happens to her in the *miḥrāb* indicates that she does not need the protection and assistance of any human being because Allah is always with her and responsive to her needs. The quality of Mary's character that the Qurʾan stresses above all others in this passage is her independence from traditional support systems and social structures. She is a young girl who is far from her family, living a life of solitude. Under these vulnerable circumstances, she does not rely on her relatives or her appointed guardian for her survival because she is alone, but not alone. Allah, "the one who hears, the one who knows" (3:34), is with her every step of the way.

Application to the Biblical Tradition

We now turn to Luke's infancy narrative, which is closer to the Qurʾan account than Matthew's is, to see if there is evidence of these same themes at work there. Is Mary depicted as autonomous and detached from the traditional locus of support for someone in her situation? Does God fill the void by being her true caretaker? Before addressing such questions, we should reiterate a point worth repeating which concerns the overall structure of the two works. Luke's gospel does not integrate the stories of Zachariah and Mary in the way the Qurʾan does. Because Mary and Zachariah never engage in conversation in Luke as they do in the Qurʾan, we might be tempted to conclude that the Islamic text cannot possibly cooperate with the New Testament one. But this would be to overlook one interesting intersection of the Mary and Zachariah traditions contained in Luke. Although the gospel does not recount a meeting between Mary and Zachariah, it does spend some time describing an encounter between her and Zachariah's wife, Elizabeth. This scene is a critical one for evaluating the relevance of the Qur'an material for the New Testament.

As noted earlier, Luke does not begin his work with a genealogy as Matthew does. Rather, he inserts Jesus' family history into the body of the gospel, almost three chapters after Jesus' birth and some thirty years into his life (3:23). This shift in the location of Joseph's family tree contributes to the general reduction of his character which can be observed in Luke when it is compared with the Gospel of Matthew. While Matthew's infancy narrative is told primarily through Joseph's eyes, the one in Luke is Mary's story. In Luke, Joseph never speaks and is much more of a secondary figure than he is in Matthew where Mary tends to recede into the background. The lack of a genealogy at the beginning of Luke suppresses Joseph's role even further and raises Mary's status in the mind of the reader. Jesus' identity is not established in relation to the family line of his mother's husband, but is slowly revealed to the reader through the actions and words of the mother herself. This is similar to what we see in the Qur'an where the mini-genealogy underscores the importance of Mary's family and she, not Joseph or any other man, is the focus of attention. An attentive reading of Luke's narrative with the Qur'an passage in mind allows this subtle aspect of the New Testament text to become more apparent and enables us to appreciate this important dimension of Mary's character in Luke.

Luke's Gospel does not present Mary's genealogy as the Qur'an does, but it does indirectly provide us with some information about her family. In 1:5, we learn that Zachariah's wife Elizabeth is a descendant of Aaron, the brother of Moses. According to the angel's words to Mary, Elizabeth is her relative (1:36) so this means that Mary, too, is part of the line of Aaron and Moses. The Greek word used here, *sungenis*, is a general term meaning "kinswoman" so we do not know the precise degree of relationship between Mary and Elizabeth that is presumed. Nonetheless, it is interesting that in Luke's infancy narrative we have more information about Mary's family than we do about Joseph's.

In Luke's Gospel, Joseph assumes the role played by Zachariah in the Qur'an text. As Mary's husband-to-be, he has a certain responsibility to take care of her and support her in time of need. During this period in Palestine, marriage was a two-step process in which there was an initial formal exchange of consent to marry followed later by the man's taking the woman to his family home where they would live under the same roof. Even though there could be an extended period of time between the two stages, the couple was considered to be legally married after the first step. The textual evidence in both Luke's and Matthew's Gospels indicates that Joseph and Mary had already completed the first step at the time Mary conceived Jesus but were not yet living together. He therefore had an obligation to her as his betrothed that was stronger than what is implied by our modern term "engaged." However, there is some cause to question how well he met that obligation in Luke's telling of the story. An examination of Joseph's role in Luke's first two chapters suggests that he is absent at key points in Mary's life where we might normally expect him to be more involved.

We first hear of Joseph in 1:27 where we are told he is a man of the house of David who is engaged to Mary. He is not mentioned again until 2:4 when he takes the now-pregnant Mary to Bethlehem to be registered in the census called by the Emperor Augustus (2:1). In between these two references to Joseph, a block of material almost thirty verses in length is devoted to Mary which describes a critical period in her life. In this section, she has the encounter with the angel Gabriel who informs her she will conceive and bear a son (1:28-38), and she journeys to visit her relative Elizabeth who is, herself, recently pregnant (1:39-56). Joseph, Mary's legal husband, is not involved in either of these two scenes, and this creates circumstances similar to those which were noted in the Qur'an. Mary is very much on her own and appears to be detached from the traditional support systems and social structures that might be able to assist her in her situation.

Normally, Joseph should have a more active role in taking care of and providing for Mary. But, as with Zachariah in the Qur'an, the person we expect to serve this function does not do so. Similarly, the lack of any mention of Mary's parents, siblings or other close family members in Luke adds to the sense of her isolation. Perhaps one reason why the New Testament text does not contain any information on her immediate family is to highlight the absence of normal companionship in her life. She spends three months with her kinswoman Elizabeth, but the description of this visit is presented in an unusual way. She enters the house of Zachariah (Luke 1:40) and greets Elizabeth with whom she remains for three months (1:56). Luke does not have Mary greet Zachariah himself and never tells us if or how Mary and Zachariah interact while she stays in his house. This lack of reference to Zachariah might be another way Luke tries to express the idea that Mary is not dependent upon him, or any other man, at this point in her life.

According to Luke, Joseph is not with Mary when she first learns she has conceived nor is he with her when she goes to spend the three months with Elizabeth. In other words, for the first one-third of her pregnancy at least, Mary is on her own, except for the company of her relative Elizabeth. This is an important element of the biblical story that is easily overlooked since the narrative is full of dramatic moments which compete for the reader's attention, like the appearance of the angel, the extraordinary message to Mary, and her encounter with Elizabeth. But Mary's lack of human support is an implicit part of all of these biblical scenes which can be brought to the surface when we recognize the higher profile the theme enjoys in the Qurʾan. As in the Qurʾan, Mary is seemingly alone, far from her betrothed, her family and familiar surroundings. At the same time, as also in the Qurʾan, Mary is not really alone because God is with her, assisting her in her time of need in a way that no human being can. She is a young girl, perhaps as young as twelve or thirteen years of age, who finds herself inexplicably with child, bereft of the support of her family and husband, embarking on an arduous journey.

A study of Mary's character throughout the Gospels points out a fascinating fact: this is the only place where it clearly states that she travels some place alone. Elsewhere in the infancy narratives, she moves around quite a bit, but it is always in the company of Joseph, and sometimes others. In Matthew, he is with her as they make their way from Bethlehem to Egypt in order to avoid Herod's plot to kill Jesus (2:13-15) and they then leave Egypt and return together to Israel after Herod's death (2:21). Similarly, in the second chapter of Luke, Joseph takes Mary with him from Nazareth to Bethlehem in order to register for the census (2:5), and it is there that Jesus is born. After his birth, Luke reports that Joseph and Mary go to present the child to the Lord at the temple in Jerusalem (2:22) and then return together to Nazareth (2:39). Later still, when Jesus is twelve years old, Mary and Joseph travel again to Jerusalem to celebrate Passover but inadvertently leave Jesus behind on the return trip, thinking he is elsewhere in the traveling party. Luke describes Joseph and Mary beating a hasty retreat back to Jerusalem and journeying back to Nazareth with Jesus once they locate him in the Temple (2:41-51). In verse 41 of this latter text, Luke indicates that Mary and Joseph were a couple who traveled together regularly. "Now every year his parents went to Jerusalem for the festival of Passover."

Outside the infancy narratives references to Mary are less common. But she is present on several occasions and the context always suggests she has journeyed some distance to be there. In each case she has traveling companions and they are usually males. Mark 3:31-35 recounts the tradition of Jesus' mother and brothers coming to see him while he is teaching in Galilee, and the parallel texts in Matthew (12:46-50) and Luke (8:19-21) tell the same story. In John's Gospel, Jesus' mother is mentioned twice and both times she has had to travel to be on the scene. In 2:1-11, she attends a wedding ceremony in the town of Cana at which Jesus and his disciples are also present. Although the text does not explicitly say they went to the wedding together, their common departure is described and this argues in favor of seeing them as traveling companions to the wedding as well. "After this he went down to Capernaum with his mother, his brothers, and his disciples; and they remained there a few days" (John 2:12). The other reference to her in John is similar in that it does not explain how she arrived at the location but it shows her departing in the company of a man. In 19:25-27, just before his death, Jesus looks down from the cross and sees his mother and the beloved disciple. He tells his disciple, "Here is your mother," indicating that it is now his responsibility to take care of her. He accepts that charge immediately as the text concludes with the statement, "And from that hour the disciple took her into his own home."

The evidence, limited though it may be, clearly suggests that in the Gospels Mary is someone who does not travel alone. The only exception to this rule is found in Luke 1:39-56, where she makes a round-trip journey by herself to visit Elizabeth. In fact, the annunciation scene and her trek to and from Elizabeth's house in Luke are the only two places in the Gospels in which Mary is not in the company of other people. By having her travel to Elizabeth on her own, Luke places Mary in a very unusual, even dangerous, situation. The gospel does not identify exactly where Zachariah's house is, but describes it as being in a Judean town in the hill country (Luke 1:39). The distance between Nazareth, Mary's hometown (Luke 1:26), and Judea is some fifty miles, and the journey between the two in those days would be an extremely difficult one taking a few days under the best conditions. The most common route would entail traveling south from the hills of Galilee, across the plain of Esdraelon, through the mountainous area of Samaria and into the hills of Judea. In attempting such a trip, Mary's status as a pregnant young female would put her at great risk. The challenges presented by the shifting terrain, natural elements, and threat of attack, which were concerns to all travelers of the time, would be multiplied in her case. Luke plainly states that during this most difficult moment of her young life, as she journeys to and from Elizabeth on her one-hundred mile odyssey, Mary is by herself (1:39, 56).

As in the Qurʾan, this is only partly true. On her way to visit Elizabeth, Mary is no more alone than she is while sitting in the *miḥrāb* in the Islamic text. In both those situations she may be far from human companionship and support, but the divine presence is ever near and ready to respond to her every need. We saw that in sura 3 Mary gives Zachariah a lesson in faith by telling him that Allah can provide anything a person asks for (v. 37). He then immediately directs a prayer to Allah that he be granted a child and this request is swiftly met. This scene is not found in Luke, where Mary and Zachariah are never shown together, but in the gospel Mary does a similar thing for Elizabeth. In Luke, Mary gives Elizabeth a lesson in faith by bringing to her the Holy Spirit. When Mary asks the angel how it is possible that she will have a child, Gabriel responds, "The Holy Spirit will come upon you, and the power of the Most High will overshadow you" (Luke 1:35). She is then told about Elizabeth's pregnancy and straightaway takes off to see her kinswoman. As Mary makes the arduous trip from Nazareth to the Judean hill country she does so filled with and empowered by the Holy Spirit. This divine gift is the biblical equivalent of the miraculous food and drink provided to her in the Qurʾan. With God's Spirit to nourish and sustain her, she needs no assistance from Joseph, her family, or any other human being to make the journey.

Upon arriving at her destination, Mary helps Elizabeth to experience the same divine favor in her own life. "When Elizabeth heard Mary's greeting, the child leaped in her womb. And Elizabeth was filled with the Holy Spirit" (v. 41). Mary brings the Holy Spirit into the house of Zachariah and this allows his wife to find it within herself. There is an interesting connection between the Christian and Islamic traditions in this regard. In the Qurʾan, Mary helps Zachariah come to knowledge of an aspect of the deity that has already been made known to her. Similarly, in Luke, Mary enables Elizabeth to be filled with the same Holy Spirit that has overshadowed her.

The Mary tradition found in the Qurʾan enables the Bible reader to recognize aspects of the story in Luke that are not central to the plot but contribute greatly to our understanding of the gospel narrative. It is natural to think of Joseph as a supportive presence in Mary's life, but Luke's text makes it clear that at key moments he is missing in action.

It can be difficult for the modern reader to appreciate the predicament Mary finds herself in as she discovers she is pregnant and then sets off on her trek to visit Elizabeth. The harsh nature of that journey and Mary's lack of companionship during it are elements of the story that are rarely considered. God's role in sustaining her with the Holy Spirit and Mary's involvement in Elizabeth's experience of that same Spirit can likewise go unnoticed. But related elements are central to the Qurʾan version and help to remind us that, as in the Islamic text, Mary in Luke is alone but not alone. As she herself states in 1:49, "The Mighty One has done great things for me, and holy is his name."

NOTES: CHAPTER 5

[1]John is the only gospel that records words spoken between Jesus and his mother, and that in only two places. In 2:1-11 she confers with him at the wedding celebration in Cana, and in 19:25-27 Jesus speaks to her as she stands at the foot of his cross. She also makes an appearance in the Synoptic Gospels when she comes to see Jesus during his ministry (Matt 12:46-50; Mark 3:31-35; Luke 8:19-21). All of these texts will be discussed later in the chapter.

[2]For more information on Islamic traditions about Mary and the relationship between the Qurʾan and extracanonical Christian writings, see Barbara Freyer Stowasser, *Women in the Qurʾan, Traditions, and Interpretation* (New York: Oxford University Press, 1994) 67–82.

[3]This is one of those areas in which we see some connection between the Qurʾan and certain Christian extracanonical writings. The Protoevangelium of James, a text from the mid-second century which purports to describe events that occurred just prior to and at the time of the birth of Jesus, contains a detailed account of Mary's birth. Some elements of this work are similar to what we find in the Qurʾan.

[4]Another reason why the word *miḥrāb* is sometimes rendered as "temple" could be Zachariah's role as a priest in the New Testament where he is shown engaging in priestly duties in the Jerusalem Temple (Luke 1:5, 8-23).

[5]The only other New Testament book containing narrative material on the conception and birth of Jesus is Matthew's Gospel. The first two chapters of both Matthew and Luke are commonly referred to as the "infancy narratives" because they describe events just prior to and immediately after Jesus' birth. The two accounts agree on very little and most scholars believe this to be the result of the different theological concerns of Matthew and Luke. The Qurʾan's material on the birth of Jesus is generally closer to Luke's version if only because Mary plays the central role there while she is virtually absent from Matthew's account. The definitive study of the infancy narratives and related

material is Raymond E. Brown, *The Birth of the Messiah* (New York: Double-day, 1993).

[6]For an excellent discussion of how commentary on the Qur³an and Is-lamic traditions have contributed to the understanding of Mary, see Jane I. Smith and Yvonne Y. Haddad, "The Virgin Mary in Islamic Tradition and Commentary," *The Muslim World* (July/October 1989) 161–87.

[7]The Gospel of Luke identifies Gabriel as the angel who spoke to both Zachariah and Mary (1:19, 26).

6

Jesus

*C*hristians are usually surprised to learn that Jesus is mentioned frequently in the Qurʾan and that he is a venerated figure in Islam. Because their opinions are often based on media reports and Hollywood portrayals of Muslims, it is common to think of Islam as a religion that places little value on Christianity and its founder and is often downright hostile toward it. Nothing could be further from the truth. Tensions and differences between the two religions certainly exist, and these need to be acknowledged and overcome. But this should not hide the fact that Muslims have a deep and abiding respect for Jesus and hold his followers in high regard as members of the people of the book. In this chapter, we will consider how Islam's sacred text portrays Jesus and we will discuss the implications of this portrayal for Muslim/Christian relations.

When we turn to the figure of Jesus in the Qurʾan, things get much more complicated for the Bible reader, particularly the Christian one. The fundamental problem is that the Qurʾan flatly denies the central article of Christian faith, the divinity of Jesus. This has not been the case with any of the other biblical figures or themes we have been studying up to this point. For example, tenets and ideas that are basic to Judaism are not explicitly refuted in the text. Nowhere does the Qurʾan claim, for instance, that God did not establish a covenant with Israel or that Moses did not lead the Israelites out of Egypt as they set out on the way to their Promised Land. Similarly, it does not reject the notion of Mary's virginal conception of Jesus but, rather, relates it as historical fact.

Only on the issue of Jesus' nature do we find a clear parting of the ways as the Qurʾan emphatically asserts the error in ascribing divinity to him. Upon learning this, many Christians are so troubled, indeed offended, by this view that the only logical response for them is to immediately dismiss the Qur'an as a tool of the devil which is intent on undermining and destroying the Christian faith. This is an understandable reaction to what appears to be an attack on what they hold near and dear to their hearts. But such an attitude only exacerbates the misunderstanding and discord that have existed between Muslims and Christians for centuries. Too often, people on each side have simply relied upon and perpetuated stereotypes that only lead to erroneous appraisals of the beliefs of the other. The best way to move beyond this predicament is to replace such distorted, uninformed perceptions with opinions that are based on accurate and factual information.

In order for them to properly assess Islam's view of Jesus and his role in its sacred text, it is essential that Christians familiarize themselves with the Qur'an by reading and studying those passages which mention him. Only then are they in a position to honestly evaluate the evidence and formulate a well-founded judgment on what Islam and its text have to say on the matter. Undoubtedly, some will reach the conclusion that the differences between the two faiths are too significant and profound to allow for any constructive conversation or dialogue between them. But others will note the many common elements in the portrayal of Jesus found in both the New Testament and the Qur'an, and this discovery will allow them to rethink their previous position regarding Islam and Muslim attitudes toward Jesus. In either case, their viewpoint will be a much more credible one because it will be based on textual evidence found in the Qur'an rather than on the opinions of others. The aim of this chapter is to help acquaint the Bible reader with the Qur'an's understanding of Jesus in order to deepen his or her understanding of Islam.

WHO DOES THE QUR'AN SAY HE IS?

Jesus is mentioned by name in 93 verses of 15 suras in the Qur'an. These numbers point to the great discrepancy that exists between the New Testament and the Qur'an regarding the amount of coverage Jesus receives in the two texts. There are almost as many chapters (89) on the life of Jesus in the gospels as there are verses on the same topic in the Qur'an. When we add to this the material found in Paul's letters and other New Testament writings which refers to Jesus, the difference is magnified even further. The Qur'an lacks a cohesive, sequential account that narrates key events in Jesus' life and ends with his death, but the Gospels represent four different versions of such a text. Consequently, the New Testament contains much more detail and information on Jesus' life than the Qurʾan does. But, as is the case with his mother Mary and other biblical characters present in the Islamic text, Muslims draw from sources other than the Qurʾan in formulating their picture of who Jesus was. He is a popular figure in nonscriptural Islamic traditions, and this material helps to fill in some of the gaps found in the Qurʾan and expand his figure considerably. As with Mary, there are a number of intriguing connections between these Islamic Jesus traditions and apocryphal Christian writings that are not included in the Bible, and this suggests Muslim familiarity with some of the noncanonical Christian writings.

The Qurʾan's denial of the divinity of Jesus, which is found a number of times in the text, is succinctly articulated in 5:17. "They have disbelieved who say, 'Truly Allah is the Messiah, the son of Mary.'" The heart of Christian belief is the incarnation, God's taking human form in the person of Jesus, culminating in his resurrection as the source of salvation for all who believe in him. According to the Qurʾan, this central article of Christian faith is an expression of unbelief, not belief. This is due to Islam's understanding of the nature of the deity. Belief in the incarnation is considered by Islam to be a prime example of the sin of *shirk*, or association. The defining quality of Allah is perfect unity, and Muslims regard any attempt to violate that divine oneness to be the most serious sin a person can commit. To ascribe divinity to Jesus, or any other person, is to associate something in the created order with the uncreated deity in a way that attempts to divide Allah's unity. To speak of Allah having a son is to imply a multiplicity within the divine nature that goes against a fundamental tenet of Muslim belief.

If Jesus is not divine in Islam, what is he? In the New Testament, as the son of God, he is the focal point of the text and of human history. In the Qurʾan, he is one of a series of focal points and, even then, he is not the most important one since he and his message will eventually be superceded by the coming of Muhammad. Perhaps the best way to get a handle on Jesus' role in the Qurʾan is to examine the titles and other designations that are used to refer to him. The two most frequent ways the text speaks of him are as "son of Mary" and "messiah." The appellation "son of Mary," found thirty-three times in the text, is the most common way the Qurʾan refers to Jesus. It does not indicate an office or function, but establishes his relationship to his mother. Consequently, it appears to be of little, if any, use in pinpointing his role since it is a fairly nondescript title that might be used for any male. Since every man has a mother, the designation "son of so and so" is not a particularly remarkable one that automatically sets a person apart from others. But this might be the very reason why it is the most frequent title used for Jesus in the Qur'an. It could be an attempt to highlight the fact that he was simply a man, no different from any other man. As we have seen, Mary's virginal conception of Jesus is mentioned in the Qur'an but there is no attempt to claim that Allah is therefore his father. The heavy use of the term "son of Mary" might have an implicit theological significance since it is a way of stressing Jesus' human nature and indirectly dismissing any declaration of his divinity.

The term "messiah" is a bit more elusive. It is found eleven times in the Qur'an and Jesus is the only individual given the title in the text. The word is of Jewish origin and most scholars believe it to be a loan-word into Arabic from Aramaic, another Semitic language that is closely related to Hebrew. While the source of the Arabic term (*masīḥ*) is easily identifiable, its meaning is not. The word "messiah" has several different meanings in the Hebrew Bible where it was originally related to the practice of anointing kings and priests to prepare them for the demands of their office. Later on in extrabiblical writings, it took on another sense to refer to a particular individual who would be a deliverer and play a leadership role within the community in times of difficulty. Recent scholarship has determined that the meaning of the term became increasingly more complex in the century or two before and after the time of Jesus since there were actually various types of messianic expectation in Israel during this period when the word "messiah" meant different things to different groups.[1]

As with other terms in the Qur'an like "word" and "holy spirit," we must avoid automatically assigning a Jewish or Christian meaning to the title "messiah." There is no evidence that the text is familiar with the significance of the term for these two communities and, in fact, nowhere does the Qur'an explicitly indicate what it means by the word "messiah." The title was certainly familiar to Muhammad and his contemporaries because the personal name ʿAbd al-Masīḥ ("servant of the messiah") is found in pre-Islamic times. But the lack of any explanation of the title in the Qur'an suggests that the early Muslim community probably had no awareness of what the title signified for Jews and Christians. In other words, in the Qur'an the title "messiah" is not a messianic one in the biblical sense of the term because the text never explains precisely what Jesus will be or will do as messiah. Nonetheless, it is a word that is uniquely applied to Jesus in Islam and this is similar to what we find in the New Testament where the title "Christ," the Greek translation of the Hebrew word for messiah, is so exclusively identified with Jesus that it is easy to erroneously consider it to be part of his name. Just as the English word "Christian" makes use of this title to designate a follower of Jesus, Islam uses the Arabic equivalent, *masīḥī*, to refer to those who believe in him.

The Qurʾan's two most frequently used titles for Jesus are therefore virtually worthless in any attempt to ascertain his role in the text. But a number of other designations which are less common are more helpful because their meanings are well known and established. One of the most important texts in this regard is 19:30 where the infant Jesus speaks from the cradle and says, "I am the servant of Allah. He has given me the book and has made me a prophet." The last word, prophet, places Jesus in the line of great figures the Qurʾan says have played that role throughout history. Like the biblical characters Adam, Noah, Abraham, and Moses, as well as nonbiblical figures such as Hūd, Ṣāliḥ and Shuʿaib, Jesus is sent to his people to instruct them in Allah's ways and warn them of the consequences should they fail to heed his counsel. The first title he uses to define himself in this verse, the servant of Allah, is a key one because it clearly places Jesus in a subordinate relationship to the deity. It implicitly argues against him sharing in the divine nature and indicates that he is to submit himself to Allah's will just as any other creature is expected to do. The reference to his having received the book from Allah is significant because it means that Jesus has another title beyond that of prophet. He is also a messenger who has been entrusted with a message for his people. Part of the reason why Jesus is held in such high regard in Islam is that he is among a handful of individuals who have been deemed worthy by the deity to play this role. Like Moses and David before him and Muhammad after him, Jesus was the recipient of divine revelation meant to guide his community to the straight path. "The messiah Jesus, son of Mary, was a messenger of Allah" (4:172).

According to the Qurʾan, the divine message given to Jesus is the *injīl*, an Arabic term related to *euangelion*, the Greek word for "gospel." The relationship between this message and prior revelation is explained in 5:46. "We sent after them (the prophets) Jesus, son of Mary, attesting to the truth already in the Torah. We gave him the *injīl* containing guidance and light and attesting to the truth already in the Torah. It is a guidance and exhortation for the pious." This verse places

Jesus in the line of the previous prophets as one who does not nullify the earlier revelation but confirms its legitimacy. The repetition of the phrase "attesting to the truth already in the Torah" underscores the idea that Jesus the messenger is not in competition with Moses his predecessor since the message of the *injīl* is compatible with that found in the Torah.

It is important to keep in mind that the word *injīl* does not refer to the Gospels or New Testament which Christians read. Islam holds that the original *injīl* was corrupted in a way similar to what happened with the original Torah. Just as the Hebrew Bible does not contain a faithful account of the revelation given to Moses, so also the New Testament is a distortion of that sent down to Jesus. The followers of these prophets introduced material into the books which is foreign to the divine message and taints it. In the case of the New Testament, for example, any references to Jesus' divinity are understood to be later additions to the original text which render it impure. Such defects are what led to the need for the accurate, final revelation which the Qurʾan provides.

An examination of the titles used for Jesus in the Qurʾan allows us to appreciate the role he plays in the text and within Islam. As the son of Mary, he is a normal human being who is no different from anyone else except for the miraculous way he was conceived. He is the messiah, a title difficult to define in the Qurʾan, but one giving Jesus special status since he is the only person so designated in the text. His important place in human history is indicated by his prophetic office and role as a messenger. The latter term highlights his uniqueness as one of a rare group of people who have been privileged with receiving divine revelation in the form of a book which is to be communicated to humanity.

In the previous chapter, we saw that Jesus is also referred to in the text as a word from Allah (3:44; 4:171) and we will note several other unique elements of his character in the discussion below. For the Bible reader, there are a couple of glaring omissions from this list of titles for Jesus. The more obvious is "son of God," but its absence comes as no surprise since its theological implications oppose Islamic belief about the divine nature. The other epithet not found in the Qurʾan is "son of man," which is a fairly common title used by Jesus in the Gospels to refer to himself that has been much studied by New Testament scholars. Although Jesus does not speak of the son of man when referring to himself in the Qurʾan, there are many passages in which he does explain his purpose and mission.

WHO DOES JESUS SAY HE IS?

One of the goals of New Testament scholarship is to identify and study the image of Jesus that emerges from the pages of the text. This is an extremely challenging and, at times, frustrating endeavor because of the nature of the sources being examined. Each of the four Gospels presents a unique portrait of Jesus that attempts to answer the question "Who was he?" in its own way. Even the material shared by two or more of the Gospels is usually shaped and edited by each to better fit the theology and concerns of the writer and address the needs of the particular audience for whom it is written. The same can be said about the writings of Paul and the other New Testament authors. Their own individual context, as well as that of the people to whom they are writing, plays a very influential role in how the person and message of Jesus is presented in the various New Testament books. The result of all this is that the New Testament actually contains a number of different christologies, or understandings of Jesus the Christ.

Things are not as complex in the Qur'an where there is a more cohesive and consistent portrayal of Jesus. This is not to say that its context has not had a hand in the compilation of the text. It certainly has, and even a Muslim who considers the Qur'an to be the verbatim words of Allah can still acknowledge the role of the context in determining the content of the text. A key difference between the Qur'an and the New Testament, however, is that the former book took shape in a narrower context. The Qur'an does not contain four separate accounts of Jesus' life, each written for a separate audience, which were originally independent and are now canonically related. Rather, its originating context was limited to a relatively small geographic area which was culturally more uniform. This contributes to the reader's impression of it being a unified text rather than a collection of separate works as the New Testament appears to be.

Although it lacks the narrative detail of the Gospels, the Islamic text is still able to communicate a fairly well-developed sense of Jesus' identity and significance. Much of this information is found on Jesus' lips since he frequently speaks in the Qur'an and many of his words are attempts to express his own self-understanding. One such text is 19:30-33, the first verse of which has already been discussed, when the infant Jesus speaks from the cradle.

> [30]"I am the servant of Allah. He has given me the book and has made me a prophet. [31]He has made me blessed wherever I may be and has

commanded me to observe prayer and almsgiving for as long as I live. [32](He has made me) obedient to my mother and has not made me proud or miserable. [33]Peace upon me the day I was born, the day I will die, and the day I will be raised to life."

We have already observed how the first sentence Jesus utters clearly puts him in his place in relation to the deity. As a newborn who is able to speak he may be a marvel, but he is not divine because he is Allah's servant. This idea is reinforced throughout his brief speech when he acknowledges that Allah is the cause of all that he is. The deity has given him the book (v. 30), made him a prophet (v. 30), made him blessed (v. 31), commanded him to pray and offer almsgiving (v. 31), and made him obedient to his mother (v. 32). He even recognizes divine responsibility for the lack of evil and suffering in his life: Allah has not made him proud or miserable (v. 32). There is also an implicit reference to Allah's authority over him in the last sentence with the mention that he will be raised to life. This grammatically passive verbal form, sometimes referred to as the divine passive, indicates that he is completely dependent upon Allah who has supreme control over what happens to him after death.

In these four verses we learn a great deal about Jesus but we also learn much about Allah from Jesus. It is a common feature of the Qurʾan's presentation of Jesus that he is always pointing beyond himself to the source of his life and abilities. We see this here when Jesus describes each of his attributes in a way that identifies them as gifts from the deity, thereby celebrating and calling attention to Allah and not himself. It is as if he is trying to explain how it is that his first statement ("I am the servant of Allah") is undeniably true because everything he has and is comes from the deity. The most intriguing thing about this mini-discourse is that it is being spoken by a baby. At this tender age, Jesus is already aware of both who he is for humanity and who he is in relation to Allah. This has a profound effect on how the reader understands Jesus' character. One of the questions often asked by biblical scholars and others who read the New Testament concerns the point at which Jesus became aware of who he was. Was it at his baptism, during his ministry, at his death, after his resurrection or at some other point? The Qurʾan leaves no room for doubt on the matter. The silent, passive infant of Matthew and Luke has here been replaced with a precocious baby who knows his role and, from the cradle, has already begun his work of reminding others of the power and authority of Allah.

A similar type of passage is found in 3:48-51, which follows imme-diately after the annunciation scene. The angel begins by explaining to Mary how Allah will instruct Jesus and then tells her what her son's message to his people will be.

> [48]He (Allah) will teach him (Jesus) the book, the wisdom, the Torah and the Gospel, [49]making him a messenger to the children of Israel. (He will say) "I have come to you with a sign from your Lord. I will make a bird-shaped form out of clay for you and then breath into it and, by Allah's leave, it will become a real bird. I will heal the blind and the leprous and I will bring the dead back to life, by Allah's leave. I will announce to you what to eat and what to store up in your houses. Truly, in that is a sign for you if you are believers. [50](I come) attesting to the truth already in the Torah and to make permissible for you some of that which had been forbidden to you. I have come to you with a sign from your Lord, so fear Allah and obey me. [51]Truly, Allah is my Lord and your Lord, so serve him. This is the straight path."

This passage is different from the previous one in that it does not quote Jesus directly but, rather, has the angel tell Mary what her still unborn son will say in the future. At what point in the future this will occur is not stated so it is unclear if the angel envisions Jesus speaking these words from the cradle, as he does in sura 19, or at a later time in his life. The content of his words also differs considerably in the two scenes. In the previous text, Jesus focuses on his own identity and the qualities Allah has blessed him with. We get very little sense of how he will involve himself in the world and accomplish his mission. Here, the emphasis is more on what Jesus will do as his miraculous works and other efforts at bringing people to faith are stressed. There are some in-teresting connections between these miracles and the New Testament material which will be discussed in some detail below. For now, it is im-portant to observe the shift in perspective as Jesus' relationship with his audience becomes the dominant theme. This is seen in the triple use of the word "sign," which is found twice in verse 49 and again in verse 50. Prior to and immediately after recounting the marvelous works he will accomplish, Jesus refers to them as a sign that is meant to instill belief in his people. The use of this term helps to highlight Jesus' role as mes-senger and bearer of divine revelation.

Despite this difference in focus, the two texts agree on one impor-tant point: it is Allah who is ultimately responsible for who Jesus is and what he does. Just as the passage from sura 19 repeatedly emphasizes the deity's involvement in Jesus' life so, too, this one from sura 3 makes a similar claim. In verses 48 and 49, the angel tells Mary that Allah will teach her son and make him a messenger. In other words, his entire identity as a prophet is divinely shaped and established. Similarly, when the angel quotes Jesus' words they call attention not to Jesus himself but to Allah. As Jesus relates the miracles he will perform, he mentions twice (v. 49) that all of these things can only be accomplished "by Allah's leave." This is an acknowledgment of a divine source outside of himself as the true authority responsible for these works. Jesus' inferior status before Allah is also underscored in verse 51 where he refers to the deity as "your Lord and my Lord." His use of the term "Lord" to characterize his relationship with Allah is a recognition of his own servant-hood and an implicit rejection of the idea of their being equal partners.

The reference to the "straight path" in verse 51 deserves some comment. As we have seen, this is a technical term in the Qur'an which signifies the religion of Islam and the spirit of submission to the will of Allah which it engenders. Its use here is meant to show that Jesus' message, like those of the prophets before him, was one that conformed to Islam and was in agreement with the revelation that would be given to Muhammad some six centuries later. This is another way in which the Qur'an implicitly critiques the idea of Jesus' divinity. In his own words, Jesus refutes this notion by referring to Allah as his Lord, exhorting his followers to serve Allah, and categorizing his message as the straight path. As is the case with other biblical figures in the Islamic text, we should not take this to mean that the Qur'an is presenting Jesus as a Muslim in the modern sense of the word. Because he submits himself fully to the divine will he is a "muslim," but because he predates the coming of Muhammad and the Qur'an by many years he is not a "Muslim" as the term is presently understood. Nonetheless, there are occasionally places in the text where Jesus and others are described engaging in activities which are prominent features of Islam. For example, in the previous passage at 19:31 Jesus remarks that Allah has commanded him to observe prayer and almsgiving. These practices, as two of the five pillars of their faith, are incumbent upon all Muslims, and so Jesus' participation in them brings him even closer to later-day Islam.[2]

Jesus' Words

As a prophet, Jesus has a definite teaching function in the Qur'an, but it is surprising how little of the content of his message is actually found in the text. This is in stark contrast to the Gospels which all contain lengthy discourses during which Jesus instructs his followers on many different matters. These sections are sometimes several chapters long as in, for example, the Sermon on the Mount in Matthew 5–7 which takes up more than one hundred verses of that gospel. The Qur'an, with less than one hundred total verses on Jesus, does not present such a detailed account of his teaching and that which it does include has a different content and form than what is in the New Testament.

The two passages just discussed are typical of Jesus' teaching style in the Qur'an. Heavy stress is placed on his identity as a messenger, but Allah's role in Jesus' life is also a very prominent theme that is frequently mentioned. The convergence of these two ideas affects how we understand Jesus' character. He is a teacher but he is also a student, since the words he speaks and message he delivers are Allah's, not his own. This idea comes out clearly in 3:48-49 which plainly states that he has been instructed by the deity. "He (Allah) will teach him (Jesus) the book, the wisdom, the Torah and the Gospel, making him a messenger to the children of Israel." This is different from the situation in the Gospels which sometimes describe uncertainty regarding the source of Jesus' knowledge. For example, in the scene depicting Jesus' return to his hometown of Nazareth, the people there wonder about the origin of his learning and powers. "Where did this man get this wisdom and these mighty works? Is not this the carpenter's son? Is not his mother called Mary? And are not his brothers James and Joseph and Simon and Judas? And are not all his sisters with us? Where then did this man get all this?" (Matt 13:54-56). The Qur'an's answer to their question is that Jesus gets all this from Allah who has instructed him and taught him all he knows.

A group that figures prominently in the New Testament as a primary audience of Jesus' instruction is his disciples. This is a term that has several different meanings in the text since it can refer, in a general way, to the crowds of people who follow him (Matt 5:1) or, more specifically, to smaller groups like the twelve apostles who are specially chosen by Jesus and enjoy a more intimate relationship with him (Matt 10:1-4). In their various configurations, his disciples are commonly found in his presence throughout the Gospels as he instructs those following him. They do not play as visible a role in the Qur'an, but in a few places, like 3:52-53, the text does identify a group which appears to be the Islamic counterpart to the biblical disciples.

> [52]When Jesus sensed their unbelief, he said, "Who are my helpers in the way of Allah?" The disciples said, "We are the helpers of Allah. We have

believed in Allah. Bear witness that we are submitters. [53]Our Lord, we believe in what You have sent down and we follow the messenger. Write our names down among those who bear witness."

The Arabic term that is translated as "disciples" is *ḥawāriyyūn*, the plural of the word *ḥawārī* which means several different things. It can refer to someone who bleaches or whitens clothes by washing them, and some of the classical Arabic dictionaries claim that the disciples are given this title because this was how they made their living. The New Testament does not support this idea because it does not speak of this as their profession and the Greek word for disciple (*mathetes*) has to do with being a pupil or apprentice, not with washing clothes. Other meanings of *ḥawārī* are more helpful in determining the disciples' probable role in the Qur'an. For example, it can also refer to a person who is pure and free of vice or someone who is a faithful friend or assistant to another person. This suggests that their own personal qualities and fidelity to Jesus are what set these individuals apart and make them worthy to be his disciples in the Qur'an.

The gospel texts which are closest to this one from the Qur'an are those that describe how Jesus called his first disciples. All four of the Gospels contain these call narratives which relate Jesus' first encounter with people who later become part of the group of those closest to him. An example of this type of scene is found in Mark 1:16-20.

> [16]As Jesus passed along the Sea of Galilee, he saw Simon and his brother Andrew casting a net into the sea—for they were fishermen. [17]And Jesus said to them, "Follow me and I will make you fish for people." [18]And immediately they left their nets and followed him. [19]As he went a little farther, he saw James son of Zebedee and his brother John, who were in their boat mending the nets. [20]Immediately he called them; and they left their father Zebedee in the boat with the hired men, and followed him.

The parallel texts in the other three Gospels differ from Mark on some matters of detail but they all agree on the focus and point of the call narratives.[3] Their initial encounter with Jesus is such a pivotal experience for these individuals that it leads to a radical realignment of their lives causing them to leave behind their former ways and move in a new direction. This change of orientation is captured well in Jesus' only words in the passage when he tells the soon to be ex-fishermen that they will now be fishing for people. They immediately leave behind their boats, nets, co-workers, even family members, to be with Jesus.

But their being with him takes a particular form since in all four Gospels the most common verb used to describe the response of someone who is called by Jesus is "follow." This is seen in the text from Mark where Jesus invites Simon and Andrew to follow him (v. 17), and that is exactly what they, and the two sons of Zebedee, go on to do (vv. 18, 20). He does not tell them why they should follow him or explain to them how and why they will fish for people. He simply issues his command and they fall in line behind him. Similarly, Mark does not record any verbal response on their part as they leave behind their boats and the tools of their trade and embark on a new career, no questions asked. The dominant theme of the passage is the allure of Jesus and the personal magnetism he exudes by drawing these men away from their familiar surroundings on the shore of the Sea of Galilee and leading them toward uncharted waters.

When we consider the Qurʾan passage in light of the biblical one some interesting differences emerge. In terms of narrative detail, the setting of the scene is not identified as it is in the Gospels and none of the disciples are mentioned by name. Rather than issuing a command to follow him as he does in Mark, Jesus in the Qurʾan asks the question "Who are my helpers in the way of Allah?" (v. 52). This change in mode of address is important because it shifts the focus of attention from Jesus to his audience. He does not play the dominant role in determining who becomes his disciple by ordering whom he chooses to follow him. This time his question, which functions as a type of invitation, leaves it up to the individual to respond affirmatively or negatively. In other words, his would-be followers in the Qurʾan appear to have more of a choice in the matter and are more directly responsible for their new status as disciples than they are in the New Testament.

Although we do not know the names and occupations of the disciples in the Qurʾan, their characters are more fully developed than they are in the Gospels because they speak and their remarks give us insight into what kind of people they are. In a word, they are believers. Their initial response to Jesus' question makes this clear. When they say "We are the helpers of Allah" (v. 52), this is the verbal equivalent to their action in Mark of leaving their nets and boats, but it is a much less ambiguous reaction than that is. In the gospel scene, the reader is unsure about the level of belief and faith commitment they possess since they could be following Jesus out of curiosity or dissatisfaction with their present way of life. In the Qurʾan, on the other hand, they explicitly define themselves as Allah's helpers, leaving no room for doubt regarding their motivation. Their self-designation as "Allah's helpers" is an interesting one in light of Jesus' question, "Who will be my helpers in the way of Allah?" This is another example of the Qurʾan's tendency to place Jesus in a subordinate position in relation to the deity. Referring to them as Jesus' helpers might blur the line between him and the deity, and their response suggests they want to avoid that outcome. In a way, this scene contains an interesting role reversal because the disciples function here as teachers of Jesus, reminding him that he and they are all servants of Allah even if he exercises prophetic authority over them.

From the outset, it is Allah, not Jesus, who is the focus of attention in this call narrative in the Qurʾan and that perspective continues throughout the scene. All of the disciples' words either concern or directly address the deity. They make an explicit statement of faith in verse 52 ("We have believed in Allah"), and then ask Jesus to bear witness that they are submitters or, as the Arabic has it, muslims. This latter request is a verbal form that is grammatically imperative, which is an interesting aspect of the passage in light of Mark's version. There, Jesus is the one who issues commands, while here his disciples direct an order toward him. Theirs is less authoritative than his ("Follow me!") since they are asking him to verify their faithfulness, but it nonetheless serves to give their relationship with him more of an air of equality.

They then turn their attention from Jesus and directly address Allah in verse 53. "Our Lord, we believe in what You have sent down and we follow the messenger. Write our names down among those who bear witness." They express their faith once again, only this time it is in reference to the divine message and Jesus as its bearer. Their final words are another command, this time directed toward Allah whom they ask to preserve them as true believers. The shift in addressee from Jesus to the deity is another subtle way of downplaying Jesus' role in the scene. This is something between themselves and Allah, not Jesus, and so he recedes into the background. How different this is from the biblical account where he is the object of attention and God is never mentioned. In the Qurʾan, the disciples express their readiness to follow Jesus, but they do so only in his role as a messenger of the divine will (v. 53). They are therefore really following Allah, not Jesus.

The shift in Jesus' role is consistent with the Qurʾan's portrayal of him throughout its text. In the Gospels, the disciples blindly follow Jesus as he exercises an almost magical control over them by convincing them to abandon their livelihoods and join him in a common venture that is still a mystery to them. The power he wields over them has a supernatural quality to it, and this creates the impression that they are in the presence of no mere mortal. The Qur'an cannot permit such a reading which allows for the possibility of understanding Jesus as more than human. Consequently, the spotlight shifts from him to the disciples who are not the same passive figures they are in the gospel. The disciples in the Qur'an are at a very different point in their faith lives than their biblical counterparts. In Mark, we do not know anything explicit about their religious beliefs when they first meet Jesus. This information is superfluous because the real interest lies in how their relationship with Jesus, which has just begun, will act as a catalyst in their spiritual development and understanding of God. The disciples in the Qur'an are an entirely different lot. They are a spiritually mature group who articulate their faith ("We have believed in Allah") and have already committed themselves to Allah. Therefore, when Jesus asks his question in the Qur'an, he is simply bringing forth what is already present within their hearts and souls. On the other hand, when he calls them to follow him in the New Testament they are still unformed, like clay that must be molded into a vessel and filled by him.

As noted earlier, the Qur'an does not directly quote much of Jesus' teaching. Where it does so, his message tends to be more general and comprehensive in nature, lacking the imagery and narrative quality of many of the gospel passages. An example of this is seen in 3:49-50, cited above. "I will announce to you what to eat and what to store up in your houses. Truly, in that is a sign for you if you are believers. (I come) attesting to the truth already in the Torah and to make permissible for you some of that which had been forbidden to you. I have come to you with a sign from your Lord, so fear Allah and obey me." Typically, the New Testament provides details on the context in which Jesus utters such words by describing the location, the audience, and other elements of the physical setting. The Qur'an rarely furnishes such information and this tends to direct the reader's attention to the words themselves rather than the situation in which they are spoken. By stripping away many of the narrative particulars, the Qur'an makes the point or message of the text, rather than the plot development or story line, its most dominant feature.

An important theme in Jesus' teaching in the Qur'an is the idea that he is not negating the previous revelation given to Moses in the Torah. Nonetheless, the text cited above indicates there is something different about his message which renders at least part of the Torah obsolete. "(I come) attesting to the truth already in the Torah and to make permissible for you some of that which had been forbidden to you." This same theme is found in some New Testament passages where Jesus acknowledges the authority of the Law of Moses while, at the same time, offering a reinterpretation of parts of it.

His paradigmatic statement on the issue is found at Matthew 5:17. "Do not think that I have come to abolish the law or the prophets; I have come not to abolish but to fulfill." This verse comes early in the Sermon on the Mount, Matthew's most comprehensive treatment of the relationship between the teaching of Jesus and the Mosaic Law. Throughout the course of these three chapters (Matthew 5–7), Jesus explains to his followers how the gospel message challenges them to reconsider their understanding of the Torah. For example, he instructs them that the command to love one's neighbor must be broadened to include love of one's enemies (Matt 5:43-48). Elsewhere in the Gospels, Jesus makes statements and engages in activities which directly defy foundational elements of the Judaism of his time including such things as the Temple, the Sabbath, dietary rules, and interpersonal relations.[4] The Qur'an agrees with the New Testament that this is a part of Jesus' message, but does not show concrete examples of his critique of Judaism.

Some of the most characteristic aspects of Jesus' message in the Gospels are not found in the Qur'an. Many New Testament scholars believe the idea of the kingdom of God, or kingdom of heaven, is the central motif of his preaching since it appears so frequently throughout the Gospels, especially those of Matthew, Mark, and Luke. But there is not a single reference to it in any of the material related to Jesus in the Islamic text. Similarly, such common gospel topics as justice, forgiveness, the end times, and concern for the poor and marginalized appear rarely, if at all, in the Qur'an's discussion of Jesus. There is a corresponding difference in the form Jesus' teaching takes in the two texts. The most distinctive genre Jesus employs to instruct his hearers throughout the Gospels is the parable, an extended metaphor or simile comparing one thing to something else. The New Testament contains dozens of such texts and many of them attempt to explain what the kingdom of God is. Some of these are very brief statements and others are more elaborate short stories in narrative form. Examples of the shorter type can be seen in Matthew 13:44-48 where Jesus compares the kingdom to three different things.

> [44]The kingdom of heaven is like treasure hidden in a field, which someone found and hid; then in his joy he goes and sells all that he has and

buys that field. [45]Again, the kingdom of heaven is like a merchant in search of fine pearls; [46]on finding one pearl of great value, he went and sold all that he had and bought it. [47]Again, the kingdom of heaven is like a net that was thrown into the sea and caught fish of every kind; [48]when it was full, they drew it ashore, sat down, and put the good into baskets but threw out the bad.

The Qur'an does not show Jesus teaching through parables as he does in the Gospels, but it does contain a number of passages which have some intriguing similarities with this New Testament genre. One such text is the rather lengthy verse 48:29, which is also interesting because it is one of only four places in the entire Qur'an where Muhammad is mentioned by name.

> Muhammad is the messenger of Allah. Those who are with him are hard on the unbelievers but merciful among themselves. You see them bowing and prostrating, seeking favor and grace from Allah. Their mark is on their faces, the trace of prostration. Their likeness in the Torah and their likeness in the Gospel is the seed which sends out its shoot, then strengthens it, then produces grain, then stands firm on its stalk, gladdening the sowers. In order to enrage the unbelievers by them, Allah promises forgiveness and a great reward to those who believe and do good deeds.

There are some connections between this passage and the parable of the sower which is found in various forms in the Gospels (Matt 13:1-9; Mark 4:1-9; Luke 8:4-8). In each text, the growing seed is compared to the true believer who, like the plant, brings forth good fruit. The faithful ones are contrasted with the infidels who, in the Qur'an, become jealous and angry because they are denied the gifts given to those who are like the seed. In the Gospels, the unbelievers are represented by the seed that falls in the places that hinder its growth: along the path, upon rocky ground, and among thorns. In both texts, a common agricultural image, undoubtedly familiar to the audience, is taken and used to teach a lesson in faith.

It is interesting to observe how each tradition adapts the idea to fit its own needs. In the Gospels, Jesus speaks these words and then goes on to privately explain to his disciples why he resorts to speaking in parables (Matt 13:10-17; Mark 4:10-12; Luke 8:9-10), followed by an interpretation of the parable of the sower (Matt 13:18-23; Mark 4:13-20; Luke 8:11-15). In the middle section in all three Gospels, Jesus stresses the connection between the parables and the kingdom as he explains why he teaches in this particular fashion. A link is therefore made between his use of parables and the kingdom, a central theme of his message. The Qur'an offers an entirely Islamic version of the parable. The rare identification of Muhammad by name sets that tone and the references to bowing and prostrating, which are actions characteristic of Muslim worship, further add to the Islamic flavor of the passage. Here, Jesus does not speak the words, Allah does, and it is Muslims who are compared favorably to the seed. The Qur'an's mention of the seed metaphor being found in the Torah and Gospel is interesting and might indicate an awareness of the importance of this parable in the New Testament.

Another text from the Qur'an which might have a possible parallel in a New Testament parable is found in 57:12-13.

> [12]The day when you see the believing men and women, their light going before them in their right hands, (it will be said to them,) "Good news to you today of gardens through which rivers flow where you will live forever." That is the great triumph. [13]The day when the hypocritical men and women will say to those who believe, "Wait for us, we want to take some of your light," it will be said, "Go back and look for light." Then a wall with a door will be put up between them. Inside it will be mercy, and outside of it, in the front, will be punishment.

Jesus relates a number of parables in the Gospels that explain the need to be prepared for the end time and the consequences that will befall those who are not ready when it arrives. The one that is closest to this passage from the Qur'an is Matthew 25:1-13.

> [1]Then the kingdom of heaven will be like this. Ten bridesmaids took their lamps and went to meet the bridegroom. [2]Five of them were foolish, and five were wise. [3]When the foolish took their lamps, they took no oil with them; [4]but the wise took flasks of oil with their lamps. [5]As the bridegroom was delayed, all of them became drowsy and slept. [6]But at midnight there was a shout, "Look! Here is the bridegroom! Come out to meet him!" [7]Then all those bridesmaids got up and trimmed their lamps. [8]The foolish said to the wise, "Give us some of your oil, for our lamps are going out." [9]But the wise replied, "No! There will not be enough for you and for us; you had better go to the dealers and buy some for yourselves." [10]And while they went to buy it, the bridegroom came, and those who were ready went with him into the wedding banquet; and the door was shut. [11]Later the other bridesmaids came also,

saying, "Lord, lord, open to us." [12]But he replied, "Truly I tell you, I do not know you." [13]Keep awake therefore, for you know neither the day nor the hour.

Both of these texts have a strong eschatological flavor which stresses the end of the world and the ensuing reward or punishment that each individual will experience, depending on the quality of the life he or she has led. This parable from Matthew is found in an extended section in the latter part of his gospel which discusses the end of the age and the judgment that will follow. An important theme throughout this portion of Matthew is the need to be ready for the final judgment, here personified in the coming of the bridegroom. The Islamic text, too, is eschatologically focused with its reference to both the reward that awaits the believers and the punishment in store for the hypocrites. This is a very common theme in the Qur'an where very elaborate and graphic depictions of heaven and hell are found in several places to serve as a reminder for the reader not to stray from the straight path.

There are some similarities between Matthew's parable and the text from sura 57 but the differences are equally noteworthy. While Matthew speaks of ten young women, half of whom are wise and the other half foolish, the Qur'an refers to both men and women and characterizes them as believers and hypocrites.[5] This division is a more theologically driven one that places the latter group of hypocrites in a far more negative light than the relatively benign designation "foolish" found in Matthew. The Qur'an, therefore, appears to highlight the faith dimension of both the saved and the damned more sharply than the gospel text does. Similarly, the unspecified amount of people in the two groups in the Qur'an, when compared to the relatively small number in Matthew, indirectly suggests that the message has wider and more far-reaching implications for the audience and might help the reader reflect more on the relevance of the passage for his or her own life.

The New Testament parable is a more highly developed narrative. The characters are more fully drawn, there is more dialogue between them, and the element of expectation as they await the bridegroom's delayed arrival adds an element of dramatic tension that is absent from the Qur'an passage. The more spare quality of the Islamic text leaves some questions in the reader's mind. Where is this scene taking place? Who speaks to the believers in verse 12? Who tells the hypocrites to return in verse 13? Who puts up the wall between the two groups? Why does the wall have a door? This last question is an intriguing one since it allows for the possibility of passage from one side of the wall to the other, implying that neither the reward nor the punishment is necessarily permanent. Interestingly, the gospel parable also speaks of a door (v. 10) which only serves to deepen the anguish of the foolish bridesmaids since the potential for entry into the banquet exists but they are prohibited from doing so. Perhaps this is the point behind the door in the Qur³an as well.

As with the previous text we studied, each version of this one conforms to its literary and theological setting. Matthew presents it as a parable, a typical example of Jesus' preferred mode of discourse when instructing his followers. The first verse relates its meaning to the kingdom of heaven, his favorite topic when speaking parabolically and a central concept of Christian faith. The Qur³an does not relate it as a parable and, in keeping with its usual literary manner, adopts a more sparse style. The theological interests of the Qur³an are clearly present in this text which conveys Allah's words, not those of Jesus. This is seen in the importance given to the theme of final judgment which is central to Islam and the key role of personal responsibility and choice in determining one's fate. The latter idea is to the fore in the verse immediately following which explains what happens to the hypocrites after the wall is erected between the believers and themselves. "They will cry out to them, 'Were we not with you?' They (the believers) will say, 'Yes, but you brought affliction upon yourselves, you hesitated, you doubted, and vain desires deceived you until Allah's decree came to pass. The Deceiver deceived you about Allah'" (57:14). The hypocrites, like the foolish bridesmaids, are prevented from gaining access through the door and it is their own fault. The punishment they now experience is the result of their bringing affliction upon their own heads by hesitating, doubting and allowing themselves to be deceived by the Deceiver, an epithet of Satan.

In a number of other places, the Qur³an uses parable-like examples to make a point, but none of these are ever attributed to Jesus. Each is a divine utterance which Allah communicates directly to Muhammad and is referred to as a *mathal* in Arabic. This word can mean "comparison, similitude, example" and its semantic range is quite close to that of the Greek word *parabole*, from which the English "parable" comes. So the Qur³an, like the Bible, makes use of this form in its teaching but does not depict human beings speaking in parables.

Interestingly, the type of speech which most typifies Jesus' instruction in the New Testament is not found on his lips in the Qur³an. As a prophet, Jesus has a teaching role in the Islamic text but we rarely get a glimpse of him functioning in that capacity. Nonetheless, the Qur'an does make a connection between Jesus and parables in a most unusual way in two verses where he himself is referred to as a *mathal*. In 43:57 we read, "When the son of Mary is presented as a *mathal*, your people shun it," and two verses later it is said about Jesus, "He was only Our servant whom We favored and made a *mathal* for the children of Israel." Most English translations render the italicized word as "example" in these two verses and there is ample lexicographical support for doing so. But if we keep in mind the other possible meanings of the term, it deepens and enhances the image of Jesus being put forward. He does not speak in parable form in the Qur'an, but he himself is a type of parable, a lesson from Allah to humanity. In other words, the messenger is also part of the message. This conforms to the Qur'an's use of the term "word from Allah" to refer to Jesus elsewhere in the text and establishes some common ground on which Muslims and Christians can meet to discuss Jesus the teacher in their respective scriptures.

A final component of Jesus' teaching in the Qur'an that should be mentioned is a text in which he apparently predicts the coming of Muhammad. In 61:6 Jesus says, "I am Allah's messenger to you, attesting to the truth already in the Torah and announcing the good news of a messenger who will come after me whose name is Ahmad." Here, Jesus adopts a role analogous to that of John the Baptist in the New Testament by pointing toward one who will come after him, a messenger called Ahmad. The three root letters of the Arabic word "Ahmad" are the same as those in "Muhammad" and the two names are commonly understood to be variations of each other. Consequently, there is a virtual consensus among Muslims that Jesus foretold the arrival of the prophet of Islam more than five centuries before the fact. It is also common for Muslims to assert that this same prediction is found in the New Testament. During a lengthy discourse at the Last Supper found only in John's Gospel, Jesus makes several references to an "Advocate," or helper, that will be sent from God to assist his community after Jesus himself departs from among them. In 14:16 he says, "And I will ask the Father, and he will give you another Advocate, to be with you forever." Similarly, in 15:26 he tells his disciples, "When the Advocate comes, whom I will send to you from the Father, the Spirit of truth who comes from the Father, he will testify on my behalf." The identification of the Advocate with Muhammad was helped by the fact that in the Syriac translation of the New Testament, to which Muslims have had access for centuries, the word for "Advocate" sounds very much like "Muhammad." Because Jesus does not refer to Muhammad in the Bible, Christians tend to see this as another example of the Qur'an putting words in his mouth. For their part, Muslims consider Jesus' announcement of the coming of Muhammad to be a validation of his prophetic office.

Jesus' Works

For the Muslim, Jesus' special status not only stems from the content of his message and what he said but is also due to certain things he did. The Qur'an agrees with the New Testament in claiming that Jesus possessed unusual powers which allowed him to accomplish acts of wonder which are beyond the ability of ordinary people. We have observed this same thing already in the case of Moses, another prophet in the Qur'an who performed extraordinary feats before Pharaoh in Egypt and among the Israelites in the wilderness. Jesus himself speaks of his miracles in 3:48-51, a text that was discussed earlier in this chapter. Another reference to them is found in 5:110-115 where Allah describes Jesus' unusual powers.

> [110]Allah will say, "Oh Jesus, son of Mary, remember my favor upon you and upon your mother when I strengthened you with a holy spirit and you spoke to people in the cradle and later in life. Remember how I taught you the book, the wisdom, the Torah, and the Gospel, and how you made a bird-shaped form out of clay by My leave and then you breathed into it and it became a real bird by My leave, and how you healed the blind and the leprous by My leave, and how you brought the dead back to life by My leave, and how I restrained the children of Israel from you when you came to them with clear signs but those who disbelieved said, 'This is plainly nothing but sorcery,' [111]and how when I inspired the disciples to believe in Me and in My messenger, they said, 'We believe. Bear witness that we are submitters.'" [112]When the disciples said, "Oh Jesus, is your Lord able to send down to us a table from the heavens?" he replied, "Fear Allah, if you are believers." [113]They said, "We wish to eat from it so that our hearts might be at rest and we might know that you have spoken truthfully to us and we will be witnesses to it." [114]Jesus, son of Mary, said, "Oh Allah, our Lord, send down to us a table from the heavens to be a feast for the first and the last of us and a sign from You. Provide for us, for You are the best of providers." [115]Allah said, "Truly, I will send it down to you, but whoever of you disbelieves after this I will surely punish with a punishment that I will not inflict on anyone else."

The two main parts of this passage will be examined separately. The first (vv. 110–111) is a paraphrase of 3:48-51 which centers on the marvelous works performed by Jesus. It was noted in the discussion on the text from sura 3 that a central theme of those verses is Allah's role as the one ultimately responsible for Jesus' miracles, and one way this can be seen is in the double use of the phrase "by Allah's leave" to explain how it is that Jesus is able to perform these works (3:49). This idea is stressed even more in the passage from sura 5 where the same phrase, "by Allah's leave," is repeated four times and each type of miracle is expressly said to be done only with divine permission. Prior to this, the text begins by asserting Allah's involvement in Jesus' life through strengthening him and his mother with a holy spirit which gives him the ability to speak as a prophet, even at a very young age. The same note is struck after the list of miracles when we are told of Allah's role in both protecting Jesus from unbelieving Israelites and inducing the disciples to accept him as Allah's messenger. There is no doubt about the main point of the first part of this passage: Allah is responsible for all that Jesus says and does. His teaching, his miracles, his safety and his followers are all due to divine favor. The tone and content of Allah's words reinforce this point since the frequent repetition of the phrase "and how I . . ." strings together a series of reminders for Jesus of all that Allah has done for him.

The reference to a holy spirit is something certain to attract the attention of Bible readers, especially those familiar with the New Testament. In the Hebrew Bible the spirit of God is mentioned frequently, but the term "holy spirit" is found only in Isaiah 63:10-11 and Psalm 51:11. It is more commonly used in the New Testament, particularly in Luke's Gospel and the Acts of the Apostles. In the New Testament writings the term is normally found in capitalized form as "Holy Spirit," and this spelling reflects the Christian belief in the Holy Spirit as one of the three members of the Trinity along with God the Father and God the Son. The formulation of this trinitarian theology was the result of a long, slow process of development which was not fully shaped until well after the biblical period during the first few centuries of the Church's history. Therefore, when they refer to the Holy Spirit, the New Testament writers are doing so without awareness of the significance of this term for later Christians. For example, it was noted in the previous chapter that the Holy Spirit plays an important role in Luke's annunciation scene and Mary's visit to Elizabeth. It would be a mistake to assume that Luke has in mind the Third Person of the Trinity as he relates this scene. More likely, his view of the nature of the Holy Spirit is probably closer to that found in the Isaiah and Psalm texts of the Hebrew Bible where it refers to God's bestowal of a spirit of holiness on an individual.

The same can be said about the Qurʾan's use of the term "holy spirit" which also needs to be understood in its own literary and theological context. It is not a concept that has trinitarian implications and should not be used to draw out a Christian interpretation from the text. With only four occurrences, the phrase "holy spirit" does not appear frequently in the Qurʾan. Interestingly, though, three of the four references to it mention Jesus. The other two which mention him besides 5:110, both from sura 2, are identical: "We gave Jesus, son of Mary, clear signs and We strengthened him with a holy spirit" (2:87, 254). All three texts which speak of a holy spirit in relation to Jesus in the Qurʾan say it is something given to him by Allah meant to strengthen him.

The other occurrence of the term is found at 16:102 which refers to its involvement in the revelation of the Qurʾan. "Say, 'A holy spirit from your Lord brought it (the Qurʾan) down in truth so that He might make firm those who believe and it might be a guidance and good news for Muslims.'" As in the case of Jesus in the other three texts, here the holy spirit also plays a strengthening role by sending the Qurʾan which helps to make firm and sustain believers. Jesus is the only individual in the Qurʾan who receives a holy spirit directly from Allah and this contributes to his elevated image in the text and for Muslims. The presence of similar ideas in the New Testament, where God's spirit is given to Jesus at his baptism (Mark 1:9-13) and is present at other moments in his life, can serve as a point of contact between Muslim and Christian christologies but caution must be exercised when considering the relationship between the two. The source of the spirit might be the same in the two texts, but the concept has different meanings for the two faith communities. Bible readers must avoid the temptation to equate this idea with their notion of the Holy Spirit and infer an implicit trinitarian theology in the Qurʾan.

When we compare the list of Jesus' miraculous works in the Qurʾan with those in the Gospels we find a great deal of overlap between the two. According to both 3:49 and 5:110, Allah gives Jesus the power to give sight to the blind, heal lepers, and raise the dead to life. All three of these feats are also performed by him in the New Testament. A key difference, however, is that the Qurʾan does not show Jesus the miracleworker in action. It simply identifies these works without ever presenting a narrative description of even one of them. The Gospels, on the other hand, contain many passages that describe Jesus performing various types of miracles. The New Testament also contains several types of miracles not mentioned in the Qurʾan, including exorcisms which expel evil spirits from people and nature miracles which show Jesus doing things like calming storms and walking on water. As was also seen with his teaching, therefore, the Qurʾan offers a less detailed treatment of this aspect of Jesus' life which is more of a summary than a descriptive account of him as a wonder-worker.

A miracle which is presented in some detail in the Qurʾan is one that has no counterpart in the Gospels. Both suras 3 and 5 refer to Jesus creating a bird-shaped form out of clay, breathing into it, and having it come alive. He does not accomplish such a feat in the Bible, but an extra-canonical Christian writing describes a similar miracle. The Infancy Gospel of Thomas is a work that might trace its roots back as far as the second century and is found in many different translations, including Arabic, from later periods. It purports to give an account of some of the things Jesus said and did as a child and youth, a period of his life about which the canonical Gospels are virtually silent.[6] In chapter two of the Infancy Gospel, the five-year-old Jesus fashions twelve sparrows from soft clay on a Sabbath. Upon being chastised for this violation of the Sabbath law, the child Jesus claps his hands and commands the clay birds to depart. To the amazement of onlookers, they immediately take flight and fly away chirping. There are a number of ways to account for the similarities that exist between the Qurʾan and extrabiblical writings here and elsewhere. Ultimately, one's opinion of the nature and origin of the Qurʾan is an important factor in determining what explanation makes the most sense. A person who is open to the idea that Christian ideas and traditions influenced the formation of the Qurʾan will be inclined to see this as an example of such influence or borrowing. On the other hand, a Muslim who considers the Qurʾan to be the immutable and eternal word of Allah would not allow for such a possibility and would probably consider speculation on the cause of such similarities to be beyond the purview of human reason.

Several things about the Qurʾan's description of the miracle of the bird deserve attention because they have implications for the image of Jesus being put forward in the text. Three elements of the passage suggest a close link between what Jesus does here and references to acts of divine creation elsewhere in the Qurʾan. The first is the choice of the Arabic verb *kalaqa* ("to create") in both suras to express Jesus' action in molding the clay into a bird-shaped form. This is a fairly common verb that is found in the Qurʾan about 175 times, and in almost every one of those cases Allah is its subject. In other words, the two passages describing Jesus' miracle with the bird use a verb that is almost exclusively reserved to express the idea of divine creation. A second point concerns clay as the material Jesus uses to make the bird. According to the Qurʾan, clay is the substance Allah uses to create humanity. In fact, of the other ten references to clay throughout the text, nine of them are used in descriptions of the divine creation of humankind. In his miracle, Jesus is using a material that is closely linked to divine creative activity.

The third thing of note is the use of the verb *nafaka* to describe Jesus' action of blowing into the clay to bring it to life. This is another verb that is very closely identified with Allah's role as creator. All eleven times it is found in the passive voice in the Qurʾan are in the context of the end of the world and speak of the trumpet being blown that signals the last days. Besides the two references to Jesus blowing on the clay, the active voice of the verb is used six other times in the Qurʾan and five of them describe acts of divine creation. Three of them refer to Allah breathing into humanity in the initial act of creation, and the other two speak of Allah breathing the divine spirit into Mary, mother of Jesus, to cause her to conceive. All of this indicates that there is a high concentration of vocabulary related to divine creation in the account of Jesus' miracle.

What does this mean? Some might wish to argue that this is a tacit acknowledgment of Jesus' divinity on the part of the Qurʾan since it seems to imply that he creates just as Allah does. But this would be to both read too much into the text and overlook an important component of it. The repetition of the words "by Allah's leave" in the description of Jesus' miracle in both suras must be kept in mind. In 3:49 the phrase is found immediately after the reference to the bird miracle and in 5:110 it is found twice in its context, once after Jesus creates the bird-shaped form and once after he breathes it to life. This establishes Allah's control over all that occurs and precludes the possibility that Jesus is somehow taking Allah's place. The repetition of the phrase "by Allah's leave" helps to keep Jesus in his place as a servant of, and not an equal to, the deity. In the Qurʾan, he is blessed with the ability to perform incredible feats of wonder, but this is due to the power and presence of Allah working through him rather than to anything he does on his own. This is an idea that is not foreign to the New Testament and is seen, for example, in Jesus' words at Luke 11:20. "But if it is by the finger of God that I cast out the demons, then the kingdom of God has come to you." Muslims and Christians believe, each in their own way, that Jesus' miracles all point to the deity's finger.

The second part of the passage from sura 5 (vv. 112–115) describes a scene that takes place between Jesus and his disciples. They ask him to call on Allah to send down a table so that they might eat from it and be assured of the truthfulness of his message. The New Testament does not relate this same episode, but it does contain several passages in which food figures prominently, and some commentators have speculated on the possible connection between these texts and the one in the Qur'an. The closest parallel is found in Acts 10:9-16 where the apostle Peter is praying on a roof and has a vision of a large sheet descending from heaven that holds many different kinds of animals. A voice tells him to kill and eat the animals and he refuses because he believes they will make him unclean. The voice then informs him that he need not worry because God has made the animals clean for consumption. The text says this occurred three times and then the sheet was taken back up to heaven. The heavenly sheet full of food is analogous to the table in the Qur'an but there are some major differences between the texts. Peter is alone on a roof in Acts while the disciples are all together in the Qur'an. Jesus is with them in the Islamic text but is absent from the New Testament one. In Acts, Peter refuses to eat and the sheet appears unexpectedly, while in the Qur'an the disciples are eager to eat and request that the table be sent down to them. These and other differences outweigh the similarities and argue against trying to compare the two texts or understand them in relation to each other.

The same can be said about other New Testament passages that associate the disciples with food. All four Gospels give an account of the "last supper," a final meal Jesus shares with his disciples prior to his being arrested and put to death. Other than the same cast of characters and the presence of food, there is no real connection between this scene and the one in sura 5 about the table from heaven. Another episode recounted in all four Gospels describes how Jesus miraculously multiplied five loaves and two fishes in order to be able to feed a large crowd of people who were following him (Matt 14:13-21; Mark 6:32-44; Luke 9:10b-17; John 6:1-15). This tradition seems to be somewhat closer to the one in the Qur'an because the disciples play an active role in the scene and Jesus acknowledges divine involvement in the miracle by either expressing thanks (John) or looking heavenward (the other three Gospels) prior to multiplying the food. But, despite such similar features, the thematic focus and point of the Qur'an text is quite different from that of these New Testament passages.

The miracle in the Qurʾan is initiated by the disciples who ask Jesus if Allah is able to send down to them a table (v. 112). The primary reason for their request is theological and not physiological since they hope this food will provide spiritual nourishment and not simply fill their stomachs. "We wish to eat from it so that our hearts might be at rest and we might know that you have spoken truthfully to us and we will be witnesses to it" (v. 113). In other words, they are asking for a sign that will verify and legitimate Jesus' message for them. This is an element commonly found in the Gospels where people are shown asking Jesus to perform signs so that they might believe in him. In many of these New Testament passages, Jesus refuses to perform the sign and takes their request as an expression of the weakness of their faith since they require some tangible evidence before they will accept him. This can be seen, for example, in Mark 8:11-12. "The Pharisees came and began to argue with him, asking him for a sign from heaven, to test him. And he sighed deeply in his spirit and said, 'Why does this generation ask for a sign? Truly I tell you, no sign will be given to this generation.'" In the three Synoptic Gospels of Matthew, Mark, and Luke, Jesus typically responds in this way to requests for signs from him and takes them as an indication of unbelief on the part of the person making the request.[7]

When the disciples ask for the sign in the Qurʾan they are doing something that is often disapproved of in the New Testament, but it is not greeted that way. This is due to the role Jesus plays as a prophet in the Islamic text. When his disciples ask that the table be sent down, their words make it clear that they do not see this as a sign that will be indicative of Jesus' own power. Rather, in keeping with the Qurʾan's emphasis on Allah, such a miracle will be a testimony to the power of the deity. They ask him if "his Lord" is able to bring the table down (v. 112). Jesus himself is simply the intermediary or agent through whom the divine work can be realized. In his prayer to Allah, he takes the opportunity to exercise his role as a messenger and highlights their shared relationship to the deity. "Oh Allah, our Lord, send down to us a table from the heavens to be a feast for the first and the last of us and a sign from You. Provide for us, for You are the best of providers" (v. 114). Jesus' choice of words here corrects any misconception they might have about who he is and reminds them that he is no different than they are. Allah is not "his Lord" but "our Lord," who is being asked to send to "us" a table to be a feast and sign for "us" that will provide for "us."

The christology of this scene is one that underscores Jesus' function as a prophetic messenger. In order for his message to be received, his role has to be accepted and validated by the community. The people attempt to do this by requesting the heavenly sign, a request which Jesus responds to affirmatively in order to legitimate himself in their eyes. The formulation of his prayer instructs his disciples about his relationship with them and their shared relationship with Allah. When the deity agrees to send down the table, it is with the understanding that doubt is no longer possible for the disciples. Once the sign has been sent, they must recognize and accept Jesus as a messenger or suffer the dire consequences. "Truly, I will send it down to you, but whoever of you disbelieves after this I will surely punish with a punishment that I will not inflict on anyone else" (v. 115). In this way, the request for a sign functions more positively in the Qur'an than it usually does in the Gospels. In the Christian text it is an expression of lack of faith, while in the Islamic one it becomes an opportunity to reach true faith.

NEAR, BUT NOT EQUAL TO, ALLAH

The Qur'an devotes a great deal of attention to refuting the trinitarian theology of Christians and their belief that Jesus is divine. This is done in very explicit language which attempts to point out the illogical nature of the idea that the deity could ever have a child. This critique is dramatically expressed several times in the Qur'an when Jesus himself rejects the notion that he is Allah's son and actually speaks out against those who hold this belief. According to the Qur'an, then, the fault lies not with Jesus, but with his followers who made claims about him that were inaccurate and gravely distorted his message. Christians, of course, counter that the Qur'an itself is a distortion of the truth because in denying the divinity of Jesus it denies an essential aspect of his nature. The end result of such conflicting opinions is predictable. Each side digs in its heels further, holding fast to its position and refusing to acknowledge the validity of the other's. An effort must be made to move beyond this impasse which allows for the possibility of mutual understanding without ignoring the serious differences that exist between Christians and Muslims on this very important point. As stated at the beginning of this chapter, the necessary first step for the Christian is to become acquainted with what the Qur'an actually says about Jesus in order to properly understand the basis of Muslim belief about him. With this aim in mind, we turn to some of the most important references to Jesus' nature and relationship to Allah in the text.

The discussion of his character in the Qur'an up to this point should make it clear that, for Muslims, Jesus was no ordinary person.

In particular, his status as a messenger, the remarkable circumstances of his conception, and the incredible feats of wonder he performed all contribute to making him one of the most exceptional people to ever walk the face of the earth. Therefore, the Qurʾan's denial of divinity for Jesus does not automatically relegate him to the rank and file of humanity, no different than the great majority of people who have lived throughout history. His was an extraordinary life marked by a closeness to Allah that only a handful of others have ever been privileged to experience. The angels' words to his mother Mary in announcing his birth to her anticipate Jesus' exalted rank. "He will be one of those brought near (to Allah)" (3:45). Christians should always keep this in mind when considering Jesus' role in Islam and this will help them remember that, like them, Muslims venerate his memory and message.

But closeness to Allah is not the same as equality. The Qurʾan frequently stresses the total humanity of Jesus and, in texts like 4:171, warns against any attempt to liken him to the deity.

> Oh people of the book, do not be excessive in your religious belief and do not speak anything but the truth about Allah. Truly, the messiah Jesus, son of Mary, was a messenger of Allah, His word which He sent to Mary, and a spirit from Him. So believe in Allah and His messengers and do not say "Three." Desist and it will be better for you for, truly, Allah is one God. It is beyond Him to have a son. All that is in the heavens and on the earth belongs to Him. Allah is the only protector.

This verse summarizes Muslim christology as it is reflected in the Qurʾan. The messiah Jesus is referred to as a messenger, a word and a spirit, and each of these titles is due to the special relationship he enjoys with Allah. But the text cautions the people of the book not to be excessive in their belief and overestimate what this means about Jesus. He is still only a person and nothing more. Because Allah's glory transcends all things human, it is beyond the divine nature to have offspring. Therefore, any expression of trinitarian belief, here depicted as saying "Three," is to speak something other than the truth about Allah.

To make false claims by ascribing a son or partner to Allah is an example of the sin of *shirk*, an offense that will be treated very harshly. The fate awaiting one who holds such a belief is described in 5:72-76.

> [72]They disbelieve who say, "Allah is the messiah, son of Mary." The messiah said, "Oh children of Israel, worship Allah, my Lord and your Lord." Whoever associates something with Allah, paradise has been denied to

that person by Allah and the fire will be their abode. There will be no helpers for the evildoers. [73]They disbelieve who say "Allah is the third of three." There is no god but the one God. If they do not desist from what they say, a painful punishment will come upon those of them who disbelieve. [74]Will they not turn to Allah and beg for his forgiveness? Allah is the forgiving one and the merciful one. [75]The messiah, son of Mary, was only a messenger, and the messengers before him passed away. His mother was truthful, and they both ate food. See how We explain the signs to them (the people) and see how they are turned away. [76]Say, "Will you worship what is not Allah, what can neither hurt nor benefit you? Allah, He is the one who hears and the one who knows."

According to this passage, anyone who claims Jesus is divine will suffer a "painful punishment" (v. 73) entailing the loss of paradise and banishment to the fires of hell (v. 72). Jesus' own words are cited in support of this as he states that he did not ask his followers to deify him. In commanding the Israelites to worship "my Lord and your Lord," Jesus explains to them the difference between himself and Allah while also reminding them that he is no different than they are.

In the Islamic view, they refused to heed Jesus' advice and chose to associate him with Allah through their belief in the Trinity. The verb that is used to express the nature of their sin is *kafara*, which is here translated as "disbelieve" once in verse 72 and twice in verse 73. Words from the Arabic root *kafara* are among those most frequently used in the Qur'an to describe people who lack faith. A basic meaning of this verb has to do with covering something in order to conceal it. That sense is then extended to refer to the act of denying or covering up the truth, and that is its meaning here. This term therefore implies a willful desire to hide the facts about Allah and set up a form of false worship in its place, a meaning that coheres with the Qur'an's portrayal of Jesus. He came to his people with a message which he faithfully communicated to them in accord with the divine will. That message was a call for them to worship Allah, the one true God, and reject all false belief. This was the truth they received, but they chose to conceal it and worship Jesus as Allah's partner. The use of the verb *kafara* underscores their guilt and personal responsibility in rejecting the message and characterizes Christian belief as a "cover-up" that denies the truth.

But all is not lost for those who are guilty of association and have violated the divine unity. In this passage and elsewhere, the Qur'an holds out the possibility for reconciliation and a return to Allah's favor for anyone who has done wrong. "Will they not turn to Allah and beg for his forgiveness? Allah is the forgiving one and the merciful one" (v. 74). Allah's capacity for mercy and clemency overrides all human transgressions so that even the most serious sin imaginable to the Muslim mind can be pardoned. The one requirement necessary to experience divine forgiveness is that offenders must sincerely repent and turn to Allah in a spirit of contrition and humbly acknowledge their error. Here we get a sense of the limitless extent of Allah's mercy and compassion in the Qur'an. No sin, not even one that desecrates the very nature of the divine being, can negate Allah's ability to forgive. "Allah is the forgiving one and the merciful one" (v. 74).

As comforting as the idea of an all-merciful deity might be, it does little to soften the sting of the point this text conveys to Christians. To be blunt, it tells them they are going to hell unless they repudiate their belief in the divinity of Jesus. The serious nature of the difference between Muslims and Christians on the matter of Jesus could not be stated in starker terms. When certain Islamic leaders and preachers, caught up in fiery rhetoric, hurl epithets like "infidels" and "idolaters" in the direction of Christians, this language has been informed by passages in the Qur'an like 5:72-76. Identifying the source of such animosity does not eliminate the distress felt by those toward whom it is directed, but it is a helpful first step in trying to comprehend its reason and basis. On some very important issues like this one, it is unlikely that Muslims and Christians will ever be able to see eye to eye or reach common ground. Perhaps the most that can be hoped for is a mutual willingness to agree to disagree in a spirit of tolerance and respect for the beliefs of others.

The reference to Mary in this text deserves some comment. "The messiah, son of Mary, was only a messenger, and the messengers before him passed away. His mother was truthful, and they both ate food. See how We explain the signs to them (the people) and see how they are turned away" (v. 75). The first sentence attempts to stress the humanity of Jesus by stating he was a messenger whose life, like those of all messengers, came to an end. This is also probably the point behind the cryptic comment in the next sentence that he ate food. If he consumed food as any other person does, this suggests he was a normal human being who was dependent upon such nourishment for his survival. It therefore might be a way of refuting any claim to divinity or supernatural status that might be made about him. But why is Mary included in this as well? Why is the text interested in reminding the reader that she, too, was a normal person who ate in the usual manner? One possible reason is that in this verse the Qur'an is implicitly cautioning against ascribing divinity to Mary as well. Another passage that mentions Mary suggests that such cautionary language is indeed a part of the Qur'an's message about her.

An explicit rejection of the Trinity is found at 5:116-118 but, by Christian standards, the belief is expounded in a most unusual way.

> [116]Allah said, "Oh Jesus, son of Mary, did you ever say to people, 'Take me and my mother for two gods apart from Allah?'" He said, "Praise be to You! It is not for me to say that of which I have no right. If I had said it, You surely would have known it. You know what is in my mind, but I do not know what is in Your mind. You are the knower of hidden things. [117]I did not say anything to them except that which You commanded me: 'Worship Allah, my Lord and your Lord.' I was a witness over them for as long as I was among them. And when You took me to Yourself, You were the one who watched over them. You are a witness over all things. [118]If You punish them, they are Your servants, and if You forgive them You are truly the mighty one, the wise one."

This text is another refutation of the Christian belief in the Trinity, but here Mary is included as one of its three members. The evidence from the classical commentaries on the Qur'an indicates that it was commonly held among Muslims that the Christian Trinity was comprised of God, Jesus, and Mary. We have noted that Jesus is sometimes referred to as a "spirit" from Allah in the Qur'an, and it is possible that this led to an identification of him with the Holy Spirit which left an open space in the Trinity that was subsequently filled by Mary. A number of theories have been proposed that try to explain why the Qur'an includes Mary as one of the Three Persons of the Trinity. It could be due to the influence of Christian popular religiosity and devotional practices which highly venerate her. To a Muslim or other person less familiar with Christian theology and ritual, it might appear that Mary is being worshiped as a deity in her own right instead of as a holy woman. It is also possible that the Qur'an's idea of Mary's divinity might have come from Christian sects present in Arabia which exalted Mary far above her usual Christian status. There is some evidence for the existence of such groups in Arabia during this time period but their precise influence, if any, on Islam is debated.[8]

Whatever the origin of the idea, this passage considers it to be another example of the distortion of Jesus' original message by his followers. Once again, his own words are quoted in order to add weight and authority to the text's condemnation of the belief in his and his mother's divinity. When Allah asks him if he had ever made such a claim, he begins his response with a cry that is a spontaneous proclamation of his faith that also implicitly establishes his innocence. His declaration "Praise be to You!" (v. 16) identifies him as a believer and the words that follow articulate further his recognition of Allah's complete authority and his own total submission to the divine will. He had no right to say such a thing but even if he had it would already be known by Allah (v. 116). The only words he spoke to the people were the ones the deity instructed him to speak (v. 117). His own existence was dependent upon Allah who eventually called him to Himself and took over as the true leader of the people (vv. 117–118). With each of these statements Jesus asserts his belief in Allah as the one God, rejects any part of the divine nature for himself, and implicates the people as the ones responsible for spreading such heretical ideas about himself and his mother. The content of Jesus' message here is identical to that found in other texts already discussed ("Worship Allah, my Lord and your Lord") and, like those other passages, he makes Allah the focus, effectively deflecting attention from himself. He conveys the latter point particularly well since each of the three verses ends with Jesus citing one or more of the divine attributes. Because Allah is the knower of hidden things (v. 116), a witness over all things (v. 117), the mighty one, and the wise one (v. 118) the only appropriate verbal response is the one that Jesus makes: "Praise be to You!"

A final text to consider which contains some peculiar ideas about beliefs among Christians and Jews is 9:30-31.

> [30]The Jews say, "Ezra is the son of Allah," and the Christians say, "The messiah is the son of Allah." That is what they say with their mouths, imitating the words of those who disbelieved before them. May Allah fight against them! How perverse they are! [31]They have taken their leaders and monks and the messiah, son of Mary, as lords apart from Allah. They were not commanded anything except to worship the one God. There is no god but He. Praise be to Him above what they associate.

This is the only text in the Qur'an which explicitly levels the charge of *shirk* against the Jews. The reference to their worship of Ezra as Allah is obscure and its origin is a mystery. Some commentators claim that this was a belief among the Jews of Medina and other areas near the birthplace of Islam, but there is no solid evidence to support this. Even the identity of the person named is uncertain. There is a biblical figure named Ezra, after whom one of the books of the Hebrew Bible is named, and many scholars see this as an allusion to him. He was an Israelite priest and scribe who lived in the fifth century B.C.E. during the time of the exile in Babylon, and the biblical text presents him as an important figure within the community who helped lead the efforts to return to the Promised Land.

The passage also states that leaders and monks, along with Jesus, were being considered lords in a way that infringed on Allah's position as the supreme authority. The word for monks, *ruhbān*, refers to Christian ascetics who adopt reclusive lifestyles and devote themselves to prayer. The other term, *ahbār*, which is translated as "leaders," is a bit broader in meaning since it refers to any learned Jew or Christian. It might be that the Qur'an uses this latter word to designate Jewish leaders only and therefore identifies a particular group within both Judaism and Christianity. However the terms are understood, the point of the text is clear: members of their communities are mistakenly ascribing divine status to these individuals. As with the reference to Ezra, the details of this charge are hopelessly vague and, in all probability, will remain so.

An issue such texts help to highlight is that of the type of Jewish/Christian presence among Muslims during the formative years of Islam. The forms of Judaism and Christianity Muhammad and his followers were exposed to undoubtedly had a profound effect on their attitudes toward these religions and the way they are evaluated in the Qur'an. If the groups they came in contact with held unorthodox views and beliefs, they were not representative of the wider Jewish and Christian communities of their own time or ours. This can have important implications for the area of interreligious dialogue and relationships. If the Judaism and Christianity described in the Qur'an do not reflect their present day forms, it is incumbent upon Muslims to replace these inaccurate images with correct ones.

JESUS' DEATH

In 5:117, Jesus seems to allude to his own death when he tells Allah, "And when You took me to Yourself, You were the one who watched over them." The Arabic verb translated as "to take to oneself" can also mean "to cause to die," so there is little doubt that Jesus is referring to the end of his life in this verse. Similarly, when he speaks from the cradle in sura 19 the newborn Jesus also mentions his passing. "Peace upon me the day I was born, the day I will die, and the day I will be raised to life" (19:33). Such passages are straightforward and unambiguous references to Jesus' demise, but the meaning of other texts that discuss his death is less clear and this has led to much debate and discussion within Islam over the issue.

The death of Jesus is the central event of the New Testament. All of the Gospels contain an extended section, referred to by scholars as a "passion narrative," which gives each book's account of the events leading up to and culminating in his crucifixion. Even prior to this, the Gospels anticipate the passion narrative and set the stage for Jesus' execution by depicting the growing tension between himself and his enemies and having Jesus speak about and predict his coming death. The letters of Paul, which are the earliest writings in the New Testament, do not offer the same type of narrative description of Jesus' death the Gospels do, but they devote much attention to interpreting the significance of the event for the early Christian communities to whom his letters were addressed. The meaning Paul gave to Jesus' death is that which has been shared by all Christians throughout history. His crucifixion was a salvific event which ushered in a new era in the relationship between God and humanity and it has the power to save every person who acknowledges Jesus as Lord and Savior.

The way the Qur'an treats Jesus' death is closer to Paul than it is to the Gospels. It is referred to in only a few passages and there is never any attempt to offer a historical reconstruction of what happened. The emphasis, as in Paul, is on the meaning of his death, but when that meaning is articulated the paths of the Qur'an and Paul diverge. There is no suggestion of a salvific or expiatory character to Jesus' death in the Islamic text. His is an ordinary passing away that had nothing remarkable or exceptional about it. The reason for this is, of course, a theological one. In Christianity, the death and resurrection of Jesus is the definitive sign of his divinity. In order for the Qur'an to remain consistent in its message that Jesus was not divine, it cannot interpret Jesus' death in the same way the New Testament does. As we will see, when the text mentions the death it does so in a way that is in keeping with its tendency to divert attention away from Jesus and onto Allah. Consequently, while his death in the New Testament is an event that allows the reader to come to know who Jesus truly is, in the Qur'an it is an opportunity for the reader to deepen his or her awareness of who Allah is.

The most important text for understanding the Qur'an's view on the death of Jesus, and the one that has generated the most discussion on the topic, is 4:157-159.

157And because they (the people of the book) said, "We killed the messiah Jesus, son of Mary, Allah's messenger." They did not kill him nor did they crucify him, but it was made to appear so to them. Those who disagree about it are truly in grave doubt over it. They have no knowledge about it and only follow conjecture. Surely, they did not kill him. 158Rather, Allah raised him to Himself. Allah is the mighty one, the wise one. 159There is not one among the people of the book who will not believe in him (Jesus) before his own death, and on the day of resurrection he (Jesus) will be a witness against them.

Muslims have commonly interpreted this text to mean that Jesus did not die on the cross. The key phrase is "but it was made to appear so to them," which allows for different readings. The Arabic text is *lākin shubbiha lahum,* and the critical word is the third one (*shubbiha*) which is a verb in the passive voice that can mean either "he was made to appear" or "it was made to appear." If one opts for the first meaning, then the subject is a person and the general sense of the phrase is that some person was made to appear to be something he was not. This is the way the verse has often been understood throughout Islamic history and it can be used to support the notion that Jesus did not die.

The most common form this belief has taken is that of substitutionalism, the idea that someone else died on the cross in Jesus' place. In this reading, "he was made to appear" means that another man was made to look like Jesus and was mistakenly crucified by the authorities who were unaware of the switch. Different candidates have been proposed by Muslims as the one who really died, with two of the most popular being Simon of Cyrene, who carries Jesus' cross for him in the Synoptic Gospels, and, in an expression of poetic justice, Judas Iscariot, the disciple who betrays him in the New Testament. Another way the phrase "he was made to appear" has been understood is to claim that it is a reference to Jesus not really being dead. He was the one on the cross and it looked like he had died but, actually, he was in a coma and was revived after being taken down. Both of these ideas, the substitution of another for Jesus and his death being only an illusion, have been held by Muslims throughout history and continue to be common ways of understanding what happened at the cross. These interpretations do not deny the eventual death of Jesus at some later point in his life, but only claim that his end did not come on the cross.

But there is another way of reading the phrase which understands it to be a statement that asserts Jesus' actual death by crucifixion.[9] If the phrase *lākin shubbiha lahum* is translated "it was made to appear to them," it could mean they did not see what they thought they saw. In other words, they witnessed Jesus' death on the cross but their understanding of how it came about and what it means is wrong. The statement found in the next verse ("Rather, Allah raised him to Himself. Allah is the mighty one, the wise one.") can help explain the nature of their confusion. The people of the book exaggerated the importance of their role in the death of Jesus and mistakenly thought they alone were responsible for it. It was made to appear to them that they had killed Jesus. The truth is, Allah raised him to Himself and was the supreme authority behind the event. This interpretation is supported by another text in 3:54-55 which mentions both Jesus' death and Allah's raising him to Himself.

> [54]They (Jesus' enemies) plotted and Allah plotted, but Allah is the best of plotters. [55]Allah said, "Oh Jesus, I am causing you to die and I will raise you to Myself and cleanse you from those who disbelieve. I will place those who follow you above those who disbelieve until the day of resurrection. Then you will all return to Me and I will judge among you concerning that on which you differ."

Islam, like Judaism and Christianity, maintains that only Allah has control over life and death. This passage explains how the passing away of a messenger like Jesus is no different. It is ultimately the deity who is responsible for the end of a person's life. When people wrongly assume that they are responsible for the death of another they have infringed on a divine privilege and claimed for themselves a power which they do not possess. Such people scheme and plot by trying to usurp the divine prerogative, as did those who put Jesus to death and then thought it was a work of their own doing. But, as 3:54 asserts, Allah is the master plotter under whose jurisdiction all things fall.

The passage in 4:157-159 is therefore a theological statement rather than an historical account. It points out the presence of human arrogance and pride on the part of those who put Jesus to death. They thought they were the arbitrators of life and death and that they could do what only Allah has the power to do. In this reading, the text is not a denial of Jesus' death on the cross, but a denial of humanity's ability to transcend its limits in an attempt to involve itself in matters reserved only for Allah. They did not kill Allah's messenger, Allah took him. When we pay attention to the immediate literary context of 4:157-159 it becomes apparent that this is indeed the point behind these three verses because the sections immediately preceding and following them talk about the excessive pride and hubris of the people of the book.

> [153]The people of the book ask you (Muhammad) to bring down for them a book from heaven. They asked Moses for a greater thing than this. They said, "Show us Allah plainly." So a great punishment came upon them for their transgression. Then they took the calf after clear signs had come to them. Still, We forgave that and We gave Moses clear authority. [154]We raised the mountain above them at their covenant and We said to them, "Enter the gate prostrating!" And We said to them, "Do not break the Sabbath!" We took from them a strong covenant. [155]So for their breaking their covenant, their unbelief in the signs of Allah, their unjust killing of the prophets, for their saying, "Our hearts are covered up," when, in fact, Allah had sealed them because of their unbelief so that they would believe only a little, [156]and for their unbelief in speaking a great falsehood against Mary. . . .

These verses, which come just before the reference to Jesus' death, focus on the sinfulness of the people of the book. The mention of Moses and the establishment of the covenant indicates that the time period being discussed predates Christianity. The term "the people of the book" therefore appears to be a reference to the Jewish community. The passage catalogues a series of offenses on their part which begins with their request that Moses show them Allah "plainly" (v. 153). This is the equivalent of saying that they want to see the deity face to face, an expression of their desire to transcend the limits of their human condition. This same spirit of rebellion is seen in the other transgressions that are mentioned. They worship the calf at the mountain (v. 153), violate the covenant, disbelieve Allah's signs, kill the prophets, ignore Allah's role in sealing their hearts (v. 154) and utter a lie about Mary (v. 156). Each of these actions is a denial of Allah's authority over them and an attempt to give themselves an inflated sense of importance. The mention of Jesus' death and their role in it comes immediately after this section as yet another example of their pride and arrogance in usurping Allah's place.

This same theme extends beyond the verses on Jesus' death to include 4:160-162.

> [160]Because of the transgression of the Jews and their hindering many from Allah's path, We forbade them good things which had been allowed to them. [161]For their taking interest even though they had been forbidden it, and for their improper devouring of people's wealth, we have prepared a painful punishment for those of them who disbelieve. [162]But those who are steadfast in knowledge and the believers among them

believe in what has been sent down to you (Muhammad) and what was sent down before you. To those who observe prayer, offer alms, and believe in Allah and the last day We will give a great reward.

This is a continuation of the inventory of sins committed by the people of the book, here referred to as the "Jews." The final verse and a half bring the list to a close by revealing the consequences for both those who are guilty of these transgressions and those who are innocent of them. The evildoers will be punished for their offenses while the blameless will experience divine favor and blessings.

The most detailed reference to Jesus' death in the Qur'an is found at 4:157-159. But when we consider the immediate literary context of those verses it becomes apparent that his death is not the focus or main point of 4:153-162. Rather, it is mentioned in order to serve as an illustration or example of the main point, which is the waywardness and insolence of the people of the book. This passage in the Qur'an is therefore more interested in instructing readers about the authority of Allah and the danger of human arrogance than it is in informing them about the details surrounding Jesus' crucifixion. This points out the very different agendas of the Qur'an and the New Testament on this issue. For the latter text, Jesus' death and resurrection is the defining moment in human history which proves his divinity and elevates him above the rest of humankind. For the Qur'an, the significance of his death is less lofty. It is cited as an opportunity to be reminded of both the human potential for sin and Allah's elevation above humanity. But this does not mean that conversation between Muslims and Christians on the death of Jesus is impossible. Despite this difference, both texts agree that the deity was intimately involved in Jesus' death. This is another point on which the people of the two books might attempt to engage in constructive dialogue since Christians can readily agree with the Qur'an's claim that only Allah has power over life and death.

For Christians, the death of Jesus is not the end of the story but, in a certain sense, its beginning. All four Gospels conclude with narratives that describe the tomb of Jesus being found empty three days after his death and go on to recount stories of the resurrected Jesus appearing to his followers. This is also an essential part of the message of Paul who understands Jesus' resurrection to be a sign of his victory over death. The Qur'an does not make any mention of a resurrection of Jesus from the dead for obvious theological reasons. This central article of Christian faith which establishes Jesus' divinity runs counter to the Islamic insistence on Allah's transcendence and is considered by Muslims to be an expression of *shirk* since it associates Jesus with the divine nature. In places, it has been seen that the Qur'an refers to Allah "raising Jesus to Himself" (3:55; 4:158), and some Christians might be tempted to see in this phrase an oblique reference to the resurrection of Jesus. Such an interpretation would be improper since it goes against Muslim theology and imposes a reading on the texts that cannot be supported. Rather than alluding to his resurrection, these texts are related to Islamic beliefs in life after death which say that when a good person dies, particularly a prophet like Jesus, the individual goes to heaven and is able to enjoy the reward and blessings of Allah.[10]

COOPERATING REVELATIONS

It might seem strange to even entertain the possibility that the Qur'an and New Testament can somehow cooperate with each other on Jesus, a figure who is understood so differently in the two texts. Such skepticism is certainly appropriate on a matter like that of Jesus' divinity, a belief held by Christians but rejected by Muslims. The great discrepancy between the amount of coverage given to Jesus in the two texts is also a problem. The New Testament contains much more information than the Qur'an on Jesus' life, and it would be pointless to try to study one of the many gospel passages for which there is no counterpart in the Islamic text. Given the nature of the material being considered it seems wiser to adopt a more thematic approach at this point rather than the text-centered one that has been used in previous chapters. Because there is hardly any narrative material that is commonly shared by the two texts, we will here consider a particular theme that is found in the Qur'an to see if it can contribute to our understanding of the New Testament. Specifically, we will remain with the topic that was discussed in the last section and attempt to examine the Gospels in light of what the Qur'an has to say about Jesus' death.

Analysis of the Qur'anic Tradition

We have noted that the issue of human pride and arrogance looms large in how the Qur'an refers to the death of Jesus. The key text is 4:157-159, which is literally surrounded by examples of such hubris on the part of the people of the book. Among other things, they violated the covenant, worshiped the calf, killed the prophets, and devoured the wealth of other people. The exaggerated importance they place on their own role in the death of Jesus is cited as another example of such sinful pride. In doing all these things, they deny Allah's authority and set themselves up in the deity's place. In the case of Jesus' crucifixion, they forget that Allah is the one who ultimately controls matters of life and death and mistakenly believe they are the ones responsible for his demise.

The focus in the Qur'an is theological rather than historical. It is interested in asking the question "What does Jesus' death mean?" not "How exactly did it happen?" As we turn to the New Testament material to see how the Qur'an might cooperate with it on the question of Jesus' death, we want to keep this focus in mind. Because the gospel texts on Jesus' death are richly detailed and artfully constructed narratives, it is easy to get caught up in the story itself as a purportedly historical document that describes the event. The Qur'an encourages us to not lose sight of the theological dimension of the texts and invites us to see if some of the same issues it identifies as central to the event's meaning are found in the New Testament as well. In particular, we want to determine if the gospel accounts also contain evidence of human pride and arrogance being a factor in Jesus' death and if God's involvement in his crucifixion is an important, if only implicit, part of the message of the New Testament.

Application to the Biblical Tradition

One of the complicating factors involved in studying the New Testament material on the death of Jesus is the presence of multiple texts treating the topic. Each of the four Gospels contains a passion narrative and no two of them are identical. The reasons for the differences among them are the same ones that were noted when we discussed the relationship between Matthew's and Luke's infancy narratives in the previous chapter. In the first place, the theological and christological interests of the various authors have played an important role in determining the way the story of Jesus' death is presented. Second, the different concerns and contexts of the audiences to whom the four Gospels are addressed have also influenced the form of the passion narrative in each text. The resulting picture is a complex one in which are found a number of different versions of how Jesus died and what led to his death. New Testament scholars have devoted a great deal of attention to trying to study and solve the many literary, historical, and theological problems that arise from the texts in their attempts to understand both the message of individual Gospels and how the four of them relate to each other.[11]

This situation also complicates our task since, unlike in previous chapters, we do not have only one version of a biblical text. We cannot simply discuss a particular biblical tradition in light of its counterpart in the Qurʾan as we have been doing. Rather, we will attempt to broaden our view and consider the evidence from all four gospel texts to see if the Qurʾan can illuminate certain aspects of it. There is an advantage to doing this in that it is an integrated approach that considers all the gospel material equally without privileging some of it over the rest. But there is also a disadvantage to this method since it may not emphasize strongly enough the differences that exist among the four Gospels and can give the false impression that they all agree on why and how Jesus died. It is therefore important to keep in mind the complex nature of the sources in the following discussion.

The length and detail of the gospel accounts make it impossible to attempt a comprehensive analysis of them here. We will limit ourselves to a consideration of several key characters in the story to see whether the Qurʾan can help us understand their roles in the text in a new light. It has been noted that the Islamic text emphasizes the pride of the people of the book as they consider themselves responsible for Jesus' death and fail to acknowledge Allah's authority over them. We now examine the issue of human responsibility as it is found in the gospel texts to see if the same element of pride is found in them. We focus on the words and actions of three characters, two of them individuals and one of them a group, who were all somehow involved in Jesus' death.

Judas

Among Jesus' disciples, none has a worse image than Judas Iscariot. All four Gospels present him as a traitor who handed over his master, and they all describe Judas leading the arresting party to the place where Jesus is captured. In the popular imagination, his name has become synonymous with the backstabbing turncoat who only looks out for his own self-interest and is ready to betray a friendship at the first opportunity. He is therefore typically understood to be one of the people directly involved in Jesus' death through his role as the one who turned him in. But when we examine the texts carefully, we see that things are more complex than this. While his role in Jesus' arrest is undeniable, some of the Gospels raise questions about his personal responsibility in the events.

Judas' complicity first becomes apparent in the Synoptic Gospels when he approaches the Jewish authorities with an offer to turn over Jesus to them. In Matthew (26:14-16) and Mark (14:10-11) he appears to do this on his own, but Luke says that Satan entered into him and then he went to the chief priests (22:3-6). In John, Judas does not go to the authorities, but at the Last Supper there is a reference to the devil that is similar to what is found in Luke. "The devil had already put it into the heart of Judas son of Simon Iscariot to betray him" (John 13:2). This is an interesting and important difference between Matthew/Mark and Luke/John. The first pair understand Judas to be acting independently when he comes to the authorities with the plan to hand over Jesus, but for the second pair Judas is not in complete control of himself since he is acting under the influence and power of Satan. In considering the role of pride or arrogance in his decision, then, it would appear that this might be less of a factor in Luke and John where he is a pawn and not an independent actor. This image of Judas comes out strikingly in John's Last Supper scene after Jesus predicts that one of his companions will betray him and they inquire as to the person's identity.

> Jesus answered, "It is he to whom I shall give this morsel when I have dipped it." So when he had dipped the morsel, he gave it to Judas, the son of Simon Iscariot. Then after the morsel, Satan entered into him. Jesus said to him, "What you are going to do, do quickly" (John 13:26-27).

Judas is a passive, almost tragic, figure in this scene. One of the hallmarks of John's passion narrative is that Jesus is always in charge of his fate. This trait is to the fore here as he determines which one of his disciples will turn him in by giving the morsel to Judas and then commands him to not delay in carrying out his task. Jesus' control of the situation and the reference to Satan entering Judas combine to give the impression that Judas' act of betrayal is not completely his own. The reader is therefore tempted to evaluate Judas' character more leniently in Luke and John because of Satan's role.

But that is not the case in Mark and, especially, Matthew. Both describe Judas going to the Jewish authorities of his own volition, but only Matthew has him ask them the question "What will you give me if I deliver him to you?" (26:15). Matthew's inclusion of this question indicates that Judas is most interested in how he can profit from turning in Jesus. There is a hint of arrogance in this scene where Judas imagines himself to be in the driver's seat, making the leaders an offer they can't refuse and confident they will pay his price. And pay they do. In Mark and Luke, the arrangement is cash on delivery as both these Gospels say that the authorities agreed to give him money, implying that he did not receive it until Jesus was in their hands. But the Greek verb used in Matthew allows for the possibility that they paid Judas up front before he had given Jesus to them, and this is how 26:15b is rendered in some English translations: "They paid him thirty pieces of silver." If we adopt this reading, it further adds to the element of pride and arrogance in Judas' character. His confident air and cocksure way have convinced the chief priests to pay him before he has even made good on his end of the deal.

This same personal quality extends to the Last Supper scene where Matthew is the only gospel other than John to refer to Judas by name. An interesting exchange is related between Judas and Jesus in 26:21-25 as the latter predicts his betrayal.

> And while they were eating, he said, "Truly I tell you, one of you will betray me." And they began to say to him one after another, "Surely not I, Lord?" He answered, "The one who has dipped his hand into the bowl with me will betray me. The Son of Man goes as it is written of him, but woe to that one by whom the Son of Man is betrayed! It would have been better for that one not to have been born." Judas, who betrayed him, said, "Surely not I, Rabbi?" He replied, "You have said so."

Judas' question "Surely not I?" is phrased in such a way that he anticipates a negative answer along the lines of "No, not you Judas." This is true of the original Greek text as well because it contains a negative particle (*meti*) which expects a negative answer to the question. In effect, by having him ask the question in this way, Matthew has Judas feign innocence before Jesus. The reader knows that Judas has already approached the Jewish authorities about turning Jesus over and has even received an advance payment on doing so. Therefore, he comes across in this scene as very insincere and gives the impression that he believes he has been able to outwit Jesus who does not have a clue about the plan to betray him. If we interpret this passage with the message of the Qur'an in mind, we are better able to recognize Judas' haughtiness and conceit in thinking he has pulled the wool over Jesus' eyes.

Another scene in Matthew which is unique to that gospel is the suicide of Judas recounted in 27:3-10. According to this passage, after Jesus is charged by the Jewish court, Judas recognizes his mistake in turning him over and, guilt-ridden, returns to the authorities to give back the money they paid him. After being rebuffed by them, Judas goes out and hangs himself. None of the other Gospels tell us what became of Judas, so in those texts we are left wondering if and how he came to terms with his own involvement in Jesus' death. Only Matthew gives us a sense of how distraught and troubled he was by what he had done, and this information underscores once again the fact that his own greed and pride led to his downfall. When he tells the Jewish leaders that he sinned in betraying innocent blood (v. 4) he is admitting his complicity in Jesus' arrest, and his return of the blood money is an attempt to free himself of the guilt he feels. But it is too late for that. In a final act of desperation he takes his own life. Ironically, this response is one last testimony to the greed and arrogance that motivated him to hand over Jesus. His suicide is, itself, an attempt to control the situation and is a direct challenge to God's role as the supreme authority over life and death. To the end, Judas in Matthew is more interested in himself than in anything else.

The character of Judas is drawn somewhat differently in all four Gospels. The Qur'an's identification of human pride as a key element in the death of Jesus is more relevant for some Gospels than others in evaluating Judas in the New Testament. In Luke and John, Satan enters him prior to betraying Jesus and this raises some question about Judas' personal responsibility for his actions. But in Mark and Matthew, Judas acts on his own and is therefore more culpable. Matthew's image of Judas, in particular, can be enhanced by being attentive to the message of the Qur'an. In that gospel more than any other, Judas' pride and arrogance help to determine what happens to Jesus.

The Jewish Authorities

The first step in the legal process that resulted in Jesus' death was his hearing before the Jewish authorities who were gathered in their deliberative body known as the Sanhedrin. The individual accounts vary on some matters of detail and, as usual, John's version differs considerably from those of the Synoptics, but the Gospels agree that this was an opportunity for the Jewish leaders to question Jesus about himself and his teaching. The primary question asked in the Synoptics concerns Jesus' identity, as all three Gospels have them ask Jesus if he is the Christ, the Son of God (Matt 26:63; Mark 14:61; Luke 22:67-70). His answer is somewhat different in each gospel, but in all three the Sanhedrin concludes that he is guilty of blasphemy and deserves to die.

There is a degree of pride on the Sanhedrin's part during this questioning that might be easy to overlook, but the Qur'an's reference to it

being a determining factor in Jesus' death enables us to be more attentive to it. The underlying presupposition behind both the questions they
direct to Jesus and their response to him is that they themselves know
what it means to be the Christ, the Son of God. As they question Jesus
they come to the conclusion that this man does not fit their idea of who
the Christ is and therefore must be a pretender. There is a great deal of
irony present in this scene as they come face to face with the Son of God
and yet fail to recognize him because he does not live up to their pre-
conceived notions. Throughout the Gospels, they have had the opportunity to see Jesus perform miraculous works and to hear him teach on
many occasions but they are still unable to see who he is. The reason for
their inability to understand who he is is that they believe themselves to
be the only authorities on religious matters and the ones most in touch
with God's will for the community. But God has other ideas which they
know nothing about and which their self-assured arrogance makes it
impossible for them to discover. The questioning of Jesus before the
Sanhedrin is therefore a scene that is rife with human pride and conceit.

A second place where the Jewish authorities play a prominent role
in some of the Gospels is in the Barabbas scene. After the Sanhedrin
finish with Jesus they send him off to Pontius Pilate who, as the Roman
prefect, was the official representative of the emperor and whose guilty
verdict was necessary to put Jesus to death. Pilate finds Jesus innocent
and then tells the people he will release at their request either Jesus or
a violent criminal named Barabbas. According to Matthew (27:15-23)
and Mark (15:6-14), the Jewish leaders then circulate among the crowd
and convince them to ask for Barabbas' release and to demand the crucifixion of Jesus. This is precisely what happens as Pilate hands Jesus
over to the executioners and allows Barabbas to go free. This is an interesting scene in light of the Qur'an's statement that the people of the
book thought they killed Jesus. By successfully stirring up the masses
and convincing them to shout for Jesus' death, the Jewish leaders undoubtedly consider themselves to be the masterminds behind his crucifixion. But other New Testament passages and later Christian
theology see a different hand behind the event and believe that Jesus'
death on the cross was the realization of the divine, not human, will. So
here, too, the theme of human pride figures prominently in the story as
the Jewish leaders wrongly assume they are the ones who have brought
about Jesus' demise.

There is also an element of irony in this scene depicting the Jewish
authorities manipulating the crowds to have Pilate put Jesus to death.

During this period, the Romans allowed the Jews to carry out the death sentence for only a limited number of religious offenses. Every other case had to be turned over to the Roman authorities who would decide its merits and determine whether or not execution was a fitting punishment. The Sanhedrin was therefore quite limited in its jurisdiction and ability to enact its own rulings. There is irony at work in the situation involving Jesus since the Jewish leaders believe themselves to be carrying out God's will yet they have to get the permission of a Gentile nonbeliever to bring it about. To paraphrase the Qurʾan, it only appeared to them that they had the authority.

In the Synoptic Gospels, the Jewish authorities are found at the crucifixion site while Jesus dies on the cross. Their comments there are in keeping with their character traits that have been observed up to this point. They mock Jesus as the Christ and Son of God, challenging him to save himself and come down from the cross so that they might believe in him (Matt 27:38-43; Mark 15:27-32a; Luke 23:35-38). Once again, their hubris has determined how they respond to Jesus. They are sure they know what being the Christ entails and Jesus does not fill the bill. To them, it is not possible that the Son of God could die such a humiliating, shameful death and the fact that Jesus continues to hang there demonstrates to them that he is a fraud. In their conceit, the thought never crosses their minds that they could be wrong and that God's will could diverge so dramatically from their idea of what it is. Here, too, they are blinded by their self-confidence and smugly claim to be acting and speaking on God's behalf.

The Jewish leaders play a somewhat different role in John's passion narrative, but two brief comments about them show that in the Fourth Gospel, too, they are a proud and arrogant group. As in the Synoptics, the authorities in John are found at Pilate's headquarters trying to make sure their request that Jesus be executed is favorably received by the Roman prefect. In this part of the passion narrative John, unlike the Synoptics, has Pilate shuttle back and forth between Jesus, who is inside the building, and the Jewish leaders who remain outside. The reason for this arrangement is given in 18:28. "Then they took Jesus from Caiaphas to Pilate's headquarters. It was early in the morning. They themselves did not enter the headquarters, so as to avoid ritual defilement and to be able to eat the Passover." According to John, if the Jews were to enter the building they would be rendered ritually impure and therefore unable to participate in the Passover ritual which was to begin the next day. They are therefore shown waiting outside the headquarters while

Pilate moves back and forth between them and Jesus. This verse, like some of the texts in the Synoptics, paints the Jewish authorities as individuals who are sure they know what God wants. In their zeal to follow the Law perfectly, they refuse to enter a Gentile's house so that they can celebrate the most important feast of their liturgical year. There is nothing wrong with such piety in and of itself and there is much to commend about it. But in the present context the incongruity between their desire to do God's will and their mission to destroy the one John presents as God's word become flesh (1:1-18) is unsettling. They arrogantly assume they are following God's will by both not entering a foreigner's house at such a sacred time and soliciting Pilate to put Jesus to death.

A second text in John which underscores the haughtiness of the Jewish leaders occurs only two verses later in 18:30. When Pilate asks them what accusation they bring against Jesus, they reply, "If this man were not a criminal, we would not have handed him over to you." Such a flippant response is especially surprising when, like here, it is directed toward a prominent official whose sympathy one is trying to win. We expect to find a more congenial, even deferential, answer even if it is completely insincere. But it offers a telling glimpse into the minds and hearts of the Jewish authorities. They are a self-righteous and cavalier group who are convinced they are in the right and believe that fact should be plainly obvious to everyone else. In its own way, then, John's Gospel also makes reference to the proud nature of the Jewish leaders.

Pilate

Pilate is another character who is generally held to have some responsibility in the death of Jesus. When we examine the texts which speak of his involvement, we can note the same element of pride that was seen with Judas and the Jewish authorities although this time it takes a somewhat different form. All four Gospels, each in its own way, draws attention to Pilate's inability to save Jesus from death by releasing him even though he knows this is the right thing to do. The main reason for his willingness to execute someone he believes to be innocent is his desire to look out for his own self-interests since he knows if he does not put Jesus to death he himself might have to pay a high personal price for that decision.

In both Luke and John, Pilate states three times that he believes Jesus has committed no crime and wants to set him free. Luke presents this within the context of a series of exchanges between Pilate and the Jews. After his first interrogation of Jesus, Pilate rules, "I find no basis for an accusation against this man" (23:4). This causes the Jewish leaders to object that Jesus' dangerous teaching has spread all around the land from Galilee, where he began, to Judea. Upon learning that Jesus is a Galilean, Pilate sends him off to Herod who has jurisdiction over that area. When Jesus is brought back from the encounter with Herod, which is mentioned only in Luke's gospel, Pilate announces, "I have examined him in your presence and have not found this man guilty of any of your charges against him. Neither has Herod, for he sent him back to us. Indeed, he has done nothing to deserve death. I will therefore have him flogged and release him" (23:14-16). Once again, this ruling leads to a strong reaction by the Jews who begin to request that Barabbas be released and to demand Jesus' death. A third time Pilate states his judgment that Jesus is innocent, and this leads to more protesting on the part of the Jews. "I have found in him no ground for the sentence of death; I will therefore have him flogged and then release him" (23:22).

John contains a more truncated version of these events which still makes reference to Pilate's triple assertion of Jesus' innocence. His first examination of Jesus leads him to conclude, "I find no case against him" (18:38). After the crowd expresses its preference to have Barabbas released rather than Jesus, Pilate has him flogged and then returns to the Jews to give them another chance to decide in favor of Jesus. "Look, I am bringing him out to you to let you know that I find no case against him" (19:4). When Jesus comes out the crowd yells for his death with shouts of "Crucify him! Crucify him!" and this evokes one final expression of dissent from Pilate. "Take him yourself and crucify him; I find no case against him" (19:6). By having Pilate repeat three times his belief in Jesus' innocence, both Luke and John leave no doubt as to the Roman prefect's opinion. Legally speaking, his view carried the most weight and this should have led to a dismissal of the charges against Jesus.

Matthew and Mark relate Pilate's view of Jesus in a different way. They never have the Roman leader come right out and say he is innocent, but in other, more subtle, ways the reader comes to learn that Pilate believes Jesus has been unfairly accused by the Jewish authorities. In Mark, Pilate reaches the conclusion that the charges against Jesus are trumped up and nothing more than a smokescreen to hide the true reason why the leaders want Jesus out of the way. The reader is given a privileged glimpse into Pilate's mind in 15:10 that discloses his understanding of the Jewish motivation for coming to him. "For he realized that it was out of jealousy that the chief priests had handed him over." Matthew contains an almost identical description of the prefect's mental state. "For he realized that it was out of jealousy that they had handed him over" (27:18).

As is often the case elsewhere, Matthew offers more detail than Mark on this point and contains some additional material which helps to further establish Pilate's conviction that Jesus is innocent. This can be seen in two scenes which are not found in any other gospel. The only New Testament reference to Pilate's wife is in Matthew 27:19. "While he (Pilate) was sitting on the judgment seat, his wife sent word to him, 'Have nothing to do with that innocent man, for today I have suffered a great deal because of a dream about him.'" Pilate does not explicitly refer to Jesus' innocence in Matthew's Gospel, but his wife does and she advises her husband to avoid punishing someone who does not deserve it. He is informed of her dream as he is about to render his judgment and we can assume he followed his wife's counsel because when the crowd demands Jesus' death Pilate asks, "Why, what evil has he done?" (27:23). This question, which is the same thing Pilate asks the Jewish leaders in Mark 15:14, might be seen as a continuation of his investigation as he attempts to get at the truth of Jesus' case. But, on another level, it might indicate that Pilate's investigation has come to an end and he has already reached a verdict of innocent for Jesus. If we understand this as a rhetorical question, rather than a way of gaining information, Pilate is asking them, "Why should I have Jesus crucified when he has done nothing wrong?" The episode of his wife's dream, where Jesus' innocence is asserted, and the following scene, which describes Pilate's distancing himself from Jesus' death, argue in favor of the latter alternative of taking Pilate's question as an implicit acknowledgment of Jesus' lack of guilt.

Pilate's act of washing his hands is another incident that is depicted only in Matthew's Gospel. "So when Pilate saw that he could do nothing, but rather that a riot was beginning, he took some water and washed his hands before the crowd, saying, 'I am innocent of this man's blood; see to it yourselves'" (27:24). With this highly symbolic gesture, coming on the heels of the message from his wife and right after he has asked his rhetorical question, Pilate disavows any connection with or involvement in Jesus' death. His disagreement with the punishment the Jewish authorities are calling for could not be any stronger since in expressing his own innocence before the crowd he is simultaneously declaring the innocence of Jesus.

If the Gospels all agree that Pilate was sympathetic to Jesus and believed him to be free of guilt, why did he not allow him to live? The answer to this question is also unanimous among the Gospels: Pilate was fearful and more concerned about himself than he was about Jesus. As the official representative of the Roman emperor in Judea, it was his job to maintain order within his jurisdiction, to quell any uprisings that might occur, and to look out for Roman interests in the area. Apparently, Pilate succeeded admirably in this office because his tenure (26–36 C.E.) was the second-longest term of office for anyone who held the position. As any politician would, he realized that one of the keys to a successful career is to avoid being identified with unpopular causes or situations that could be personally damaging. If Rome were to get wind of any problems that might develop in Judea on his watch, Pilate's head would be the first to roll. Each of the Gospels exhibits an awareness of this political fact of life and understands it to be part of the reason why Pilate acquiesces in the face of Jewish pressure.

Matthew gives a clear reason why Pilate caves in to the demands to crucify Jesus even though he disapproves of the act. According to 27:24, discussed above, he gives up and decides to wash his hands of the matter when he sees "that he could do nothing, but rather that a riot was beginning." It is his fear of a melee, which might quickly get out of control and lead to carnage and bloodshed, that forces Pilate to concede. But whom is Pilate most concerned about? Is it the general population, whose safety would be threatened if the violence were to escalate to dangerous levels? Possibly, but Pilate is more likely thinking of himself and the ramifications social unrest and discord might have for his career and position within Roman society.

We see a similar concern on his part, expressed somewhat less dramatically, in Mark 15:15. "So Pilate, wishing to satisfy the crowd, released Barabbas for them; and after flogging Jesus, he handed him over to be crucified." Pilate does not want the crowd to get angry over his decision and so goes against his better judgment and signs off on Jesus' death warrant. In other words, public pressure and the desire to maintain his political office override the responsibilities of that office and lead him to make a ruling that goes against his principles. The same fear of a riot, which is articulated in Matthew but unexpressed here, has probably influenced his decision in Mark.

Luke hints at Pilate's self-preoccupation and desire to avoid conflict with the citizens of Judea in several interesting ways. The first place is in his decision to send Jesus off to be interrogated by Herod (23:6-12). When

Pilate discovers Jesus is a Galilean, he immediately transfers his case to Herod, who was the provincial governor of that part of Palestine but happened to be in Jerusalem at the time (v. 7). This maneuver seems strange in light of the fact that the charges were brought up by residents of Judea, which came under Pilate's control. It therefore raises questions about Pilate's motivation in attempting to have Jesus tried as a Galilean. It could be that it is a way for Pilate to evade personal involvement in Jesus' case. In other words, this is Luke's equivalent of Matthew's hand-washing. If Herod were to reach an unpopular decision regarding Jesus, Pilate would be politically unscathed by it and perhaps might even be able to claim that the case would have had a different outcome had he been allowed to rule on it. This scenario is particularly compelling when we recall that Luke mentions that Pilate and Herod were enemies at this point in time (v. 12). The decision to send Jesus off to Herod therefore works to a double advantage for Pilate since it both distances him from involvement in Jesus' trial and has the potential to sully the name of his rival ruler.

Another place Luke raises doubts about Pilate's character is in the description of his turning over Jesus to be executed. The other Synoptics simply say that he released Barabbas for the crowd and delivered Jesus to be crucified (Matt 27:26; Mark 15:15). Luke adds a couple of things not found in Matthew and Mark. When he refers to the release of the other prisoner, Luke does not identify him by name as Barabbas. Rather, he identifies him by his crime and says, "He released the man they asked for, the one who had been put in prison for insurrection and murder" (23:25a). The reference to Barabbas as the man "they" wanted released underscores the fact that this is not Pilate's choice but he has given in to their demands. Luke then spells out exactly who this person is: he is someone guilty of insurrection and murder. This unflattering description serves as a reminder to the reader that Pilate has agreed to free someone who is deserving of the punishment about to be inflicted on Jesus. After learning of the role "they" play and about the contemptible nature of the one set free, the reader is left wondering about the basis for Pilate's decision. Luke's closing comment on the trial in 23:25b answers this question. While Matthew, Mark and John all state that he delivered Jesus to be crucified, Luke has "but Jesus he delivered up to their will." It is the will of the crowds and the Jewish authorities, not that of Pilate, that is being carried out. In his selfish desire to avoid conflict with them in order to remain in his powerful office, Pilate has ironically become powerless and Luke portrays him as nothing more than a puppet responding to the wishes of others.

John is probably the most blunt about pointing out the political aspect of Pilate's decision to have Jesus put to death. In 19:12 the crowds know just how to convince him to come around to their way of thinking. "From then on Pilate tried to release him, but the Jews cried out, 'If you release this man, you are no friend of the emperor. Everyone who claims to be a king sets himself against the emperor.'" They lay out the choice before Pilate in stark terms that he is bound to understand because they only identify the implications of the decision for him personally, not what it means for them or for Jesus. If he opts to free Jesus, he will no longer be considered a friend of the emperor. If he loses the support and backing of the ruler, Pilate's career will come to a screeching halt and his reputation will be ruined. Their words to him are not a reminder, but a veiled threat. If he fails to meet their demands for Jesus' death, the effects on his personal life will be devastating. As in the other three Gospels, Pilate's ambition and pride win out in the end and he orders that Jesus be executed.

In the Gospels, as in the Qur'an, Jesus' death is surrounded by examples of human pride and arrogance. This analysis of the three characters most often implicated in the death of Jesus has revealed that all of them were governed and motivated by their own self-interests. Each of the characters expresses this hubris in a way different from the others but it serves the same function in all of their lives. In the case of Judas, it takes the form of overconfidence and an inflated sense of self as he plays the power broker in working out a deal with the Jewish leaders and then smugly feigns his loyalty to Jesus. With the Jewish authorities, it is seen in their mistaken belief that they know what it means to be the messiah and son of God, and in their inability to consider the possibility that the divine will is something beyond their comprehension. Pilate's pride is found in his selfish personal and career concerns which lead him to assent to Jesus' crucifixion even though he knows it is unjust. All of these elements are present in the New Testament but easily overlooked and rarely given the attention they deserve. After reading the Qur'an's treatment of Jesus' death in 4:153-162, which highlights the role of human pride, we are better able to recognize its presence in the Gospels when we revisit them.

NOTES: CHAPTER 6

[1]An excellent study of the development of messianic expectation around the time of Jesus can be found in John J. Collins, *The Scepter and the Star* (New York: Doubleday, 1995).

[2]The other three pillars of faith for Muslims are reciting their confession of faith, fasting during the month of Ramadan, and, if possible, making the pilgrimage to Mecca at some point in their lifetime.

[3]The other texts are found at Matthew 4:18-22, Luke 5:1-11, and John 1:35-51. As is often the case, Matthew's version of the event is most similar to Mark's and John's is the one that is least like the others. The differences are due to the unique theological perspective of each work.

[4]The difference between the gospel message and Law of Moses is most forcefully articulated by Paul, the earliest New Testament writer, who argues that Jesus' death and resurrection has rendered the Law totally obsolete for the Christian. Much of his letter to the Romans attempts to explain why this is so.

[5]The presence of males and females in both these groups is clearly expressed in the Arabic original where the words "believing" and "hypocritical" are found in both the masculine and feminine forms. This type of repetition of the same word with a shift in gender is not a common feature of the Qur'an where the masculine plural is typically used alone and commonly refers to both men and women.

[6]Luke is the only gospel to contain any information on Jesus' childhood. In 2:41-52 he describes how Mary and Joseph left Jesus in Jerusalem when he was twelve years old and had to return to the city to look for him. They found him in the Temple in the presence of some of the learned religious leaders. The Infancy Gospel of Thomas concludes with an account of this episode.

[7]The word "synoptic," which comes from Greek and means to "see together," is used to refer to Matthew, Mark, and Luke because of the many similarities of structure and content that exist among these three Gospels. John's Gospel has less in common with the other three and contains many passages not found in them.

[8]One group of this type was the Collyridians, a sect that began in fourth-century C.E. Arabia. According to ancient historians, their devotion was centered on Mary and their rituals included offering small cakes to her.

[9]Much of the material in this section of the chapter is based on the work of Professor Mahmoud M. Ayoub in his influential article, "Towards an Islamic Christology, II: The Death of Jesus, Reality or Delusion," *The Muslim World* 70 (2) (1980) 91–121. Another informative article which discusses the role of this Qur'an text in interreligious dialogue is Michael G. Fonner, "Jesus' Death by Crucifixion in the Qur'an: An Issue for Interpretation and Muslim–Christian Relations," *Journal of Ecumenical Studies* 29 (3–4) (1992) 432–49.

[10]As often occurs with such figures, the nonscriptural Muslim traditions add information on Jesus not found in the Qur²an which have been influential in shaping the ideas Muslims hold about him. Included in the details found in this material is the belief that he will return to the earth and kill the antichrist, live his life as a good Muslim, die, and be buried next to Muhammad in Medina.

[11]The most thorough study of the passion narratives is Raymond E. Brown, *The Death of the Messiah*, 2 vols. (New York: Doubleday, 1993).

Bibliography

THE QUR'AN

Texts

Al-Qur'an. Trans. Ahmed Ali. Princeton: Princeton University Press, 1988.

The Koran. Trans. N. J. Dawood. New York: Penguin, 1990.

The Meaning of the Glorious Qur'an. Trans. Mohammed Marmaduke Pickthall. Chicago: Kazi Publications, 1983.

Noble Quran. Trans. Muhammad M. Khan. Chicago: Kazi Publications, 1995.

Studies

Cragg, Kenneth. *The Event of the Qur'an: Islam in Its Scripture*. Oxford: Oneworld Publications, 1995.

Esack, Farid. *Qur'an, Liberation & Pluralism*. Oxford: Oneworld Publications, 1997.

Gatje, Helmut. *The Qur'an and its Exegesis*. Oxford: Oneworld Publications, 1996.

Haleem, Muhammad A. *Understanding the Qur'an: Themes and Style*. New York: St. Martins Press, 1996.

Parrinder, Geoffrey. *Jesus in the Qur'an*. Oxford: Oneworld Publications, 1995.

Rahman, Fazlur. *Major Themes in the Qur'an*. Minneapolis: Bibliotheca Islamica, 1980.

Robinson, Neal. *Discovering the Qur'an*. London: SCM Press, 1996.

Seale, Morris S. *Qur'an and Bible: Studies in Interpretation and Dialogue*. London: Croon Helm, 1978.

Stowasser, Barbara Freyer. *Women in the Qur'an, Traditions and Interpretation.* Oxford: Oxford University Press, 1994.

Watt, William Montgomery. *Companion to the Qur'an.* Oxford: Oneworld Publications, 1994.

MUHAMMAD

Armstrong, Karen. *Muhammad: A Biography of the Prophet.* San Francisco: HarperCollins, 1993.

Newby, Gordon Darnell. *The Making of the Last Prophet: A Reconstruction of the Earliest Biography of Muhammad.* Columbia: University of South Carolina Press, 1989.

Peters, F. E. *Muhammad and the Origins of Islam.* Albany: State University of New York Press, 1994.

Schimmel, Annemarie. *And Muhammad Is His Messenger: The Veneration of the Prophet in Islamic Piety.* Chapel Hill: University of North Carolina Press, 1985.

Watt, William Montgomery. *Muhammad at Mecca.* Oxford: Oxford University Press, 1979.

_____. *Muhammad at Medina.* Oxford: Oxford University Press, 1981.

ISLAM

Brown, Stuart. *The Nearest in Affection: Towards a Christian Understanding of Islam.* Valley Forge: Trinity Press International, 1995.

Esposito, John L. *The Islamic Threat: Myth or Reality?* Oxford: Oxford University Press, 1996.

_____. *Islam: The Straight Path.* Oxford: Oxford University Press, 1998.

Rahman, Fazlur. *Islam.* Chicago: Chicago University Press, 1979.

Renard, John. *Seven Doors to Islam: Spirituality and the Religious Life of Muslims.* Berkeley: University of California Press, 1996.

_____. *Windows on the House of Islam: Muslim Sources on Spirituality and Religious Life.* Berkeley: University of California Press, 1998.

Schimmel, Annemarie. *Islam: An Introduction.* Albany: State University of New York Press, 1992.

Watt, William Montgomery. *A Short History of Islam.* Oxford: Oneworld Publications, 1996.

Index of Subjects

Index of Bible Passages

Index of Qur'an Passages